D1382795

The Newark Teacher Strikes

The Newark
Teacher Strikes

Hopes on the Line

Steve Golin

Rutgers University Press

New Brunswick, New Jersey, and London

Publication of this book was assisted by a grant from the New Jersey Historical Commission, a division of Cultural Affairs in the Department of State.

Library of Congress Cataloging-in-Publication Data

Golin, Steve, 1939-
   The Newark teacher strikes : hopes on the line / Steve Golin.
      p. cm.
   Includes bibliographical references (p.) and index.
   ISBN 0–8135–3057–1 (alk. paper)
   1. Strikes and lockouts—Teachers—New Jersey—Newark—History—
20th century. 2. Labor disputes—New Jersey—Newark—History—20th
century. I. Title

LB2844.47.U62 N494 2002
331.892'813711'00974732—dc21

2001048608

British Cataloging-in-Publication data for this book is available from the British Library

Manufactured in the United States of America

For Sophie Golin (1906–1992), activist teacher in Brooklyn, who taught me right from wrong, and Essie Conyers (1903–1972), migrant from the South, who taught me love.

Contents

Acknowledgments

The people who made this book possible are the fifty-two teachers who took the time to sit down and talk to me. First and last, I thank them. They invited me into their homes, or came to mine; they put up with my questions, my ignorance, my curiosity. Some dug up documents or photographs. Many helped me find other people to interview. All collaborated in the process of creating this book.

Other people also helped me find people to interview. I want to thank Ann-Marie Batista, Allison Capel, Pat Cheatham, Rogelio Hernandez, David Kilbourn, Sylvia Lehrick, Mark Levitan, Paula O'Connor, Wendy Oxman, and Richard Ryan.

When I started, I knew little about Newark. Rich Wesley gave me a lovely orientation, using his high school yearbook and his knowledge of Newark. Bob Blackwell, Charles Cummings, and James Osbourn helped me discover the treasures of the New Jersey Room in the Newark Public Library. Later, Elena Scambio gave me the benefit of her rich experience in trying to bring about school reform in Newark.

Norman Eiger shared with me his invaluable interviews from 1974 to 1975, with leaders of negotiations on both sides of the 1970–1971 strikes and with mediators. Paul Lappé loaned me a wonderful document: the tape of his wife, Jeanette Lappé, discussing her jail experience, made shortly after she left jail.

Joe Del Grosso opened the Newark Teachers Union to my inquiring eyes. I am grateful, because before he became president, I was not allowed to use the Union archives in the basement, or to connect with the staff.

Bloomfield College gave me precious time. I enjoyed two leaves, in 1995 and in 1999–2000. In late stages of my research and manuscript preparation, I leaned on the expertise of two people who work at the college: Mark Jackson, librarian, and Cynthia Romero, humanities division secretary. I also benefited in the late stages from the suggestions and criticisms of Marlie Wasserman, director of Rutgers University Press, and Willa Speiser, copy editor.

Seven people read the entire manuscript at earlier stages. The first was my wife, Alice Golin, who read drafts of chapters as I wrote them, encouraging me as only she can, and critiquing my writing as only she can. Alice was my consultant on every tough decision I had to make; she helps me be who I am.

My friend Ron Aronson read a draft, looking at the overall scheme and the details, the content and the form. He deepened my understanding of what I was doing. My friend Barbara Machtinger made great suggestions for changes and additions. She annotated her draft with a detailed, running commentary that was an author's joy to read.

The other four readers were Newark teachers. Vic Cascella, despite his poor eyesight, checked the manuscript for errors of fact or interpretation. Harold Moore, Jim Lowenstein, and Carol Keeran (Carol Karman in the book, her name at the time of the strikes) read the chapters as I wrote them, telling me what they liked, what they didn't like, and why. Beyond all the things they taught me, I am grateful for the passionate seriousness they brought to the task, which allowed me to glimpse, in the present, the spirit that animated their strikes.

Which brings me back to Newark teachers. This book is about them. It is also, to an unusual extent, by them. They are the authors of the events and coauthors of the book. I made the final decisions, and am responsible for them. But above all, I am grateful to the teachers. This book, in a sense, is my way of saying thanks.

The Newark Teacher Strikes

Introduction

A complexity clings to teachers. We are working people. And we care, or want to care, about our students. Social workers and nurses are also torn between their need to defend their interests and their need to connect. But I'm a teacher. Since 1973, I've been teaching at Bloomfield College, a mile from the Newark border; many of my students come from Newark schools. Writing about teachers, I was able to use what I've learned from teaching, and to learn more.

I decided to write a story, because movies and novels and my favorite histories tell stories. We remember and imagine in stories; we become ourselves through the stories we tell. I wanted to write a story about teachers making sense of their work and of themselves as workers—a story about teachers in the process of self-transformation.

I found my story in the New Jersey Room of the Newark Public Library: the strikes of 1970 and 1971. Reading the *Newark News* and *Star-Ledger*, I discovered a terrific story about teachers who went on strike for more than three weeks in 1970, and eleven weeks in 1971. Many went to jail. What, I wondered, did they learn about the system and themselves by acting together? What were their hopes when they joined the Newark Teachers Union, when they went out, picketed, were arrested, jailed? Did they want money? Job security? A chance to really teach? What happened to their hopes?

I needed to know not only what teachers did but why they did it. I contacted a strike leader, the brother-in-law of the cousin of a friend of mine. I contacted a teacher who went to jail, the friend of a friend of my mother-in-law. What did

1

the strikes mean to them? They suggested other teachers. Following where suggestions led, I interviewed fifty-two people who taught in Newark during the strikes or earlier. I asked them not only about their experiences, but about their thoughts—when they joined the Newark Teachers Union or the Newark Teachers Association, went on strike or went to work, picketed or crossed the picket line.

I knew I was not writing a history of the Union. My story was about the teachers who built the Union. Through the strikes, and through the struggle with the Newark Teachers Association that preceded the strikes, Newark teachers transformed their relation to their employer and their ways of seeing. Striking teachers learned to see through the media, one teacher told me. She meant that when teachers compared their experience of the strikes with the version presented by newspapers and television, they learned that the stories the media told were constructed by people who had different interests from those of working people. She questioned me about my politics, because she understood that the story I told would be shaped by my values.[1]

My focus is on what teachers learned as a result both of teaching and of refusing to teach. My method is to use their words. As they told me their stories, they re-created the meaning of what they did. I used what they said the way Erich Auerbach used fragments of Homer and Stendhal and Virginia Woolf in *Mimesis*, as texts to be studied, explicated, interrogated, connected.[2] Like Auerbach, I didn't worry whether I'd covered everything or everyone important, in some external sense. Some people were no longer alive; some I never got in touch with; a few did not want to speak to me. Like Auerbach, I assumed that if I went deeply enough into the material that presented itself, I'd make new discoveries.

This study of the Newark teacher strikes is grounded in the stories of people who went on strike. In writing the book, I've tried to honor the trust they put in me. I could not uncritically accept everything they told me. Sometimes they deliberately left things out. Often they misremembered dates, or combined memories from the two strikes. Always, they constructed and reconstructed the meaning of their experience, even as they were telling me about it. I analyzed the stories they told me, looking for their assumptions and angles of vision, for what was then and what is now. But I hope that, when they read the book, they find that I treated them with respect, I honored the spirit that moved them, I showed how much I cared.

The first chapter introduces Jewish teachers—leftist, egalitarian, and socially committed—who shaped the Newark Teachers Union in its formative decades in the 1940s and 1950s. And Italian teachers who, committed to collective bargaining, made the Union into an effective force in the 1960s. And Black teachers, who took time on the job before they found their way to unionism. Instead of lumping Jews and Italians together as "white," I learned to appreciate their differences and to question my own assumptions (inherited from my mother, a teacher unionist in New York who was both Jewish and leftist) about what a teacher union should be.

The first chapter examines the dialogues between teachers about professional identity and working-class identity. According to the dominant ideology, teachers were professionals, who belonged in the professional organization, the Association; if they joined a union, they lowered themselves to the level of other workers, became cogs in the AFL-CIO machine, and lost their professional identity. As a college teacher, I was not surprised to find teachers defining themselves in terms of the idea of professionalism. What surprised me was how directly some teachers challenged that idea during the 1960s—how they deconstructed, and reconstructed, the idea of professionalism.

The second chapter surveys the long-range effects on teaching and teachers of the 1967 riot/rebellion. When violence spread to Barringer High School, its faculty acted together to limit violence, restore order, and make teaching possible. I'd always thought of the issue of discipline in schools as a right-wing issue, until I talked to teachers. Across Newark, many teachers recognized that their old methods were not working with the children of migrants from the South. Some blamed the children. Others tried new ways of teaching after the riot/rebellion. The most exciting experiment was School Within a School. The second chapter tells the stories of Barringer and School Within a School.

The second chapter also tells the stories of the large cohort of young people who began teaching in Newark after the riot/rebellion. I was interviewing two friends, who began teaching in 1969, when one said that the movement for teacher power was a sixties movement. The other disagreed, insisting that teacher unionism was a labor movement in the tradition of the thirties. The first went away to college; the second went to college locally. I realized that young teachers who commuted to college were likely to embrace a bread-and-butter version of unionism. Those who went away to college were generally changed by the popular campus protests, and brought some of the expansive spirit of 1960s movements to the Newark Teachers Union.

Chapter 3 explores what Newark teachers meant by power, and what they did in 1970 to get it. From newspapers, articles, and monographs, I received the impression that either striking teachers aimed primarily at the good of the children, as the Union claimed, or they aimed primarily at more money, as the Newark Board of Education claimed. Talking to teachers, I found the dichotomy was false, not only because most striking teachers wanted to make more money *and* improve the schools, but also, and especially, because they wanted a third thing: teacher power. I discovered that more than anything, striking teachers hoped to end the tyranny of principals and of the Board of Education.

Most writing about the 1970 strike focuses on the Union leadership and the Board of Education. Much of it was useful to me, and some of it invaluable— particularly the 1976 dissertation of Norman Eiger, based on extensive inter- views with Union leaders and Board of Education members. Eiger and Robert Braun, the *Star-Ledger* reporter who wrote a chapter on the strike in his 1972 book on teacher unionism, talked to Union and Board officials and staff.[3] Their groundwork enabled me to focus on the experience of rank-and-file teachers, their hopes, their words, their ways of constructing meaning. The third chap- ter tells the stories of teachers as they argued with strikebreakers, pleaded with parents, were torn by the claims of their own families, let themselves be arrested, and experienced the high of solidarity.

Chapter 4 tells how the conflict between the Board of Education and the Union became reframed in racial terms. Newark elected a Black mayor, who created a nonwhite majority on the Board during the year between the strikes. Simultaneously, a Black woman won real power in the Union for the first time. I analyze how the Union became cast as white, even as a Black woman took control of it.

The new Board made "nonprofessional chores" a centerpiece of its anti- Union campaign. I didn't understand why the Union freed teachers from non- professional chores such as hall and cafeteria duty. A leader of the Union explained that he was so angry about the way elementary school teachers were ordered to perform duties that he didn't care about the consequences. In the contract negotiation, and in the implementation of the contract after the 1970 strike, he pushed the issue. The fourth chapter examines how the elimination of nonprofessional chores increased racial polarization and cemented the Board/parent alliance in 1971.

The fifth chapter describes the violence of the 1971 strike. There was far more violence than was reported at the time—violence to strikers, and espe- cially violence by them. Teachers who coordinated attacks on nonstriking teach- ers told me how it was done. Listening, I realized that striking teachers used violence not incidentally but as a matter of policy, to make up for insufficient numbers. In 1971, unlike 1970, most Black teachers did not strike. Partly for that reason, the brutal 1971 strike was widely seen as white versus Black: white teachers versus Black Board and Black parents. But seen up close, from street level, it was worse. It was Italian versus Black. The Italian community mobi- lized behind the teachers. The fifth chapter tells how two communities, two peoples, faced off in 1971, pushing Newark toward civil war.

When I first read about the 1971 strike in the New Jersey Room, I rooted for the striking teachers. I identified with their militancy, their solidarity, their hopes. I saw that they could lose everything—their strong contract, with its machinery for keeping the authorities honest; their hopes of improving the schools; their Union, which they had built—if they lost the strike. But the more I learned about the 1971 strike, the less I rooted for either side, and the more I rooted for peace. A powerful peace movement emerged late in the strike. I learned much of what I know about it from the tapes of Norman Eiger's interviews, which he shared with me. The fifth chapter tells the story of the successful move to end the violence and the strike.

Most writing about the 1971 strike was done only a few years after it. Most writers chose sides, embracing the either/or of class or race. Choosing class, some treated racial conflict as an abnormal intrusion on working people's struggles to achieve collective bargaining.[4] Choosing race, others saw striking teachers as clinging to racial privilege and trying to check the advances of the Black majority.[5] Race and class offer legitimate partial perspectives on the 1971 strike. The fifth chapter suggests how the opposing views might illuminate each other.

The sixth chapter describes the responses of teachers to jail. As a result of the strikes, 189 Newark teachers went to prison. What happened, I wondered, when professional men and women were treated as criminals? How did they react to jail? To other inmates? I was moved by what I found. On the one hand, many teachers became angry and depressed in jail. On the other hand, many supported each other, forming a kind of prison community; reaching out to other inmates, they organized protests for prisoner rights. The line between these two different responses tended to be the line between the sexes.

The epilogue focuses on the question of democracy in the Union. Many liberals and radicals praise union leaders for progressive stands on national issues. But I believe that the ways in which leaders treat their members matter more. Is there free speech in the union? Is there accountability of the leadership? Do members experience the union as their own power, or as another power against them? From the beginning of my study of Newark teachers, I pursued these questions. From the beginning, too, I wondered about the possibilities of educational reform. At the end of the book, I describe the fate of union democracy and educational reform in Newark, and argue that they are linked.

My story of the Newark teacher strikes stays close to the experience of the teachers. By taking their experience seriously, I've been able to explore ways that gender, class, and race mattered. How did male high school teachers see female elementary school teachers? How did elementary teachers see themselves? How did teacher professionals redefine themselves as workers? How did white teachers respond to the blackening of the student body or the presence of militant Black adults in the schools? How did Black teachers respond? How did Black teachers experience the conflicting loyalties of race and class in 1971? How did women teachers create an activist style of their own in faculty rooms, and in jail? These questions are an integral part of my story, giving it shape and meaning.

I've stayed close to the language of the teachers. If they referred to Jim, not James, I say Jim. Because the story comes first, I've used people's names when they enter. If a teacher got married after the strikes and changed her name, I use her maiden name. I don't use people's names if they didn't talk to me and weren't prominent in the public record, to protect their privacy. Most of the time, I say Black, rather than African American, because Black is what people said in 1970. (But I capitalize Black, both as noun and as adjective, because I capitalize Jewish and Italian.) The function of changing Jim to James, or Black to African American, would be to create more distance between them and us, then and now. On the contrary, I want to get as close as possible to their lived experience.

This story of Newark teachers crosses the boundaries of many fields of historical inquiry. It is urban history as the history of education, it is labor history brought up to date as the unionization of public-sector workers, and it is a study of ethnicity, gender, and race in class formation. It is, particularly, a book about the 1960s, one of a growing number of local studies. Only local studies can reach beyond the famous leaders of the decade and re-create the democratic hopes that drove the struggles.

The national movement for teacher power is sometimes seen as a sixties movement, sometimes as merely a continuation of thirties unionism.[6] Studied on a local level, the either/or dissolves. As teacher activists shaped the oppositional culture of the Newark Teachers Union, they drew on rich traditions of democratic control. Older activists remembered how the CIO once struggled to democratize the workplace and the larger society. Younger activists, especially those who went away to college, were influenced by the Student Nonviolent Coordinating Committee (SNCC) and the Students for a Democratic Society (SDS) and the contemporary struggle for participatory democracy.

Charles Payne, in his wonderful local study of the freedom struggle in Mississippi, observes that "SNCC . . . did a great deal to invent the sixties." Newark teachers participated in the reinvention of the possibilities of the sixties and in the closing out of those possibilities. Somewhat like early SNCC, the Newark Teachers Union identified and developed grass-roots leaders during the sixties, instead of smothering them under bureaucratic and hierarchical control. Like SNCC, the Union was powered by the idealism of its members and became a kind of democratic community of activists. Like the SNCC community, the Union community was torn apart partly as a result of its success.[7] Newark teachers drew on the energy and forms of struggle of the grass-roots movements of their times, but could not transcend the limits of those movements. This is their story.

Chapter 1

The Teacher Activists

Teachers created the Newark Teachers Union (NTU) because they wanted an alternative to the Newark Teachers Association (NTA). From 1919 to 1936, the Association was the only organization of educators in Newark. Then a rival was born. On Christmas Eve 1936, the American Federation of Teachers (AFT) granted a charter to Local 481.[1] On Christmas Eve thirty-five years later, more than one hundred Newark teachers would be in jail. This chapter tells the story of the formative years of the Newark Teachers Union, when some teachers developed commitments that would carry them all the way to jail.

The Jewish Teachers Who Shaped the Union

Local 481 of the American Federation of Teachers was not an immediate hit. Most Newark teachers preferred the Newark Teachers Association, an affiliate of the National Education Association. They were attracted to the Association's ideology of professionalism and its inclusion of administrators, who often provided leadership. Some teachers joined because the Association offered one of the few routes of advancement open to women, some because they were pressured to join by the principal of their school. The few teachers in Local 481 felt like underdogs and relished the role. By excluding administrators and claiming the status of a union rather than a professional association, teachers in Local 481 embraced the idea of conflict and struggle in the school system.

Local 481 was not a typical local of the American Federation of Teachers. At the founding of AFT, in 1916, male high school teachers elbowed aside militant female elementary school teachers. Like AFT as a whole, Local 481 was dominated by high school teachers. In other respects, however, it was more egalitarian. In 1938, Local 481 criticized national AFT for using an insurance company that sold only to whites. The teachers who joined the union in Newark wanted to improve their salaries and working conditions. But they also wanted to improve the world.[2]

The political and ethnic composition of Local 481 made a difference. It was predominantly left wing and—by the 1940s—Jewish. Equality—of both race and gender—was a core value. Newark elementary teachers were paid less than secondary teachers. Such pay differentials were common nationally, reflecting the assumption that elementary teachers deserved less money because they were not graduates of four-year liberal arts colleges, and needed less because they were women. (The maximum salary in 1939 for Newark high school teachers was $4,600; the maximum for elementary teachers, even with a master's degree, was $3,600.) Union leaders rejected the pay differential as not only discriminatory but also divisive. They went to the Board of Education with a proposal to forgo a raise for high school teachers—that is, for themselves—and to use the money to equalize the scale. In 1950, prodded by other local trade unions in alliance with Local 481, the Board finally ended the differential.[3]

By 1943, when Local 481 officially changed its name from the Essex County Federation of Teachers to the Newark Teachers Union, it had demonstrated its commitment to fight for the equality of women and men, Blacks and whites, and white ethnics. Italian and Jewish teachers tended to remain substitutes in Newark, unable to get regular appointments. Teachers in Local 481 formed the Newark Substitute Organization to press the Board of Education to hire permanent subs as regular teachers. The Substitute Organization was so successful in getting Jews and Italians regular positions in Newark that it lost members and eventually disbanded.[4]

Italians, Jews, and Blacks—members of marginalized groups just breaking into teaching—were attracted to the Newark Teachers Union. Jews especially flocked to the Union, to the point where one member, himself Jewish, suggested the "itskys and steins" should keep in the background.[5] In the time of the Spanish Civil War, World War II, and the Popular Front, it was less daring to be publicly identified as an organization of liberals and radicals, even socialists and communists, than as an organization mostly of Jews.

Years later, Allen Ginsberg recalled parties in Newark during the Popular Front in the 1930s, when he sang Spanish Civil War songs while his Aunt Rose collected money for the Loyalists in Spain. His poem also mentions his Aunt Honey. Hannah (Honey) Ginsberg Litzky grew up in Newark, the youngest sister of Allen's father, Louis. Leftist political arguments were routine in the family. Hannah's Russian-born parents had socialist leanings and were members of the Workmen's Circle. When she became a teacher, Hannah Litzky viewed political questions as inseparable from educational ones. Members of the Newark Teachers Association "were satisfied with the status quo" and "always currying favor with the downtown administration. . . . They were in political philosophy reactionaries, and that's something I was not." To Association members, a union member was "a laborer, a workingman, not a professional, not a college graduate. And they didn't identify at all with that class."[6]

Litzky identified with the working class. When the call went out for forming a union, "given my background I immediately felt that was what I wanted to do. But I didn't have a regular appointment. So there was a risk." She was a permanent sub in 1936 when she attended the organizational meeting of Local 481 in a basement store on Halsey Street in Newark. Despite the risk, she joined in 1937. The Union embodied her hope of change in the educational system and—acting with other workers and other unions—in the larger society. She went on to serve as corresponding secretary and as delegate to the Essex Labor Council, where she met with leaders of the Painters, the Steamfitters, the Carpenters, and other trades. As the only female delegate, she listened rather than spoke. But she was not easily intimidated, especially when acting with other women. Years later, when she was a grandmother, serving the Union as a prisoner in the women's wing of the Essex County penitentiary, she would speak up at the decisive moment, and trigger a prison rebellion.[7]

When Litzky attended the founding meeting of Local 481, Bob Lowenstein was a speaker. He was a radical and intellectual, with a Ph.D. in Romance languages from Johns Hopkins. He had completed his course work in 1933, with only his dissertation on Voltaire to write. But he couldn't find a college job. It was the Depression, and being Jewish didn't help. He taught high school, in Trenton and then in Newark, where he had been born. He gave up the hope of college teaching, of autonomy. But he wouldn't give up hope of preventing the interference of people who happened to be above him in the hierarchy. (Like Rousseau, he believed that if we can't be free, we must be equal.) Tenured friends in the Union urged Lowenstein to wait a few years before joining, but characteristically ignoring the advice of his elders, he joined in May 1937, becoming the Union's thirty-second member. He joined out of "self-respect. I didn't want to be a servant."[8]

Philip Roth was Lowenstein's student in Newark. Afterward, they became close. In *I Married a Communist*, Roth drew on Lowenstein to create Nathan Ringold, a Newark high school teacher. "I threw myself into organizing our union," says Ringold. "I burned with zeal to establish the dignity of my profession." Roth captures Lowenstein's tone, and his bill of particulars. "The personal indignity that you had to undergo as a teacher when I first started teaching—you wouldn't believe it. Being treated like children. Whatever the superiors told you, that was law. Unquestioned. You will get here at this time, you will sign the time book on time. You will spend so many hours in school. And you will be called on for afternoon and evening assignments, even though that wasn't part of your contract. All kinds of chicken-shit stuff."[9]

The Union became Lowenstein's way to make the lack of independence tolerable. He was a driving force in the effort to get the Board of Education to pay extra for extra work. "They just assumed they could make the faculty come back in the evening, and never give them anything for it." Before Local 481, he was active in the Newark Teachers Association, "but . . . soon became dissatisfied with that, because it was dominated by administrators." He wanted an end to domination by administrators, an "end to cronyism" and "bootlickers." Even today, like an intellectual Humphrey Bogart, Lowenstein speaks the hardboiled language of masculine independence. "The classroom was the toughest job." By contrast, the job of guidance counselor, which some friends saw as a way out of the classroom, "was a lot of crap."[10]

Hannah Litzky and Bob Lowenstein embodied the strengths of the early NTU. They were committed to fighting for the rights of teachers and the rights of students, and refused to choose between the two. Their political egalitarianism shaped their vision of unionism. The Union's demand for smaller classes was meant to bring students and teachers closer, and to enhance teaching and learning. The same Union that insisted teachers be paid to attend after-school functions also insisted Newark develop a citywide food program for needy children. Litzky, Lowenstein, and their Union colleagues never imagined that their efforts would benefit teachers alone. On the contrary, their bedrock faith was in the convergence of struggles by working people everywhere. They were part of what Michael Denning calls the "laboring of America," the left-wing culture of the 1930s and 1940s that drew strength from the CIO, and encouraged office workers, government employees, and teachers to identify their struggles with those of industrial workers.[11]

Lowenstein was brilliant, courageous, rebellious. He became an executive board member of the Union soon after joining and remained a leader for three decades. To counteract the need for bootlicking, the Union fought for, and won, promotion by examination. After twenty-five years of classroom teaching, still loving it, Lowenstein would take the examination and become department chair, even though it meant leaving the classroom. "For self-respect I became a department chairman," he explains. "Because I was humiliated to take dictation from department chairs I could not respect."[12]

Through the 1940s and 1950s, the Newark Teachers Union remained strongest at high schools, particularly Weequahic High. When Litzky received a regular appointment, it was to Weequahic; Lowenstein was already there. Built in the mostly Jewish South Ward, completed at the beginning of the Depression, Weequahic quickly became one of the strongest academic high schools in the nation, the focal point of Newark's Jewish community, and the center of the Teachers Union.

Alice Saltman, a young art teacher, was transferred to Weequahic in 1937 on the request of her principal, who told her she'd be happier there; she still wonders if the remark was anti-Semitic. She *was* happier. She found strong Jewish faculty teaching motivated Jewish students. Saltman had grown up in the Ironbound section of Newark's East Ward, one of two Jews in her elementary school. She thought Weequahic—not only the school but the neighborhood— "was wonderful. It was a close community. It was like a ghetto. But," she adds, laughing, "it was an upper-class ghetto."[13]

Saltman became part of a group of radical teachers at Weequahic. "Everybody at the time from my group were not necessarily communists. . . . A lot of them were. You know that's the way it went in those days. If you were liberal, you were very close to communist thinking." Saltman didn't join the Party. But she did join the Union, because the outstanding teachers like Lowenstein, whom she knew by reputation even before transferring, were in it. And she joined because "I had a background." Her mother, an immigrant from Russia, joined the Industrial Workers of the World, was arrested while picketing in New York City, and went to jail. Almost six decades after her mother's arrest, Alice Saltman would come out of retirement to picket for the Union, get arrested, and at the age of 72, go to jail.[14]

If Weequahic was the heart of the Union, faculty rooms were the arteries. "People always talk," explains an NTU activist, "and out of that dynamic of faculty rooms something emerges." Faculty rooms were segregated by gender through the 1950s. At Weequahic, Litzky explains, "straight-laced WASPS" mainly used the second-floor teachers room for women. Jewish and left-wing women came together in the third-floor teachers room. "We would talk politics. We also had group therapy sessions—we didn't know that's what they were then, but they were. Many of us were by then married, and had children. We had a lot of mutual common problems. We used to talk about that. Then as younger teachers came into the school, some of them joined us."[15]

In the faculty rooms of the secondary schools of the city, teachers forged common ties that would carry them into strikes, even to jail. Some were carried too far. Esther Tumin began teaching at Weequahic in 1959, as a mature woman, and joined NTU two months later, becoming a regular in the third-floor teachers room. She joined "because I'm a liberal, and because I approved of the unionization of teachers. And most of the people I knew in the schools whom I admired, the master teachers, were all very active in the Union." Teachers in the Association "considered [us] radicals, and they considered themselves professionals, and felt that strike was a dirty word because professionals don't strike." Tumin believed, on the contrary, that only the Union would protect the professionalism of teachers.[16]

She always wanted to be a professional. "I wanted to be a doctor." As a Jew, she would have faced quotas in medical schools. She did not apply. She was defeated by a combination of factors. "In my day, women just did not go into medicine, and certainly children of milkmen didn't go to medical school." Teaching science was next best. She saw teaching as a step up from the working class, from "milkmen, and shoemakers, and tailors—you know, the generation that came in the early 1900s." Later she would strike to protect her professional middle-class status, and finding herself in jail, would be shocked to discover how little her status mattered. And would be defeated again.[17]

By "master teachers," Union members meant teachers who had high standards and believed in the students' ability to meet those standards. Seymour Spiegel experienced those standards and that belief as a student at Weequahic. He graduated in 1951 but wasn't planning to go to college. He couldn't go away to the college of his choice, because his father was very sick; he felt angry at the world, and depressed. Jeanette Lappé, NTU activist and regular in the third-floor teachers room, was cleaning out her classroom at the end of the year when she saw Spiegel and asked about his college plans. She did not accept his answer. Lappé had failed him in social studies because he would not outline the "News of the Week in Review" from the *New York Times*. But he was going to college. Physically taking charge of the paper work, Lappé got Spiegel to apply to the Newark campus of Rutgers University. She changed the direction of his life.[18]

Spiegel came back to the Newark school system five years later, as a teacher. He joined the Union in his second month. "I felt the men and women in the Teachers Union were the brightest and the most informed and the most committed of all the teachers." Teachers in the Association seemed more concerned with the privileges of the profession than with the students. "I remember the long arguments of the Union meetings were seldom about increase in salary. They were almost always about teaching conditions," like overcrowded classes. "The function of the Union—more than protecting our rights—was to improve education." Spiegel became an educational leader, with a primary focus on turning around kids who were in trouble. Later, after the riot/rebellion of 1967, he would launch Newark's most important educational experiment.[19]

The ability of the Newark Teachers Union to attract creative and committed educators like Spiegel was one of its strengths. But it grew slowly. The brilliant oratory of Union leaders impressed young teachers but also intimidated them. When Spiegel began attending Union meetings in the 1950s, he found Bob Lowenstein's intellect "electrifying" and "overpowering" and knew he could not compete. Feeling "honored to be there," another young teacher was quiet at meetings, "because the competition and the articulation of those around you was too much of a challenge." He would agree with Lowenstein, but silently. "To stand up and raise 'a point of order, Mr. Chairman—oh, forget that. They were too intellectual for me."[20]

The competitive, masculine style of intellectual debate kept some men and perhaps even more women from participating. The sheer length of meetings also discouraged those with family responsibilities. In the 1950s, meetings frequently lasted until eleven o'clock; sixty people might be there in the beginning, and only fifteen or twenty at the end. Lowenstein explains, "Our meetings were so democratically run we never got out. Anybody who wanted to say anything at all was given the floor repeatedly. . . . The meetings lasted too goddamn late. People got turned off, got bored."[21]

The style and substance of the early Newark Teachers Union reflected the concern for autonomy voiced by men like Lowenstein. These men reached out to women, not only female secondary teachers like Litzky—that was easy—but women in elementary schools as well. Yet prejudice against female elementary teachers lingered within the Union. Ben Epstein, who served as the Union's legislative chair for seventeen years, supported the campaign to equalize pay between elementary and secondary school teachers, because the wage differential hurt the Union. He did not, however, believe teachers were equal. Elementary school teachers were less militant than secondary school teachers, he maintains, because they knew less. Stressing the difference between a two- or three-year education degree and a bachelor's degree, he contends that "the educational level, and the broader university graduate view, was in the secondary schools. The guy who taught social studies all the time, you see, knew more about society than did the lady who was handling the kindergarten."[22]

Epstein was one of many male high school teachers whose class and gender prejudices converged in a disparagement of elementary school teachers. Union leaders with degrees in the humanities often looked down on teachers with educational degrees. "You can't hide contempt," observed a younger activist. Was the "lady who was handling the kindergarten" really less intelligent than "the guy who taught social studies," or was she more isolated? She had few opportunities to meet with colleagues during school, and no department chair to provide a buffer between her and the principal; when the principal pressed her to join the Association, she was not in a position to refuse.[23] The prejudice within the Union toward female teachers of small children limited its capacity for growth.

The Union's growth was also limited by its reputation as the organization of Jews and radicals. To many teachers, the Union was the preserve of Jewish high school teachers who challenged administrators, and was the opposite of professionalism. Still, the NTU was able to recruit new members among marginalized groups (Italians and Blacks, as well as Jews), until it ran into organized anticommunism.

Communist-dominated locals in New York and Philadelphia were expelled in 1941 by AFT, which hoped to gain more support from the anticommunist American Federation of Labor. But in Newark, throughout the 1940s and early 1950s, communists, socialists, labor liberals, and other more or less radical teachers continued to meet, debate, and sustain their distinctive Union culture. Then in 1955, the House Un-American Activities Committee came to Newark. Bob Lowenstein and two other teachers refused to answer the Committee's questions. For twenty years Lowenstein had been one of the most respected teachers in the system. Now he was fired because he refused to name names. "He protected many others," says Spiegel. "There were many others who would have gone down."[24]

The New Jersey Supreme Court sent the case back to the Board of Education. "On the one hand," Lowenstein told the Board, "you have a record here of over 20 years of unblemished, competent and devoted service to children, to teachers, to American principles and ideals. On the other, you have an allegation of insubordination and conduct unbecoming a teacher that presumably makes me unfit to teach." He left the choice to the Board, offering only this: "I told the Superintendent of Schools that I am not a member of the Communist Party and that I have not been since the summer of 1953." He would answer no further questions about his beliefs or associations. He doubted "our state supreme court intended to sanction an invasion of my privacy to such an extent that I would be stripped naked of my constitutionally protected self-respect."[25]

Whether constitutionally protected or not, Lowenstein took his stand on self-respect. The Board of Education unanimously fired him. To support his family, he worked in a liquor store, sold insurance, sold mutual funds. Vinnie Young, the Union president, visited him, and asked if he was bitter. He said no: "What I did, I did for myself, as a teacher." He meant that if he violated his core integrity, he would have nothing left with which to teach. The Union helped him. Local affiliates of the AFT in other cities abandoned communist teachers during the crunch years of the witch-hunting in the schools. Not so the Newark Teachers Union, which stood by Lowenstein and pushed the state and national Union to back him. Some Union members had money taken from their salary to help. Six years after he was fired, Lowenstein was reinstated by order of the New Jersey Supreme Court, the last of the three dismissed teachers to regain their positions.[26]

From a high of about 425 members, at the beginning of the 1950s, the NTU slipped to a low of about 125 members at the end of the decade. Some teachers "hated the Union because of its left politics," says a member. "The old Jewish, Communist Union. They didn't want anything to do with that." Others were sympathetic, but afraid to be associated with "reds." After three decades of protest, the Newark Teachers Union remained much smaller and less organized than the Newark Teachers Association. The Union was idealistic, principled, and amateurish—a gadfly, remembers Ben Epstein, "making good speeches, trying to get good publicity, but never acting as a power bloc. We were the inspired leaders of a cause without force."[27]

During the 1960s the Newark Teachers Union acquired force.

The Italian Teachers Who Transformed the Union

From 1946 to 1960, there were no teacher strikes in Newark and only eleven brief strikes in New Jersey. Before collective bargaining, teachers had little power. The tone of relations between teachers and boards of education in the pre-bargaining era was captured by one historical study.

> A group of teacher representatives appeal to the local school board for a $300 salary increase and an extra $150 for all teachers at or reaching maximum step on the salary scale. The board first would thank the teacher representatives for their presentations. . . . Then the board president would state that financial conditions prevented the school board from granting more than a $150 raise and an additional $50 to all teachers on maximum step. The teachers would thank the board for its generosity and then return to their seats.[28]

This pattern of going to the board of education with "hat in hand"—the phrase is Ben Epstein's—was broken in 1960 by a one-day strike in New York City. The strike forced the New York City Board of Education and the city's mayor to hold an election to determine which teacher organization would represent teachers in collective bargaining. Impressed, nine representatives of the Newark Teachers Union went to talk to the New York leaders. In 1961, the New York local won the representational election. In 1962, it followed up with another strike, forcing the Board of Education to sign a collective bargaining agreement.[29]

In 1962, NTU launched a campaign to become the collective bargaining agent. What the New York local accomplished in 1960–1962 shaped the strategy of the Newark local from 1962 to 1970. First build up membership; then force a bargaining election, by striking if necessary; gain enough votes from nonmembers to win the election; and force the board of education to sign a contract, again by striking if necessary. In 1963, an NTU vice president told the Board: "We no longer accept the archaic system by which this Board, or any Board, unilaterally arrives at a decision and in effect says to the teachers 'This is what you will live with.' "[30] The days of hat in hand were over.

No longer a gadfly, the Union began a struggle for power. It wouldn't go smoothly. Elections would be lost. Strikes would be terribly costly. But now there were people in the Union who knew not only where they were going but how to get there.

Tony Ficcio was NTU's earliest, most consistent advocate of collective bargaining. Born in Newark, a graduate of Barringer High School, he began teaching in 1954. "The principal called me in and told me he had always had 100 percent membership in the Association." Unprotected by tenure, Ficcio joined the Association. Soon "a teacher came to me very quietly, when we were alone, said that he was a member of the Newark Teachers Union, and would I be interested in joining." Ficcio's father belonged to the Carpenters Union; Ficcio saw the labor movement as a "progressive force." He joined NTU and "kept it very quiet," because joining was dangerous. "You didn't get fired. All you did was you were not rehired for the next year." He was now a member of both teacher organizations. His official and visible membership meant nothing to him, the way membership in the Anglican church meant nothing to a seventeenth-century Puritan in England. His secret and invisible membership became his life.[31]

Ficcio paid his way to AFT national conventions in the late 1950s and met delegates from the New York local. He went to New York and sat in on their meetings. What fascinated him was their focus on collective bargaining. He was particularly impressed by a national staff representative named Dave Selden. Later, as president of AFT, Selden would go to jail in Newark to support the striking teachers. At the end of the 1950s, Selden was organizing for AFT in New York, and pushing collective bargaining. Bargaining for public employees was a new idea for most people, and it galvanized Ficcio. Never inspirational, a plugger and transmitter rather than a creator, he brought the gospel back to Newark.[32]

Ralph Favilla and Vic and Joe Cascella were childhood friends, Newark-born Italian Americans who, like Ficcio, joined the Union in the 1950s and spearheaded its drive for collective bargaining in the 1960s. They were more adept than Ficcio at rooting the new doctrine of collective bargaining in the experience of teachers. Vic Cascella was drafted after graduating from high school; Favilla dropped out of high school, joined the service, then followed Vic's twin brother, Joe, to Newark's Central Evening High School, where he got his diploma. By the time the three veterans became teachers, they were mature men who had a sense of their rights and hated being pushed around.[33]

At the evening school, Joe Cascella met older Union teachers and became a socialist like them. But the Cascellas and Favilla were no carbon copies of the NTU's left-wing leaders. From the beginning their orientation was more practical. They were impatient with extended debate and focused on issues of money and power. Before he even began teaching, Vic Cascella drove around Newark with Joe, helping him conduct an NTU survey on teacher salaries. After the 1962 victory in New York, the Cascellas and Favilla were ready to lead the charge in Newark. They regarded themselves as the Union's "Young Turks" and saw their mission as pushing the "Old Guard," the older, mostly Jewish leaders, into the era of collective bargaining.[34]

Favilla began teaching elementary school in 1958, and was asked to join the Association, but declined. He had already joined NTU. That year he began recruiting teachers into the Union. To put him in his place, the principal observed him, the supervisor of elementary schools observed him, and the assistant superintendent of schools observed him—all in the same day. The next year, at a new school, the principal circulated a notice in support of the Association, and deliberately sent it to him first. "Principals were gods," says Favilla. "They could do no wrong. And that was unacceptable to us." In big red letters, Favilla wrote on the principal's notice that it was intimidation. The notice went to the other teachers with his comment. Favilla used the effort to silence him as a means of illustrating the tyranny of principals. He became one of the Union's most effective recruiters.[35]

As elementary school teachers, Favilla and Vic Cascella brought new issues to the Union, and a new anger. Cascella expresses a resentment felt by many elementary teachers toward secondary, and postsecondary, teachers. "High school teachers, they have the racket. The lower you go in school, the harder you work. That's why I know you don't work too hard," he said to me, slyly.[36]

Elementary teachers were assigned to many nonteaching duties. Cascella was eating lunch one day when the principal announced it was his turn for cafeteria duty. "I went to see Mr. Vincent Young, president of the Newark Teachers Union, and Joe Cascella, executive vice president of the Newark Teachers Union, and I said, 'I had to stop eating lunch to do cafeteria duty.' " Even the army gave people a chance to eat, he complained. But his brother and Young were not impressed. " 'Oh Vic, you got to expect to do some of these things. They're professional. They're professional chores.' That phrase rang in my mind." Years later, when the first contract between the Union and the Board freed teachers from "nonprofessional chores" like cafeteria duty, Vic Cascella was the Union officer who would insist on strictly enforcing the contract. "And that was because I was an elementary school teacher. These high school people, it didn't bother them. They stood in their doorways [on hall duty], b.s.-ing each other and stuff, whatever they did."[37]

The school population swelled in the 1950s and 1960s, and teaching became harder. Small children need individual attention. "With overcrowded classrooms, you could never get to the child who needed it the most," Favilla explains. Cascella taught with "desks and chairs in the hallway, for crying out loud." His school was on double sessions. He taught thirty-nine students in the morning, forty in the afternoon. "Double registers, double report cards, double plans, double this, double that." Still angry, he asks, "What do you think forty kids in a classroom [are] getting out of a teacher that taught thirty-nine in the morning?" It was bad for students and for teachers. "You couldn't do anything about it, because you had no power. You worked at the prerogative of the Board, under their rules and regulations. And we needed some way to say, 'Wait, halt! This is abusive treatment.' "[38]

Vic and Joe Cascella inherited their unionism from their father, who was active in the Musicians Union. Don Nicholas, another activist pushing for collective bargaining, inherited his unionism too. His great-grandfather was in the Knights of Labor, his grandfather in the Miners Union, his father in violent mining strikes in Scranton, Pennsylvania; in New Jersey, his father became president of an ironworkers local. Don Nicholas was already committed to the labor movement when he came to teaching. On his third day, he joined a Union demonstration and joined the Union. With the Cascellas, Favilla, and Ficcio, Nicholas prodded NTU toward becoming a real union.[39]

AFT leaders were excited about the possibilities of organizing in cities where conditions were similar to New York: overcrowded classes, old schools, insufficient supplies, low salaries, breakdowns in discipline. They wanted their urban locals to challenge National Education Association affiliates by campaigning for collective bargaining. Public-sector unionism was growing, aided by a 1962 executive order by President Kennedy. Teachers, police, firemen, garbagemen, transit workers, postal employees, and social service workers were organizing. With the United Automobile Workers leading the way, the AFL-CIO backed the unionization of teachers as a way of countering the decline of industrial unionism. The Industrial Union Department (IUD) of the AFL-CIO put several organizers of teachers on the payroll and sent one to New Jersey, with primary responsibility for Newark.[40]

Ficcio, Favilla, Nicholas, and the Cascellas knew there was local talent to do organizing. What they wanted from IUD was money, to pay a Newark teacher to go on leave and organize full-time, or pay three Newark teachers to organize part-time. The idea of payment grew out of the collective bargaining campaign and was the beginning of professionalizing NTU; in the days of the amateur union, from 1936 through 1961, everything was done on a voluntary basis. In 1963, a New Jersey Committee of IUD agreed to small stipends for three part-time organizers. Along with the money went advice: "The other union leaders at the meeting further suggested that the Newark Teachers Union attempt to find a Negro, an Italian, and an Irishman to fill these organizing positions." The labor leaders evidently believed organizers would be most successful in reaching teachers of their own race or ethnicity. Then why not hire a Jew? Perhaps they thought there were already enough Jews in NTU. Accepting the advice, NTU hired Favilla (Italian), Rolston Gaiter (Black), and Don Nicholas (mother half Irish, father Welsh).[41]

IUD and NTU leaders did not treat gender as they did race and ethnicity. Although most teachers were women, the IUD did not ask NTU to hire a woman. All national AFT organizers were men. The leaders of NTU, AFT, and the AFL-CIO shared the assumption that labor organizing was men's work. The civil rights movement was pushing them to take racial difference into account; the modern women's movement had not yet emerged to pressure them to take gender difference seriously. In the collective bargaining campaign of the 1960s, NTU organizers were men who thought of their own style as the universal style and were not especially sensitive to the nuances of gender.

President Young was opposed to paying anyone for Union work. He hesitated to risk NTU's limited resources on a campaign for collective bargaining. Perhaps he also didn't want to risk the Union's purity. But when the Union held its first meeting of the 1962–1963 school year, in the words of the newsletter: "The announced subject was COLLECTIVE BARGAINING; it was the best attended meeting in many years, and many of the faces were new."[42]

Ficcio, Favilla, Vic Cascella, and Nicholas made organizing their second, usually unpaid, job. They worked every day after school, from 3:15 to dinner, and went to meetings two or three nights a week. Nicholas edited the *NTU Bulletin*. Cascella and Favilla organized teachers wherever they found them, beginning with the playgrounds of the summer recreation program. In 1963, the Association had six full-time staff, and a membership perhaps ten times as great as NTU's. To overtake the Association, the union depended on the unpaid or underpaid labor of dedicated members. "We had no social life," Favilla says. "That was the social life," counters Cascella.[43]

Most dedicated of all, considered fanatical by fellow organizers, Ficcio was the nuts-and-bolts man of the collective bargaining campaign, supervising the distribution of literature, giving the building representatives things to do, trying to anticipate problems before they arose. Led by Ficcio, the Union in the fall of 1963 sent three first-class mailings to every teacher in Newark, plus five permit mailings and seven mailings of *Bulletins* on collective bargaining. In addition, organizers put information in teachers' mailboxes where principals allowed the practice.[44]

Teacher-organizers knew that support for the association was softer than it looked. An internal NTU report in the fall of 1963 noted that the association relied on school administrators to do the organizing. "There are very few teachers who are dedicated members of the NTA. (You are rarely dedicated to an organization in which an administrator urges you to join.)"[45] Union strategy would depend on teachers urging teachers to join—school by school, teacher by teacher.

During the campaign for collective bargaining, from 1962 to 1969, Union leaders learned more about teachers than they had ever known about them, or would ever know again. In the 1940s and 1950s, the Union had a reputation for being a bit exclusive. Teachers were rumored to have been denied membership because they were not considered good teachers, or because they were politically conservative; what probably really happened was that they just weren't asked to join. Bright and committed to good teaching and progressive politics, NTU activists tended to look down on those who seemed less bright or committed. Not everyone felt welcome in Weequahic's third-floor teachers room.[46] But once the collective bargaining campaign began in 1962, the Union needed votes and could not afford to dismiss anyone.

NTU leaders recognized that many elementary school teachers saw unionism as a threat to their professional status. In 1962, the newsletter specified what collective bargaining could do for elementary teachers: limit class size, free teachers from nonteaching duties, provide a duty-free lunch period and a preparation period. In 1964, Sidney Rosenfeld, the new NTU president, listed the ways elementary teachers benefited from the contract in New York, and then pointed to the less tangible but decisive benefit: "Elementary school teachers have achieved professional status!" The argument that unionism made professionalism possible would become the Union's most important argument, especially with elementary school teachers.[47]

Jerry Yablonsky liked talking union to teachers in the Association. Yablonsky began teaching full-time in 1961, after a stint in the army, and joined the Union during his first school term. Like many members, he was Jewish, grew up in Newark, and went to Weequahic. But like many Italian teachers, his roots were in the trade union movement: his uncle, Pete Yablonsky, was president of the local Painters Union, a past member representing labor on the Newark Board of Education, and a powerful friend of the Newark Teachers Union. Jerry

Yablonsky was predisposed to join the collective bargaining campaign and make the NTU more like a regular union. When the Union needed to replace one of its part-time organizers, he was recruited by Young, and Ralph Favilla became his instructor.[48]

The pay was very part-time and the hours full-time. But he didn't mind, because he believed in the work. He phoned teachers and asked to meet with them in their homes. He arranged meetings with small groups after school or on weekends, in their schools or in restaurants, diners, or delicatessens; IUD money paid for the food. Teachers told him that labor unions were corrupt and bullying; they were repelled by the idea of a percentage of NTU dues going to the AFL-CIO. Would NTU take money from teachers to organize custodians? Why did teachers need a union when there was already a professional association for them and administrators? Yablonsky answered that the "interests and needs" of principals and superintendents were not the same as the interests and needs of teachers, "and therefore we weren't all on the same team."[49]

Trying to put himself in their place, Yablonsky imagined why teachers resisted joining a union. "'What kind of a professional am I, being in a union like Uncle Joe, who was in the union when he went to the factory?'" Many teachers were the first in their family to go to college; they came from the working class, and their claim to professional middle-class status was still fragile. Yablonsky and other NTU organizers simultaneously challenged the class prejudices of teachers and assuaged their class anxiety, their fear of losing middle-class status by joining a union. One teacher raised her hand at a small after-school meeting with Yablonsky. She expressed doubts about unions, citing the exorbitant hourly wage of electricians. "I said to her, without missing a beat, 'Wouldn't you like to make that?'" Once a teacher asked Vic Cascella, " 'Do you think I want to go to a union meeting and sit next to a carpenter or an electrician?' " Cascella responded, "Snobbery is not going to get anything for teachers in this country."[50]

Ficcio made the same point by telling teachers a fable. Once there was a meeting, he would say, and at this meeting of teachers there was a representative of another union, "in this case the electrical workers union, who's a member of the Labor Council in the area. And in the question period a teacher got up and said, 'If I joined the union would I have to associate with plumbers and electricians?' And the electrician said, 'Let me answer that question.' He says, 'In a society, as you know, people usually associate with other people who are in the same socioeconomic bracket. So you don't have to worry about associating with me, because I make a helluva lot more than you do.' " Ficcio was suggesting a redefinition of class. Class was really about money. The rest of it, the professional dress and style and aspirations, served to mystify class. Only by giving up their sense of superiority, and joining blue-collar workers in the labor movement, could teachers actually improve their class status. "So 'professional,' the word 'professional,' was an empty word."[51]

If focusing on money enabled organizers to demystify the idea of professional, focusing on working conditions gave them a way to reclaim the idea and transform it. Ficcio: "We would always define professionalism: professionalism is when a group of workers have a very great and influential and strong voice in determining their working conditions." Yablonsky: "We pointed out to them that most professionals set the terms of their employment. And we as teachers did not do that. That unless we had the right of collective bargaining, with enforceable contract, we would never be able to set our own working conditions." In this way, the Union stood the Association's appeal to professionalism on its head. Joining the Union, even striking, became not the obstacle to professional status but the only way to achieve it.[52]

Vic Cascella saw the idea of professional as contested territory. "The asskissing type, many of them were very 'professional' to the administration, and if the administration determined who the hell professionals are, you'd have a problem." The conferred status of "professional" left teachers dependent on administrators, who did the conferring. "But in the eyes of the Union, one of the criteria of professionalism was—I won't say a leftist attitude but—you had to be concerned with civil rights, you had to be concerned with the learning of the kids."[53] Cascella's definition of professional preserved the key meanings of the old Union. You were a professional if you stood up to the administration and if you cared about the education of the students and civil rights. Under the influence of his socialist brother, Vic Cascella kept alive the spirit of the old Jewish and left-wing Union, even as he and his colleagues were transforming it into a vehicle for collective bargaining.

Union teachers never ceded the idea of professional to the "professional association." As Bob Lowenstein insisted, either teachers joined together to fight for respect and the right to participate in decisions or they were servants and bootlickers. The premise of the Union, from the beginning, was that real professionalism must be taken, not granted. Union teachers rejected the choice framed by the Association: workers or professionals? Instead, they fashioned a complex class identity as working-class professionals.

But were they really working class? Who is working class? Many social workers in New York, especially during the thirties and forties, also defined themselves as professional workers, and organized around their rights as workers. Do we invent a proletarian who has only his or her time to sell, and use this abstraction to determine that social workers and teachers are not working class? Of course teachers are working class. Of course they are not working class. That's what it means to be working class: to be defined by your role as worker, and to struggle to be more than your role.[54]

Persuading teachers to join together as working-class professionals was one thing; creating an effective organization was another. Ficcio was "certainly trying to sign up as many as possible, but really the focus was to get building reps." The building rep at each school distributed Union literature, talked to teachers, signed them up, kept them involved. Before the collective bargaining campaign, many schools had no representative; at others, the rep was inactive. Yet potentially, the system of building reps was the backbone of the Union. "How much more must it be improved before we act?" asked an internal report in 1963.[55]

Favilla took on the task of improving the building-rep network, with help from Yablonsky and teacher-organizer John Schmid. "We targeted the dead schools," explains Schmid. They asked a New York organizer how to do it. Then they identified teachers willing to represent the Union and put them through a training program, teaching them how to approach others in their buildings.[56] The building reps became reliable links between the Union office and the members. In 1970, the network of building reps established during the collective bargaining campaign would serve as the strike network.

How effective was the organizing drive? An imperfect measure was the number of people who joined the Union—imperfect because the membership book shows who joined, but not who kept paying dues. Some joined, let their membership lapse, then joined again. Still, the figures are revealing. During the 1940s, an average of 79 teachers joined NTU each year. In the 1950s, at the time of the anticommunist crusade, the average fell to 58. From 1962 to 1966, in the first four years of the collective bargaining campaign, the annual average was 290.[57]

Union membership remained smaller than Association membership, because teachers were still afraid to be identified with the Union, and Union dues were higher; it cost more, in both senses, to join the Union. But the Union was ready to challenge the Association. It circulated a petition, threatened a strike, and in December 1964 forced the Board of Education to hold an election to determine which organization would represent teachers.[58]

The election is a better measure of the growing Union strength. "We really didn't think that we stood much of a chance," says Vic Cascella. The vote "was a complete surprise for everybody," says Ficcio. Given a secret ballot, 1,447 teachers voted for the Union and 1,466 for the Association. For the first time, the Association would represent all Newark teachers in negotiations with the Board. But the vote vindicated those who were pushing for collective bargaining. "That was the end of the debating society," says John Schmid. The Union was no longer the ghetto organization of left-wing Jewish high school teachers. Now it was the organization of all teachers who saw militancy as the answer to the unchecked power of the principals and Board.[59]

Who voted Union and who voted Association? Clara Dasher and Edith Counts illustrate the differences. Dasher and Counts were both African Americans who began teaching elementary school in Newark before the collective bargaining campaign began, and originally joined the Association. They posed the question of supporting the Union in almost identical terms. "I guess I felt that it was a labor movement and not a professional movement," says Counts. "I felt that we were first of all more workers than mere professionals," said Dasher.[60] Dasher supported the Union, and Counts did not. What differentiated them was how they constructed their class identity.

Counts was proud of her professional status. A graduate of Barringer, she took pleasure in the fact that her mother had gone before her, when Barringer was the only public high school in Newark. Counts returned to Newark after teaching several years in South Carolina. She found the situation of teachers in Newark "wasn't that bad," and she focused on the professional obligation to serve students. As a teacher in Newark, Counts arrived at a position where she felt both able and obliged to put others first. She voted for the Association against the Union and remained a member of the Association even after the Union became the bargaining agent.[61]

Dasher was proud that she was a second-generation Union member. Her father was a teamster, "a strong union member." As a teacher, she felt she was still arriving. She was frustrated because "the teachers used to gripe constantly but never take it any further than that." She left the Association because "they didn't fight strong enough, for not only teachers' rights but for pupil rights as well." She wanted the Union to take teachers further, and hoped students would be carried along. Dasher joined the Newark Teachers Union in 1964, and became an officer in 1966, a vice president in 1969, and remained one of the two most important people in the Union for a quarter of a century.[62]

The decisive question for teachers was whether they saw themselves as part of the working class. Many still rejected NTU because it seemed more a labor movement than a professional organization.

In college, Ellen Cunniff became an officer of the student wing of the New Jersey Education Association. She wanted to go into educational administration, and she knew that the Association and administration were intertwined, with each recruiting for the other. As an elementary school teacher, she was pressed to join the Newark Teachers Association. "You didn't have to belong, but depending on the school you were assigned to you'd better belong." But she didn't mind, because the Association was one of the few routes open to women who wanted to move up.[63]

In 1965, when Cunniff began teaching, she was approached by two Union activists. She listened to their arguments and told them she was going to join the Association. She didn't like what Union recruiters said, or how they said it. "With the Union there would be a lot more emotion. They were trying to stir people up. Drinks flowed more freely. You bought your own at the Association." Association members "were not rebels, they were not placard holders at all, they were going to go through the system." Many Union members were rebellious young high school teachers who looked down on elementary teachers as less qualified. They also had an attitude of " 'Don't trust anyone over thirty.' Everyone in the Association was over thirty."[64]

Cunniff was a woman hoping to move up in the system rather than change it, an elementary teacher who resented the superior attitude of Union secondary teachers and preferred the more sober style of the Association. And she adds, "I guess I'm shaded by my parents' impressions too." After World War II, her father's union rejected the company's final offer; when he lost his job, he blamed the union. "He always said, 'There's an agenda among many unionists.'" On every ground, Cunniff preferred the Association.[65]

Like Cunniff's choice of the Association, Pat Piegari's choice of the Union was overdetermined. By 1965, teachers were joining the Union for different reasons. Some experienced the arbitrary power of the principal as intolerable. Others were frustrated by the Board of Education's unwillingness or inability to provide the supplies children needed. Some inherited their unionism. Others joined because they were impressed with the caliber of teachers in the Union. And others, like Piegari, joined because of all those reasons.

Piegari had grown up in Newark and wanted to give something back. Like Cunniff, he began teaching in 1965. He came into an elementary school where the educators he most admired, the teachers who seemed "pro-kids," were also pro-Union. As a teacher of industrial arts, he couldn't get the supplies and materials he needed. He bought the compasses and pencils and notepaper. To get wood, tools, and equipment, however, he needed the support of the Board of Education. The Board didn't seem to care. In his second month, unable to teach without wood, Piegari drove his car to the Board office depot and just took what he needed.[66]

In his first month of teaching, Piegari joined the Union. He grew up in the Ironbound, a solidly blue-collar section. He worked summers on the docks of Port Newark, where he was exposed to strong unions. His parents were in unions, "and I wouldn't think of crossing a union picket line. So it was my roots."

The conditions he found on the job and the example of outstanding Union teachers ratified his predisposition.[67]

Like Piegari, many Italian American teachers had union roots. The labor movement was part of their communal identity; fathers or uncles were members, sometimes leaders, of local unions. As children of the labor movement, many Italian teachers saw the Newark Teachers Union as the best way to advance their interests and protect their rights as working people. They were drawn to the NTU because of its militancy, but they did not necessarily share its vision of social and political change.

Joe Ciccolini and Felix Martino prided themselves on their pragmatism and lack of susceptibility to ideologies of any kind. Although new teachers in the 1960s, they were mature men, born in the Depression, who approached unions in terms that they inherited. Ciccolini's father was an immigrant from Italy, a Roosevelt Democrat, "a strong labor man . . . in the coal mines." As a youth, Joe went in a different direction. Graduating from Barringer High School, in the predominantly Italian North Ward, he went to the University of Pennsylvania's Wharton School of Business and into business. But when he became a teacher of business at Barringer, he also became a loyal supporter of the Newark Teachers Union.[68]

Felix Martino also graduated from Barringer, and taught there. His father was a famous, and feared, Newark teacher of physics and chemistry. Felix came to teaching after training at the Special Warfare Center in North Carolina. He joined NTU while he was still a long-term substitute. Neither Martino nor Ciccolini expected unions to reform the world. But they assumed unions and strikes were necessary for working people. "You see, I grew up with that attitude," explains Martino, referring not so much to his father as to his extended family and neighborhood.[69]

Martino hated the arbitrariness of authority in the schools. Once, when he was a sub, the principal, who had a grudge against his father, walked in and just took over the class, embarrassing him. Later, after he hit a student who had hit him three times, the administration pressured him into admitting a guilt he did not feel, because the family was suing. Principals had power to do as they pleased. "Teachers would ask to leave the building early for an emergency. This was strictly within the purview of the principal. And quite frankly, some principals would play favorites. Some teachers: sure you can. Other teachers: no you can't." What he wanted from collective bargaining was a grievance procedure, so conflicts with administrators "would be settled in a noncapricious manner."[70]

Martino and Ciccolino brought their practical skills to the movement for teacher power. Pete Petino brought a tradition of labor violence. His uncle, an organizer for the International Ladies Garment Workers Union, was shot and stabbed in Pennsylvania. Petino learned about picket lines while growing up in Bayonne. "I think I was born with a labor attitude." Once, while driving a truck during summer vacation from college, he was confronted by pickets. " 'You know what a picket line is?' I said, 'I sure do, and I'm not crossing.' " Petino's boss ordered him to cross or be fired. He told the boss, " 'You want to cross, you want to go in front of those two dudes, you go. You get your ass kicked. I'm not.' " He began teaching at South Eighth Street school in 1965 and gravitated toward the Union, becoming a building representative and then an area coordinator. In the brutal 1971 strike, Petino would be at the center of the violence.[71]

Petino, Martino, Ciccolini, and Piegari saw themselves as working people who were taking the next step up. In their Italian families and neighborhoods, they grew up with the attitude that without unions, working people were defenseless, and without the threat of strikes, unions were nothing. As teachers, they were not embarrassed to be called trade unionists, nor did they think the Union had to be primarily a vehicle for improving education. They tended to a bread-and-butter unionism, which focused on the protection of teacher rights, including the right to make a decent living. The Association's appeal to teachers to behave like professionals rather than workers was not persuasive to these teachers. To them, the Association just seemed wimpy. "The NTA did not want to be identified as a union, you see. I never felt that way," explains Martino.[72]

Responding to NTU's growing focus on collective bargaining, many Italian Americans joined during the 1960s and strengthened the tendencies that Ficcio, Favilla, and the Cascellas had helped create. The Italian-flavored version of teacher unionism that gained strength in the sixties was articulated by Ficcio. The older, Jewish-flavored version, which retained considerable power, continued to be articulated by Bob Lowenstein. Ficcio and Lowenstein both identified with the labor movement, aspired to collective bargaining, and embraced the necessity of strikes and struggle. They disagreed on the scope of demands and the relation of the Union to society. The quarrel between them was really a family quarrel.

Ficcio began with the fact that "there was a great deal of antagonism toward collective bargaining. It was not the professional thing. . . . Even quite a number of Union members were quite uneasy about collective bargaining." As a result, he always drove home the tangible benefits of bargaining, such as improved salary and working conditions, and freedom from nonteaching duties. "I'd sort of hit them with the bread-and-butter issues."[73]

Lowenstein had a different approach.

I liked Tony very much, but he would push very hard to stick to bread-and-butter issues. He'd say you'd get around to those [other] things later. We'd try to explain that bread-and-butter trade unionism had never done the trade union movement any good unless they had a larger political perspective. We tried to point out that you could get a real good salary schedule, but if that's all you're interested in you're not going to accomplish anything for the students or the profession. You can be bought up.[74]

In the 1960s as in the 1930s, Lowenstein wanted the Union to fight not only for teachers but for all the oppressed, including the children of Newark. Ficcio wanted the Union to focus on issues it could directly confront, at the bargaining table. He knew that while many teachers felt the way Lowenstein did about larger issues, many did not. He believed that if the NTU were to be strong enough to beat the Association and the Board, it would have to stick to the issues that all teachers, as teachers, had in common. Ficcio himself had broader values; like his mentor, Dave Selden, he regarded himself as a socialist. He believed, however, that NTU was doing its share toward building a good society by getting its members the best possible wages, benefits, and working conditions; other groups of workers could do the same. But to Bob Lowenstein, unless other people, including the students, were included in the goals from the beginning, the Union was more likely to become a vehicle of integrating teachers into the existing society (teachers being "bought up") than a vehicle of social change.[75]

Everyone active in the Union during the 1960s was aware of a conflict between the new strand of bread-and-butter unionism and the older strand of socially committed unionism. Not everyone experienced the conflict in ethnic terms. Many Jewish teachers thought of ethnicity as incidental to identity, and focused on social and political differences. Contesting my emphasis on ethnicity, two Newark teachers ask, Doesn't ethnicity hide class? Weren't Jews really more middle class, and Italians more working class?[76] Most older Jewish teachers in the Union and most younger Italians came from working-class families. But their class orientation, the way they constructed their working-class identity, was not the same. Italian teachers in NTU tended to speak of themselves as "working class," which they defined in terms of relations on the job: employees versus management. Jewish teachers were more likely to define the working class politically, in terms of what it had already accomplished in transforming American society and might yet accomplish; they identified with what the working class could be. Ethnic identity and class identity mutually reinforced each other.

Ethnicity influenced, but did not determine, the position of individual teachers. A young Jewish teacher like Jerry Yablonsky, with his trade-union background and bread-and-butter orientation, was closer in his thinking to Ficcio. A young Italian teacher like Angela Paone, who was developing broad social commitments, was closer to Lowenstein's position.

In college, Paone realized she wanted to teach in an urban school. A graduate of Barringer, she came back to Newark. "I guess there was a sense of idealism, in wanting to do something, change something in the system. I think there was a social consciousness that was budding there." Her principal "had the old idea of what a teacher should do, in or out of the classroom." A colleague told Paone, " 'You know, the boss really likes our teachers to be a member of the Association.' Well, that's all she had to say. . . . I wouldn't join." Paone began to develop her own idea of what a teacher should do. She dated Ficcio, who took her to hear the socialist Michael Harrington, and introduced her to NTU. All her mother's brothers were in unions; one was president of a local. But in her mind, NTU was not primarily about bread and butter. Idealistic, rebellious, increasingly radical, Paone was attracted to the Union's left-wing atmosphere.[77]

So was Janice Adams, who became friends with Paone in college. Growing up in Newark's North Ward, Adams was one of the very few African Americans in the neighborhood. In elementary school, she was accused by a teacher of stealing a pencil; no matter what she said, the teacher was certain she was guilty. Adams never forgot. As a teacher, she feared the abuse of power. Attending NTU meetings, she was impressed: even without power, the Union seemed like "a watchdog" that kept the administration straight. The Union spoke to Adams's broad interests in the labor movement, civil rights, and peace. "The level of dialogue was much higher than it [later] became. You had a lot of progressive thinkers at that time." In the early 1970s, after the Union came to power, Adams, Paone, and a few other radical women would become watchdogs, trying to keep the Union straight.[78]

During the collective bargaining campaign, the Newark Teachers Union aggressively courted African American teachers like Adams. But unlike Italian and Jewish teachers, Black teachers rarely joined immediately. Their hesitation was caused less by NTU's actions and attitudes than by the actions of the American Federation of Labor. Apart from the newer CIO unions, most national and local trade unions had a history of discriminating against Blacks.[79] Consequently, few African American teachers grew up with deeply ingrained pro-union attitudes. Whereas most Italian teachers had relatives in local trade unions, often in high places, and most Jewish teachers were raised to regard unions as essential to progressive change, most Black teachers did not come to teaching with a pro-union orientation. They hadn't grown up with the ethic of "Don't cross the picket line." Clara Dasher, with her teamster father, was the exception. Charles Nolley and Harold Moore were the rule.

Nolley arrived at unionism the hard way, through experience on the job. He graduated from Arts High School in Newark, and in the mid-1950s, began teaching art in a Newark junior high. His classes were jammed, with as many as sixty-five students in a room with only thirty-five seats. Sending half the students to the blackboard to work on pinned-up newsprint paper, he solved the overcrowding problem. What he couldn't solve was the problem of the principal's power. Having announced the school was going to lead Newark in support for the United Fund, the principal held faculty meetings after school every day, until 100 percent of the faculty made the pledge. "I was the last holdout, and my colleagues were after me." It was a decisive experience for Nolley. He could have gotten angry at his colleagues, who pressed him to give in. Instead he got angry at the system, which gave unchecked power to one person. "How could a person tell you you're going to stay here until after work, you're going to remain here with no extra pay, until I say you can go home, unless you do what I say? That's bondage."[80]

Solidarity became, for Nolley, the way to end a system of bondage. He attended a few Association meetings. "No one spoke up if there was an injustice. They just wanted to mumble about it, but nobody wanted to do anything." He understood: "Historically teachers have always said that it's undignified to fight for your right." During his eighth year of teaching, he joined the Union and began to proselytize. Patiently, he explained to hesitant colleagues that a militant organization that made demands was more practical than one that only made requests. "We come on our hands and knees with hat in hand and ask. They just look at us and turn up their noses, and turn their backs. You have to have people who are united and who can do something that hurts." Bob Lowenstein spoke from a long tradition of masculine independence when he described the alternatives as Union or servitude. Posing the issue similarly, Charles Nolley was speaking from a specific historical memory of bondage.[81]

Harold Moore also went to Arts High, where he experienced outstanding teachers and a sense of interracial community. It was a "small school, you knew everyone, there was a closeness, there was a warmth." He became certified in elementary education and special education—his lifelong vocation became working with hearing-impaired students—and came back to Newark in 1953 to teach. "It was home. It was something good, and I wanted to be part of something good. That sounds like a joke now, I'm sure." Moore liked his students, liked the system, and found some good even in the Board of Education. "There was a kind of administrative paternalism exercised by the Board. I mean they weren't always bad guys. If you were a nice guy, they could do things for you. If they didn't like you, they could shaft you."[82]

With his upbeat feeling about his job and the educational system, Moore was an unlikely candidate for unionism. In fact, he joined the Association. But in 1965, in his thirteenth year of teaching, Moore switched to the Union. He was frustrated because he couldn't get the supplies he needed for his students. "There was a lot of electronic equipment that I needed, like a group hearing aid; I needed an audiometer. . . . It was like pulling teeth to get that kind of material." The system of power, "with everything flowing from the top down," was not working for the benefit of the children. "I felt that the Union would make it possible for those things to be provided to teachers; they could put enough pressure on the powers-that-be to get us what we needed to do the job." Five years later, on strike with the Union, he would rediscover the sense of interracial community that he had experienced as a student at Arts High.[83]

The Union appealed to a range of people in the 1960s. Adams, Paone, and Moore were drawn to the Union because it was serious about change in the school system and society. Petino, Martino, and Nolley were drawn to the Union because it was serious about protecting teachers. The conflict between the tendency embodied in Lowenstein and the tendency embodied in Ficcio was healthy. The strength of Italian-flavored teacher unionism was its grounding in trade union experience and practice, and its willingness to reach out to all teachers, regardless of their educational or political beliefs. The strength of Jewish-flavored unionism was its refusal to separate practice from theory, what benefits teachers from what benefits students and society. What was healthy was the dialogue between the two positions, a dialogue that flourished in the democratic and open atmosphere of the NTU.

Union versus Association in the Era of Collective Bargaining

In the spring of 1965, the adherents of bread-and-butter unionism challenged the socially committed unionists for control. Favilla, Yablonsky, Nicholas, Vic Cascella, and a few others ran for NTU office against the ticket headed by then-president Sid Rosenfeld. The main issue for the challengers was the leadership's reluctance to go all out for collective bargaining. A second issue was NTU's continued orientation toward high school teachers. In the election campaign, the conflict within the Union was fought out not as Italians versus Jews—the terms were only approximate, and the public discourse on ethnicity was not yet kosher—but as Young Turks versus Old Guard.[84]

Young Turks accused the Old Guard of foot-dragging. But Rosenfeld had become president in 1964, replacing Young, partly because he was more committed to collective bargaining. Rosenfeld and his allies rounded up votes and trounced the challengers. For the advocates of bread-and-butter unionism, it was a setback; they had misjudged their support from the rank-and-file. (As if recognizing his strength was not in open battle, Ficcio did not support the challengers, and became one of the new vice presidents.) On the day after the election, in a gesture Favilla still appreciates, Lowenstein came to him and praised the Young Turks, encouraging them to remain active in the Union.[85]

The conflict within the Union in 1965 reflected anxiety about the future. When the Association won in 1964, it won the right to represent all teachers and signed an agreement with the Board on their behalf. Now that there was collective bargaining in Newark, there was no room for two teacher organizations. The Union, in its drive for power, had created a winner-take-all situation. Either the NTU drive would soon culminate in victory or it would be eliminated as a viable organization. Most AFT affiliates in New Jersey would in fact be defeated in the struggle for exclusive representation rights, and they would eventually disappear. Nationally, some AFT affiliates refused to pursue collective bargaining, because being a gadfly was preferable to being nothing. In Newark, NTU was feeling the pressure and looking for ways, in the anxious words of its newsletter, "of showing that the Newark Teachers Union is very much alive."[86]

The stakes had gone up for the Association, too. As bargaining agent, it needed to deliver. Having (barely) beaten the Union in December 1964, it now had to confront the Board. How could the Association force the Board to make concessions? With what weapons? Would it threaten to strike? Could it strike? Was it a union? The Association's narrow victory plunged it into an identity crisis.

During the winter of 1965–1966, both teacher organizations led strikes. Bargaining on salaries for the next school year was supposed to begin on December 1, 1965. Union leaders took the position that the Association did not possess a mandate to negotiate beyond its one-year agreement. At a membership meeting, they proposed a strike beginning November 22, to force the Board to halt negotiations and call a new election. But the Board had obtained an injunction prohibiting the proposed strike, and most Union members were afraid to go forward with one. A majority at the meeting, hoping not to strike, forced a postponement until after December 1. A minority opposed even this compromise on the grounds that any strike by public employees was illegal and would be punished. Divided and hesitant, NTU stumbled toward its first strike.[87]

The strike began December 2. At Barringer High School, only 22 teachers picketed; 96 of the school's 141 teachers crossed the picket line. At Arts High, 35 of 45 teachers went to work; at Clinton Place Junior High, 58 of 83. The strike was even less effective at elementary schools, where most teachers simply ignored it. A total of 2,600 teachers went to work; only 600 stayed out. On December 3, about 200 more teachers were out, but there were still three Newark teachers going to work for every one striking. Almost half the number of people who voted for the Union in the 1964 representation election were not willing to strike with it in 1965, even for one or two days. Union support was much broader than it had been in 1962, at the start of the collective bargaining campaign, but it was not yet deep enough to win a strike. John Schmid, who helped organize the strike, acknowledges "it was a dumb thing to do." The strike alienated some teachers and "probably cost us the next election."[88]

There were exceptions to the rule of a failed strike. Rolston Gaiter led 11 pickets at Bragaw Avenue Elementary School, and 36 of the school's 41 teachers stayed out. At Weequahic High School, there were 82 Union members and a proud Union tradition; 91 of Weequahic's 118 teachers went out on December 2. Weequahic principal Ben Epstein, the former NTU activist, fulfilled his duty to the Board by identifying Tony Ficcio, Sidney Rosenfeld, and others he saw on the picket line.[89]

In 1970, as assistant superintendent for secondary education, Epstein would again identify pickets, thereby sending them to jail and alienating some old friends. But no one went to jail in 1965, and no friendships were lost. The feelings of which-side-are-you-on, of loyalty and betrayal, were not yet strong. This was not a war. The Board invoked the injunction, and the Essex County Superior Court cited the Union and its officers for contempt. The Union called off the strike. A face-saving agreement set up a fact-finding panel. The panel ruled there would be no election until spring but stipulated that there could be no bargaining until the election determined which organization would represent the teachers.[90]

The Union and the Board showed restraint. The Union instructed picket captains regarding proper strike behavior. The instructions seem modeled more on the dignified stance of the early civil rights movement than on the labor movement. "Dignity and good appearance are all-important." Pickets "must be thick-skinned," ignoring provocations and giving none. "No one who crosses a picket line should be insulted." In the light of what would happen on the picket line in 1970 and 1971, the 1965 instructions appear absurd. But the idea of teachers striking was so radically new in Newark that it needed to be clothed in respectable garb. The audience was not so much administrators or parents as teachers. "Remember, we want him [sic] to vote for us, and an insulting remark may cause him to vote otherwise."[91]

The Board did not feel threatened and was not punitive. It announced that it would not punish striking teachers and asked Superior Court Judge Ward Herbert not to jail them, although they had violated the injunction against striking. Herbert fined NTU one thousand dollars and fined ten officers personally for contempt of court.[92]

Newark's first teacher strike settled nothing. But all participants learned something that they would use in the 1970 strike. The Board and the court learned the power of the antistrike injunction. Union leaders learned that NTU could not strike if it was divided, that the issues must be clear, and that there was no point in striking if the Union was not prepared to stay out until it won. Nearly eight hundred rank-and-file teachers learned they could defy the administration and the Board.

Elementary school teachers took the biggest risks and learned the most. It was hard to be militant in the heart of Association territory. Striking at Weequahic, surrounded by friends, was one thing. Striking at an elementary school, where you could be almost alone, was another.

At Fourteenth Avenue Elementary School, Bob Clark was one of the two teachers on strike. Clark, a young funeral director, had begun substitute teaching as a second job. When he received a regular appointment at Fourteenth Avenue in January 1965, there was no one to approach him on behalf of the Union; he joined the Association, like almost everyone else in the building. But his father had raised him to support unions; uncles and cousins were union members. He attended an NTU monthly meeting and was impressed by the aggressiveness, determination, and "brilliance" of the veteran Jewish leaders. Betty Rufalo, a young Union officer, recruited Clark and another man to become the Union presence at Fourteenth Avenue. Other teachers at the school looked down on them as irresponsible and unprofessional. When the strike came, the two young friends were afraid to picket at their school, because they could be fired, or made miserable in other ways. They picketed at West Side High, a few blocks away.[93]

At Dayton Street Elementary School, another pair of young friends was also alone. Carol Karman, who was Armenian American, grew up in Jersey City. Her father, a committed radical, took her to Spanish Civil War commemorations. She learned more from him than from school. "I never had a teacher who taught us to read between the lines. I learned that from my father." She developed a skepticism toward authority. When she began teaching in 1964 at Dayton Street, she had a difficult class but received no support from the administration. Her skepticism was reinforced. Elementary school principals acted as "petty tyrants in their fiefdom." Reading between the lines, Karman worked out her own analysis of principals. "They view the teachers, particularly in elementary school, as children. They [the principals] came out of the classroom, and now they view us as if we were the children that they have to push around and tyrannize."[94]

With her left-wing background, and her lack of deference, Karman didn't hesitate. She joined the Union immediately. One Union demand particularly resonated with her: the demand for a preparation period for elementary teachers.

> There were no preparation periods. None. I was going from week to week, from the minute that kids came in, in the morning, to the minute you dismissed them, and never have a moment's relief. I don't know if you've ever been in a classroom, but that's like being on the stage, and you've got all these little people in front of you, and you have to orchestrate that stage. . . . I think teachers need a break.[95]

Karman's friend at Dayton Street was Carole Graves. Graves grew up in Newark's East Ward and graduated from Arts High. She knew there were downtown areas where Black people did not go. When she worked briefly at the phone company, she was the first Black in her office. She was one of only eleven Blacks in her graduating class at Newark State College. She learned about segregation; she also learned about solidarity. Her father was in several unions. Her mother's brother was a porter, and she heard about A. Philip Randolph, who founded the union of Pullman porters. Her mother, who worked for RCA, was angry at other women for backing a company union. "There were some things—dos and don'ts of the workplace. And I think probably I got most of that from my mother."[96]

Graves began teaching special education at Dayton Street in 1960. She joined the Association. Then the Union began its collective bargaining campaign. Graves talked about the Union with her younger sister, who was an activist, and joined in 1964. She and Karman quickly became friends at Dayton Street, where they *were* the Union; Graves was building rep and Karman was assistant rep. They reached out to colleagues, and found fifteen interested in striking. But when the time came, Graves and Karman were the only ones committed enough to picket. They chided people crossing their two-person picket line, but did not get nasty.[97] Clark and other striking elementary teachers challenged the Association's definition of professional. But by picketing at their own elementary school, Graves and Karman were making visible cracks in the Association's fortress.

The Union's militancy created a dynamic that drove the Association beyond where it intended to go. To prove the Union wrong for calling the Association a "company Union" and ridiculing its first agreement with the Board as a "sweetheart deal," some Association leaders proposed striking. Months before, when the Union staged a protest at City Hall for an early election, the Association followed with a counterdemonstration at the Board of Education. Demonstrations suited the Union's style, noted the *Bulletin*: "A little noise on the sidewalk in front of an underprivileged school will do far more to bring conditions to the attention of the public than all the quiet 'conferences' carried on behind closed doors." But the Association had perfected the style of quiet conferences. In forty-six years of existence, the Newark Teachers Association had never demonstrated. During the 1965–1966 school year, forced to play the Union's game of representational elections and collective bargaining, the Association found itself matching the Union demonstration for demonstration, and strike for strike.[98]

In February 1966, for the first—and last—time, the Newark Teachers Association led a strike. The idea of teachers striking was gaining adherents, even in the Association. On the day before the strike, the president moved to postpone the action but was overridden by the members. The contrast is telling: whereas in the Union the leaders pushed members to strike, in the Association the leadership lagged behind members. During the two days of the Association strike, about half of Newark's 3,200 teachers stayed out. Some were Union members. Although the Association had condemned the Union strike in December and urged its members to cross the picket line, the Union voted to honor the Association strike. Union activists were bound by the never-cross-the-picket-line ethic. And they sensed that militancy, even by the Association, worked in their favor.[99]

The Board of Education agreed to submit the salary issue to an arbitrator, who gave the Association most of what it wanted. The Superior Court fined twenty-three pickets five hundred dollars each for violating the injunction; it was the first time rank-and-file teachers were punished for striking in Newark. The New Jersey Educational Association (NJEA), a step ahead of the National Educational Association (NEA) in recognizing the necessity of militancy, supported the strike. In the long run, NJEA's aggressive strategy of collective bargaining, backed when necessary by strikes, would effectively head off the AFT threat in all but a few New Jersey school districts.[100]

The attempt to match the Union's militancy seemed to be succeeding even in Newark. In the second representational election, held four months after the Association strike, the Association defeated the Union by a slightly wider margin (1,534 to 1,481) than it had previously and attempted to lock the Board into a five-year agreement that would put the Union on the sideline for the duration; during the five years, only salary would be renegotiated. The five-year proposal suggests the Association was more concerned with destroying the power of the Union than curbing the power of the Board. The Union protested, and the Board agreed to limit the second agreement to three years, from February 1, 1967, to January 31, 1970.[101]

The Union entered a protracted period of being unable to bargain for the teachers or force a new election. One national education expert, noting that some of NTU's most capable leaders had moved into administration or retired, thought he observed weariness among those who remained. He predicted the Union would never recover and pointed to its militancy as the cause of its weakness: "It would appear the NTU has alienated NTA, the board and administration, the mayor, the courts and significant segments of its own membership." Indeed, recruitment fell off. Organizers and building representatives could find only sixty-five new members to sign up in 1966–1967.[102]

By achieving a three-year agreement with the Board, the Association seemed to have decisively beaten back the Union challenge. During the course of the agreement, however, it was not the Union but the Association that fell apart.

The issue on which the Association foundered was power. In both the first and second agreements, the Board relinquished none of its prerogatives. During the first negotiation, the Board attorney insisted that the Board would not tie itself down, that its agreement with the Association was not a contract. There was nothing in the first agreement (1965–1966) that forced the Board to honor it. Mocking the agreement, the Union observed that "the elaborate grievance machinery ends in a whimper." Grievances ended in advisory arbitration, which meant that a teacher could go through each of the four steps, to principal, superintendent, Board, and finally arbitrator; the arbitrator could rule that the Board had violated the agreement; and the Board could ignore the arbitrator. The concept of "advisory arbitration" undermined the entire agreement.[103]

In the second agreement (1967–1970), the Association won a modification. Now the four-step grievance procedure culminated in binding arbitration when the issue required interpretation of the language of the agreement. In all other cases, arbitration remained advisory. Again the Union pounced. "This so-called 'binding arbitration' is really a subterfuge," NTU executive vice president Edith Jaffe told the Board, "since the language itself is clear enough in the agreement, and the Board states its unwillingness to relinquish any of its discretionary powers. It is in this area of discretionary powers that the areas of disagreement would arise."[104] For the next four years, through the big strikes of 1970 and 1971, the goal of the Union would be binding arbitration for all grievances.

The Newark Teachers Association was hampered by its history of accommodation and its inclusion of principals, and was never able to develop a coherent strategy for wresting significant power from the Board. Unlike the Association, the Union focused on the question of power. Its position was that the Board would not give up any power unless forced to do so. Legal power, in the form of binding arbitration, would grow out of the exercise of illegal power, in the form of the strike. An AFT pamphlet by Dave Selden pointed out that teachers were in the same position industrial workers had been before the creation of the National Labor Relations Board; the 1935 legislation establishing the rights of workers in the private sector had excluded public employees, who could only protect themselves through the exercise of their own power.[105] Sobered by the failure of the strike of 1965, NTU strategists patiently prepared teachers to embrace the strike as their only weapon.

The Association could not confront the issue of power without questioning its assumptions about class. Would teachers forfeit their professional status if they acted like members of trade unions? Were they superior to blue-collar workers, or could they learn some things from them? In Newark, the Association was unable to outgrow its identity crisis. In most other New Jersey cities, including Jersey City and Paterson, the local NJEA affiliate evolved a new identity and turned back the challenge of the AFT affiliate. If the Newark Teachers Association had had space enough and time, perhaps it too might have made the same difficult transition.

But the Union gave it no space. With its gadfly history and activist membership, the Newark Teachers Union was unusually energetic and articulate. Union officers, organizers, and building reps, utilizing the communications network they had worked so hard to create in the mid-1960s, offered teachers a running critique of everything the Association did and didn't do. Constantly on the defensive, the Association leaders had little chance to learn from their mistakes.

And as it turned out, they had no time. Before their three-year agreement was a year old, the race issue exploded in Newark. Called a riot by some and a rebellion by others, the events of July 1967 changed the way business was done in Newark and created tremendous pressure for change in the educational system.

Chapter 2

After the Riot / Rebellion

The Newark schools were in crisis after 1967. In reality, the schools and the city had been in decline for a long time. What made it a crisis was that people were fighting back. The violent uprising of Black people in Newark, in which twenty-three people were killed, seventeen by city and state police and the National Guard, transformed the way everyone looked at the city and the schools. Some white teachers gave up and left. Younger white and Black teachers took their places. They preferred the Union to the Association.

The Crisis in the Schools

African Americans came to Newark from the South in great number during the 1940s, 1950s, and 1960s. In 1940, Blacks were 11 percent of Newark's population. By 1970, they constituted 54 percent. Only Washington, D.C., and Gary, Indiana, experienced a more rapid change.[1]

The migrants from the South placed new demands on the city's resources. But the city was losing resources, and people. From 1958 to 1970, Newark lost over 20,000 manufacturing jobs—almost one-quarter of its jobs in that category. During the 1960s, 40 percent of Newark's white residents left.[2] The flight of industry and of middle-class taxpayers impoverished the city, leaving it unable to cope with the enlarged need for jobs, housing, social services, and education. Meanwhile the civil rights movement was creating higher expectations in Newark's Black community. The mass violence of July 1967 and the sporadic violence in the schools in 1967–1968 were the result of rising expectations and diminishing opportunities.

Told this way, from a great distance, the violence in the city and the crisis of the schools appear inevitable. But the facts have an appearance of solidity that is misleading. People make policies, and policies make facts.

The blight in the central city was created as a matter of policy, even before massive numbers of migrant Blacks were forced to live there. Newark authorities of the 1920s and 1930s created a housing shortage: through zoning ordinances, they limited residential development in the central city, favoring commercial development instead. The Newark Housing Authority, established in 1937, built segregated housing projects: two Irish, two Italian, two Jewish, and one Black. Then the Federal Housing Administration and the Home Owners Loan Corporation gave loans to people leaving Newark for the suburbs and refused loans to people staying in the central city.[3]

Property taxes in Newark rose catastrophically not only because of plant closings and urban renewal but also because powerful Newark institutions manipulated government to avoid paying their share. In 1935, the Essex County tax board reduced the tax assessments of nine of Newark's biggest corporations. In 1945, the New Jersey state government gave a major property tax reduction to insurance companies. In the 1960s, the Prudential Insurance Company got its taxes reduced again. By the end of the 1960s, the property tax rate in Newark was almost twice the suburban average. The high tax rate encouraged more middle-class people to move to the suburbs, leaving the poor behind to pay and suffer the consequences of depleted city funds.[4]

In 1953, a few teachers, members of the Newark Teachers Union, went to the Essex County Hall of Records to document the decline of Newark's tax base. They discovered that the corporate beneficiaries of the postwar boom were not paying their share. They found "offices and apartments crammed to overflowing. Over 100 million dollars in new construction. Corporate and business profits at new high peaks." And a shrinking tax base, because "tax payments are low for owners of some of the biggest commercial and industrial properties." The city was wealthy, but its wealth was not reaching its citizens and employees. So although the city government pleaded poverty or pointed to the high tax rate as the reason new revenues could not be raised, both the poverty and the high tax rate had been created in part by that same government.[5]

The high property tax and the housing shortage didn't just happen. Powerful people created them. And the flight of industry to the South and the southern Black migration to northern cities were responses to circumstances that powerful people had shaped. Both the migration of people and the migration of factories were propelled by conditions in the South, conditions rooted in anti-Black and anti-union policies. African Americans came to Newark seeking the jobs, citizenship rights, safety, and education they were denied in the South. The conditions that they—and their children, and their children's teachers— found in Newark were shaped by decisions previously made by other people, living and dead, in Newark and the nation.[6]

Superintendent of Schools Franklyn Titus preferred to treat the facts as given. "The Newark school system is beset with all of the problems common to most large, old, crowded slum ridden, metropolitan cities from which there has been an exodus of great numbers of small families of substantial means and an influx of even greater numbers of new large families of small means," he said in 1965. White flight and crowded Black slums were beyond anyone's control and "beset" school systems. The only hint of human agency contained in the superintendent's analysis of the crisis was his reference to the "large families" of the Black migrants.[7]

Titus was making the Board of Education's case for an injunction against the 1965 strike by the Newark Teachers Union. Separating effects from causes, absolving himself and the Board from responsibility for the suffering of Black children, the superintendent wielded that suffering as a weapon against Newark teachers. "A large percentage of Newark school children come from disadvantaged homes and deprived environments, and interruption even for one day in the instruction and guidance they receive at school will constitute a great and irretrievable loss to many of them."[8] Seen as natural, the massive failures of Newark's educational system could be used to block challenges to the educational status quo.

But the failures were not natural. Many of the decisions in Newark that directly shaped education were racially motivated. The history of education in Newark is the history of deliberate segregation. For eighty-one years Newark had a "colored school," the Baxter School. In 1909, when Newark closed the school and ended formal school segregation, the great Black migrations had not yet begun, and the Black population was only 2.7 percent. Blacks were not yet feared. Still, Newark remained segregated in other ways. Downtown theaters and stores continued to be segregated; there was still a "colored Y" in the 1940s.[9] In the 1950s, segregation took on new life where it mattered most: in education.

Segregation returned in 1949 as Board of Education policy, built on a base of increasing residential segregation but extending beyond it. Many white parents were frightened by the great influx of Blacks. They wanted to be able to transfer their children out of mostly Black schools in the Central Ward. Black parents argued for neighborhood schools. The Board of Education sided with the white parents. By 1950, more than four thousand white children had been transferred from predominantly Black schools. The Board hired Black teachers, assigning them to Black elementary schools. Qualified Black teachers were excluded from secondary schools. Of 120 African Americans teaching in Newark by 1953, only one was teaching in a high school.[10] The Board of Education treated African American students and teachers as inferior, creating a racially stratified system.

By 1960, half the students in the Newark public school system were Black, and most attended overwhelmingly inferior schools. The NAACP compared Newark's predominantly white and predominantly Black schools and found that class size in white schools was well below the city average; sometimes there were empty classrooms. The Black schools were so overcrowded that they often had double sessions. Newark's social tensions all funneled into the school system. Education was a more necessary route to upward mobility for Blacks than for ethnic whites, who could get good union jobs and move up. Most Newark unions, with the exception of the CIO unions that began in the late 1930s, excluded Blacks.[11] Forced into decaying residences by housing policy, barred from most good jobs by union policy, and condemned to overcrowded schools by educational policy, most Blacks in Newark were trapped.

One response was the five days of destruction in July 1967. The violence of July 1967 appears in the rest of this story as a given to which teachers responded. But in another story, the violence would appear as a response by Black people in Newark to the trap in which they found themselves.

The Newark riot/rebellion heightened the pressure for change not only on the mayor and the Board of Education but also on the Association and Union. The students were now mostly Black. On the eve of the riot/rebellion, with principals doing the counting, 74 percent of the students were classified as nonwhite. All the principals themselves were white, and there was only one Black vice principal. Counting was easier at this level. Fred Means, a high school teacher who was the founder and head of the Organization of Negro Educators (ONE), called in June 1967 for the hiring of Blacks at all levels of the school system. After the uprising in July and the racial violence in the schools during 1967–1968, the Board found such calls irresistible.[12]

For years before the riot/rebellion, Blacks had charged that oral examinations for regular appointment as a teacher and for promotion to administrator were racially discriminatory. Scoring of orals was very subjective and had been used to keep Blacks as permanent substitutes and to prevent Black teachers from becoming administrators. After the violence in the city and the schools, it was no longer a question of abolishing the orals but of abolishing the written exams as well. The Board announced in the spring of 1968 that it was going to appoint Blacks as principals and vice principals, to suspend the promotion list based on the written and oral exams, and to give permanent appointments to Black teachers who had not passed any exams.[13]

The Association, as legal representative of the teachers, was in a bind. Many white teachers hoped to pass the exams for promotion and become administrators; indeed, facilitating the passage of teachers into administration was one of the Association's strengths. At the same time, most white teachers and administrators realized that they could not, by themselves, effectively manage a system in which the students were mostly Black. Trying to act responsibly, an Association team negotiated with the Board over the summer of 1968 and worked out an agreement to suspend the exams for promotion. But the Association was dragged down by its history. Its president, Michael Limongello, had passed the written exam and was expecting promotion. He rejected the compromise hammered out by his negotiating team and got support from members. The Board went ahead and abolished the exams for promotion, thereby violating its agreement with the Association. The Association looked weak, and the splits within its leadership never healed.[14]

The Association was coming apart under the pressure of the city's racial crisis. The Union had a different history and responded differently. Its longstanding commitment to racial equality had deepened in the sixties. In 1963, addressing the Board, Joe Cascella noted, "This meeting takes place on the eve of the March on Washington." Five years later, at a meeting of the Union's executive board, "Don Nicholas reported on the preparations for chartering buses to the Poor People's March." More important for NTU than participating in national marches was its series of demonstrations at overcrowded schools during the 1964–1965 school year. In return for the Union's militant efforts to reduce class size, the Congress of Racial Equality (CORE) supported the Union's 1965 strike.[15]

As the pressure to promote Blacks grew, the Union experienced the same conflict as the Association, between what was good for the school system and what was good for its white members. But the Union drew on its commitment to racial integration and its tradition of democratic debate. At a membership meeting in the fall of 1967, the Union held a panel on whether the written and oral exams for becoming a regular teacher should be cancelled. Joe Bruder, a former NTU president, argued that if the exams were abolished, "jobs will go to those who exert the most pressure." Carole Graves, speaking not only as a member of the Union's executive board but also a member of ONE, broadened the debate. "There is a crisis situation," and the exams for becoming a teacher *and* the exams for becoming a principal or vice principal should be abolished.[16]

When the Union's nominating committee put forward candidates in the spring of 1968, Carole Graves headed the slate. NTU leaders wanted a Black president. Graves says they approached Clara Dasher first, thinking they could more easily control her. But Dasher did not want to be president. Graves's younger sister, working for the AFT in Washington, suggested Carole, and other leaders pushed the idea. Graves was committed to the collective bargaining campaign. She had picketed in 1965 and learned the fine points of debating and *Robert's Rules of Order* from Joe Bruder, whom she describes as "my coach." She was unanimously elected the Union's first Black president.[17] Because the racial question was so dominating, no one observed that she was the first woman, and first elementary school teacher, to head the thirty-one-year-old organization.

Graves's election in the spring of 1968 helped the Union hold together while the Association was coming apart. One of Graves's first duties was to inform the Board of Education of the Union's position on promotion. The superintendent should promote people in the pool of qualified candidates "who most suitably relate to the needs of the students, community, and faculty." That is, within the pool of those who had passed the exam, he could give preference to Blacks.[18] This compromise fell short of Graves's own position in 1967, when she advocated abolishing the exams. But she did not control the executive board, which had shaped the compromise proposal; its members had picked her. Not until the next election of Union officers, in 1970, would she have the opportunity to pick her own executive board. Until that time she would remain one leader among others, more than a figurehead but less than a chief.

Meanwhile, teachers and students faced violence in the schools. In the system as a whole, from September 1967 through the riots following Martin Luther King's murder in April 1968, there were one thousand incidents of vandalism, eighty-four assaults by students on students, and four assaults by students on teachers.[19] The violence, familiar today but shocking then, raised questions it had never before been necessary to ask: How was it possible to teach in schools where violence was constantly erupting? What could teachers do to make themselves and students safe?

The violence began earlier and lasted longer at Barringer High. During the early 1960s, a large building was erected to replace the old one and was immediately caught in racial conflict; CORE led demonstrations against discrimination by the construction unions. The new Barringer, completed in 1964, drew students not only from the Italian North Ward but also from the Black Central Ward. By 1967 the school was 40 percent Black. In October, three months after the riot/rebellion, some students began to fight with each other. The police came and school was closed. The next day a full-scale riot broke out in the cafeteria, involving seven hundred students; groups of Black and Italian students continued the battle out on the street. Nine were hurt and thirteen arrested. There was more violence in November. This time a student hit a teacher.[20]

Barringer was contested territory, the focal point of Newark's civil wars. Two angry, self-conscious communities met head-on. To Italian Americans in the North Ward, Blacks seemed invaders. Unlike Jews, most of whom left Newark before 1967, most Italians planned to stay and fight. They had transformed their neighborhoods in Newark into communities that felt like home, and they did not want to leave or share them. The anger of Italians was expressed by Anthony Imperiale, who in response to the riot had formed the North Ward Citizens Committee, a vigilante and nationalist group that would, he said, use its guns and a tank if necessary to protect the North Ward. The anger of Blacks was articulated by the poet and playwright Amiri Baraka (formerly LeRoi Jones), who graduated from Barringer in 1951, was arrested during the rebellion—"One of the first cops to whip my head during '67 rebellion was an Italian I knew from Barringer, where Italian language was part of the curriculum"—and emerged as the principal spokesman for Black Power in Newark.[21]

Both Baraka and Imperiale became familiar figures inside Barringer, entering at will, recruiting students. "So you could go down to the lunchroom, which was always the scene where these battles would start," remembers Andy Thorburn, "and you'd see Imperiale in person, surrounded by his escort of Brownshirts, and you'd see LeRoi Jones surrounded by his escorts of African bodyguards." The principal, paralyzed by the unprecedented disruption, retreated to his office. Felix Martino went downstairs one day and saw a policeman on horseback in the cafeteria. "There is nothing in any classroom in any university that prepares you for the events that took place."[22]

Thrown back on their own resources, unable to teach, Barringer faculty members seized the initiative in the fall. "What happened," explains Thorburn, "was the faculty of Barringer sort of spontaneously rose up and said we've had enough. The administration is not doing crap to try to get this back to a teaching environment. And so they called a spontaneous meeting after school one day." Knowing they had the support of the Barringer PTA, which wanted racial peace, the faculty met almost daily, especially during the first weeks. Most of the 150 faculty came. They were themselves diverse; the largest ethnic group among them was Italian, but the desire to restore order and make teaching possible was stronger in all groups of faculty than the tendency to side with any group of students.[23]

The faculty elected a chair: twenty-four-year-old Andy Thorburn, who was a permanent sub. Thorburn thinks he was chosen partly because his wife, who was also on the Barringer faculty, was Black; in Newark after the riot/rebellion, whites felt they needed to prove they weren't racists. The faculty formulated demands, and Thorburn took the demands downtown to the Board of Education. Two demands focused on preventing nonstudents from entering the school. Two others aimed at maintaining the suspension of older disruptive students and creating "permanent in-school facilities" for younger disruptive students. In November, 300 Black and white students from Barringer marched on the Board, demanding safety in their school, and the Barringer faculty threatened to strike. The Board agreed to most of the demands.[24]

The faculty acted before receiving permission from the Board. Thorburn closed school early many times. Taking the microphone out of the hands of his ineffective principal as soon as trouble started, speaking on behalf of the faculty who had elected him, he sent students home. During one early dismissal, Thorburn and the principal were standing at an exit and someone in Branch Brook Park shot at them. Thorburn sealed off the exits facing the park. Although what he did was illegal, he knew he was carrying out the will of the faculty. "Maybe we'll get killed in a fire," he thought, "but in the meantime we won't get shot at."[25]

Having reduced the flow of outsiders into the school, Barringer teachers moved to identify and isolate troublemakers. Each teacher wrote down the names of three or four of the most disruptive students. Then they collated the lists. A dozen names showed up again and again, students who rarely went to class and often started fights but were not yet sixteen and could not be expelled. They put these students in two classrooms of their own. Not waiting for the Board to find space, the faculty agreed to give up two faculty rooms. Thorburn took the six boys, and a Black woman took the girls. They worked with their groups separately for the first ninety minutes of each day, then brought them together. They did very little teaching, in the usual sense. Their aim was to prepare as many students as possible to return to regular classes.[26]

Thorburn began by seating the students around the table in the faculty room and asking each one why, in his own opinion, he was there. One by one, each maintained angrily that he'd done nothing wrong. The next day Thorburn asked again, and again the students blamed the teachers, or racism. "I'm here because I hit a white kid over the head with a chair." "Do you think that's why you're here, because you hit a white kid over the head with a chair?" I said. "Do you think you'd be here if you hit a Black kid over the head with a chair?" "I'm here because I hit a white kid over the head with a chair." Then Thorburn asked the next student. Every morning started the same way. He never argued. But gradually, they began to tell him why they were there. "'You know, when there was the big fight, I was on the second floor, I dropped my geography book on some kid's head and he went to the hospital.'" It was the beginning of taking responsibility.[27]

Two of the six boys changed their attitude, returned to regular classes, and went on to graduate. Others never changed; once, when Thorburn left them alone, they lighted paper towels and started a small fire.[28] Thorburn and his colleagues could not eliminate violence. Violence and disorder, at lower levels, continued at Barringer for the next few years. But the effort of self-organization paid off. The faculty succeeded in staying together and outlasting the worst disruptions. By April, fifty or sixty teachers were still meeting regularly, and the racial violence, erupting now at Vailsburg High, was ebbing at Barringer.

During the 1967–1968 school year, Barringer teachers made the Board of Education, the Association, and the Union react to their initiatives. The Association sent a representative to attend a Barringer faculty meeting and spoke to the Board on behalf of the Barringer faculty. The Board negotiated with the self-constituted faculty group, then looked the other way during the crisis while the faculty ran the building. But it was the Union that aligned itself publicly with the Barringer faculty, publishing their demands and advocating a similar program for disruptive students throughout the system.[29]

President Rosenfeld called in November for the establishment of special classrooms at schools throughout the city, with medical, psychological, and social services, and a maximum of ten students. The *NTU Bulletin* emphasized that "[o]ne of the decisions that relieved the crisis at Barringer was to remove a number of disruptive students from the regular classrooms." Moving quickly to endorse and extend the program hammered out by Barringer faculty, the NTU demonstrated its support for teachers on an issue that was crucial for them. The Union's readiness to support this initiative by classroom teachers gave it an edge over the Association. Barringer had never been a strong Union school; in the Union's 1965 strike, two-thirds of Barringer's faculty crossed the picket line. In 1970, Barringer's faculty would be overwhelmingly pro-Union and pro-strike.[30]

Teaching the New Students

Restoring order would make teaching possible. But was it possible to teach in traditional ways? Would teachers need to lower their expectations and water down the curriculum? Or were there more creative ways to respond to the changed nature of the school population, ways that might result in more learning rather than less? How would the Newark Teachers Union respond? If teachers themselves initiated change, would the Union support them?

Many teachers did not want to change. The Barringer faculty protested against the widespread tendency to blame them for students' troubles. Teachers "find it strange that the remedial measures they, out of their first-hand experience, have formulated, receive scant attention, while most of the remedial measures offered TO them boil down to this: the teachers have to do a different and better job."[31] As a protest against buck passing by the Board, this defense of the wisdom of classroom teachers was persuasive. As a response to what was happening in classrooms at Barringer and throughout the city, however, the protest was inadequate and self-serving. Restoring order was a necessary but not sufficient step toward making teaching and learning possible. As the students changed, teachers and their techniques also had to change.

Throughout Newark, many teachers could not change. According to Thorburn, there were "old-fashioned" Barringer teachers who could not connect with the students. "You can't change the teachers at that point." He removed difficult students from the classes of these teachers, bypassing the classroom assignments made by the Board, and placed them in the classes of people who could reach them, who usually were young. At West Side High, where the student body had become almost entirely Black, a number of older teachers decided to leave or retire. "This is where you saw a changing of the guard," says Charles Malone, a Black teacher who shared the high standards of the departing teachers. "It was a shame, because they were the real teachers. But they didn't know how to handle this new breed. And this new breed had no respect for age, or—how do I say?—the teacher's position."[32]

At Weequahic, where the standards had been so high, many faculty experienced the late 1960s as a painful time. The student body changed rapidly from middle-class Jewish to southern Black. The new students who came—or whose parents came—from the Jim Crow schools of the South had not developed the literacy skills that Weequahic teachers took for granted. One confessed: "I teach English literature—but I realized from the very beginning I had to throw out Shakespeare. I tried getting the kids to read newspapers. Too difficult for them. Finally, I was able to have them read the comic strips."[33]

Many Weequahic teachers became "a little hopeless," says Esther Tumin. In her own field of physics, "standards had to go way down. There was no way of teaching these students the kind of physics we had always taught, without failing most of them, because they came to us with a very bad preparation in mathematics." Like many conscientious teachers, Tumin did not know what to do. "I was working with a young man at his lab table and he pointed to a number and he said: 'I don't know what this dot is.' And the dot was a decimal point. At this point it suddenly struck me: what am I doing here?" Tumin took a refresher course in earth science and helped create a course that required no math and was taught "on a very very superficial level."[34] It was a kind of giving up.

Weequahic also dropped its interdisciplinary humanities course. In other ways too, faculty retreated. Weequahic had rules about conduct in the halls, Tumin explains. "We stopped asking the kids after a while. . . . Some of them were very big kids, some of them were very hostile kids. A teacher alone, especially a woman teacher, didn't stop a big kid in the hall because he was without a pass or wearing his hat kind of defiantly, because we were a little bit afraid."[35] Unlike the conflict at Barringer, which drew media attention, the conflict at Weequahic was played out quietly, in the classrooms and halls of the high school, between mostly Jewish faculty and mostly Black students.

Shocked by the rapidity of change, many Newark faculty experienced a loss of authority. The presence of angry parents in school added to the sense of intimidation. One teacher admitted, "Every time I go to discipline a child or give a failing grade, I hesitate a moment, wondering what might happen." Teachers at Madison Avenue Elementary School, in the South Ward, staged a one-day boycott to protest against parent intimidation. At Weequahic, Tumin felt under siege. "Black activist parents began to invade the classroom . . . with impunity." This was her school, her classroom, yet she could not defend it. Elayne Brodie, head of Newark's Title One program, walked the halls with three or four Black men, and came into classrooms.[36] In her honesty, Tumin says what many white teachers think but will not say, or will only say if the tape recorder is turned off. She experienced the influx of Black children and of Black activists as part of the decline of the school system.

To Tumin, the rapid change in the student body made teaching difficult, and the rise of Black activism after the riot made it impossible. She blamed the activists for preventing teachers from helping the children of migrants. Weequahic began English as a Second Language (ESL) for students from Eastern Europe, Israel, Latin America—and Blacks from the South. For a few hours a day, students worked on improving their English; during the rest of the day, they took subjects like math, which did not require much English. The plan was to keep students in the program for about six months. Tumin thought it was a hopeful approach. "The reason we stopped it was really a very cynical reason. One of the Black activist groups . . . accused us of segregating Black children in ESL to keep them out of the school population. The Board caved in immediately, and the ESL was discontinued."[37]

As a teacher, Tumin lost hope. In her mind, dropping ESL for southern migrants, substituting earth science for physics, dropping the humanities course, failing to enforce rules in the halls or protect classrooms from outsiders, were all part of the same decline of a once-proud school. "It was very hard for the teachers to keep lowering and lowering and lowering [standards]. . . . And when you combine that with the fact that we didn't feel protected, that our classrooms were invaded, that kids were becoming very, very confrontational, that was about as well as I could describe the atmosphere of the school," she says. "The whole atmosphere was one of powerlessness."[38]

One change Tumin and many Newark teachers made was to move out of the classroom, to work individually with students as guidance counselors. One on one, a connection could be forged. But here too, she experienced powerlessness. She remembers one young man with whom she developed real rapport. She was pleased that he was planning to go to college. "Then just a couple of weeks before graduation he told me he wasn't going to college, he had made a young girl pregnant, he had to work either to make her money to support the child or to have an abortion—I don't remember if it was an abortion or a child or what—and I thought to myself: Oh God, what am I doing here?"[39] Tumin's uncertainty about the fate of the baby is significant. The story is not about the baby, or even the young man. The story is about her despair.

Other teachers tell similar stories of hope and heartbreak. Whatever they tried, whenever they got their hopes up, the circumstances of their students' lives could overwhelm those hopes. "We couldn't buck it," explains Tumin. "It was like all the weight of the culture, the society in which these Black children lived, their constant mobility from address to address, the absence in the home of a father or mother who worked very hard, their obsession with fancy shirts and lizard shoes and everything—we just couldn't buck it. Forget it. It's a lost cause. I think that's the way I really ended up feeling about it."[40] As Tumin describes her experience, her description of African American students and their parents shades into caricature. Frustrated in her hopes, hurt by the blame placed on teachers, angry that she was not able to use her talent or training constructively, she blamed Blacks and their culture.

The tendency to blame Blacks was widespread throughout the system, especially among experienced white teachers, who described the new students as "unruly" and "unmotivated." At Bergen Street School, in the South Ward, older white teachers constantly complained to each other about the new students and their parents. They questioned the ability of the new students to learn and criticized parents for not being involved in their children's education.[41]

Edith Counts heard similar complaints at Peshine Elementary School in the South Ward. When she began teaching there in 1961, the students were predominantly Jewish. By the late sixties, the student body was predominantly Black. "I can remember once being in the teachers' cafeteria—I was sitting there with a group of teachers—and they were discussing how the school had changed because of the children coming in from the South. That was the reason why. These were white teachers saying it." Counts wanted the teachers, most of whom were Jewish, to question their assumptions about the migrants.

She told them her family was already living in the South Ward when Jews were the newcomers who were despised. "The area started changing," so her family moved to the North Ward. "That was a little bit of a hit that I was giving them."[42]

Counts agreed, however, that it was more difficult to teach the new students, because their needs were greater. Teachers had to work harder in order to continue to be effective. She observed that some young Black as well as older white teachers were not willing to work that hard; they put in their time and left at 2:45 each afternoon. Dedication was necessary, but not sufficient. "You were not teaching children perhaps who came in with all the skills that you needed. So it meant that you had to change your attitudes or methods."[43]

In the Central, South, and West Wards, wherever the migrants lived, experienced teachers had to change their attitudes and methods if they hoped to be successful. Nothing in their training prepared them for the work they now found themselves doing. Not only did they have to work harder, they also had to create, through trial and error, techniques and approaches geared to students who had been born, or whose parents had been born, in the segregated South.

Hannah Litzky lived in the Weequahic neighborhood. "Quiet Weequahic, once Jewheaven now is Route 66 of Black desire," wrote Baraka. But Hannah and her husband, Leo, stayed in the neighborhood long after most Jews left, still hoping—and working—for integration. Their first child had graduated from Weequahic in 1959. "There were a few Blacks in her class," Hannah remembers. "There were parties at our house where the kids mingled." The student body changed quickly. By 1966, Weequahic was 70 percent Black. Hannah and Leo discussed their youngest child's experiences, seeing the change as a challenge, not a catastrophe.[44]

Litzky tried to rise to the challenge as a teacher, as well as a parent and neighborhood resident. She experimented, letting students choose the subject of their talks. "And then it was so disappointing to me when, let's say, a student was scheduled to give his talk that day and he was absent. This would happen again and again." She went on sabbatical to Oxford. "I was inspired by my exposure to literature in the country where our cultural history began. I came home in the fall of 1968 very anxious to see if I couldn't be more inspirational. But I found I couldn't win. It was very frustrating. I couldn't reach the kids the way I like to."[45] Her assumption that American cultural history began in England—an assumption that African Americans were beginning to challenge—may not have made reaching students easier.

Determined to connect with the new students, Litzky gave up classroom teaching, becoming a full-time guidance counselor. As a counselor, she again experienced success and felt useful. "I helped a lot of Black kids who had no thought of college, or who had not been able to get into college." But the defeat in the classroom rankled. "The fault was mine I suppose. I just couldn't reach the kids in some way, or they weren't willing to meet me halfway." Litzky never fell back on racial stereotyping, never gave up. But the defeat was particularly painful, because she had been regarded for decades as one of Weequahic's outstanding teachers. "I was a good teacher, I was a successful teacher, except at that time."[46]

Some teachers tried bigger changes. Jeanette Lappé, another veteran of the third-floor teachers room at Weequahic, used prejudice, including the prejudice of her students, as a learning opportunity. She asked what kinds of things were said against Blacks. Blacks were described as kinky-haired, having thick lips, having rhythm, being stupid, the students said. Then she asked them to look around the room and check out the stereotype. They saw it was inaccurate—except for rhythm: they wouldn't give on that. Then she did the same with Jews. Jews were big on education, were stingy, wouldn't give credit to Blacks, students said. One added: if you think Jews are stingy, try asking a Black merchant for credit. They got the point: stereotyping was silly.[47]

Seymour Spiegel wanted teachers to change. "I knew after the riots we could not continue with the schools the way we were." When he began teaching at South Side High in 1956, a majority of the students were Black. South Side had been the school of working-class Jewish students in the South Ward, as Weequahic was the school of middle-class Jews. By the time of the riot, Spiegel was chair of the English department at South Side, Leo Litzky was principal, and almost all the students were Black. "We were actually failing all these kids. Not because they didn't have ability, I believe, but because we were doing just a lousy job." In the months after the riot, he worked out a proposal for a School Within a School (SWAS). The premise was that "the inner-city high school student can achieve the same standards of academic excellence achieved by more affluent students."[48]

Assistant Superintendent Ben Epstein helped get the Board of Education's approval for the experiment. Litzky gave space in the building. Spiegel began recruiting. Speaking to PTAs and eighth-grade classes across the city, he found 116 students willing to begin in the fall of 1969. During the first two years, whoever applied from any eighth-grade class in Newark got in, no matter how low their test scores, if they made a commitment to do homework and go to school for eleven months, and their parents agreed to be involved. SWAS could suspend students who didn't follow the rules. The success of SWAS in holding students to high standards suggests that the approach could have worked wherever teachers, administrators, and parents committed to it.[49]

The key to School Within a School was to turn power over to the teachers. Spiegel looked for teachers ready to try something new. "Teachers don't change because you order them to"; they change because they feel that their ideas matter. An interdisciplinary team of five teachers met every day for forty minutes, without a supervisor. Making decisions as a team, they created the curriculum and then created the daily schedule to fit the curriculum. If the biology teacher needed four hours for a lab, she asked the other teachers for the time, and gave it back later in the week. The five teachers also used the meeting time to reflect together on their practice.[50]

The daily meeting was controversial from the beginning, Spiegel says. "Because the Board of Education, they don't like teachers to sit around and talk." The meeting cost the Board no money; teachers made up for the time by teaching larger classes. But it cost the Board power. The meeting gave concrete expression to the idea of teachers taking ownership of the curriculum. "School administrators are so afraid that they're going to lose control that . . . they impose restraints on teachers that are making it impossible to teach effectively."[51]

Spiegel's faith was that motivated teachers would motivate students, and motivated students would improve their skills. The structure of School Within a School—the team approach, flexible schedule, rigorous program, and interdisciplinary courses—was designed to help teachers to transform first their own approach to learning, and then the approach of their students. The program had to be rigorous because it aimed not only to get students into college but to keep them there. Spiegel had seen too many of South Side's best students go to college unprepared and return defeated. Students at School Within a School took four years of science, four of math, four of foreign language, and four of an integrated English and history program. While Weequahic abandoned its interdisciplinary humanities program, teachers at SWAS chose a theme and taught it across the disciplines.[52]

SWAS was confirming as well as challenging. Teachers would call students to a team meeting to tell them how well they were doing. Teachers received support, too. Spiegel told new teachers they could not fail in their first year, that they would get a satisfactory rating. He told them: If you try ten things, and eight don't succeed, you have two good ones for next year. This approach to faculty development grew out of his experience. During his first, frustrating year at South Side he once taught a successful lesson and tried to tell his sarcastic chair about it. "I went to him and I said, 'It was so great. I did this and the kids did that.' And he said, 'My God, this is wonderful. I think I'm going to have an orgasm.' "[53]

The students at SWAS were overwhelmingly Black and, according to a Prudential study of the graduates, overwhelmingly successful. But the Board was never comfortable with SWAS. From the beginning, Spiegel turned to the parents and the Union. "This is the idea of unionism," says Spiegel, "that the teacher is a professional person, and that the union enhances that professionalism." He fully enlisted parents, who became active in hiring teachers and powerfully involved in lobbying downtown. He was less successful with the Union. The Newark Teachers Union was always represented on the board of SWAS and helped when required, but was not a strong advocate for the program.[54]

The Union was not innovative in the area of improving teaching and learning. Union leaders wanted to demonstrate that they were as committed to professional standards in the classroom as the Association was. The 1964 edition of the NTU *Handbook for New Teachers* was full of commonsense advice about the importance of "meticulous planning" and "good discipline." It contained little to encourage creativity or experimentation, advising teachers to consult the teacher's edition of textbooks for "excellent suggestions on how to present the material to your class." Given the magnitude of the problems in Newark's schools, the Union's approach to teaching and learning was pretty tame.[55]

As the educational crisis in Newark deepened, the Union embraced the rhetoric of school reform. But beyond smaller classes, it lacked a reform program of its own, and without much debate adopted the American Federation of Teachers (AFT) More Effective Schools program. Ten days after the riot/rebellion, the Union asked the Board to establish a More Effective Schools Program in Newark. "We copied it right out of Shanker's thing in New York City," says Andy Thorburn. More Effective Schools—an expensive program, requiring substantial additional funding—was the Union's answer to the crisis in the schools. In effect, when asked what it would do about the challenge of teaching Newark's new students, NTU fell back on a prepackaged program. Although the School Within a School was pro-teacher, subversive of school hierarchy, developed in Newark by a Union member, and staffed by Union teachers, the Union never pushed the program or adopted it as its own.[56]

By contrast, the Union's program regarding discipline was largely homegrown. NTU leaders knew that the union in New York had worked out demands regarding safety and discipline in the schools.[57] Nevertheless, the NTU endorsed the program developed by Barringer teachers, adapted it, and pushed it. NTU leaders did not show the same interest in initiatives from below when it came to new ideas about teaching and learning. The issue of violent and disruptive students was one that tended to unite teachers; perhaps that was why the NTU tackled it so aggressively and with such sensitivity to the ideas of teachers themselves. The issue of whether teachers had to change when students changed often divided teachers, partly along generational lines; perhaps that was why the NTU handled it in a formal and somewhat empty manner.

School Within a School was the most visible of the attempts in Newark to find new ways to teach the new students. But many teachers, mostly young ones, driven by hope and desperation, were trying experiments of their own.

If Spiegel was hoping to help Newark graduates survive in college, Ken Waters was hoping to help Newark students graduate from high school. Waters was teaching health and physical education at West Side High. He was looking for "ways to deal with the problems which beset us—racial conflict, drugs, violence." He and a colleague received federal funding for a program focused on students identified by teachers as likely to fail or drop out. These students still went to West Side High for some academic courses, but for most of the day, they were in a nearby building, where West Side teachers ran innovative programs addressing attitudes as well as skills. The experiment was only partially successful, because the teachers were not allowed to take full ownership. The Board of Education would not let them decide which students to admit to the program. "Taking this function away from West Side teachers reduced the teachers' sense of control and interest in our program," says Waters.[58]

Angela Paone tried an experiment at Abington Avenue Elementary School in the North Ward. Abington students were mostly white. But in the fall of 1966, Black children from the overcrowded South Tenth Street School were bused to Abington; the Board agreed to busing after the Union threatened to picket at South Tenth. Abington's principal did not construe busing as integration. He kept the new students separate. Paone, with her developing social conscience, volunteered to take an all-Black seventh-grade class. At first she could not connect with the students. She turned to Harold Moore, the special education teacher, saying, "I don't know what it is. I don't know if they don't trust me as a white person or what. But they are such a sullen group of kids that I don't seem to be able to break through to them." Moore sat in her class, talked with her students, and confirmed they were sullen. But somehow, after his visit, things began to go better for Paone. "They really accepted that I was trying to help."[59]

Then she took a significant step. She asked the principal to let her have the same students again in the eighth grade. It had taken them so long to trust her that she didn't want them to have to begin again, or to begin again herself.[60] Implicit in this approach of staying with a group of children for more than a year was the recognition that bonding between teacher and student was more difficult than ever to achieve, given the racial divide separating most students from most teachers, and that such bonding was more important than ever, given the skill and motivation problems of the students.

In their two years together, Paone and her students learned about race from each other. One girl asked Paone if she was white. "I said 'yah. Why do you ask me?'" You let us use your comb when we were getting ready for the play, said the girl; you let us drink soda from the same container you were using. "White people don't act like that," concluded the girl. "I nearly fell over," says Paone. Another student went to see Martin Luther King Jr. when he came to Newark and wrote a powerful piece about the Poor People's March. "It was very, very moving. So the kids had their own social conscience, and political consciousness, at the time." The experience transformed Paone. "My dedication . . . to the whole question of equality and civil rights and all of that I think really developed through my connection with those kids."[61]

Paone and Spiegel and the staff at SWAS supported the Union, seeing it as the best hope for change in the system; Ken Waters also joined the Union in 1968.[62] The Union was not in the lead on educational questions, but it was not so far behind that it was losing the young experimental teachers. On the contrary, because of their frustration with the Board and the Association, they were attracted to the NTU. As the Association's three-year contract increasingly exposed its weakness and the rifts in the Newark school system widened, the Union also galvanized the hopes of experienced teachers like Esther Tumin, who wanted more security and more money, as well as Harold Moore, who wanted supplies for his students.

"We were very angry," says Tumin. "We desperately wanted an acknowledgment that that the whole nature of the teaching situation had changed." The desire for more money was linked to those changes. "When you were teaching kids of whom 50 percent would go on to be Ph.D's, it was a pleasure; you'd pay for the job. When you were teaching students where you struggled and worked and really were so concerned all the time about whether you were doing anything at all that was of value, we felt that deserved a better salary."[63]

Tumin wanted the Union to lessen the pain of the transition to mostly Black and poor students. She was frightened by the new students and community activists; she felt disrespected and disheartened. She experienced the racial change as purely negative and hoped the Union would protect her and others like her. If the Union could get the Board to restore order in the schools, to reduce class size and provide remedial services, and to compensate teachers financially for their sacrifice, it would make an unbearable situation bearable.[64]

From his different perspective, Harold Moore saw the Union as expressing the militancy of the sixties. The Association, to which he had once belonged, "was really a big zero. . . . There were no changes as a result of anything they did—anything that I can remember. And the Union was militant, strident, and that was in keeping with the time, I think. Those were strident times in our history." The sixties, particularly the nonviolent protests of young Black people across the country, fanned Moore's idealism. As Tumin speaks for the powerlessness and despair experienced by all urban teachers some of the time, Moore speaks for the hopefulness experienced by many teachers at that particular time.

> We were not intimidated by the system. And we believed. . . . We believed in America in those days, and in what we called America. We just assumed that the little guy, that individuals, could make a difference, that we could change things, that we could make it better. . . . Even though, as a Black person, I took a lot of that stuff with a grain of salt, and "Liberty and Justice for All" didn't mean a thing to me, really, but there were certain things about being an American that just kind of stuck to you and you just believed. If you looked around, you saw the same kind of thing happening all over the country. People *were* making a difference. Individuals were coming together to make positive change.[65]

The Union embodied the hopes of the majority of teachers at the end of the sixties, even when those hopes were in conflict. The Union, not the Association, was the organization that captured teachers' desire to change the educational system in order to make it work, as well as the desire to be compensated fairly for working in the present system. The Union was the organization that expressed the teachers' need to reach the new students, as well as their need to be protected from the new students.

The forces that tore apart the Association strengthened the Union. In the collective bargaining elections of 1964 and 1966, the teachers had been almost evenly split between the two organizations. But the riot/rebellion of 1967 shifted the balance toward the Union. As Black principals and vice principals began moving into the offices, many white teachers left Newark.[66] In the late sixties, it was no longer hard to get a teaching job in Newark. Newark was hiring on a grand scale. Most of the people who filled these openings were fresh out of college. Many came as permanent subs, "provisionals" who would get their education credits while they were teaching. In the competition for the allegiance of these new young teachers, the Union had all the advantages.

The Class of 1969

After the riot, some education students in colleges refused to practice teach in Newark. Many parents, especially, objected to their sons and daughters working in Newark.[67] The young people who chose Newark after 1967 were willing to be part of the postrebellion city.

Phyllis Salowe was a rebel. At Boston University, she protested the war in

Vietnam; she and her friends once harbored an AWOL soldier in their apartment. She found practice teaching in a Boston suburb bland. "I always wanted to teach in an inner-city school." When she graduated from college in 1969, she applied only to Newark. Her parents, who originally came from Newark, thought she was crazy, but she wanted to be where she was most needed, and where there would be other young teachers. "Newark seemed to be on the cutting edge at that time." She joined NTU in her second month of teaching. Four months later, Salowe took illegal action, which, unlike her illegal action in college, led to arrest and imprisonment. It would be the first of many arrests in her activist career.[68]

At the University of North Carolina, Beth Blackmon joined a demonstration and rode a bus to Washington to protest the war. When she graduated in 1968, she applied to Newark. "I didn't apply to places that were all white and middle class." Newark was slow responding, so she took a teaching job in her New Jersey hometown, then reapplied to Newark. She wanted to be where "the biggest need existed." In 1969 she was assigned to Barringer, where the need was certainly big. Despite ongoing racial tension, or because of it, she found Barringer "very exciting." She would stay there as a classroom teacher for twenty-five years. During her first months, representatives from the Association and Union came to speak. She chose the Union. "One reason was that the people who were involved were newer, younger. . . . The Association seemed old, tired, much more traditionally based, willing to compromise."[69]

Phyllis Cuyler was a student at Arts High from 1961 to 1965. Her algebra teacher did not seem interested in her learning, and she did not do well. Years later, as a teacher, she shared a teachers room with him (during the sixties, teachers rooms stopped being gender specific) and heard him boast how he taught algebra to the top 10 percent, how he didn't have time for the rest. "I suppose he took those 10 percent to their highest level. But how about the other ones? And I was one of the other ones."[70]

Cuyler began to sort out her own thoughts about "the other ones"—those considered less valuable—at Howard University. She read Marxist philosophy, which struck a chord. "The workers were exploited and it seemed to be a great idea for the workers to run the government, to share in the wealth of the society." Encouraged by the nationwide Black movement, she majored in history. She participated in the pivotal campus takeover "to get ROTC training not to be a mandatory thing," and to get more Black history in the curriculum. The people she most admired nationally—Angela Davis and the Black Panthers—were people who addressed the intersection of class and race. She began to think of herself as not only Black but working class.[71]

Cuyler returned to Newark as an elementary school teacher. She felt change coming. "The sense of a new Newark, even in '69, might have been triggered because of the riots. Even though it looked like Newark was devastated, the Blacks had a sense of power after that." Carole Graves was also an Arts High graduate, and Cuyler gravitated toward her, becoming part of the group of socially committed young people around her. "She wasn't such a rebel that I couldn't identify with her. And she wasn't so bourgeois, so involved in the system. She hadn't taught so long; she was a relatively young person. So I could relate to an educated person who wanted to see some changes for the people, for the average worker." Association leaders, by contrast, "were administrators themselves, or former administrators," who seemed "more bourgeois," and "would sell out to the Board of Education."[72]

Cuyler was the daughter of migrants from the South; Salowe was Jewish; Blackmon's ancestors were from northern Europe, and her husband was Black. Salowe and Blackmon came to Newark to help others. Cuyler came back to Newark to help herself as well as others. Cuyler was angry about how little teachers were paid; Salowe was happy to be self-supporting and thrilled with the salary. But the three young women were all daughters of the sixties. When they came to Newark in 1969, they were drawn to the excitement of participating in change, an excitement they had tasted at college. They were drawn to the Newark Teachers Union because it embodied the value of struggle. "I think it's somewhat of a carryover from the sixties," says Cuyler, "where a lot of young teachers felt obligated to fight for rights that weren't granted you any other way."[73]

By 1969, Jim Lerman was already on the Union's executive board. He graduated in 1968 from Brown University, where he was involved in demonstrations for peace and fair housing. For Lerman, the Union "meant a continuation of the activism I'd been involved in as a college student." He came to teaching as "a sixties person who thought I could change the world." Within a year he was editing the *NTU Bulletin*. The position entailed membership on the executive board. "Here was a chance to be involved in policy issues and citywide stuff and get to meet other people and be treated in a nonpatronizing manner, which is the basic way teachers were, and unfortunately continue to be, treated." In his first year of teaching at West Kinney Junior High, Lerman experimented with having students write in journals. No one in authority knew or cared. He was an employee, isolated in his classroom, forced to work within the existing structures. In the Union's inner circle he was planning how to transform those structures.[74]

The energy of youth pulsed through the Union in the fall of 1969. Andy Thorburn, who was also on the executive board in 1969–1970, maintains that "there's no way a young person could . . . [have joined] the Association." Carole

Graves recognized the contributions of young activists to the Newark Teachers Union. "Now you had young teachers who had been through demonstrations in the South, who had been through the civil rights demonstrations and the peace demonstrations, who had been through the Peace Corps and VISTA."[75] With its youthful president and young leaders like Thorburn and Lerman, the Union was a beacon to new teachers.

Hundreds of young teachers, wanting change in the educational system, joined the Union. They were all hopeful. But their hopes were not the same, because their experiences were not the same. Cuyler, Blackmon, Salowe, and Lerman chose Newark, as a way of putting their college ideals into practice. Other young teachers never left Newark in the first place.

Students from Newark who commuted to colleges in northern New Jersey often found themselves on the margins of campus, lumped together as "Nicky Newarkers." It was a derisive term, a term of prejudice. It meant not only that you were from Newark but that you had a working-class attitude. It could also be embraced, as an identity. "I was a Nicky Newarker," says Tom Lawton. Lawton grew up in Newark and went to nearby Bloomfield College. "I wasn't into college life." He just wanted "to make enough money to get married and start a family." He worked as a butcher and belonged to a union before starting to teach in 1967. He was attracted to the NTU. "I liked the idea of a membership that was for each other, protecting each other against the administration."[76]

Some students from Newark took the bus together to Montclair State College, ate lunch together, hung out together. They did not participate in campus activities, including protests, and called the students who participated "collegiate." In turn, they were called "Nicky Newark" by "collegiate" students. Coming together because of their common experience of marginalization in college, they discovered they "had the same kind of background, whether you went to Barringer or Essex Catholic, West Side or Central." They were male or female, Italian, Irish, Jewish, or Black. They were the first generation in their families to go to college, and they hoped to be upwardly mobile. They had part-time jobs. The guys wore Italian knits and pants, in contrast to the Levis and plaid jackets of the "collegiate" kids. They were said to have an attitude. Some professors would say: " 'Well, yeah, you're a hard guy from Newark.' " After the riot, another note crept in: " 'How could you still live in Newark?'—if you were white."[77]

Walter Genuario graduated from Barringer and went to Montclair State, where he joined a small fraternity of students from Newark and other urban centers. While in college, Genuario substitute taught at Barringer, was caught in the violence, and knocked against the wall of the cafeteria. His first full-time teaching job, at West Side High, seemed more chaotic. He taught six classes in six different rooms in five different subject areas and was given no help or support. "I felt used." His students, who were Black, would not salute the flag. He asked the principal what to do. When the principal told him not to make an issue of it, Genuario knew he was on his own. He joined the Union for protection and support. He insists that "the mainstream in the Union" wanted to improve working conditions, not change the world. For some people, joining the Union and striking was "a liberal thing, but for most people it was [a result of] the fear and abuse they were taking."[78]

Genuario deeply respected his parents and was not rebelling against them but rather trying to live up to their ideals. In the 1930s, his father, a second-generation Italian American, fought prejudice to get into the Painters Union, which had been Irish, and "when he got in he did the opposite, he opened it up." In the 1950s, under the leadership of his father and Pete Yablonsky, the Painters Union became the first of Newark's construction unions to accept Black members. It is this history, the unfashionable history of the labor movement, that Genuario finds inspiring, not the history of sixties movements. In contrast to students who went away to college, he never protested for civil rights or peace, never tried marijuana. "My protests were all union movement. . . . I always remained a Democrat."[79]

While he was still a boy, Genuario went to the Essex Trade Council at the Labor Lyceum in Newark with his father, where he heard "brilliant" men like his father and the NTU's Bob Lowenstein discussing issues of concern to working people. "It was like an education, a colloquium, to be there." The experience shaped his image of vibrant intellectual exchange. As a boy, he also did volunteer work at Kennedy headquarters in Newark. The labor movement and the Democratic Party, the twin pillars of his father's life, became the pillars of his own life. Walter Genuario was not lacking in idealism. But unlike Jim Lerman—or Bob Lowenstein—his idealism was channeled within the existing institutions of the AFL-CIO and the Democratic Party.[80]

"I think the term 'sixties' is a terrible term," says Steve Shaffer. He means that the rise of teacher unionism was not related to campus-based movements. Upon reflection, he admits he is generalizing from his own experience. His parents were separated. His mother, who did not have a high school education, worked hard to support three children. "When I went to Rutgers-Newark, I had to come home, and I had to deliver papers every day. I had a job to deliver newspapers to God knows how many families. . . . I never went to a teach-in, I never was part of a civil rights demonstration, because I never had time for that."[81]

Shaffer began teaching in 1969 and joined the Union on his first day. Like

Genuario, he inherited both his unionism and his politics. His father, a member of the Ironworkers Union, was an active member of the local Democratic Party. Shaffer, who had no time for sixties protests, made time to ring doorbells and put literature under doors for Democratic candidates. He grew up in what he calls "the political culture of Newark." Through his father, he knew about Don Nicholas's father and Bob Lowenstein. When he met Lowenstein and Joe Bruder for the first time, in the Newark Teachers Union, it was like meeting people he already knew. "I said: 'Do you know who I am?' In a sense I almost became part of the brotherhood."[82]

Shaffer, who is Jewish, and Genuario, who is Italian, came from a working-class reform tradition, which seemed to them much more solid and real than campus-based radicalism. Their fathers were active in the Democratic Party as an extension of their roles in the labor movement. Within the context of their family histories, becoming a teacher and a teachers union member was the next step up. Shaffer "was watching what was going on in New York and seeing how the folks in New York were trying to improve the schools, the status of teachers, have a role and a voice in what was going on."[83] Genuario and Shaffer looked to NTU to protect their embattled, newly won status as teachers.

The Union appealed to Nicky Newarkers and sixties activists in 1969. Later, it would be unable to keep the faith with all its young adherents, in part because they embraced different faiths.

Some young teachers embraced a third faith: Black nationalism. In 1968, 25 percent of the teachers and substitute teachers in Newark were African American. Then the exams were abolished, and hundreds of Black substitutes immediately won regular appointments; meanwhile, new Black teachers were recruited as they graduated from college. Hired after the rebellion, and partly as a result of it, young Black teachers were less willing than their elders to compromise with prejudice. Most of them drew encouragement from the national and local Black Power movements. They were not interested in the Newark Teachers Association, with its history of compromise and collaboration. The choice for them was between the Organization of Negro Educators (ONE) and the Union. ONE was new, and geared to the nationalistic mood of the late 1960s. Nevertheless, most Black teachers chose the Union.[84]

Martha Nolley began substitute teaching in 1968 at West Side, where some founding members of ONE taught. They approached her, but she turned them down, because she believed they could not win. "There was a little splinter group called ONE," she says, "but not too many people joined that because they realized that it wouldn't have the political clout." In October 1969, still a sub, she joined the Union. "I could see it coming, the Union coming." Her husband, Charles, adds that he chose to stay with the Union rather than shifting allegiance to ONE "because I felt the families in the city weren't all Black. And it was a teacher thing. It wasn't exactly a Black thing."[85]

To Avant Lowther, Jr., however, it *was* a Black thing. His father was a teacher in Newark. When Lowther was a boy, he saw Black substitute teachers come to the house for advice about how to clear the hurdle that prevented them from becoming regular teachers. That hurdle was the oral exam. He thought about why his father's friends—bright, articulate people—couldn't pass the oral, why they remained permanent subs, why racism was so strong. Outside Newark, racism was worse. At Montclair State, he found himself the only Black among fifty chemistry majors. "Those four years were a living hell for me, because I had not ever run into that kind of prejudice." When he graduated from college in 1968, he turned down an offer from a white suburban school district and gladly returned to Newark.[86]

Lowther knew a leader of ONE but would not join. "You had a lot of folks that will support an organization, but if it's geared toward Blacks or Hispanics or any other particular type, they'll back off. So I just logically felt that ONE would never be strong enough to carry us, even though the number of Black teachers was growing. And that was the main reason why."[87] He did not reject ONE because he thought racism was no longer a problem, or because he thought there were more important problems. On the contrary, he rejected ONE because "there was still too much prejudice in Newark for an organization like ONE to become the bargaining agent." He joined the Union right away, beginning a career of Union activism unbroken except by the 1971 strike, when his loyalty to Black nationalism would come into conflict with his loyalty to unionism.[88]

"Younger Blacks like myself," Lowther notes, "were more militant and more aggressive" than their fathers, who were born in the South. His father, and his father's teacher friends, came North after World War II. "The younger Blacks, most of us were born up here."[89] They wanted to fight racism and build Black Power in Newark. If they gave their allegiance in 1969 to the Union, it was because they believed the Union could wrest some power from the Board and principals, and ONE could not. Phyllis Cuyler worked out a theoretical position combining race and class. But the younger Lowther, Martha Nolley, and many other young Black teachers experienced a tension, and sometimes a conflict, between their identity as Blacks and their identity as workers. In 1971 they would be torn, and most would cross the picket line.

Another group of young teachers was drawn to the Union in 1969. Unlike most, who intended to make teaching their professional home, these young men were just visiting. Teaching kept men out of the war in Vietnam. For some, like Steve Shaffer and Jim Lerman, avoiding the draft was one factor among many in deciding to teach, and they remained teachers after the war.[90] But for others, like Dave Lieberfarb and Marty Bierbaum, the draft was the determining factor.

Lieberfarb had always wanted to do newspaper work, but journalism did not carry a deferment. He was a teacher for three years, leaving to become a journalist when it was safe. But during that time he supported the Union, struck with it, and went to jail for it. He supported the Union out of the same idealism that led him to oppose the war. "We were young. We felt the Union was pretty democratic and idealistic." To Lieberfarb, who was not committed to teaching as a career, his starting salary was not important. What was important was that teachers, as working people, should have some control of their lives. The Union was "trying to improve the schools, and trying to put a little more power into the hands of the professionals who did the actual work in the schools. . . . I was sort of: 'Power to the people!' "[91]

As an undergraduate, Marty Bierbaum commuted to the Newark branch of Rutgers University. Then he went to the University of Michigan for a master's degree and became involved, for the first time, in "the music, the protests, the drugs—marijuana." In 1968, realizing his student deferment was ending, he came back to Newark to teach, becoming part of the group of young experimental teachers at Bergen Street. In 1969 he joined the Union, not because the Union turned him on, but because the Association was "not militant enough and sort of a milk-and-cookies kind of professional teachers association." He noticed a difference within the cohort of young, white, male teachers. Like him, some Jewish men went into teaching in a tentative way, while sitting out the war. They were committed to their students but not to teaching as a profession, and they did not ask the Union to protect their future or their status. Other men at his school—although glad to miss the war—looked on teaching as a career and hoped eventually to move up into administration. He remembers "young, white, mostly Italian, males from North Newark feeling that they had much more at stake than a lot of us did, and therefore [they] identified more strongly with the Union." Eventually, in 1971, Bierbaum and some other young Jewish teachers at Bergen Street would feel torn between their students and the Union, and would cross the picket line.[92]

The large number of new teachers pushed the Union over the top. Many, particularly those who had gone away to college, had participated in movements for civil rights or peace. Many more had been touched by the spirit of the sixties: a distrust of authority, a belief in people fighting for their rights, a faith in the possibility of change. For these young idealists, the NTU was a people's movement, battering down the establishment in education, transforming the schools. Most of the young Black teachers were touched in addition by the spirit of Black Power. They chose the Union because it alone seemed able to defeat the Board of Education and get teachers what they needed. But many young teachers who had commuted to college identified more with Newark, and with the trade-union movement, than with any sixties movement. In their more conservative vision, the Union's mission was to restore status to teachers and discipline to the schools. In 1969, the Union was all these things to these young people.

The young teachers, says Jim Lowenstein, "went to the union, and that's how it got the big push through." Jim is Bob Lowenstein's son, raised in the community of the Newark Teachers Union. His idea of the Union came from knowing Hannah Litzky, Jeanette Lappé, Joe Bruder, and other women and men like them. "They were not people who would go out on strike just for salary. They believed people were entitled to a living wage. But they were very truly committed to improving classroom conditions: reducing class size, expanding course offerings, increasing professional autonomy for the staff." He went to Weequahic High School. "People who I knew on a first name basis by the time I was three and four and five years old were now my teachers. So it was a little awkward not knowing how to address them." The idealism Jim Lowenstein brought to the Union—which would later bring him into conflict with it—grew out of its early history.[93]

Jim was involved in campus movements as an undergraduate at Johns Hopkins, where his father had been a graduate student. He came back to Newark in 1969 and was assigned to Weequahic. There had been roughly equal numbers of Black and white students in 1965, when he graduated. When he returned, all the students were Black. "It was a bit of a surprise." He had come back to teach Black students but was hoping for some diversity. "I remember getting my rosters a day or two before the kids actually showed up, and reading down the names, just trying to familiarize myself with names and so on. Oh good, Lynn Cohen, there's still one Jewish kid here; you have a little of a diverse population. And a kid named Kevin Bohanan, oh, an Irish kid." But both were Black. If there was less diversity in the student body, however, there was more in the Union. "The Union was much more mixed than it was just a few years earlier, and it was one of the few places where you have meaningful ongoing relationships with different racial groups." Jim joined the Union his very first day of teaching.[94]

He identifies three generations of Union activists, all coexisting in the Union in 1969. There was the thirties generation, "my parents' generation, in the later

stages of their career, but still there, many progressive, lifelong trade unionists." There was the sixties generation, his generation. "Many of them brought
with them the same idealism and activism that they had displayed on college
campuses and in community and other organizations," where they were "active in civil rights, incipient woman's movement, student movements. . . . They
gravitated toward the Union as a matter of course." And there were middle-
aged people, who "tended to be more bread and butter: 'Here's a chance to
get a little more remuneration for the work we're doing.' Not quite as political,
if you will, but involved for their own reasons, which I think were defensible."[95]

The description is perhaps weighted toward the radical idealism of the old
and young. But Jim Lowenstein captures much of the diversity of the Newark
Teachers Union in 1969, a diversity that was not only racial and ethnic but generational and ideological. This diversity was the great accomplishment of the
Union's self-transformation during the 1960s, and became, briefly, its greatest
strength.

Victory

During the spring of 1969, anticipating an election in the fall, NTU
leaders increased dues and fine-tuned the system of building reps. Tony Ficcio
was working full-time for the State Federation of Teachers and spending most
of his time in Newark. "And it was great. 'Cause I was full-time, I was able to
meet with all these building reps." The leadership asked the reps to gather
ammunition from teachers. What are "the chronic complaints"? How about class
size? The physical condition of the school? Which nonteaching chores "can
and should be eliminated"?[96]

In June, the building representatives got more than two thousand signatures
from teachers in sixty-two schools on a petition requesting a new election. This
triumph of efficient organization was completed in three days. The Public Employment Relations Commission (PERC), which was created by the New Jersey Legislature in 1968 to regulate representational disputes, scheduled the
election for November 18. The 1968 legislation clarified the concept of exclusive bargaining rights: it would be a winner-take-all election.[97]

The Association was in trouble. During the five years it represented the
teachers in Newark, salaries did not keep up with inflation, or with salaries in
neighboring districts. By 1969, Newark—once the New Jersey leader in teacher
salaries—had the lowest starting salary in Essex County. Salary negotiations
for the final year of the Association's three-year agreement with the Board began in December 1968 and went nowhere. The city, pointing to the shrinking
tax base, refused teachers a raise. Money could be found, as the Union proved

a year later, if it was necessary. But in 1969 it wasn't necessary. With the Association too weak and divided to pose a credible threat, the Board of Education kept stalling. From December 1968 to August 1969, with the teachers watching, the Board refused to grant a raise. In August, it voted a seven-hundred-dollar increase to each teacher, which was promptly vetoed by the mayor. Powerless, the Association asked the Board to submit the dispute to an arbitrator. The Board refused. Teachers began the fall without a raise.[98]

Despite pressure from his own rank and file, Association president Limongello favored taking the cancellation of the raise to the courts, not the streets. He observed in September that "the choice is between the more militant methods of the union and the reasonable legal procedures that we are using." One day later, the superior court turned down the Association's reasonable procedure, but still Association leaders did not act. Turning on each other rather than on the Board of Education and the mayor, they descended into factional warfare. In October, Association members voted narrowly to strike, but Limongello refused. The New Jersey Education Association, which saw Newark slipping away, pressed him to resign, and the new leaders said they would strike. But given the chaos in the organization and the closeness of the vote, they were unable to act. The raise was dead, and so, in Newark, was the Association.[99]

"After [Mayor Hugh] Addonizio promised us a raise and didn't give it, people went to the NTU in droves," observes Martha Nolley. The movement to the Union was especially noticeable among young teachers, who preferred militant methods. A reporter observed that when the Association failed to strike, "many of the younger teachers, most of them in the high schools, were incensed." Hoping for action, many young teachers had attended the Association meeting in August after Addonizio cancelled the raise, but another reporter noticed that few returned to the next meeting in September. "There were fears last night that many of those newer teachers had drifted away to the union when the association failed to take militant action."[100]

The November election was "a mismatch," says Andy Thorburn; the Union was "better organized" and had "better resources." The union in New York sent money and people to Newark, including an Italian organizer for Barringer. The national AFT lent the NTU twenty-five thousand dollars and sent five organizers for the election campaign, including Vic Cascella's brother Joe and three men who would play a significant role in the strikes: Bob Bates, Larry Birchette, and Vinnie Russell. During the campaign, Birchette and Bates ran workshops for NTU building reps and assistant reps; seventy or eighty teachers attended each workshop.[101]

Ron Polonsky took charge of the logistics of the campaign. Polonsky had joined the Union in 1961 and helped make West Kinney Junior High a strong Union school. His specialty was mentoring future Union leaders, including Avant Lowther and Jim Lerman. Local 481 paid Polonsky to be its organizer in the fall of 1969, making him its first full-time employee; even Graves, as president, was still teaching. Less committed to sixties movements than Graves, Polonsky was still young and in tune with the energy and hopefulness of the time. He was good at details and even better at inspiring solidarity. "While the association's leadership tore their group apart," observed the *Star-Ledger*, "Ron Polonsky, the activist vice president of the union, issued appeal after appeal for teacher unity."[102]

Polonsky hired Thorburn on a day-to-day basis, calling the Board to get him excused from teaching. Thorburn was out of school more than he was in it, working harder on the campaign than he ever did as a teacher. Polonsky, Thorburn, and Ficcio held lunch meetings and after-school meetings; where the Union was weak, they provided cocktails instead of just coffee. Teachers asked why the Union did not allow principals to join. Thorburn answered: "One of the things we're going to try to get for teachers is a grievance procedure, and the principal's on the other side of that."[103]

The Union's message was clear and consistent throughout the campaign: an enforceable grievance procedure would protect teachers from abuse. Power in the streets was needed to counter the Board's institutionalized power; willingness to strike would enable teachers to be taken seriously as professionals. In October, the Union reproduced an article on the Association's latest will-o'-the-wisp, the hope that the state would supply money for a raise, and added: "You do not bargain teacher conflicts in Trenton."[104]

During the campaign, from September to November, the Union added 350 new dues-paying members. Recruiting had lagged during the first two and a half years of the Association agreement. Though the Union would not admit it publicly, there were only about 400 dues-paying members at the end of the 1968–1969 school year. A high percentage of these—perhaps 20 percent—were activists, including building reps. Now the activists began to transform their energy into numbers.[105]

"There was a lot of excitement in the air," says Lerman. "There was a sense that there would be some progressive change, and the teachers would really get an advocate." The dramatic surge for the Union during the campaign was the culmination of a learning process in which teachers saw their problems as common. They were "divided ethnically, they're divided by gender, they're divided by secondary school and primary school," Thorburn explains. "What you have taking place over a period of two or three years . . . is a tremendous movement on the part of the rank-and-file members . . . toward being militant about their working conditions and being a unified body."[106] Teachers were becoming a self-conscious group, aware of their rights and strength. The Union was becoming, for the first time, the expression of their unity.

The Association and the Organization of Negro Educators each made desperate moves to widen their bases during the campaign. The Association elected a Black president. ONE announced it was considering changing its name to Organization of Newark Educators, to appeal to whites. These moves only highlighted the fact that the Union was the most interracial organization of the three, one of the few citywide organizations of any kind in Newark where Blacks and whites in significant numbers worked together and talked to each other.[107]

In the end, ONE decided to retain its name and its focus on Black issues. A flyer in October claimed "ONE bargains for students as well as teachers" and pointed to its fight for more Black administrators and its advocacy for Black substitutes. ONE's strategy was the opposite of the Union's. Whereas the Union attempted to cut across racial lines and unite all teachers around their common class interests, ONE attempted to cut across class lines and unite all Black teachers, aides, and administrators around their common racial identity.[108]

Each strategy grew out of a strong nationwide movement of the late 1960s: the movement for teacher power and the movement for Black Power. Throughout the 1960s, NTU cited the example of New York City as the place where the teachers union set the standard for teachers. ONE cited New York too, pointing to the 1968 struggle in Ocean Hill–Brownsville between the Black community and the teachers union as a negative example of what can happen when teachers organize apart from the community.[109] In the context of 1969, and of Newark—a time and place for taking sides, for militant struggle—ONE represented a more serious challenge to the Union than the Association did.

ONE could not hope to win a majority of teachers and moved to split the election. PERC agreed: there would be one election for teachers and another for aides and per diem subs. Most aides were parents hired from the neighborhood around the school; they were Black, like most subs. On November 18, ONE received more votes from aides and subs than the Union did, but narrowly missed a majority. In the runoff election between the Union and ONE, three weeks later, the Union won the right to represent the aides and subs.[110]

The November 18 election to decide who would represent the teachers was not close: 3,400 certified teachers and permanent subs were eligible to vote, and more than 3,000 voted. ONE received 428 votes, the Association received

571, and 2,020 chose the Union.[111] There would be no runoff. The Board of Education and the mayor, taking a hard line, had demonstrated the Association's impotence. Now, partly as a consequence, they would have to deal with the Union.

That night, with AFT president Dave Selden in attendance, NTU celebrated. The next day, strike preparations began.[112]

Chapter 3
The 1970 Strike

Most teachers believed the Board of Education did not take them seriously. Their belief was grounded in experience. As employees, they had found the Board unresponsive to their ideas and concerns. They watched it go through the motions of negotiating with the Association and saw that it would not voluntarily share its great power. They expected to have to strike as a way of forcing the Board to take them seriously.

Strike Preparation

NTU leaders simultaneously prepared for negotiations and for the failure of negotiations. After winning the bargaining election, they approached contract negotiations "with the feeling that we were not going to gain a contract without striking," explained Carole Graves. "And we prepared to go on strike." Painstakingly, the Union negotiating team collected more than three hundred demands from members and presented them to the Board team. The real audience for this drama was not the Board but the teachers, most of whom were not NTU members. The Union leadership wanted to convince teachers that they could not get what they wanted unless they were willing to strike. In this way, the negotiating process became part of strike preparation.[1]

Negotiating was a technical business, requiring expertise. The Union negotiating team was led by Robert Bates, a former teacher and experienced negotiator sent by AFT. The Board team was led by Jacob Fox, a Newark attorney, who had conducted negotiations with the Newark Teachers Association and came out of retirement to help the Board again. The Board needed Fox and

NTU needed Bates because neither organization had anyone on staff who had ever negotiated a contract. Fox's experience, however, was in dealing with the Association. Fox "waltzed the NTA around repeatedly and thought he could do the same with the NTU," said Bates. Bargaining with the Association had been "relatively simple," observed Ben Epstein, a member of the Board negotiating team in 1970. "So really there was an underestimate of the situation."[2]

Fox assumed that what teachers really wanted was higher salaries. The rest of the 300 demands were window dressing. "I said to Bates and Graves at the very first meeting: 'You've got some very fine things here. You want to make it a better school system; you want a voice in administration. . . . You want smaller classes. You want all the nice things that educators want for pupils. But right now, we're making a budget. I would like to negotiate your money demands.' " To Fox, it all came down to money. Reach agreement on salary, and everything else would fall into line. His job as negotiator was to cut through the "nice things" and get to the bottom line. "I was ready," he said later. "They wouldn't do it. It was incredible. They wanted to go on with all these fancy items of a purely academic nature. . . . I called it 'bunk' at that point."[3]

Fox didn't realize that many teachers cared passionately about making the school system better. They really wanted smaller classes. More fundamentally, he didn't realize the key demands were neither "purely academic" nor about money. The key demands were about power. "The Board will take advice," he told the Union team, "but make all the decisions." Looking back, four years later, he still didn't grasp the significance of the grievance procedure the teachers won in 1970. "The Union got some things I wouldn't have agreed to, but they weren't crucial; just on paper."[4] Fox never understood the difference between the Board's paper agreement with the Association and its paper agreement with the Union. Trying to be shrewd, in his focus on money, he was not shrewd enough.

The decisive demand was for a grievance procedure with binding arbitration. Teachers would have the right to initiate grievances, to protect themselves. The Union would also have the right to initiate grievances, to protect the contract. And to protect the grievance procedure, there would be binding arbitration. "We can argue for educational improvements from now until next year," said Carole Graves, "and unless the board puts it in writing, we have no way of being sure their promise will be kept." According to Bates, Fox "would give you a paragraph or more of language on some agreed to item but he would then throw a hook into it that would make it virtually meaningless." Unless the Union could do what the Association had never been able to do—tie the Board down by language that was binding and enforceable—nothing it might negotiate concerning class size or other working conditions would matter very much.[5]

The Union had compiled its list of proposals to give teachers a stake in the process. In January, the Union team let the Board team know that many of the three hundred demands were not essential. But the team also informed the Board that certain nonsalary demands were crucial: the demand that class size be reduced, that seniority be respected in the transfer or reassignment of teachers, that teachers be freed from nonprofessional chores such as cafeteria or hall duty. Above all, in the words of bargaining scholar Norman Eiger, the NTU team demanded "a broad definition of what would be grievable" and a grievance procedure culminating in binding arbitration.[6]

Each key demand, except one, was directed toward a particular constituency. The elimination of nonprofessional chores especially appealed to elementary school teachers, who had almost no free time during the day. Smaller classes especially appealed to the idealistic young teachers who were developing more individualized ways to teach the children of the migrants. Respecting seniority in transfers and reassignments especially appealed to the veteran white teachers who feared the growing power of Black parents and administrators. But the demand for a broad grievance procedure with binding arbitration was crucial for all teachers. Among the fundamental demands in 1970, binding arbitration was the most fundamental.

Most Newark teachers did not understand the legal subtleties of binding arbitration. What they understood was that the Association had not been able to force the Board to keep its word or share its power. "After all," Epstein explained, imagining himself a Board member, "I'd become a Board member in order to have power." Tom Malanga, a Board member since 1965 and on its negotiating team in 1970, could not understand how teachers claimed a share in decision making. "If they want to be partners with us," said Malanga, "why don't they get the mayor to appoint them to the Board of Education?" Board members were not paid, but there were many perks, not the least of which was the opportunity to tell thousands of people what to do. When teachers began telling the Board what to do, the Board began preparing legal weapons to restore the normal order of things. Its other attorney, Victor De Filippo, got the injunction from 1965 ready to use if teachers went on strike.[7]

Fox hoped it wouldn't come to a strike. "Top dollar," he told the Board, "will settle this thing." Fox and the Board brushed aside the teachers' nonmonetary demands and made a final salary offer: a raise of thirteen hundred dollars annually for every teacher. On Sunday, February 1, just before teachers voted on whether to strike, the Board placed a big ad in the *Newark Star-Ledger*, addressed "to the CITIZENS and TEACHERS of Newark." It only mentioned salary. Fox and the Board were trapped in patronizing assumptions. They learned little from weeks of talking to the Union team.[8]

If money was the overriding issue, as Fox assumed, teachers would accept the raise, because it was substantial, and because they would lose money each day they were on strike. The Board offered a raise, said Hannah Litzky, "but the teachers were more concerned with working conditions and the welfare of pupils, which the Board negotiators refused to discuss." The Union's executive board said 'no' to the Board's final offer. "What do you mean this can't settle it?" an enraged Board member said to Bates. "We just gave you thirteen hundred dollars. This is it." Board negotiators complained the Union was trying "to get us to contract away our responsibilities." Union leaders complained the Board was "trying to buy us off with a thirteen-hundred-dollar salary increase." Both were correct: the Union wanted the Board to share some of its decision-making power, and the Board wanted to only give money.[9]

Bewildered and angry when their final offer was refused, Board members began to give up on negotiations. At a special meeting on January 31, they adopted a budget that contained money for the proffered raise but no funds for the other proposals. Upon hearing the news, the members of the Union team angrily walked out of the negotiation room. "Happy strike, fellas," said Fox. "See you in jail." De Filippo went to get the signature of Superior Court Judge Ward J. Herbert on the antistrike injuncton.[10] The Board counted on the fact that it had the power, legally, to force the teachers to work. Under the injunction, rank-and-file teachers as well as Union officers were liable to arrest if they went on strike. Having underestimated the teachers and tried to buy them out, the Board would rely on force—and underestimate them again.

In a way, the Union also underestimated teachers. Ron Polonsky, Tony Ficcio, and Andy Thorburn imagined teachers voted against the Association in November rather than for taking it to the streets. "Our biggest burden to these members who voted for us was to demonstrate that we did not have our minds set up that we were going to strike," says Thorburn. Polonsky, Ficcio, and Thorburn saw their central task as "trying to build support for what we knew fairly early was a virtually inevitable strike."[11] They feared they were too far ahead of most teachers on the issue of a strike; they saw themselves as the actors, and the rank and file as the acted upon.

Polonsky, Ficcio, and Thorburn used the network of building representatives to shape the climate in the schools. "By the middle of January," Thorburn explains, "we're going to the schools again, just like the collective bargaining campaign, we're going to every school, getting them ready for a strike." At Belmont-Runyon Elementary School, Phyllis Salowe recalls, "there was probably a month of talk about the strike, before it actually happened." At Vailsburg High School, a woman asked Thorburn if it was true that under state law she could lose her tenure if she went on strike. Thorburn saw the question as a threat to strike preparation and ducked it by pointing to his own lack of tenure.[12]

"WHY MUST WE PREPARE FOR A STRIKE?" asked an NTU leaflet. "Because the Board of Education could prolong negotiations indefinitely; therefore, we must prepare to flex our muscles." Union leaders knew, but didn't say, that threatening to strike would not be enough. If there was a strike, the leaflet then asked, "WILL THE STRIKE LAST MORE THAN ONE DAY?" Again the answer was equivocal: "Teacher strikes are almost invariably of short duration. We must prepare to fight, however, until the battle is won." No one in the leadership thought the strike would be won in a day. Toward the end of the leaflet, teachers and aides were assured that they would be able to get loans from the Union during the strike. From threatening to strike might do it, to just one or two days might do it, to loans will be available: step by step, Union leaders led the rank and file toward the predetermined conclusion.[13]

Union leaders met just before the mass strike meeting on Sunday, February 1, "to go over the last little details of who was going to do what," Thorburn explains. At the mass meeting, Bates would emphasize the deadlock in negotiations; so would Graves. Then Graves would recognize the raised hand of a building rep, and he would recite the strike resolution. Tony Ficcio and his colleagues wanted everything to go smoothly in front of the teachers and TV cameras. "Tony believed that these meetings should be absolutely totally controlled, in the sense of no spontaneity," says Thorburn. "Ficcio was scared to death that we didn't have the strength."[14] The assumption behind the careful preparation was that teachers, left to their own devices, would not want to strike, or would at least be split.

Yet when the time came, it was the leaders who were split. "We had a fight with Carole." To President Graves, scripting the details of the strike meeting seemed unnecessary. She had more confidence in the teachers. Graves was outnumbered and lost the argument, but the tension lingered. Ficcio, Polonsky, and Thorburn were already angry that she did not put in the hours they did. Now they began to question her grasp of tactics. "The break with Carole . . . was becoming more and more evident."[15]

When the mass meeting began, in the Grand Ballroom of the Military Park Hotel, the script broke down. The teachers seized control of their story, becoming its authors. Thorburn narrates:

> We saw the people coming in the building, parking their cars, walking in the main doors of the hotel, and we're standing in the mezzanine, and you could tell within five minutes that they were going to rip that building apart, and there was no chance that you could not go on strike. You could see it in their

eyes, you could hear the muttering. Some of them carried signs in, spontaneously, that they'd made up on their own. Strike signs. . . . We didn't ask
anybody to bring signs.[16]

While Bates was telling the audience of twenty-five hundred about the dead-
lock, he saw that "teachers were standing up all over the hall, calling for a
strike." According to Thorburn, "the listeners were ahead of the speakers."
Responding to the mood of the teachers, the leaders spoke openly of the
Board's weapons and the coming war. "This audience led us," says Thorburn.
"This audience carried us away on a wave of militancy."[17]

Then a teacher who was not in the script took over. Pat Piegari had become
intensely frustrated by the Board's refusal to give him the support he needed
to teach. He didn't want to become cynical, to "tune myself off to these children who are educationally dying." The only hope was to strike. "Very impul-
sively," he ran forward, stood on a chair, held his hands in the air, and roared
above the crowd: "Strike! Strike! Strike!"[18]

Harold Moore, Piegari's colleague at Abington Avenue, recalls the moment.

It was Pat Piegari who jumped up on a folding chair . . . and started yelling
"Strike! Strike! Strike!" And everybody picked up the chant. And that moved
us over the top on that. Later I found out that the officials of the Union had
everything orchestrated. They knew what they were going to do. . . . And
there was somebody else who had been assigned to get the ball rolling. Pat
did it prematurely. . . . He just spoke the spirit.[19]

Before Graves recognized the building rep who made the formal motion,
the teachers had already voted. "Even though we might have been underdogs,"
says Moore, "we really felt a sense of power. And we felt like we were going
to win."[20]

Teacher Power

The power experienced by teachers on Sunday continued to build on
Monday. Defying the Board and the Court, 2,925 teachers, or 78 percent, observed the strike on Monday. These were Board figures. For the first time in
the history of the Newark teachers, the great majority demonstrated their solidarity with each other. Throughout the first week, more than 75 percent of the
3,800 teachers stayed out. After the first day, with so few teachers in school,
more than 70 percent of the 78,000 students were out as well.[21]

The 1970 strike cut across racial and geographical lines. It was less solid in
the Black Central Ward than in the Italian North Ward, or in the East Ward,
which was strongly blue collar and pro-union. But at West Kinney Junior High,

in the Central Ward, 37 of 50 teachers went out Monday, thanks to organizing by Polonsky, Jim Lerman, and other activists. And at South Eighth Street Elementary School, in a Black neighborhood in the West Ward, three-quarters of the teachers were out; Betty Rufalo, Clara Dasher, and Pete Petino had done their homework. The strike also cut across previous organizational lines. At Fourteenth Avenue Elementary School, a former Association stronghold, only three teachers reported for work. At Vailsburg, the high school where the Association was strongest, 60 of 85 teachers were out. The strike was citywide and effective.[22]

Most striking teachers hoped to force the Board to make changes that would be good for them and for students. At Arts High, only a quarter of the teachers came in on Monday, but students taught some classes themselves. "Ironically," said the *Newark News*, "many of the classes conducted yesterday by students were outlined beforehand by teachers who presumed they would be on the picket lines instead of in classes." Ironically, the *News* reporter assumed, because striking teachers were not concerned about students' learning. On the contrary, the point of the strike, for Carole Graves and her friends, "was beyond just that contract and the money and anything else—that we could make a difference in terms of the school system itself."[23]

Looking back, many teachers are almost apologetic about their idealism in 1970. Remembering his hopes, Harold Moore speaks of "a certain naiveté." The self-description as naive comes up frequently. "It's almost naive," says Angela Paone. "We thought that if we had more control, teachers had more control, more say in the educational process, that we could improve things throughout the system." Paone wanted classroom teachers, who knew what students needed, to have a role in shaping policy. "We wanted to be on committees throughout the city, we wanted representation. We wanted to have a voice in what was happening in the district."[24]

The hope of participating in decision making, which was common to sixties movements, was a driving force in the 1970 teachers strike. It was the motivating force for Dave Lieberfarb, who wasn't thinking of teaching as a career and "didn't give a hoot" whether his salary was raised. "I felt that the strike was primarily about trying to improve the schools and trying to put a little more power into the hands of the professionals who did the actual work in the schools, in terms of determining class size and curriculum and things like that. It may have been a naive idea at the time."[25]

Teachers would use the power they won to help students: the idea didn't seem naive in 1970. Like Lieberfarb, Phyllis Salowe was in her first year of teaching, and like him, she wasn't thinking about a raise. She was thinking about the supplies she couldn't get for her third-graders, supplies abundantly available in the Boston suburb where she had done her student teaching. What she wanted from the strike were new books, modern facilities, "smaller class sizes, more remedial services—all the things that would take a child who was operating at a lower level of performance and bring them up. The kinds of things that I had seen in Brookline, Massachusetts." She adds: "I was pretty naive."[26]

The word "naive" cuts two ways, saying something about now as well as then. It was naive to think, like Salowe and Lieberfarb, that money wasn't of vital concern to most teachers, or to assume that parents would see the strike as a way to improve education. But it says more about the present—the reduced sense of possibility, the loss of public hopes—that teachers think they were naive to have once hoped to use their emerging power to make Newark schools better, even as good as suburban schools.

One way to resolve the tension between the hopefulness of 1970 and the present pessimism is to collapse the difference between then and now. According to Joe Ciccolini, who came to teaching from business, the strike was really about money. Ciccolini was on strike in 1970, and heard what teachers said. Whatever they said, "no one was striking for the kids." To support his argument, he asks: "What do they do now? Do they go to extra meetings, or stick to the two in the contract?"[27] Employing a cynical materialism that has become fashionable, Ciccolini reads the present into the past, the outcome into the intent.

For some, the strike was about money. Avant Lowther made the decision to strike based on a kind of calculus, weighing the pay lost by striking against the raise a strike could bring. "I was willing to sacrifice my present to try to preserve my future." Unlike most of the cohort of 1969, Lowther was already married and had a child; money weighed heavily in his decision. But the decision to strike was almost always shaped by more than money. Growing up, Lowther heard criticisms of the Board by "my mother, my father, and all their friends, the Black educators and the close white ones that came to our house." As a young teacher, he heard veteran teachers "constantly complaining about how the Board of Education was using them and taking advantage of them." Activists at school "told us—the young ones—this [strike] is good for you, because it will give us more power over the Board. So my answer was yes, let's do it."[28]

As a demand, money is not as simple as it seems. Teachers who chose to fight for money were usually angry about their loss of status and control. Beth Blackmon, who taught history, contrasts "the thirties and the forties and the fifties, where teachers were revered and respected," with the sixties, when "the changes in urban areas and the riots seemed to put a big hole in the issue of respect." Older colleagues felt that if "we're not going to get any respect, the very least we can do now is get paid decently." During the sixties, in the cities, teachers experienced a loss of respect; at the same time, "teachers were sort of coming into their own." And Blackmon correctly links the two developments. Recognizing they could not get respect (or support or supplies) as individuals, teachers turned to collective action to assert professional pride and control.[29]

Teachers wanted the power to demand respect. A reporter asked "some of the most sensitive teachers" why they were on strike. He knew there was a "relatively generous" salary offer. Then why were good teachers really striking? "One thing which galls the union members, perhaps more than anything else, is what they regard as a paternalistic attitude taken by the board toward teachers." But here the reporter's assumptions got in his way; he viewed concerns about power as the selfish concern of the Union rather than the legitimate concern of classroom teachers. Therefore, despite what they told him, he was at a loss to explain why "many of the city's best teachers take to the picket line—in the context of New Jersey law a serious criminal act which threatens their freedom, livelihood and even their certification as teachers."[30]

One teacher wrote to the *News* during the strike, detailing the frustrations of Newark's classroom teachers and explaining how good teachers could reach the point of trying to effect change themselves. The letter is a bill of particulars, more specific than people's memories.

> Parents complain to the teachers. Teachers, being teachers, generally listen. Teachers complain. Who listens? No one.
>
> Why should a teacher have 50 in one class, a class of 40 in an old shower room, 70 scheduled for one class and 35 for another? . . .
>
> Why should a teacher spend three or four hours of her own time marking extra papers?
>
> Why should a teacher put up with undisciplined students when others want to learn?
>
> Why should a teacher have to use books from 1945? Why should a teacher have an insufficient number of books?
>
> Why should a teacher have to use archaic equipment—if there is any at all?
>
> Tolerating conditions, hoping they will get better, is one thing. Tolerating conditions, knowing they are getting worse, is another.[31]

The teacher blamed worsening conditions on "people who are in the position to effect a change [who] sit comfortably in their offices." The new idea for teachers in 1970 was that they did not have to tolerate working conditions that were bad for them and bad for their students.[32]

Striking teachers wanted to curb the Board's power. Curbing the power of principals was also important, especially to elementary teachers. "The principals . . . ruled by divine right," says Bob Clark. One of the original three hundred demands was for teachers to evaluate principals; the Union dropped this demand as too extreme but still insisted that teachers be relieved of non-professional chores. To Clark, the power of the principal to assign lunch duty or playground duty was a symbol of tyranny. The strike demand that teachers be freed from these chores was aimed at the principal "having so much power, and the rest of us having no power, and no say." Clark expected teachers whose rights were guaranteed to be better teachers. "We were idealists."[33]

A reporter observed that there was no single reason for striking. "Each teacher has his 'most important reason' for striking—better schools, more money, more teacher power."[34] But if money was most important for some, and better schools most important for others, teacher power was a key demand for all. Experienced teachers might, like Bob Clark, hope for better teaching and learning, or might, like Esther Tumin, focus their frustration on money. But together they identified strongly with Union demands that confronted the issue of power in the schools.

New teachers like Walter Genuario, who had commuted to Montclair State, and Marty Blume, who went away to college and participated in Students for a Democratic Society, embraced teacher power. Although each cared about his students, who were predominantly Black, only Blume saw the More Effective Schools program as an important strike demand. Whereas Blume was excited by the possibility of renewal in the city and the schools after the rebellion of 1967, Genuario was upset by the breakdown of order in the schools. But what Genuario and Blume had in common, when they struck in 1970, was a desire to address the imbalance of power between classroom teachers and management.[35]

At West Side High, Genuario was experiencing not only a lack of supplies and inadequate facilities but also "no support, getting abused." Power, in the form of a strong contract, was his answer to abuse. "After what I took at West Side, you better believe I was ready to strike." Blume, teaching elementary school, knew that if a teacher took a stand or disagreed with a principal, "you could easily be transferred. Done." What was needed was a grievance procedure to "level the playing field," or if not quite level it, at least give "some form of protection." Still in the system, Blume now sees that a strong grievance procedure "can work both ways—it can protect incompetents." But in 1970, Blume and Genuario and other young teachers who wanted to help their students were more worried about protecting teachers against administrators than about protecting students against teachers.[36]

The 1970 strike was about power. What the Union meant by power was a contract with binding arbitration. What individual teachers meant by power varied, teacher by teacher.

Felix Martino defined power narrowly. In his ten years of teaching, he had suffered the arbitrary power of administrators. He wanted the protection of a strong contract. Martino, who was not given to enthusiasms about changing the schools or transforming the system, was very specific about why he struck. "I went out on an issue that was nonsalary, the binding arbitration. It meant that should a problem with the contract appear, or should a teacher have a problem, that it would be settled in a noncapricious manner."[37]

Janice Adams took a broader view of teacher power. Teachers believed they were underpaid and wanted a raise. "Of course that was part of it," acknowledges Adams. "But there just seemed to be a higher level of idealism among [teachers at that time], because there were old-timers out on strike, but there were a lot of young people out on strike, y'know? I mean," she adds, laughing, "even I was young at the time." For Adams, teacher power included the power to improve the schools. But like Martino, she wanted a grievance procedure to protect teachers from the arbitrary power of the administration. "We needed some leverage within the school system," she explains. "If they wanted to transfer you, they would transfer you."[38]

Adams's emphasis on transfer reminds us not to see the 1970 Newark strike as primarily about race. In Newark, many African American teachers wanted protection from the tyranny of administrators. "At that time there was also a lot of harassment, administrators to teachers," says Martha Nolley, who began teaching in 1968. The chair of social studies at her school, "a lecherous guy," pursued one of the women until she got a transfer, because she had no other way to protect herself. As for the principal, "he thought he was a god." Martha Nolley wanted teachers to have power, like her husband, Charles, who regarded teaching without rights as a kind of servitude. The 1970 Newark strike cut across the color line. Black and white teachers joined together to curb the power of management.[39]

To some white teachers, however, management was beginning to be tinted Black. Jerry Yablonsky was striking for the protection of a binding contract. He organized teachers during the 1960s "so that we could control our working conditions through an enforceable and binding contract, so naturally when we went on strike for that reason, . . . I would support it." Claiming to strike for the kids "wasn't all phony. Part of it was public relations, of course." Power for teachers could benefit students, but teachers came first. "Number one, we had to protect ourselves through a contract, or how long could you keep working like that?" Yablonsky hints that the administrators he especially wanted protection against were Black. "In an urban area, with all the pressures we had, you needed protection. Especially as more and more political administrators were appointed."[40]

The racial changes in the Newark schools were part of why some white teachers, like Yablonsky, Walter Genuario, and Esther Tumin, went on strike. They wanted to protect themselves against the decline in academic standards that they associated with Black students, or the incivility of some Black students and parents, or the new preference given to Black administrators. They wanted teacher power partly to protect themselves as white teachers.

Race was also a factor, but in a different way, for Angela Paone, Janice Adams, and Anna Blume. They wanted to end racism, especially as it affected children.

Anna Blume did not strike for the same reasons as Yablonsky. "I really didn't look at the Union as more benefits for teachers. I looked at the Union as putting a focus on education. And getting away from what was going on in Newark: 'they can't learn because they're Black. They can't learn because they're stupid. They smell.' This tendency to blame Blacks flowed from the top down. "There was still a white power structure in the Mayor's office and downtown, and there was still a white power structure in the schools, over the hill, unable to realize the change." Wanting "more radical Black representation" to lead the charge for racial justice in the schools, Blume placed her hopes in the Union. Graves was Black, and "she was bringing in new people, and they were all a little more radical, and they were looking to shake things up."[41]

As Blume talks of prejudice, it's hard not to connect her passion with her history. She was born in a displaced persons camp in Germany. Her parents, Polish Jews, survived the Holocaust. When she was two, they moved to Newark. She went to Newark schools and then to Rutgers-Newark, where she turned against the Vietnam War after seeing on the cover of *Ramparts* magazine the now-famous photograph of a girl burning from napalm. Blume could never bear the persecution of helpless children. She went on strike for the same reason she protested against the war. Witnessing the continued destruction of Newark—"the real estate agents in town trying to scare people out so that they could sell homes"—she made a connection. Indifference to human life and human suffering were destroying Vietnam and Newark. Blume took injustice personally and felt she had to do something about it.[42]

She was in her second year at Bergen Street Elementary School, where she liked both the principal and her students. "When we started teaching in Newark, we really did start with: We're going to work our butts off, and we're going to make a difference." The shock came when new teachers saw their class-rooms. "One of the reasons we all struck that first year [1970] is that you started teaching in Newark with nothing. You walked into a classroom; there was nothing there. . . . There weren't desks. There weren't pencils. . . . I remember when the supply room opened and you'd go down there, you'd have to kind of beg to get ten pieces of colored paper."[43]

Blume thought about the lack of supplies. "There's got to be money here. How come it's not coming into the classroom?" She concluded that the system had to be changed. She believed Union leaders shared her commitment to reforming the system and helping the students. That's what "our thinking was, when we started—and were later to find out was naive."[44]

Carol Karman fits Blume's description of the new, more radical people whom Carole Graves was bringing in. After picketing with Graves in 1965, Karman left the Newark school system but stayed in touch with Graves. She returned to Newark in 1969. "The main reason I came back to Newark, as opposed to going anyplace else, was I wanted to be involved in the Union. It looked like things were heating up. It really looked like we were going to win the [bargaining] election, and I wanted to be there, and she wanted me to be there."[45]

Like Bob Lowenstein and Hannah Litzky, both of whom she admires, Karman embraced teacher power as part of working-class power. The 1970 strike, for her, was never primarily about money. It was about the power of the people who did the work to change the world. Karman had a more sophisticated analysis than Anna Blume of education, racism, the war in Vietnam, and the role of the Union in bringing about change, and she was closer to the centers of power in the Union. But at bottom, her faith was very similar. "I thought that through the Union I could help to influence the opinions of other teachers and to make them conscious of the world they lived in and try to make the world a better place that way. That was my vision."[46]

Karman sensed that teachers could make history in Newark. "When I came back I was very excited to be there. . . . There was a lot of momentum." She brought her energy, clarity, and sense of social justice to the campaign against the Association. When she went on strike, it was with high hopes. "We all were young and didn't have mortgages or children." Looking back, Karman does not call her hopes—or those of her friends, Black and white—naive. Acknowledging the gap between then and now, she has the strength to reaffirm the power of then. "We were young adults, on the top of the world; you know, you think you know everything; and we stood up for what we believed in, and we did it together. It was very exciting, a tremendously exciting thing. That's why you're writing about it."[47]

Close Combat

Every teacher faced the choice of striking, crossing the picket line, or just staying home.

Hundreds stayed home. Calling in sick daily, presenting a doctor's note when the strike was over, these teachers chose the path of least resistance. They avoided conflict with the Board and the Court, because, in a legal sense, they were not striking. They avoided conflict with the pickets and Union, because they were not crossing the line and were counted with the thousands who were out.[48]

But even staying home had costs. Elena Scambio was advised by older teachers to "call in sick, don't strike." Scambio, a new permanent sub, reported sick every day. A sympathetic doctor wrote "phony notes" for teachers who wanted them. The deputy superintendent called Scambio in after the strike and asked about her note. "I'm sure my face was bright red because I wasn't being honest, but I sat and swore that I was sick." What hurt was lying. "It killed me. It killed me." What also hurt was not being true to her working-class values. She grew up in the North Ward. Her mother, who worked all the time, believed unions protected workers; her cousin was president of a Teamster local. "So I had a respect for the worker and the rights of the worker." In the next strike, Scambio would be on the picket line.[49]

For teachers ready to confront the Board, the picket line was the place to be. They attended the daily meetings and the big Sunday rallies. They made phone calls, or even house calls, to teachers who were crossing the line, to get them to join the strike or at least call in sick.[50] But picketing, which directly challenged the Board's authority, was their full declaration of citizenship in the strike.

The AFT organizers tried to control what pickets said and did. Larry Birchette, a skilled strike strategist for national AFT, was chief spokesperson for the strike, as Bates was chief negotiator. Birchette ran the daily meetings and big Sunday rallies. Local leaders deferred to him and learned from him. When a TV newsman wanted to interview striking teachers, NTU insisted he interview Birchette or no one; there was no interview. A chain of command ran from strike headquarters—from Birchette, Polonsky, Ficcio, and Graves—through area coordinators, to picket captains.[51]

But there were as many front lines as there were schools. And teachers were not soldiers, trained to follow orders. Despite the centralizing tendencies of the strike, pickets created their role as they went along. That was the strength of the 1970 strike, and its beauty.

Teachers usually picketed their own schools. Sometimes the picket captain asked them to go where there weren't enough pickets. Pete Petino notes that some teachers preferred to picket where they didn't teach, because they were less likely to be identified. Vic Cascella adds a more telling reason: some teachers found it easier to say "Scab!" to people they didn't know.[52] To confront your own colleague, someone you knew and would work with again, exacted a kind of price.

The NTU issued detailed instructions to pickets, as it had done in 1965. Pickets were to arrive at school by 7 AM, early enough to shame teachers going in. But pickets themselves decided what to say and how to say it. Bob Clark would get to Fourteenth Avenue every day at 6:30. Twenty minutes later, a kindergarten teacher, one of two teachers who came every day to the school during the strike, would arrive on her bike. "Mr. Clark, you're not going to block me from entering the building, are you?" Every day, he would respond: "No, Gertrude, not at all," as he swung the door and held it open for her.[53]

Phyllis Salowe was friendly to teachers going to work at Belmont Runyan. She was trying to gain concessions from them, not make them angry. By observing the technique of veteran teachers on the line, Salowe learned to approach strikebreakers as they arrived in their cars. "That was a big deal. If you could go get somebody before they got out of their car: 'Give us one more day. Go home.'" Some did go home. Others told her they could not afford to lose the money and went in. Still others listened sympathetically, then went in the back door.[54]

Many pickets insulted teachers who crossed the line. They were angry at colleagues who ran no risks, who went to work and got paid, but who would get the same raise and working conditions as strikers. Janice Adams asked teachers why they should "reap the benefits" of the strike when they were doing nothing to gain those benefits. Sometimes she yelled "Scab!" She also yelled "some not very nice things," which she declined to repeat to me. Adams picketed her own school, Webster Avenue Junior High, and other schools when assigned. It was on the picket line at another school that she met Carol Karman. "The two of us," says Adams, "were screaming at the top of our lungs." They bonded on the picket line and have been close friends ever since.[55]

Many teachers did things on strike that would have been unthinkable when they were teaching. Some strikers stopped students on the way to school and encouraged them to go home. Sometimes, strikebreakers who parked near school found their aerials broken or tires slashed. Some of Walter Genuario's colleagues thought striking teachers were acting "like hoodlums." They said: "It's not professional to strike." He argued: "We're workers. Look at the way we're being treated. We're a different kind of professional."[56]

Worker or professional, hoodlum or helper, some strikers found it difficult to integrate their role as pickets with their role as educators. Pat Piegari developed almost a second personality. With his students, inside or outside school, he was consistently caring and supportive. "These kids became my extended family; I still remember their names." But his frustration over what the system was doing to children and to the teachers who cared about them drove him wild. After triggering the strike, he became picket captain at Abington Avenue, and the most vocal and most aggressive on the line. As he walked up and down, angrily confronting teachers crossing the line, he wore a black ski mask. He thought he did it because of the cold, and because the authorities were taking pictures. Years later, talking about his efforts as a teacher to help students and his combativeness as a picket, he mused about his split identity in 1970, and made a discovery. "I was a Dr. Jekyll and Mr. Hyde. Maybe that's subconsciously why I wore a black ski mask."[57]

Tom Lawton was torn in a different way: he felt conflicting loyalties. On the one hand, he felt almost filial respect toward administrators. "Being young at the time, and the administration being older, I came with the idea that I didn't want to upset the older adults. They're the same age as my parents." A self-described "Nicky Newarker" who supported the war in Vietnam, Lawton respected authority and deferred to it. When he first started teaching at Garfield Elementary in 1967, the real authority was the vice principal. "I was probably just as afraid of him, if not more, than the children were afraid of him. I felt like a child rather than a professional. . . . If you heard him coming, you cringed."[58]

When the strike came, he wanted to join. But he was afraid of hurting the authorities and being punished by them. NTU activists helped him work out his identity as a striker. "The difference was, the Union people explained to us, they're not our parents. They were our employer, they were our evaluators. I was saying, These people are going to get me when I go back. And we were assured that in unity there was solidarity." In the end, Lawton embraced unionism as a counterpower that enabled him to overcome his fear of the vice principal—"to talk back to him and tell him he was wrong."[59]

Having made his choice, Lawton enjoyed picketing. He took pleasure in plotting the next day's moves against colleagues crossing the line, not only "how to respond to what they would say" but also how to "put a banana or a potato into their tailpipe, after they'd park the car and go inside." The recognition he got for his picket line activities helped solidify his new sense of himself. "I think some of the greatest times that I had was when, after picketing, we would get together, my particular school, at a back room at a local store, and people from the Union would come in and tell us how great a job we were doing."[60]

If it was hard for teachers to make sense of their role as pickets, sometimes it was harder for their spouses. Lawton's wife, an Association member in another district, gave him "heat." Avant Lowther's wife also was upset by his role in the strike. Lowther was comfortable on the line, where his strength and aggressiveness protected him; he would go wherever pickets were needed, with other young teachers from West Kinney. But at home, he was vulnerable to the tears of his wife. "She was really upset. A lot of times during the night she'd be crying. . . . 'They may fire you. We have the baby. You may lose your job.' " Moved by his wife, he struggled inside himself to believe that what he was doing was right. Whereas Lawton remembers the 1970 strike as a good time, Lowther remembers the inner struggle.[61]

Teachers who chose to picket faced criticism from the community. In the mostly Italian, pro-union North Ward, most community members offered support. About twenty teachers were walking back toward Barringer High School after picketing at Summer Avenue Elementary School. An older woman they didn't know, who knew they would be coming back her way, came out on her porch and invited all of them into her home for coffee and doughnuts. Rarely sentimental, Felix Martino was touched by her gesture.[62]

But conversations between strikers and community members in the mostly African American wards—the South, Central, and West Wards—were likely to be painful. Despite low attendance, most schools stayed open. Strikebreakers, substitutes, young volunteers, and parents came to teach the children who showed up, or at least to babysit. Some of these community members were angry. At Bergen Street Elementary School, in the South Ward, where parents counterpicketed the striking teachers on the first day, charging that teachers had betrayed them, "teachers and parents clashed verbally," observed the *Newark News*. Bergen Street was Anna Blume's school, where she picketed; she knew the parents and cared about them. She had "a lot of conversations" with parents but failed to convince them that the strike was the only way to get supplies into the classroom.[63]

Phyllis Salowe visited the home of the PTA president at Belmont-Runyan "before the first picket, to just say this is why we're doing it. We were very earnest and believing that we were striking for the kids. And getting mediocre response." Salowe came to teaching committed to "parental involvement, community involvement." On strike, she was "flabbergasted about the negative reaction we got from parents."[64] The arguments with Black parents shook the assumptions of Salowe and Blume, leading them to question the meaning of what they were doing. In 1971, recognizing they had to choose between solidarity with parents and solidarity with teachers, Salowe and Blume would make opposite choices.

Arguments about the strike followed Salowe home. Harold Hodes, Newark's human rights commissioner, lived in the same apartment building that she did.

Salowe knew Hodes from her hometown, where he had been a lifeguard; she liked and respected him. While she was in college, he encouraged her interest in teaching in Newark, helping her get work as a substitute during her vacations. Now he criticized her involvement in the strike and warned her there were going to be mass arrests. She ignored the warnings but could not ignore the criticisms and argued with him at length.[65]

Martha Nolley also could not get away from the strike when she went home. She received calls from a respected teacher and strikebreaker with whom she taught at West Side High, where both were part of an interracial educational reform project that included parents; the man led the group. He did not believe in the strike and may have feared it would antagonize parents and split the group along racial lines. "He used to call me every other day [and] say: 'Come back, Martha, you've made your point.' "[66]

Strikers engaged in difficult dialogues with people to whom they felt connected. Dorothy Bergman was striking; her older sister Eleanor was not. When Dorothy was growing up, her father insisted she become a teacher, because it was a secure job for a woman. Having deferred as a daughter, she deferred as a young teacher. She began teaching at Weequahic High in 1951, six years after she graduated from the school, and continued to address her colleagues as, for example, Mrs. Litzky and Mrs. Lappé, just as she had as a student. "I didn't have to call them [that], but I was intimidated." Bergman let the older faculty pressure her into joining the Union. But she did not feel comfortable with them. "I was still a student, going to the third-floor teachers room!"[67]

In the 1960s, teaching now at South Side High, Bergman became an activist. She went to the monthly Union meetings, which were exciting, and stuffed envelopes at NTU headquarters and delivered literature to schools. Reassigned in 1968 to Boylan Street Elementary School as a special education teacher, she found herself for the first time at a school with almost no Union presence. Her new principal threatened her over a minor issue. She was surprised by her response. "I was so mad that I didn't care what I said. I didn't get mad very often. . . . No one ever spoke to Mr. Modell that way."[68]

During the strike Bergman usually picketed Boylan Street, but one day she was assigned to picket her sister's school. They had never been very close, but Dorothy wanted to avoid a final breach. She called and said, "Ellie, I'm going to be picketing at your school tomorrow. I wish you would stay home." Eleanor came to work. Once more, in front of the school, Dorothy pleaded with her. "Please don't go in, just for today." Saying she didn't believe in unions, Eleanor crossed the line. It was a decisive moment for Dorothy. "I never felt the same about her."[69]

Jim Lowenstein experienced no inner conflict over picketing and no conflict with family. As an exception, he confirms the rule. He did not have to forge a new identity for himself as a picket. He inherited an identity that combined professionalism with activism, teaching with a lack of deference. His father supported the 1970 strike from inside, as many department heads did. "Without letting ourselves be quotable," department heads would talk to individual students, asking them not to come to school, "which was insubordination on our part," Bob Lowenstein proudly admits. As for strikebreakers, "I felt sorry for them. For centuries it's been a rather gutless profession."[70]

Picketing did not challenge Jim's assumptions about who he was. "It was sort of like the natural extension; it's almost like the good guys and the bad guys. For me, given my family experience, the Board of Ed and its hired hands—that is, its bureaucracy—were the bad guys." During the strike, "I was out on the picket line every day. They said seven o'clock on the picket line, I was out there seven o'clock on the picket line."[71] Unlike Jim, most strikers did not have an inherited sense of good guys and bad guys to guide them through the multilayered conflicts to which picketing exposed them. They had to improvise not only actions but also their sense of self.

Nevertheless, many teachers, especially those who were young and without children, remember the 1970 strike as a good time. "It was bitterly cold," recalls Jim Lowenstein. "But we were out there, lots of good spirit." Jim Lerman remembers it was "almost a party, almost a celebration." Carol Karman says simply: "Seventy was a very up strike." For Anna Blume, "even walking on the picket line was buoyant and so optimistic and hopeful." What made the strike feel hopeful and good was that most teachers were striking for the students as well as for themselves. That's why Andy Thorburn, thinking about the labor movement as a whole, says, "This teacher strike is one of the last good strikes."[72]

Inevitably, these memories are tinged by nostalgia. The emphasis on the 1970 strike as a good time and a good strike reflects a longing for a time when the issues were simple. Teachers' memories of 1970 are constructed not only out of their experiences at the time but also out of their knowledge of the struggles and disappointments that came later. "My memory of the first strike was it was sort of fun," says Beth Blackmon. "People really weren't hurt financially by it," because they were later allowed to make up many of the days they missed. "It also seemed to bring a sense of cohesiveness among teachers." Joe Ciccolini emphasizes that the strike lasted only three weeks and teachers were allowed makeup days. "The first one was a good time," he says, "a little vacation."[73]

The "first strike" only appears as a vacation in contrast to the much longer, more violent 1971 strike. In lived experience, though, the 1970 teachers strike was longer than anyone imagined it would be. It was recognized at the time as the longest and most bitter teacher strike in New Jersey history. Strikers did experience genuine closeness, but the resulting "cohesiveness" did not include the 25 percent of teachers who crossed the line, nor the others who just stayed home. Strikers did not know there would be makeup days and did not know what the consequences would be for breaking the law. More precise than most, Felix Martino captures the mood of many. He too recalls "a feeling of camaraderie." But he adds, "It was a mixed feeling. One part of it [was] like unity together. But on the other part, there was a certain amount of anxiety." The anxiety came from not knowing how the strike would end. "Remember that was our first experience. Three and a half weeks seemed like an eternity to us."[74]

Getting Arrested

The Newark Board of Education used mass arrests in 1970. For the first time in New Jersey, rank-and-file teachers were arrested for striking. Two union officials had been jailed in 1967 during a strike in Woodbridge.[75] But what Board members did in Newark was new: a legal offensive directed against the teachers themselves. They did not want to engage in dialogue with teachers, which would also have been new. Instead, they wanted to force teachers back to work.

When a court issues an injunction and a union persists in striking, the union officers are usually charged with contempt of court, and then the court selects a date to hear their case. Board members and attorneys believed the usual procedure would take too long and asked the Essex County superior court to issue immediate arrest orders against NTU officers during the first week of the 1970 strike. The court complied, ordering the arrest of Carole Graves, Don Nicholas, Betty Rufalo, Jim Lerman, and three other officers.[76]

The Board and the superior court knew that arresting NTU officers would not, by itself, break the strike. While moving against the officers, they prepared to crush the rank and file. During the first week of the strike, superior court Judge Ward Herbert ordered the Essex County prosecutor to assemble evidence for mass arrests. The Board and the county worked together. The prosecutor's staff took hundreds of photographs of pickets; the Board—with the help of principals and Assistant Superintendent Ben Epstein—identified teachers in the photographs; the Court issued individual arrest orders. By the second week, the arrest orders were ready.[77]

On Wednesday, February 11, early in the morning, sixty uniformed Essex County sheriff's deputies spread out across the city. The day was clear, cold, and windy. Deputies read the order to disperse at more than a dozen schools, using bullhorns. Teachers were faced with a choice: stop picketing or get arrested. Many stopped. Some continued to picket. The deputies arrested a total of twenty pickets at six schools, handcuffed them, and drove them to the Essex County Courthouse. Four claimed they didn't realize what was going on when the deputies arrived, and were released. The other sixteen teachers offered no excuses or apologies. They were fingerprinted, photographed, and arraigned. They would be convicted and sentenced without trial by jury. Technically, their crime was not disobeying the Board, but disobeying the Court.[78]

Jerry Yablonsky was one of the sixteen. Before leaving home, he received a call from Ron Polonsky, warning him that the arrest of pickets was about to begin. He could have stayed home. Instead, he went to picket at East Side High, where he had been teaching since 1961 and picketing since the beginning of the strike. He let himself be arrested—"I could have left; I knew they were coming to arrest me"—because the NTU leadership was encouraging teachers to get arrested. The idea, Yablonsky explains, was to pressure the Board "through the force of public opinion, once middle-class teachers were arrested." He became skeptical of this tactic shortly after his arrest. But the other reason he didn't run away was because he felt an obligation. He had been a part-time organizer for NTU. Now he was picket captain of his school, a strong Union school. "I wasn't going to run away when I'm leading the pickets. I mean, how much I was leading them I don't know, but I was the picket captain."[79]

Bob Hirschfeld remembers "bundling up like crazy. It was just an effort to physically picket." The moral dimension of picketing was easier. He began teaching in 1961 at Quitman Street Elementary School, an Association school. To him, the Association seemed "in bed" with the administration, so he joined the Union, becoming Quitman's building representative and picket captain. As the sheriff's deputies pulled up at Quitman on February 11, Hirschfeld simultaneously saw someone who was "not one of ours," a strikebreaker or an administrator, approaching the school. "I said they're not coming to the school without crossing the picket line, and I grabbed a sign and started picketing . . . , knowing that the chances were pretty strong that the police would grab me."[80]

The teachers who were arrested during the strike were deeply committed, a minority of a minority. They set the standard for others. They went to picket when arrest was likely and refused to run when arrest was certain. They did not yet know whether they were going to spend time in jail. They only knew that they would not allow the Board or the Court to break their strike. They had come too far, together, to back down.

The arrests of rank-and-file teachers changed the strike. The big Sunday rallies became more vital to sustaining teachers' spirits. On Sunday, February 15, Bayard Rustin, the civil rights leader, and Albert Shanker, the teacher union leader, came from New York to speak. On February 17, to further encourage

Newark teachers, national AFT President Dave Selden flew to Newark. Selden, more than Shanker, had been active in Newark during the 1960s, sealing envelopes in the NTU office, helping shape a strategy for winning collective bargaining. Now Andy Thorburn met Selden at the airport and drove him to McKinley Street School, where both men raised picket signs in front of police and photographers. They were immediately arrested. To protest the law whereby public employees could be jailed for striking, Selden refused bail, remaining in jail until the strike was settled.[81]

Thousands attended the Sunday rallies; hundreds attended the daily strike meetings. But they were the active strikers. They would picket, go out for coffee in small groups, then come together late every morning at the American Federation of Musicians Building on University Avenue. Once mass arrests began, they felt an increased need for each other. "There were rumors all over the place," says Harold Moore. By attending daily, activists kept in touch with the latest news—the status of negotiations, the events on the picket line, the number arrested, the number still out—and with each other.[82]

"Probably the worst thing in any strike is for the strikers to feel isolated," observes Moore. "And I think a big thing was getting people together, because you'd kind of feed off each other's energy." Hearing each other's stories made a big difference. "It was a great thing," says Jim Lowenstein, "because you got to meet a lot of your colleagues from throughout the city, people who were in the same fight as you, [with] slightly different experiences." The daily meetings would "get us all hepped up," says Phyllis Salowe, who was new to unions and strikes. Even Vic Cascella, an old pro, needed the lift. "If I looked at my school, and saw [only] one teacher from West Side picketing with me, God, I may well have thrown in the towel. But then I'd go down to the rallies, and you see the people from all over, and other schools. They were down there cheering and carrying on with the successful stories that they had, and that reinforced you and carried you through."[83]

Picketing changed too. Only the most committed teachers were still willing to picket. Strike leaders could no longer put pickets at every school; instead, they concentrated pickets at a few schools each day. Meanwhile, they tried to turn the Board's legal offensive into political advantage, encouraging pickets to let themselves be arrested, and finding ways to use the repression to win public support.[84]

The publicity campaign began February 12, the day after the first mass arrest, with a "funeral for justice." In front of the courthouse, more than four hundred teachers buried the casket, led by Bob Clark, a licensed funeral director as well as teacher, who wore a derby hat and chesterfield coat. Also starring in the street theater was a teacher's aide dressed in widow's weeds, who announced, "My husband, Mr. Justice, had been sick for some time. He died yesterday." She declared she could no longer provide for herself or her eighty thousand children.[85]

On Friday, February 13, the Union mounted a march of protest. Throughout the strike, the labor movement in New Jersey—led by Charles Marciante of the AFL-CIO, but spearheaded by the Industrial Union Council—gave reliable financial and political support. Now labor leaders from other New Jersey unions marched with strikers to show their solidarity in the face of repression. The march snarled downtown traffic. Nine nonteachers, including labor leaders, were arrested when they refused to put down picket signs. Eighteen teachers were also arrested, including Jim Lowenstein, who called the march "classic out of the South." He meant that, like civil rights marchers, the teachers and union leaders were peacefully protesting legalized oppression.[86]

The mass arrests led to a reframing of the strike. At the beginning, everyone saw the 1970 teachers strike primarily as a labor dispute. But in the second week, the courts and state and media cast the strike as defiance of law and order. With the youth rebellion of the sixties approaching its zenith, law and order were widely perceived as under siege. The *Newark News* was carrying reports on the simultaneous trial of the Chicago Seven, the antiwar protestors who were challenging the authority of their judges. Striking teachers were perceived as also challenging the system of justice, setting a bad example for youth. With fifty-seven rank-and-file teachers already arrested, the *News* called for more repression. "City and state administrations have demonstrated patience, or weakness, but little else."[87]

New Jersey Supreme Court Chief Justice Joseph Weintraub viewed the strike as "an attack upon the state." Judge Nelson Mintz of the county superior court, as he presided over contempt proceedings, saw himself defending "an orderly society." On February 19, he sentenced a Union officer to the Essex County penitentiary for three months. The Union's lawyer argued that civil disobedience was an American tradition. But Mintz insisted that the conscientious objection to laws made the lawbreaker more guilty rather than less so. "It cannot excuse, on the contrary, it emphasizes the deliberate nature of the violations."[88]

New Jersey officials and judges criminalized the teachers strike, linking the arrests to the national campaign for law and order. Governor William Cahill denounced teacher strikes because they "encourage our youth to further challenge authority and the laws of the state and nation." Cahill threatened to decertify striking teachers for a year. Privately, deputy attorneys general of New Jersey met with the Newark Board of Education to discuss decertifying teachers, or even firing them outright. But the Board vetoed these suggestions. By

performed a dance at Barringer, allowing both to do their jobs without any-one getting hurt. Felix Martino analyzes the tactical situation with the relish of an expert; he had been trained in guerrilla war at the United States psycho-logical warfare center. Police would approach Barringer from one side, sirens blaring. The sirens signaled pickets to exit on the other side, through the park-ing lot. Martino picketed every day but was never arrested, because "many of the police officers were sympathetic, unofficially," and because "I ran." He did not go to Vailsburg High to picket, because he didn't know the neighborhood and wouldn't know where to run. But it was different on his home turf. Al-though "the Union at times encouraged people to get arrested," Martino prac-ticed "hit and run, hit and run. I looked on the strike as guerrilla warfare."[96]

Fred Klock, who taught at Barringer, was arrested on February 19 at Sum-mer Avenue Elementary School. Klock was helping pickets avoid arrest and was charged with violating the injunction against striking, even though he was not picketing. The judge found that he "would blow his horn and wave his hand to direct picketers to leave when the official [police] car was arriving in the area."[97] Klock's job was to warn people so they could run.

Some teachers didn't believe in running. Phil Basile, another Barringer teacher, was arrested at Elliot Street Elementary School on February 19. Strik-ing for students as well as teachers, "all fired up" by the daily meetings, Basile was ready to be arrested. "I just didn't go too fast." Dave Lieberfarb, who taught at Weequahic, was picketing at Miller Street Elementary School on February 19. He had a chance to get away when officers appeared. Because he saw the strike as a way for working people to achieve some power, he accepted the price. "I let myself get arrested."[98]

During the third week, teachers who went on the picket line were willing to be arrested. In a sense, they chose arrest. At the beginning, Dorothy Bergman and a friend picketed their own school, Boylan Street Elementary. When the Union told them to go to Summer Avenue on February 19, they knew the risks. Bergman took the bus; the friend drove. At Summer Avenue, Bergman spotted her friend's car and went over to chat. "Three men jumped out of nowhere, I think three, they just jumped out. They said, 'Are you a teacher?' I said yes. They said, 'Did you call in sick?' I said no. So they said, 'You're under arrest.' I said, 'All right.' "[99]

Carol Karman went to picket at Miller Street on February 19. "There were maybe six or seven schools at that point being picketed in the whole city. So we knew we would be arrested if we went there, and we went there anyway." Having chosen to be arrested, she just climbed in the paddy wagon. "I didn't struggle. At that point many people had been arrested, and we had decided the more the merrier." *We had decided*: Karman, who returned to Newark in

1969 to join the fight, did not look on herself as a foot soldier who took orders. She participated in making decisions and felt an obligation to carry them out. Being arrested was a way to make a point about the Board's policy of repression. "Let them look totally ridiculous. How many teachers can they arrest?" She does not sound cool, or tough, about it. "The arrest was the big deal. You don't get arrested every day of your life."[100]

When Howard Goeringer was arrested on February 19, it was a very big deal, because it was his second arrest. Goeringer was a minister as well as a teacher. He was "a true community-type person," according to a colleague at West Kinney Junior High, extremely idealistic, dedicated to "doing everything to improve the daily lives of people." At the daily strike meeting, on the day before his first arrest, Goeringer spoke to teachers about the strike: "The name of the game is power."[101] He allowed himself to be arrested twice because he believed people could defeat powerful and oppressive institutions, if they were willing to pay the price.

The price was high for Esther Tumin. "We knew we'd be in for a fight, we'd lose salary, there might be some unpleasantnesses on the picket line. . . . But well into the strike, jail was not one of the options anybody thought about. And then suddenly, it became *the* option." Tumin continued picketing, "knowing that we probably would be arrested," and was one of forty-five teachers apprehended on February 19. She resented the fingerprinting and mug shots. "I remember feeling the humiliation of the process. We were after all, I thought, pretty special people. Many of the people were master teachers, incredible teachers. And here we were going through a process that criminals go through, with little girls at typewriters who persisted in calling us by our first names, as if we didn't deserve the dignity of our name."[102] Little girls in the courthouse, like big boys in the halls at Weequahic, failed to show respect. The struggle to reclaim the dignity and status of a professional was already proving more difficult than Tumin had imagined when she chose to strike.

Pat Piegari had avoided arrest. "It may have been instinctive, growing up in the city. I could run fast." But one of the forty-five teachers arrested on February 19 was his close friend. Now solidarity overcame instinct. "The next day I got arrested because I wanted to show my friend . . . he had support." Angela Paone, married to Piegari at the time, remembers. "He sort of sacrificed himself, literally, because . . . our very good dear friend was arrested out on the line, and my husband felt guilty about that, that he hadn't gone out on the line with him that day. So he knew what the dangers were. He wouldn't let me go out on the line; he was not going to let us both get arrested, because we had the baby. So he went out the next day . . . where he knew he could be a sitting duck, and didn't run, and got arrested."[103]

Alice Saltman also showed support to a friend. Saltman retired in 1968 after thirty-eight years of teaching in Newark. Hannah Litzky was still teaching, however, and Litzky was Saltman's best friend. Litzky, in her fourth decade of teacher activism, picketed daily. "We were told where to picket," she says simply. "At first we picketed at our own school. Then the Union decided to send some of us to other schools, knowing full well that the people were going to be arrested on the picket line. We went wherever we were told to go." Saltman went out on the line with Litzky and was arrested with her. Saltman had not picketed regularly. "But I picketed the day we got picked up. And that may have been why I went that day. I was gonna make my statement. If they're gonna do it, then I want to be in it too."[104]

Activist teachers persevered to the end. Their ties with each other were too powerful for the Board or Court to sunder. Litzky, Saltman, Piegari, and the seventeen others arrested on February 20 would be the last. On that day, negotiators for the Board of Education agreed to the key Union demands. A total of 188 Newark teachers had been arrested.[105] It is hard to imagine the members of the Board would have begun the mass arrests if they had known how strongly teachers felt and how far they would go.

The Settlement

The Board strategy was to make a decent money offer, arrest Union officers and active strikers, break the picket line, and force the majority of teachers back to work. The Board underestimated teachers at the bargaining table and then underestimated them in the streets. Force did not defeat them. Although fewer teachers picketed, and some returned to work, most stayed out. Throughout the third week, according to Board figures, two-thirds were still out. The way the Board treated teachers confirmed their view that it would not listen to them unless they spoke as one.[106]

While the teachers maintained solidarity, the Board split wide open. When Mayor Hugh Addonizio pressed for a settlement during the third week, a majority on the Board agreed to give teachers what they wanted. Reluctantly, the mayor and the Board acknowledged the power of the teachers. Carole Graves was not grateful. She emphasized that teachers had won the strike themselves. "It was won on the streets, on the picket line, unfortunately." Ben Epstein, who was on the Board team, also gave the teachers the credit. The mayor "found out that he was dealing with a legitimate force, that the teachers were able to get people out on the streets. That makes injunctions and all that alright, but they weren't going to solve the problem."[107]

Addonizio was under indictment because of his mob connections and the pervasive corruption of his administration; soon he would go to jail, for much longer than the teachers. But in February 1970 he was still mayor, still hoping to be reelected in the spring. He opposed the strike when it began, hoping to keep the city's labor costs down. So long as it seemed that the legal offensive could break the picket line, he removed himself from the struggle. The teachers' solidarity changed his mind.[108]

Pressed by Newark and New Jersey union leaders, Addonizio abandoned his allies on the Board and presented himself as the man who would restore order to the city. On February 16, he sat in on the on-again, off-again talks for the first time and pressed Board members to modify their opposition to binding arbitration. On February 18, the Board negotiating team accepted the principle of binding arbitration. On February 20, the mayor fully joined the negotiations, summoning the Board team to the Robert Treat Hotel and instructing them to stay there, day and night, until the strike was settled. The Board team, chaired by Dr. Michael Petti, did as told. Described by a member of the Board team as "an Addonizio man," Petti put aside his personal feelings, and gave up the struggle.[109]

Jacob Fox would not surrender. The chief negotiator was convinced the Board could not and should not contract away any of its powers. The Union concentrated its fire on Fox. Privately, Union leaders complained to the mayor about him. Publicly, Charles Marciante, the AFL-CIO leader in New Jersey, blasted him. Marciante called for the removal of Fox because his "intransigent and arrogant attitude" blocked a settlement. Fox was disturbed when Addonizio attended the talks on February 16. "He was clearly ready to give away anything. It bothered me." He was more disturbed when the Board began to reconsider binding arbitration. "You people tell me no arbitration, no arbitration. You put me out on the limb and you cut me off."[110] Fox was not invited when serious negotiations began on February 20, and he resigned.

Even with Fox gone, reaching a settlement took four and a half days of round-the-clock bargaining. Board President Harold Ashby opposed binding arbitration and objected to being bullied. Another Board member, Dr. E. Wyman Garrett, was furious about the contract. NTU leaders were also not happy. They knew that the Union would be paying fines, and paying to defend 188 teachers, for a long time. One officer was already sentenced to three months; three more received three-month sentences on the very day of the settlement.[111] Graves's comment that the strike "was won on the picket line, unfortunately" expressed the bitterness of NTU leaders that they had to bankrupt their Union and go to jail in order to get an agreement whose fundamental terms were visible early on to almost everyone, including the mediator provided by the state.

The State of New Jersey had chosen Theodore Kheel as mediator, under the 1968 law regulating public-sector bargaining. Kheel brought the twenty-seven-year-old Lewis Kaden to Newark and left him in charge. Kaden's suggestions on February 10 for ending the strike included a grievance procedure with binding arbitration. Board negotiators, including Fox and Epstein, were enraged by Kaden's suggestions, immediately rejecting them as "the union demands in better English." Skillful as he was, keeping the teams in separate rooms and shuttling between them, Kaden could create no movement for settlement until the mayor's pressure on the Board gave him an opening. Then he limited each team to five members and brought them together in one room, where they hammered out a contract.[112]

On February 25, after a seventeen-day strike, the teachers won a comprehensive grievance procedure with binding arbitration. Dave Selden, emerging from jail, termed the binding arbitration clause the best in New Jersey. Going him one better, the Union claimed that Newark teachers had won "the best grievance procedure in the country."[113] What mattered to Newark teachers was that for the first time they were protected from the arbitrary power of the principal; what they had won was a measure of self-respect.

Now teachers could hold the Board accountable. Everything in the contract took on more weight, because there was a mechanism for enforcing what was written. For example, the contract limited class size to thirty. Although the language gave the Board some flexibility, teachers believed that they could finally control the number of students per class. It was no longer a question of asking the Board. If the Board did not live up to its word, there was a way to keep it honest. The Board also pledged to hire 252 teacher aides to take the place of teachers in cafeterias, playgrounds, and halls. Vic Cascella, on the negotiating team as the representative of elementary teachers, saw to it that these "nonprofessional chores" were included in the settlement. Cascella knew the Union could force the Board to honor its pledge through the grievance procedure.[114]

Third parties who helped get the contract were called mediators; third parties who settled conflicts under the contract were called arbitrators. Arbitrators were more powerful, because their decisions were final, whereas mediators only recommended. But either way, they were experienced people who did not assume management was always right. Their very training as arbitrators and mediators was based on the idea that conflict between labor and management was legitimate. When arbitrators were called in to resolve a grievance, or when mediators helped resolve a strike, they implicitly recognized that teachers had legitimate claims on the Board, and not just vice versa. This recognition, in itself, represented a victory for teachers.

At the same time, the grievance procedure and arbitration process encouraged teachers to put their trust in experts and lawyers rather than in their own strength. Handling grievances became the Union's business, requiring specialized training and technical knowledge. Teachers would be protected by Union staffers, Union lawyers, and professional arbitrators. In the long run, teachers might forget that the Union's power was their power. They might forget their role in the 1970 strike, or remember it nostalgically, as something they did once and long ago.

But for now, there was no chance to forget. The struggle was not over. On February 26, teachers voted by three to one to ratify the contract and return to work. Most were happy. But when Bates told them, "It is time now to go back and live together," they yelled back, "No!" Many were angry at teachers who had crossed the picket line and gotten paid. The strike had required real sacrifice, leading some to want revenge, and others to raise their expectations. Twenty-five percent of the teachers wanted more from the settlement, especially money. The final salary package was very similar to the Board offer at the beginning. Meanwhile, many teachers lost seventeen paid days; the settlement allowed them to make up only ten. One teacher heckled Graves at the meeting, complaining the Union hadn't won anything.[115]

Board members would not have agreed with him. At their ratification meeting, they expressed misgivings about the concessions they were making. At the last minute, they balked. They realized the salary package—raising the starting salary from $6,700 to $8,000 and the maximum to $13,100, and reducing the number of steps needed to reach maximum—would cost $740,000 more than they had figured. But it was too late. Petti, forced to defend the agreement he had negotiated, looked "haggard and like a loser in a battle against his personal judgment."[116]

Before they voted, Board members listened to parents and other community members denounce them for capitulating. Then they voted five to three for the contract, with one abstention. Ominously, in terms of the future, the "no" votes were cast by the three African American members. Ashby and Garrett were known to oppose the settlement. But Gladys Churchmen was going to vote yes before she heard the parents and community leaders speak so passionately.[117] The strike was over, but a new struggle was just beginning.

Figure 1 Sheriff's deputy reads the injunction to pickets, 1970.
(Newark Teachers Union)

Figure 2 Arrested teachers after booking and fingerprinting, 1970.
(Newark Teachers Union)

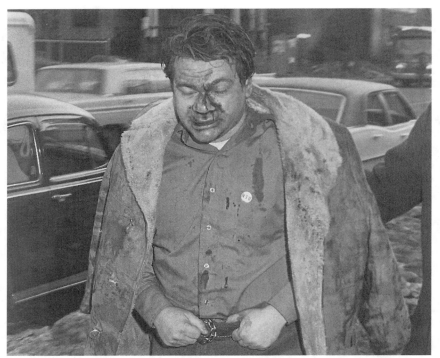

Figure 3 Terry Elman outside NTU office after beating, February 2, 1971.
(Newark Teachers Union)

Figure 4 Carole Graves, Don Nicholas (second from left), and Frank Fiorito (far left) had just been sentenced to six months, February 25, 1971.
(Newark Star-Ledger)

Figure 5 Harold Moore and his son, celebrating the end of the 1971 strike, April 18, 1971. *(Newark Star-Ledger)*

Figure 6   Essex County Penitentiary.
(Newark Teachers Union)

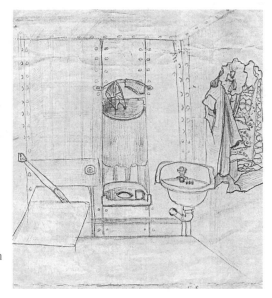

Figure 7   Alice Saltman's sketch
of her jail cell, December 1971.
(Alice Saltman)

Figure 8   Jim Lowenstein teaching at School Within a School, late 1970s.
(Jim Lowenstein)

Chapter 4

Black Power Between the Strikes

Striking teachers defeated the Board and won a contract in 1970. But their victory heightened racial conflict. During the year of the contract, Blacks took power in both the Board and the Union and prepared to go to war with each other.

Race in the 1970 Strike

A tendency toward racial polarization existed throughout the 1970 strike. Amiri Baraka and Tony Imperiale developed opposing projects from the beginning. Baraka formed New Ark Community Coalition to staff the schools and keep them open. On the first day of the strike, Baraka supporters physically confronted a teacher picketing at the Robert Treat School in the Central Ward. From the third day of the strike, Imperiale—as head of the North Ward Citizens Committee—used force to prevent Puerto Rican and Black volunteers from working with children in the McKinley Street Elementary School.[1]

Union leaders tried to contain the tendency toward racial polarization. In the Black-majority city, they feared teacher power would be perceived as white power. That is why, in 1968, after the riot/rebellion, they chose an African American for president. That is why, in the 1970 strike, they selected an African American building rep to present the strike resolution, and why they welcomed Larry Birchette, an African American, as leader and spokesperson of the strike. That's also why they invited Bayard Rustin to speak at the big Sunday rally of 2,500 teachers on February 8. Rustin's presence challenged the tendency to see the strike as white. He brought to the strike his immense prestige as organizer of the 1963 March on Washington, "a living legend," in the words of Jim Lerman.[2]

Rustin held high the restraining order that officers of the court had served on him as he entered the hall, the same order served on NTU officers during the week, and he spoke slowly and powerfully. "I have been told that if I counsel you to picket, congregate, parade, etc., I will be in contempt of court, so, I counsel you to picket, congregate, parade." The crowd roared. Rustin returned the following Sunday, risking arrest, and was given a standing ovation. For many striking teachers, his speeches were a high point. They cite his "ministerial style," "beautiful voice," "wonderful speech." Esther Tumin goes deeper: "A Black like Bayard Rustin came to us, gave us a great deal of prestige in terms of Blacks, and the fact that Black teachers were on strike, and Black teachers went to jail, meant it was not a Black/white issue."[3]

Rustin confirmed the teachers' belief that their strike was not about white over Black. From the point of view of NTU leaders, Rustin was the ideal speaker. They knew he would emphasize what Black and white working people held in common rather than what separated them. An outspoken critic of Black nationalism, Rustin focused on issues of class; he had even supported the teachers union in New York during the 1968 Ocean Hill–Brownsville strike. Yet his legitimacy came from his long and prominent involvement in the civil rights struggle. NTU leaders knew that having Rustin speak would decrease the tendency toward racial polarization.[4]

But Al Shanker could have the opposite effect. Carole Graves opposed inviting him to speak. She argued that an invitation to Shanker—the leader of the Ocean Hill–Brownsville strike—would offend Blacks in Newark. Ron Polonsky, Tony Ficcio, and Andy Thorburn, the three activists who dominated the executive board, wanted to invite Shanker. To them, Shanker was a hero of the struggle for teachers' rights; his local in New York was contributing resources to their strike. They marshaled enough votes on the executive board to override Graves.[5]

The argument about whether to invite Shanker is an early example of conflict between Graves and her executive board, and the argument turned on different views of race. To Polonsky, Ficcio, and Thorburn, Shanker's image in the Black community was not relevant. He embodied teacher power, and they were glad to associate their struggle with his. To Graves, Shanker embodied white power, and she wanted to distance her struggle from his. Graves was sensitive to the views of Black people in the community and wanted to send NTU speakers to Black churches and organizations. According to Thorburn, "It's one of the things we had a lot of trouble with Carole on. Carole was into community support." Ficcio believed that if teachers maintained their picket line and did not go back to work, they would win; the community had little effect on the outcome. Thorburn quotes him from memory. "'They're not gonna walk your picket line. If they support you, what are they going to do? . . . So don't waste your energy. . . . You're not going to win a strike because of community support.'" Ficcio was not racist, according to Thorburn. It was just that he wasn't concerned about the community, whether white or Black. But Thorburn recognized that Ficcio's exclusive focus on class—on employees versus employer—sounded racist to Graves. "Well, to Carole it sounded like you're anti-Black, because community to her means Black."[6]

After the strike, racial issues would contribute to the first split between NTU leaders. But during the strike, when the Union was fighting for its life, leaders compromised. Graves lost the argument on Shanker but prevailed on community support. By reaching out to African Americans, the Union helped prevent racial tensions in the city from derailing the 1970 strike. Graves wrote to Black leaders before the strike, offering to discuss the Union's position and asking for "a unified front against the administration of this city." Such contacts were intended not so much to win over Black groups as to neutralize their opposition and prevent the formation of a united front against the strike. Thorburn spoke to Black community groups. "I convinced, I converted nobody. But the fact is that the hostility level was still low enough that a white spokesman could stand up [and] be listened to."[7]

The hostility level remained low in 1970 partly because of the efforts by rank-and-file teachers. Some striking Black teachers set up a private meeting with Baraka and a few NTU leaders. The meeting, which took place on the fourth day of the strike, was "helpful but difficult," according to a Union source. Baraka went on to publicly position himself as a third force, not aligned with either the Board or the Union. He criticized the Board: "I still believe these schools are the worst on the planet." And he criticized the Union: instead of striking, it should have joined with community groups "to make the board give in and try to improve these schools." But Baraka gave the teachers something which, considering his position in the city, only he could give. Commenting on the tension between parents and striking teachers, he said: "I don't really think it has become too much of a black-white issue yet."[8] Union leaders gave Baraka a tacit acceptance of the presence of parents and college students in the schools. They did not try to close the schools. NTU leaders instructed teachers to say nothing to the parents and college students who were crossing the picket line.[9] They did not want to turn the strike into a "black-white issue."

Many pickets were Black. Harold Moore, Janice Adams, and Charles and Martha Nolley picketed every day. Phyllis Cuyler and Avant Lowther Jr.

picketed many days. Some African American teachers stayed home; they too contributed to the perception of the strike as interracial. Others crossed the picket line, but they were not alone: many older white women, teaching in elementary schools, also crossed the line. The line was not a color line. All observers agreed that the percentage of Black teachers who struck was lower than the percentage of white teachers who struck. But it was high enough to counter the view that the strike was white. "The presence of black teachers on the picket lines and a few white teachers in the classrooms during the strike has considerably settled fears that the walkout would become a racial issue," commented the *Star-Ledger* during the first week.[10]

Fred Means, president and founder of the Organization of Negro Educators, nevertheless maintained that the strike was racial: white teachers were asserting themselves at the expense of Black children and parents. Carole Graves had reached out to Means before the strike. "As I see it, at this point, an individual can support either the teachers or the Board," she wrote. "There is no other tenable position."[11] Means agreed there was no other tenable position. He chose the Board.

Means framed the strike as a conflict between the movement for Black power and the movement for teacher power. Blacks were organizing in Newark to take power over the institutions that affected their lives, including the schools. "The Newark community will never allow teachers to control one of its most important institutions," he warned. "By its unabashed thrust for power, NTU has charted a course that will polarize teachers on one side and the community on the other." With the Black community on one side and teachers on the other, where did that leave ONE? Eugene Campbell, a vice president of ONE, observed during the strike, "We're in a trick bag—so much so that we've become strange bedmates with that other monster, the Board of Education."[12]

It was an awkward position for ONE, which had been critical of the Board. In a 1974 interview, Means claimed that ONE supported the Board in 1970 because the Union was the oppressor. He argued that Newark's "traditional white power structure" was represented not by the Board, nor—as the interviewer suggested—by the Prudential Insurance Company, but by the Newark Teachers Union. Ficcio, like many trade unionists, dissolved race into class. Means, like many Black nationalists, dissolved class into race.[13]

The strength and limit of the Black Power movement derived from its exclusive emphasis on race. This emphasis was a strength, because many Blacks were able to band together to force their economic and political advancement, as they did in Newark. It was also a weakness, because, as also happened in Newark, class was denied but reemerged: Blacks who advanced tended to become separated from those left behind. Disillusionment was built into the model. In 1974, Means acknowledged that ONE's emphasis on race—on getting Black people into positions of power—had not turned out as he and his colleagues had hoped. Selfish class and political concerns now came first for Blacks on the Board, he said, not the idealistic concerns that the movement had envisaged.[14]

In terms of the model of racial conflict that Black groups embraced, those who struck the schools were oppressors, or dupes of oppressors. In terms of the model of class conflict that the Union embraced, those who opposed the strike were oppressors, or dupes of oppressors. Everyone claimed to be on the side of the people. Emotionally as well as intellectually, it was hard for either side to acknowledge the absence of a single, unitary people from whom all legitimacy sprang. If teachers, as working people, had a legitimate reason to strike, then those who opposed them became oppressors. If Black people, as students and parents, had a legitimate stake in the schools, then those who struck the schools became oppressors. The explosive element in the Newark strikes of 1970 and 1971 was rooted in the way that the protagonists denied each other's legitimacy. The explosion did not occur in 1970, but the widespread and mutual disrespect was, already, a kind of violence.

Many Black parents made an effort to see the teachers' point of view. But their children were either not going to school or were going to schools without teachers. "The strike, I am afraid, is going to devide [sic] the community," wrote one parent, early in the strike: "Teachers on one side and parents on the other." The letter, handwritten by M. J. Porter to teachers at Avon Avenue School in the South Ward, expressed a parent's complex feelings about the strike. Porter acknowledged that the Board had given teachers reason to strike. "Truthfully, most teachers are looking forward to better working conditions and [expecting that] in the end the products will come out better." But Porter doubted the strike would actually decrease class size and that the Union would protect only good teachers. "I don't truly believe the union will ease away the burden of the school system." So "I wish I could just say to you 'please come back to school, your students misses you' and that would be enough." But that wasn't going to happen. And the longer the strike continued, the greater the "possibility of temper flare-ups in the community."[15]

Temper flare-ups became common by the third week of the strike. Parents packed the Metropolitan Baptist Church in the Central Ward in response to an invitation from strikers. They listened quietly to Jim Lerman and Evelyn Johnson, white and Black teachers respectively at West Kinney Junior High. Johnson and Lerman emphasized that they were striking not primarily for money but for the "power to govern the circumstances surrounding [our] jobs." Then Dick Parish, a Black vice president of AFT, spoke. Parish had good credentials for community outreach: in New York, he had opposed the Ocean Hill–Brownsville strike. But in Newark he was an outsider. When he asked Black parents to support the strike, the cry from around the hall was "Never."[16]

Parents' frustration broke into the open, and the meeting spun out of the strikers' control. Eugene Campbell, the ONE vice president who was an acting principal, questioned the right of striking teachers to be in a Black church and argued that a Union victory would slow the promotion of Black teachers. The Reverend Henry Cade, chair of the New Ark Community Coalition, hit a nerve. "Just because a few whites get thrown into a few wagons they start crying that justice is dead. I'm here to tell you that justice for the blacks has been dead in the land for 350 years." Strike opponents took over the meeting. When it ended, Johnson stood at the exit. "I'm sorry I asked you to come," she said to parents. She had hoped to hear their "questions and feelings on the problem [of the schools], but all we got were representatives of different groups and factions tonight."[17] The dialogue between parents and teachers, always difficult, was becoming impossible.

Like parents, students wanted teachers to come back to school and became more militant as the strike went on. Initially, student activists were skeptical of both the Board and the Union. A small sampling of student opinion taken by the *Newark News* on the first day of the strike showed no pattern, with some supporting and others opposing the strike. Larry Hamm, a sixteen-year-old junior at Arts High, refused to take sides that day but noted that "the teachers have been handicapped in many respects." Hamm, an African American, identified with the teachers' difficulties in getting supplies from the Board.[18]

Hamm joined with students from other high schools in organizing Students for Better Education to fight for the rights and interests of students. The leaders were Black, representing every high school except East Side. Jim Lerman met with Hamm and other leaders of the group several times during the strike. Lerman says that the students understood the labor issues in the strike. "And for a while they were sympathetic, but ultimately they got pissed off," because teachers weren't teaching and they weren't learning. Students and parents attended a Board meeting in the third week of the strike and condemned both sides, but especially the teachers.[19]

During the third week of the strike, Students for Better Education intervened. "The union and the Board are both tools of the establishment," they complained. They staged a sit-in at the Board office. From the Board office, they sent a delegation to meet with the Union negotiating team, but it came back frustrated. "I can see why they're called 'professional negotiators,' " said one. "They talk so much you forget what you came to discuss." Supporting the sit-in, a large group of students confronted teachers and trade union supporters who came to hold a previously scheduled protest against the Board. Charles Marciante, New Jersey AFL-CIO head, immediately called off the protest. Inside, the Board lost patience with the sit-in on the second day and forcibly ended it; as the students were carried out, they went limp in civil rights style. About six hours later, they disrupted a mass meeting of strikers, which Birchette ended quickly.[20] Strikers were still trying to avoid a fight with Black students and parents, but doing so was getting harder.

Two things helped teachers escape confrontation. One was that their critics were not yet united. In 1970, student activists maintained their independence from other community groups. For example, when settlement was near, Black adult leaders wanted the Board to hold out for better terms, but student leaders argued for the quickest possible end to the strike. Black community groups were themselves divided in relation to the Board of Education; Baraka and CFUN (Committee for a Unified Newark) opposed the strike without supporting the Board. The Board itself, instead of joining together with Black groups, kept them at arm's length in 1970. When the New Ark Community Coalition pressed for a role in negotiations, the Board shunted it aside.[21]

The other thing that prevented confrontation was the timing of the settlement. The more the strike became racialized, the greater became the pressure on Mayor Addonizio to end it. One day after the parent meeting at the Metropolitan Church, on the same day students were evicted from the Board office, a group of about forty angry Black parents met with Addonizio. They warned of a danger of "confrontation that could return the city to 1967." The flash point would be the McKinley School, they predicted, because Imperiale's men, patrolling the grounds with dogs, continued to prevent volunteers from coming into the school. Responding to the growing racial tension and fear of a new wave of violence in Newark, the mayor intensified his attempt to settle the strike.[22]

Union leaders knew that they were near victory. But they wanted a victory the Black community could live with, so they gave ground on some crucial issues. In addition to their overriding demand for binding arbitration, on which they would not compromise, they had made three potentially inflammatory demands. The three demands concerned promotion, transfer, and nonprofessional chores. In the end, the Union made concessions on two of the three.

On promotion, the Union retreated from its demand for reinstatement of the written exam for principal. Union negotiators dropped this demand during the second week of the strike, stating that if they got binding arbitration of grievances, they could settle for language on promotion that would prevent the Board from acting arbitrarily. In the settlement, the new contract specified the criteria for promotion, including "the welfare of children and the community," which allowed the Board to continue to promote Blacks ahead of whites.[23]

Racial politics had everything to do with why NTU negotiators made the original demand, and why they dropped it. White teachers who resented and feared the promotion of Blacks were part of the Union constituency; hence the demand to restore the written exam. But many striking teachers, white as well as Black, wanted students to see more Blacks in positions of authority. And in any event, the door to Black promotion had been opened by the riot/rebellion, and it would be unwise for the Union to try to close it. Hence the Union dropped the demand for restoring the written. The issue of promotion was, for Blacks, "hotter than a two-dollar pistol,"[24] Superintendent Franklyn Titus provocatively observed. By ratifying and formalizing the racial change that was already taking place, Union leaders dodged a bullet.

The Union also made concessions regarding transfer. One question was: Who should get preference in reassignment to a new school or to a new position within a school? The Union agreed to give up its original position—seniority should shape the decision—in return for spelling out the criteria, which would now include "integration of staff and the welfare of children and the community."[25] In other words, race could be taken into account. This was the easy part.

The trickier question concerned involuntary transfers, where teachers were removed from a school against their wishes. Here teacher power and Black power met head on. "If you put one teacher whom we do not like in a school, we will boycott the school until someone gets him out of there," warned Jesse Jacob, a former president of the Newark PTA. The settlement specified no involuntary transfer could take place "except for just, fair, and equitable cause." But a tiny last-minute change muddied the water. Initially, the agreement acknowledged the needs of "the children in the community." The final draft, produced by Board staff, changed "in" to "and." Union negotiators balked, sensing danger, but finally capitulated, putting their faith in the grievance procedure. By using the phrase "*and* the community," the contract seemed to say that in addition to the needs of students, the Black community had needs of its own that could legitimately affect transfer decisions. Through this tiny opening, militant parents and citizens would later pour.[26]

Promotion and transfer were highly visible issues. By contrast, the assignment of nonprofessional chores was not an issue that anyone in Newark outside NTU had thought much about. Black leaders did not focus on it during negotiations, and Union leaders were not forced to soften their demand. As a result, the contract provision on nonprofessional chores would be more damaging to relations between teachers and parents than anything else in the contract.

In New York, teachers were freed from nonteaching chores in 1962. Nationally, teacher union leaders saw the change as enhancing the professional status of teachers and lightening their work load. In Newark in 1963, Vic Cascella's brother Joe raised the demand that teachers be "released from all nonteaching chores."[27] Now, in February 1970, the Board agreed to hire teacher aides to relieve teachers of much of their supervisory work, including cafeteria duty and hall duty. In the following year, as teachers stopped doing these tasks, many parents felt hurt and angry. It was hard for them to see teachers spending less time with their children while getting paid more—especially, as Means emphasized, when the children were mostly Black and the teachers mostly white. A militant Black parent asserted that nonprofessional chores were "the only human aspect of the teaching," and that teachers who didn't want human interaction with his child didn't belong in the schools.[28]

The Union victory in 1970 led to the war in 1971: the new conflict was built into the settlement of the old. The settlement postponed confrontation but did not resolve the underlying racial issues, and in some ways inflamed them. Involuntary transfer, nonprofessional chores, and binding arbitration would all become battlegrounds.

On a deeper level, the very fact of teacher power was galling to many Black parents and residents. In the devastated city, the ability of teachers to organize, fight, and win was infuriating. As they watched the teachers take to the streets—illegally—and get what they wanted, some parents felt resentful and probably envious. Teachers had won a powerful voice in the strike and the contract, a voice they could use to speak up for themselves. Who would speak for the children? Carole Graves and Jim Lerman and Angela Paone tried to say, We will speak for the children. During the strike, they insisted that they wanted power not only for themselves but also for students. Their message neutralized opposition and helped them win, but their victory galvanized opposition.

"The community cannot live with binding arbitration," said a leader of the New Ark coalition when the settlement was announced. "We are working now on our strategy to test it." The frustration of Black parents and community leaders boiled over at the crowded Board ratification meeting on February 26. When Carole Graves spoke, only the few teachers present cheered. Nearly everyone else booed. Graves was protected by police when she finished speaking and was escorted through the crowd of angry parents. She acknowledged that she had been the target of hostility before, "but not [from] a part of my community."[29]

Community leaders and parents simultaneously condemned the teachers for striking illegally and threatened illegal action of their own. Voicing the confusion of many, a member of the overflow audience at the ratification meeting called out, "When Martin Luther King broke the law, he paid for it. They [the teachers] broke the law and they should be punished." But as the audience knew, the teachers were about to be rewarded with a contract. Already possessing some access to resources and power, teachers would now be protected by binding arbitration. The contract was the symbol of their victory and the guarantor of their power. Jesse Jacob reminded the Board how, as a volunteer, he had served the restraining order on many striking teachers and testified against them. Then he dared the members of the Board to implement the 1970 contract.[30] Six months later, Jesse Jacob would become the new president of the Board of Education, responsible for implementing the contract.

Two Elections

In the spring of 1970, the members of the Newark Teachers Union elected a new slate of officers, and Newark citizens elected a new mayor. These two elections, which no one connected at the time, transformed the Union, the city, and the relationship between them.

The Union election was considered a formality. A group of activists around Ron Polonsky controlled the election machinery, via a three-member election committee that put forward the slate of candidates. Carole Graves, as president, could suggest people to serve on the election committee, but the executive board, which had the final say on its membership, was dominated by Polonsky's allies. "So essentially the election committee that year was in the hands of Polonsky, who was not even on the executive board, but two of the three people [on the committee] were his close associates," says Andy Thorburn.[31]

Polonsky and Thorburn (Ficcio had moved on to a position in the state federation) needed Graves to head the ticket, even though they were critical of her. She came to the office late and took long lunches. They saw her as not really serious, as more committed to a political agenda—pro-Black, antiwar—than to unionism. But during the strike, they were not nearly as visible as Graves, who as president became the symbol of resistance to the Board of Education and the courts, and the best-known and most popular figure in the Union. "We couldn't break with her, because we just weren't popular enough without her," Thorburn explains. "So we put up a slate of candidates with Carole at the head, but which we controlled."[32]

Their plan went smoothly. The election committee nominated Graves, and a majority of candidates for the seventeen other executive board positions who were closer to Polonsky than to Graves. The only problem was that "it was not easy to find Blacks." Bill Troublefield, an activist at Polonsky's old school, West Kinney Junior High, was on the slate. "He was Polonsky's guy," says

Thorburn, "more likely to support us than [to support] Carole. That was a perfect out for us, because we couldn't be accused of not putting Blacks on the slate." Clara Dasher was also on the slate; Polonsky and Thorburn imagined she was in neither camp. But race was the wild card, the one thing Polonsky and Thorburn could not control. They thought they could count on Troublefield. "But because of the pull of Carole being Black, we gradually lost control of him."[33]

At the April membership meeting, Polonsky and Thorburn expected nominations to close after the election committee presented its ticket. But they underestimated Graves. She took the microphone and announced that she was withdrawing from the slate nominated by the election committee. Dasher resigned with her. Then from the floor someone nominated an entire new slate headed by Graves. "It was a brilliant, brilliant coup," says Thorburn. He assumed Graves herself was not smart or hardworking enough to plan the coup. "I don't know who was advising her, but it was a brilliant move and she really screwed us royally."[34]

"Carole did it, I did it, and Clara did it," says Vic Cascella. Dasher went to Graves and told her that the dominant faction wanted Graves to continue as merely titular head. Graves called the initial secret meeting with Dasher and Cascella. The three conspirators carefully expanded their planning group, choosing people who would keep the secret. Bob Hirschfeld and Bob Clark were among those asked to join. Hirschfeld remembers six to ten people gathering at private houses to prepare the coup; Clark recalls meeting in South Orange to plan exactly what would take place at the April membership meeting. What would happen at the membership meeting, Cascella explains, "was prepared in advance. In those days people took time to work out the floor arrangements on things."[35]

There were two slates after the April membership meeting. There was the official slate, with no one at the head, and the "Presidential Slate," as it was called, the people nominated from the floor, including Graves, Dasher, Cascella, Hirschfeld, Clark, Don Nicholas, Ralph Favilla, and Carol Karman. They seemed to many members like a breath of fresh air. Six of the eighteen were women, seven were elementary teachers, nine had been arrested in February. As the Presidential Slate, they were publicly committed to supporting Graves.[36]

When the average member, who was not part of the plots and counterplots, looked at the ballot, the choice seemed clear. "Most of us were behind her," says Charles Nolley. "She stood up for the Union. She was just excellent. And we had so many people who just idolized her." Thorburn understood: "Here's a slate of officers which Carole is *not* at the head of, all her enemies are, and here's a slate of officers that she is at the head of."[37]

Graves, Dasher, and Cascella outmanipulated the master manipulators. The slate headed by Graves won all eighteen contests easily, sweeping from power the group around Polonsky and Ficcio, which included not only Thorburn but also Betty Rufalo, John Schmid, and Eddie Tumin. By means of the coup, Graves took the symbol of leadership from the 1970 strike and turned it into power. All participants agree that, in Cascella's words, "The coup was to support Carole in running the Union."[38]

The motives of those who supported Graves were complex. Graves herself did not want to enter the next round of contract negotiations "with someone controlling me, and especially if it was someone white, in terms of how the community would view it." She also recognized "a philosophical split" between "bread-and-butter" unionists like Ficcio and those who took "the broader view" of benefiting students and the community as well as teachers. Graves and her friends "had some kind of ideology beyond collective bargaining; we had a social mission." The struggle between the factions had intensified in March, as a result of a dispute over the jail sentences. Graves wanted to appeal all sentences. Rufalo, supported by Thorburn, decided just to serve her time. Graves saw Rufalo as breaking ranks. "It was clear that there was a schism that could not be repaired," says Graves.[39]

Cascella would challenge Graves for the presidency five years later. Why did he act with Graves and Dasher in 1970 against Polonsky and Thorburn? He answers, hesitantly, in terms of Polonsky's and Thorburn's style. At a Union meeting, before he got to know them well, he looked at the head table and saw Polonsky and Thorburn. "I guess in those days we called them beatniks or whatever. Long flowing hair, my God!" They looked unprofessional to Cascella. "So they kind of rubbed me the wrong way, with their outlook on things. They were too far out, for even me." To Cascella, Graves and Dasher seemed closer to the norm of teacher unionism than did "beatniks" like Polonsky and Thorburn.[40]

Angela Paone's understanding of the coup was closer to Graves's than to Cascella's, but she focused more on gender. Paone wanted to give real power to a woman who was socially committed; she wanted to get traditional trade unionists of the Ficcio mold out of leadership. "As a matter of fact it was Carol Karman and myself and Janice Adams and a few other women who—and there were other men in this group too . . . —we sort of allied together with Carole and Clara Dasher to actually have a coup and throw out that old guard that was represented by Tony [Ficcio] and all the other guys who were there at the time, and to move someone like Carole Graves in, who I guess represented more of a social consciousness." The two other women Paone names are African American, as is Adams. To Paone, a woman-centered alliance that cut across race "really threw out the old guard," which was predominantly white guys, and gave a progressive Black woman the power to lead.[41]

"I encouraged her [Graves] to do this thing," says Carol Karman, "to get rid of the people she didn't want to have to deal with any more. Some of the old leadership: people like Betty Rufalo, Andy Thorburn. People she felt were patronizing to her and treated her like a mascot." The old leadership "really had patronizing attitudes toward Blacks." But Karman, a close friend of Graves since their time together at Dayton Street, was disturbed by one conversation with her friend. During the planning for the coup, Karman asked Graves whether Clara Dasher could be trusted, given her relationship with Betty Rufalo; at South Eighth Street School, Rufalo had originally encouraged Dasher to become active in the Union. Graves's answer disturbed Karman. "She said something like 'Blood is thicker than water'—or a similar racial expression. So I felt: I'm the wrong color, I guess. I found that very shocking. I thought we were best friends."[42]

The Presidential Slate had the same number of Blacks as the slate originally put together by the nominating committee. But it was chosen by Graves and loyal to her. In 1969, during the collective bargaining campaign, observers noted that Graves seemed only nominally in charge. People behind her were passing notes to her, whispering in her ear, telling her what to say. According to persistent rumors within the Union, Graves was not calling the shots; in a more specific version of this rumor, Graves was a figurehead and Jews were still calling the shots. After winning the 1970 election, Graves consolidated her power within the Union. This election resulted in a purge of the losers. It was not like 1965, when Bob Lowenstein encouraged Ralph Favilla to stay involved. The stakes were higher now that the Union had won. Control of the Union brought control of access to full-time NTU staff positions and a share of power in the city and in national AFT. Thorburn's career in the Union was over. Polonsky was kept on as the organizer, but Graves never trusted him; after his success organizing the 1971 strike, he would be brutally purged. Rufalo was forced out of leadership and not allowed even to serve on committees.[43]

"We got them out," says Paone. "That changed the entire course—for better or worse—of the [Newark] Teachers Union." Hirschfeld expresses the same combination of pride and doubt. "We were people who—for right or wrong, better or worse—who backed her and enabled her to obtain power and to mold her own programs, agenda, what have you."[44]

For better or worse: May 14, 1970, proved a turning point for the Union. In the years following the 1970 coup, those who tried democratically to limit Carole Graves's power would be portrayed as aiming to restore her figurehead status. Those who did not follow her without question or debate seemed to be acting to restore the so-called Old Guard, the white guys who had run the Union during the first two years of her presidency. Calls for democracy became tainted with the appearance of racism. Gradually the power of the Union would be monopolized by Graves and her chosen associates. And the teachers who brought the Union to power, who defeated the Association and the Board, would exercise less and less of that power.

Ken Gibson came to power at the same time as Carole Graves, and for a while, the city was not big enough for both of them. In May 1970, as the Union was voting to give real control to a Black woman, Newark was voting to give control to a Black man.

Teacher power and Black Power emerged on parallel tracks in Newark. In November 1969, the Union beat the Association, and the Black and Puerto Rican Convention selected Gibson as its candidate for mayor. Gibson finished first in a field of seven candidates for mayor in May 1970, and Graves swept to power in the Union election. In June, Gibson defeated Addonizio in the runoff.

Many teachers, including Graves, voted for Gibson. He "was the first Black," observes Phyllis Cuyler. "So this whole thing of being part of a new Newark is what we felt too." Angela Paone recalls the riots and corruption that were dividing people in Newark. "I had this idealistic notion that Gibson was gonna bring us all together." Elena Scambio had similar hopes: "I thought he really was for the people."[45]

Gibson was an integrationist whose civil rights work was with moderate organizations. He was committed to fairness, to reform, and to Newark. His family had moved to Newark from Alabama when he was in elementary school. He graduated from Central High and went to engineering college in Newark. He became an engineer for the city of Newark; his brother was a Newark policeman. In 1966 he made a run for mayor and did surprisingly well. He was not charismatic, but he wanted to replace the corrupt and racist government of Newark with a government for all the people.[46]

The Black and Puerto Rican Convention that nominated Gibson was designed to build Black power by selecting one Black for each office. Baraka, a charismatic urban revolutionary, had created the convention for city council elections in 1968. If Gibson spoke for the desire of African Americans to succeed within the American system, Baraka spoke for their desire to transform the system. During the 1970 campaign, Baraka brought leaders and entertainers—Bill Cosby, Dick Gregory, James Brown, Sammy Davis Jr., Harry Belafonte, Ruby Dee, Ossie Davis, Adam Clayton Powell, Ralph Albernathy, Shirley Chisholm—to Newark to give Gibson publicity he could not afford to buy. With his small radical organization, Baraka also brought a street style of tireless leafleting and speaking.[47]

LeRoi Jones had returned to Newark in 1965. His new name—Imamu Amiri Baraka—linked him to Africa: *Imamu* means "priest" in Swahili. Rejecting integration, rejecting whites, rejecting Christianity, a convert to Black nationalism in the mold of Ron Karenga, Baraka wanted to build Black power in Newark. "They ask if we are separatists. If we want a separate state. We have always been separate here. . . . Ever hear of a ghetto? That's separate." Whereas the Black Panthers sought tactical alliance with white leftists, Baraka had no interest in working with whites. In California in 1969, Karenga's group fought a gun battle with the Panthers. In Newark, Baraka articulated the aims of a separate Black city-state: "To own and operate the businesses. To own and operate the politicians, for our own benefit."[48]

Indeed, Addonizio supporters claimed that if Gibson won, Baraka would run the city.[49] Gibson was not owned and operated by anyone, however. The truth was that there were two powerful Black men in Newark.

Two separate staffs worked for Gibson's election. Gibson's own staff calculated that white votes were needed to win the runoff election, knew many whites were disgusted with Addonizio's corruption, and hoped some whites would respond to Gibson's emphasis on good government. Baraka ran his own campaign for Gibson and did not seek white votes. He wanted Blacks to liberate themselves. "The election in Newark of a Black and Puerto Rican slate ie a mayor and 7 of 9 possible councilmen is not to us an end in itself. It is the beginning of national construction." He sketched what Blacks would do when they took control of Newark. "We will nationalize the city's institutions as if it were liberated territory in Zimbabwe or Angola." The city-state of Newark would run the schools, police, and economy. This radical restructuring was just the beginning.[50]

Baraka threatened, Gibson reassured. To many whites, they seemed a classic bad cop/good cop team. It was not an act, though. Right after the election, Baraka criticized Gibson for appointing a white police director; by the end of Gibson's first term, four years later, Baraka and Gibson would be enemies. During the seven months between Gibson's inauguration and the beginning of the 1971 teachers strike, however, his relationship with Baraka was strained but not broken.

Mayor Gibson thought Baraka was naive in believing Black government in Newark could work revolutionary change; he criticized people who "talk about changing the system." The federal government could simply crush them: "the power structure can push a button on you tomorrow." And the greatest power was not government but big corporations like the Prudential Insurance Company. "Believe me, folks, if I could take over Prudential Insurance, you all could have city hall."[51]

Baraka regarded Gibson as naive for thinking Blacks could achieve justice within the existing racist system. More than Gibson, Baraka recognized the psychological barriers to Black pride and power, the internalized racism. More than Baraka, Gibson recognized the intractability of power in its military and economic forms. But though their goals and strategies were opposed, Baraka and Gibson sometimes agreed in practice. For instance, they agreed that in the 1971 contract negotiations, Newark teachers could not be allowed any further gains.

Baraka was angry at Newark teachers for enforcing white values. "Our children in most of these so called schools are not being taught anything. And when they are taught something it is usually to hate themselves." Bright Newark kids succumbed to the "cool scholarship game which turns stone killers alabaster by graduation time." Baraka wanted children to be taught pride in their blackness. He wanted a curriculum that was Afrocentric, a school system that taught revolutionary Black values instead of assimilation into the white middle class. "We will build schools or transform the present curriculum to teach National Liberation." He hoped the Newark public schools would become a training ground for parents as well as students. In the struggle for control of the schools, parents would transform themselves.[52]

Baraka blamed the schools for teaching white middle-class values, and particularly blamed Black teachers for internalizing those values. In a 1961 poem, he ridiculed a Black teacher who didn't "like to teach in Newark" because there were "too many colored in her classes."[53]

Through all his changes from Beat poet to Black prophet, Baraka's view of Black teachers remained negative. In 1965, he imagined a Black teacher—socialized as a student by Newark schools—boasting about his transformation. "Boy, we cool even tho we teach school now and disappeared in our powder-blue coats." In 1970, he mocked the bourgeois attitude of Black educators, who were thinking: "Look at those poor niggers back there; and look how hip I am here by myself." Seduced by the privileges of class, Black teachers abandoned their race and perpetuated a racist system. The fact that a Black teacher was the head of the Newark Teachers Union did not impress Baraka. To him, she had become part of the system of white power. He hoped the next step in building Black power in Newark, after Gibson's election, would be the defeat of the Teachers Union.[54]

Gibson's position on Newark schools was very different. "Our schools are producing another generation of porters," he said. The problem was that Newark schools were not preparing Blacks to move into the middle class, "even as I was prepared through my upbringing and education in Newark." What Gibson wanted was money to invest in the schools. But everyone—his budget people, the city council, the local corporations—told him that there was no money. "With a critical need for more money to modernize and upgrade the entire school system, we find ourselves with a $21 million deficit in our school budget, passed on by the previous administration."[55]

Gibson was angry. Poor schools produced poor people, and a poor city. But how could he break the cycle? He asked for emergency state and federal aid. Speaking to Congress, he pointed out that Newark spent less than $650 per student, whereas New Jersey suburbs averaged more than $800. But the ruling Republicans in Trenton and Washington were not responsive. Newark was in a fiscal crisis, he said in December, "because of the way we live in this country—the way we set up priorities." The United States was "willing to spend billions of dollars to go to the moon and pick up some rocks to look at and spend billions in Vietnam."[56]

Desperately he put together a new tax package, placing a 2 percent income tax on people working in Newark, most of whom lived in the suburbs. Led by suburban districts, the state legislature defeated his tax and vetoed his proposal of a tax on jet fuel at Newark Airport. In January 1971, Gibson brought what was left of his tax package to the Newark City Council, and all hell broke loose.[57]

All six Italian councilmen opposed Gibson's tax proposal, primarily because they opposed Gibson, and any form of Black power. Many Italians felt that just as they were coming into their own—Addonizio had been the first Italian mayor in Newark, after years of Irish mayors, and one Jewish mayor—Blacks were taking it all away. But Black citizens were so angry at the council majority that the council adjourned the hearing on Gibson's tax package in order to avoid violence. The confrontation in January showed the fault lines in the city on the eve of the 1971 teacher strike: Mayor against council, Black against Italian. Before the strike began, violence was already in the air.[58]

When Gibson chose three new Board of Education members in July, he was thinking about race—his appointments created a nonwhite majority on the Board—but he was also thinking about money. He was afraid that the city could not afford another raise when the teachers' contract expired on January 31, 1971. That is probably why he chose Jesse Jacob.[59]

Jacob was an open enemy of the Newark Teachers Union. A Housing Authority employee in 1970, he volunteered to pass out injunctions, help arrest striking teachers, and testify against them in court. Jacob regarded the contract the teachers won in 1970 as "asinine" and "outlandish." He was particularly angry about binding arbitration, insisting that the power gained by teachers came at the expense of students. Mayor Addonizio had given the teachers 65 percent of the power in the Newark school system, said Jacob.

"Every child in this school system is sorry he did it." Jacob claimed a powerful role as the voice of Newark's children. His mission on the Board was to take back the power that the teachers had won.[60]

Jacob's sense of mission developed in 1968, during the Ocean Hill–Brownsville strike in New York. He followed the strike in the newspapers and talked with friends teaching in New York, concluding that "Shanker and his hoods" ruined the educational system in New York. Jacob wanted to prevent the same thing from happening in Newark. Rhody McCoy, the administrator of the Ocean Hill–Brownsville district, came to Newark during the 1970 strike and told Black activists that he was "amazed at the audacity of NTU to have Shanker speak in Newark." Maintaining that the struggle in Newark was similar to the one in New York, McCoy argued that Newark gave Black people a second opportunity to defeat "white supremacy and racism."[61]

To Jacob, Means, Baraka, and other Black nationalists in Newark, Ocean Hill–Brownsville set the pattern of Black resistance. "They followed a pattern that had been set in another area, that did not have the same kind of political structure that we had," said Clarence Coggins, a Black community organizer appointed by Gibson.[62] Coggins saw that Newark was not New York. Decentralized community control, which was the battle cry of Black militants in Ocean Hill–Brownsville, made little sense in Newark, where Blacks were the majority, the mayor was now Black, and the Board of Education had a nonwhite majority.

The teachers were different too. Teachers in Newark were 38 percent Black during the 1970–1971 school year, in contrast to teachers in New York, who were 90 percent white at the time of the Ocean Hill–Brownsville confrontation. And the leadership of the Newark Teachers Union was different. "You know we're not an Al Shanker," said Clara Dasher. But in the months before the 1971 strike, "We had to work under the gun, so to speak, of the Ocean Hill–Brownsville situation." Graves also protested that, despite the number of Black teachers on the picket line during the 1970 strike, "The spectre of Ocean Hill–Brownsville was raised, and they played that up to the hilt."[63]

The specter of Ocean Hill–Brownsville—white teachers and white union against Black parents and Black community—didn't fit Newark. But Jerald Podair points out that the underlying question in the Ocean Hill–Brownsville conflict was, Who is to blame for the school failures of Black children? The teachers union in New York blamed the families and culture of the children. Black nationalists blamed the teachers and the culture of the schools.[64] At the psychological level of assigning blame, the Ocean Hill–Brownsville model did fit Newark. For Jesse Jacob, the struggle against the Union in Newark was aimed at placing the blame where he believed it belonged, on the teachers.

Gibson—who did not hate the teachers—was pointing a weapon at them when he placed Jacob on the Board. Graves and Dasher knew they couldn't work with Jacob. Graves told the press, "I have some misgivings concerning working with a man who was instrumental in sending me to jail for three months." Jacob shot back that if the teachers dared strike again, "I will not only see that you go to jail, but see that you get out of the school system altogether."[65]

The Board elected Jesse Jacob president. The Union asked to begin negotiations for the new contract on October 1, as stipulated in the contract. Jacob did not reply. His hope was not to negotiate with the Union, but to destroy it. In October, he hired Don Saunders as full-time specialist in labor relations. Saunders had no experience in school negotiations or in Newark. But Jacob believed that as a professional negotiator, Saunders could match the professionals sent by national AFT, and that as a Black man who had been active in the civil rights movement, he could rally Black parents and citizens behind the Board.[66]

Now Gibson's and Baraka's strategies came together. Baraka wanted to mobilize the Black community around school struggles. Gibson wanted to balance the budget. Before the start of negotiations, Gibson told Saunders the new contract must cost no more than the old one. Saunders concluded he had nothing to negotiate with and would be forced "to develop fake issues—in order to have a negotiation process." The fake issues were binding arbitration and nonprofessional chores. They were fake because the teachers had already won them and were not going to give them up. But Black parent and community groups wanted to rid the contract of binding arbitration and nonprofessional chores. "I had to side with the public even though I knew as a professional they were not really real issues."[67]

Saunders employed Black groups as a battering ram against the Newark Teachers Union. Elayne Brodie, Newark's Title One coordinator and head of the local NAACP Education Committee, sponsored him, smoothing his way in the Black community. In November and December, he spoke to groups all over the city, asking what they wanted, saying he was the "representative of the community on the Board."[68]

If Saunders had had money to offer the teachers, he would never have involved Baraka in the negotiation process. But he had no money. When he finally began negotiating, he used the symbol of Baraka to set the tone. He asked Baraka to be present in the hall and took several conspicuous breaks from the table to meet with him. Saunders was sending a message: these were not going to be ordinary labor/management negotiations. To emphasize the message and enhance the symbolism, Saunders wore a dashiki to meet with the Union team, though he had worn a business suit when he met with the mayor.[69]

There were only three weeks left in the 1970 contract when Saunders began negotiations. Still he kept stalling, staging a kind of filibuster. "I wasn't bargaining in good faith," said Saunders. "I knew a strike was inevitable, based on what Gibson had said to me." He played with the NTU negotiators. "I could take a proposal and tie them up for six hours." And his tactics were "contagious," according to Pete Curtin, who was on the Board team as a representative of Mayor Gibson. "People forgot that they were there to negotiate. They thought they were role playing, some of them rather enjoying it." The intent, according to the mayor's other representative on the team, was to force a strike. "It was all delaying tactics," said Clarence Coggins. "I sat there, I heard it, I participated in it."[70]

Graves and Dasher knew Saunders and Jacob had no interest in negotiating.[71] They began to hunker down, to look for allies, to prepare for war.

On November 10, Graves wrote to Archer Cole, a leader of the Industrial Union Council of New Jersey and one of the NTU's most important allies, who was scheduled to meet with Mayor Gibson. Gibson must not let the Board keep stalling, she wrote, or "teachers will be forced onto the streets." Graves wanted Cole to tell Gibson that "[t]eachers and trade unionists in general do not want to take over the city; they do require, however, a legitimate participation in the circumstances of their employment."[72]

But when Cole and other prominent trade unionists asked Gibson to intervene, he said no. Gibson did not originate Saunders's strategy of simultaneously stalling the talks and mobilizing Black groups, but he didn't object to it. Also, he could not tell Saunders what to do. Although Saunders reported to Gibson as well as to Jacob, it was Jacob who had hired him, Jacob who gave him his instructions. And Jacob wanted nothing more than to force an all-out confrontation with the Newark Teachers Union. When he got that confrontation, in the form of the 1971 strike, Jacob thought, "Well, look, if there has to be a year of attrition, then it might as well be now as be later."[73]

How did the two elections in the spring of 1970 lead to the war of 1971? Blacks came to power in both the Union election and the mayoral election. Why were they so quickly on opposite sides? Certainly the inadequate resources of the city exacerbated tensions and pitted groups against each other. The 1970 strike left some teachers bitter about arrests, and some parents bitter about nonprofessional chores and binding arbitration. Like most sixties groups, both NTU and CFUN regarded themselves as the true representative of the people. But the fact that a woman won one election and a man the other also matters.

One woman wrote after the election that she "voted for Kenneth Gibson despite the fact that the Black and Puerto Rican Convention, which nominated him, snubbed women in its nominations. I sincerely believe he will live up to his promise as 'mayor of all the people.' . . . So many of our politicians seem to forget that included in 'all the people' are women." But in his initial appointments, Gibson selected fewer women than Addonizio. There were so few women in the Gibson administration—no department heads, no staff members except secretaries—that a columnist wondered why. Women had "played major roles in Gibson's mayoral campaign. However, there has been some suggestion that the male dominance in the administration may reflect the philosophy of the Committee for Unified Newark, which also had a key role in Gibson's campaign."[74]

Throughout America, even in SNCC, the Black Power movement led to a backlash against women's leadership in the movement. In Newark, CFUN taught women in the organization to submit. They had no say even in naming their babies. "Once the Imamu has selected the name it is given to the head of Social Development, and in turn given to the mother." Baraka did not believe in equality. "We cannot understand what devils and the devilishly influenced mean when they say equality for women. We could never be equals." In Baraka's 1969 play *Madheart*, the hero slaps the woman into psychological and sexual submission. Later, after Baraka became a Marxist, he was embarrassed by the play, "because of the whole kind of attack on black women"; earlier, his relationship with his Greenwich Village companion and first wife had been rooted in mutual respect.[75] But in the early 1970s, when he supported Gibson's candidacy and opposed the Newark Teachers Union, Imamu Baraka—like fundamentalists everywhere—wanted to put women back in their place.

Phyllis Cuyler, the young Howard University graduate, toured CFUN's Spirit House but was not comfortable. "All the women and all the babies were in one room, as if they were babysitting all day—so submissive to Baraka. . . . That was a turnoff." Cuyler recognized that "[t]he aim was African. But it didn't appeal to me, because the women—and I had learned this from Angela Davis in that struggle—women have a part."[76]

If CFUN repudiated the idea of equality for women, NTU embraced it. Decades earlier, NTU had advanced the claims of elementary school women teachers for pay equity with high school teachers. In 1970, Graves aimed to increase the power of women. She wrote to Gibson a week after his victory about the Board appointments he was going to make. "We would ask for two trade unionists, neither of them from the customary source (the building trades)." Also, there should be more Blacks. And also, she stated bluntly, "There should be a more equitable representation of women." When Gibson chose Jacob and two other men for the Board, Graves publicly criticized him for not appointing women.[77]

Like Baraka and Gibson, Graves spoke nationally for Blacks. She supported the Black Caucus within national AFT, opposed Shanker, and defended the goal of community control of schools in New York. But she faced humiliations Baraka and Gibson did not face. During the 1970 contract negotiations, Jacob Fox, the Board negotiator, made fun of the Union demand for a paid honeymoon. He turned to Graves, the only female negotiator in the room, and said: "Hey, honey, you want we should buy you the hot-water bottle, too?" A man on the Union side of the table joined in the laughter.[78] Male bonding at the expense of women was part of the way business was done, including the business of contract negotiations. When Graves took control of Newark's most powerful union in May 1970, at the head of a slate that was one-third female, she was implicitly challenging the way business was done.

Graves now appeared confident and powerful, no longer taking direction from anyone. However, Jesse Jacob still treated her as a puppet. On January 5, he refused to meet with a negotiation team headed by Graves, calling her a lackey. Later, he dismissed the leaders of the Newark Teachers Union as "a puppet kind of leadership. . . . They had a colored woman who supposedly was the leader but who in fact was not the leader. They played games, they told her what to do, and she did it."[79] The phrase "a colored woman" expressed the same contempt for assertive Black women as the slap in Baraka's play.

Graves had to fight triply for respect: as a working person, an African American, and a woman. Perhaps that's why she became so fierce. Nationally, the conflicts between leading Black women and men were usually played out in private. In a conflict Ella Baker attributed to gender differences, she and Martin Luther King clashed behind the scenes of the southern civil rights movement in the late 1950s.[80] In the spotlight, Graves and Dasher fought Gibson and Baraka and Jacob, Black women publicly defying Black men. Perhaps that is one reason why the two elections in Newark in 1970 led to such a terrible struggle.

Two Schools

Parents and teachers shared an interest in making schools better. In the year between the strikes, they joined together at several schools. These efforts in the spring and fall of 1970 are important, because they indicate what might have been; they suggest the possibility of a citywide alliance for school reform between parents and teachers. Most notable was an educational experiment at Bergen Street School, where teachers found new ways of reaching students and parents supported them. But at one school, South Eighth Street, lines were drawn, and parents and teachers became enemies. This school shaped the future.

Bergen Street was a large elementary school in the heart of the South Ward ghetto. An informal group of ten to fifteen young Bergen Street teachers talked teaching with each other, even when socializing, and experimented with open classrooms. Many were frustrated because their students were reading far below grade level. Marty Blume explains: "If you have a kid who comes to you in the fourth grade and he's already reading on a first-grade level, and he's three years behind, even if you did a great job, and caught him up a year and a half, he'd still be behind the next year."[81]

Five young men, including Marty, reached a decision. They went to the principal and proposed staying with the same children for four or five years; each teacher would have a specialty, and each child would experience all five teachers. The principal agreed to the proposal. The teachers asked for a section of the school, starting in the spring of 1970, and he gave them the basement, with five classrooms and a big play area.[82]

The basement experiment at Bergen Street was based on the same principles as School Within a School at South Side High School. In place of the usual large factory-type school, the educational unit was small. In place of the usual isolation of the classroom teacher, the teachers worked together. In place of the usual hierarchy, the group of teachers took control of decision making. In place of the usual bureaucracy, the group was free to remake the rules. No wonder that the experiment at Bergen Street, like the one at South Side, was a success.

One rule said you taught reading with the school district's reading textbooks. Marty Blume and the other basement teachers scrapped the books, basing their reading program on the children's experience. "I said these kids can't read but they have great oral vocabulary." Like Sylvia Ashton Warner teaching Maori children in New Zealand, teachers asked the students about their lives. The children told about fires, police, crime, violence. Taking a sentence from every child, the teachers wrote a continuous story on the board. They used this story to teach reading. They did phonics with the words in the story; they did vocabulary. "Then what we did is we printed the stories. And so in a matter of months, we had a whole reading book of their stories. And the kids were involved in the whole process, writing the stories."[83]

Like despair, energy is contagious. The principal helped get a grant to pay for instant cameras. The basement teachers gave the cameras to the children and told them to take pictures in their community. These pictures became the basis of new stories and books. Beyond the basement, Anna Blume and a female colleague started with a group of first-graders and took them through two years. (When these two years ended, the two women repeated the process with a new group of children.) "You can go so much further," Anna says. "You don't have to start . . . the year getting to know, and trying to figure out, the youngsters."[84]

The principal and the young teachers reached out to parents. Bringing parents into the school as volunteers was one of the most radical aspects of the experiment, according to Marty Blume. "The last thing [older] white teachers wanted to see in this Black area was parents coming in. 'Cause their rationale was . . . parents were drunk, they were dirty, they weren't interested in their kids." Rejecting racist assumptions about the parents as they rejected racist assumptions about the children, young Bergen Street teachers invited parents into their classrooms. Soon, led by the principal and encouraged by the young teachers, the parents were fighting successfully for the school at the Board level.[85]

Bergen Street and School Within a School show what might have happened in Newark. When given a chance, teachers could teach, children could learn, and parents could help them both.

In 1970 teachers often took the lead in fighting for educational reform; parents often took the lead in fighting against overcrowded and unsafe conditions. The parents at Garfield Elementary School were mostly white; at Weequahic High and Miller Street Elementary School, they were mostly Black. White or Black, these parents were angry with the Board and welcomed the teachers' support. Angry about filthy conditions at Miller Street, parents called a boycott, which lasted four days. At Weequahic, a group of parents, students, and teachers fought against the imposition of split sessions. Garfield was so overcrowded that classes were held in the halls, cafeteria, and even the ladies' room. Parents called boycotts and teachers eventually joined them. In response to the combined pressure from parents and teachers, the Board fixed most of the problems at Miller Street, called off plans for the split session at Weequahic, and met with Garfield parents to discuss solutions to overcrowding.[86]

The main story line about the Newark schools in the year between the strikes does not run through these three schools, or through Bergen Street. In terms of the direction of change in Newark, these parent-teacher alliances represent a road not taken. The main story is about the South Eighth Street Elementary School. The alliance that emerged from this school was not between parents and teachers, but between parents and the Board of Education, with teachers as the common enemy.

All the major currents flowed through South Eighth Street. The Union, faced with enormous fines from the 1970 strike[87] and more than 180 court cases, wanted to implement the grievance machinery it had won at such cost. The Board wanted to sabotage binding arbitration rather than share power. Parent groups wanted teachers to continue to perform nonprofessional chores. It was the confluence of these three currents that made South Eighth Street into a storm center in the fall of 1970.

The Union leadership encouraged teachers to implement the contract by aggressively filing grievances. Training sessions for building reps, which formerly focused on how to recruit members, now focused on "how to handle a grievance on the local level." Activist teachers were eager to file grievances. They knew they would keep their power only if they used it. Early in the contract year, teachers at two schools used grievances to get windows fixed that had been broken for a long time; the *NTU Bulletin* quickly informed all teachers of the result, so that they would file grievances too. The *Bulletin* explained why grievances over lack of supplies or unsafe conditions were quickly settled. "The Board can afford neither the cost nor the bad publicity which would result from its forcing to arbitration a grievance which benefits the children."[88]

Grievances flooded the system. In the spring, Jim Lerman sent teachers in his building a questionnaire asking "if they had a desk, if they had a working chair, if they had a file cabinet and a storage cabinet, working windows and working shades." Using the information, he filed a grievance; he "wanted to show people they could make the contract work for them." In the fall, the teachers won their grievance and West Kinney got more than one hundred thousand dollars' worth of furniture. All over Newark, teachers initiated grievances. "The reason for the Union's being was to handle these grievances," says Vic Cascella, chair of the grievance committee. In the year between the strikes, the NTU won about two hundred grievances concerning physical conditions or lack of supplies or staff.[89]

Other grievances concerned conflict between a teacher and an administrator. Ron Polonsky kept a file of thank-you notes from teachers grateful for his help in these grievances. One teacher wrote for himself and for his wife, whose dispute with an administrator at Vailsburg High had been resolved "quickly" and "professionally" by Polonsky and the Union. "I now see that my many cold mornings on Picket-lines at Barringer last February were not at all in vain."[90] The battle fought on the streets of Newark in 1970 between the teachers and the Board was waged more quietly but no less importantly in the year following the strike. Thanks to their excellent grievance procedure, the teachers kept winning.

Teachers were feeling their power, and principals and Board members were not used to it. They had no experience of negotiating with teachers who had enforceable rights. Principals refused to settle grievances, even when the contract language was clear. The Union sent the grievances to the next level, to the superintendent and the Board of Education, where—as the Board ducked and dodged—grievances began to pile up. Assistant Superintendent Ben Epstein found the number of grievances irritating. "We had more grievances than U.S. Steel in its entire history. Everything was grieved." In October, Board member John Cervase protested that two hundred grievances had already reached the Board level; in his three years chairing the Board's negotiating committee, during the Association's agreement, only a total of six grievances had reached the Board.[91]

Cervase didn't say that under the Association's agreement, teachers had little to gain by grieving, since the Board itself was the final arbiter. Now the final arbiter was impartial. As cases began to reach the arbitrator in October, the Board began to lose. Twenty cases went to binding arbitration during the year of the contract. The Board lost eighteen.[92]

NTU leaders knew that they had the Board on the ropes. Graves characterized the Board's attitude as "if you don't like it grieve it—which is what we did. So we ended up with about 500 grievances." Cascella says simply, "We killed the Board with grievances." Dasher likened the attitude of the Board to that of kids. "When playing a game, all at once they realize that they've lost the game completely. . . . They really had no idea that once the contract was written, that it would be strictly enforced. Because again, prior experience: our contracts had *never* been enforced by the Association."[93]

The grievance procedure institutionalized the power of teachers. On the day Newark celebrated the inauguration of its first Black mayor, Graves celebrated teacher power. She sent Al Shanker a newly printed copy of the contract, with this boast:

> When you spoke to us at the N.J.S.F.T. [New Jersey State Federation of Teachers] Convention on November 1, 1969—before we won the collective bargaining election—you said that you wanted us to have in our contract something better than exists in your contract, so that you could point to it in future negotiations with the New York Board of Education and say, "They have something better than we." We do! We believe that our grievance procedure is better than yours.[94]

The grievance procedure meant the principal and the teachers had choices. They could not prevent conflict in their school. Indeed, there had always been conflict, but the forces had been so unequal that it was possible to mistake the quiet for peace. Now they met on a more level playing field. If the principal could accept the new state of affairs, new ways of resolving conflict became possible.

Bob Clark was building rep at Fourteenth Avenue Elementary School, where his job was to enforce the 1970 contract. The principal was anti-Union, but because he did not want grievances from his school going to the Board, he learned to work within the contract. For his part, Clark believed if "the teacher was at fault, we couldn't back them." The principal cited a teacher for frequently cutting short his school day, and the teacher wanted to grieve. Clark told him that the principal was right. The principal, the teacher, and Clark met in the principal's office. The teacher never committed the infraction again.[95]

Fourteenth Avenue was an exception. The school was small, with only about thirty teachers. The principal, though anti-Union, was capable of responding to changed circumstances. The building rep was not vengeful. The exception shows that if the principal accepted the new rules and the rep exercised good judgment, there was a chance to channel the conflict in a constructive direction. As a rule, though, the principals and Board resisted a grievance as long as they could, and the Union pushed as hard as it could.

One grievance pushed by the Union was the elimination of nonprofessional chores. The contract stipulated that teachers would be relieved of hall duty (in secondary schools), playground and cafeteria duties (in elementary schools), and other nonteaching duties. Vic Cascella had been the force behind the demand. As chair of the grievance committee, he became the force behind the effort to implement the contract provision.

Against his colleagues in the Union leadership and against the Union lawyer, Cascella argued for using the grievance procedure to take the Board to arbitration over nonprofessional chores.

> Nobody wanted to. They were right. From their point of view they were right. They felt that if we brought it to arbitration and won, it would do so much damage in the community. I didn't give a damn. I felt the community had abused the elementary school teachers for long enough. . . . I didn't care about the parents. This was a Union issue, as far as I was concerned.[96]

Cascella prevailed. In his frustration at the disrespect with which elementary teachers were treated, he lumped parents in with the Board and triumphed over both. His triumph would help cement a Board-parent alliance.

In April 1970, the Union specified nonprofessional chores as a contractual area of disagreement with the Board. The Board stalled, claiming that it had never agreed to relieve teachers of hall or cafeteria duty, that the definition of "nonprofessional chores" was solely up to the superintendent. In May, the Union sent its first set of seven grievances to binding arbitration, including one on nonprofessional chores.[97]

While the grievance proceeded toward arbitration, Union leaders encouraged teachers to stop doing nonprofessional chores, in order to force the Board to hire aides, as specified in the contract. Most teachers, however, continued to do their chores. Union leaders warned that the teachers who had already stopped were vulnerable to charges of insubordination unless all teachers stopped. Privately, the leaders were worried. Polonsky reported at the May meeting of the Union's new executive board that he and Graves went to schools to urge teachers to stop doing nonprofessional chores. In the words of the minutes, "Reaction unfavorable in many of the schools."[98]

Many teachers did not want to stop doing hall or cafeteria or playground duty. Their replacements, the aides and security guards, had not yet been hired. They worried about the children. Even when aides and security guards were hired, would they bond with the children? The members of the Union had never debated the idea of relieving teachers of nonteaching duties. Faced with a decision, school by school, most teachers kept performing the duties.

Elementary teachers had the most to gain by the elimination of the duties. Carol Karman was glad to be free of cafeteria duty, because she had no other preparation time. But she wished teachers could have a different free period and be able to eat lunch with the children. Bob Clark now thinks that it was a mistake for teachers to stop doing playground duty. But he supported the change in 1970 as a way of curbing the principal's power to tell teachers what to do. Harold Moore had doubts at the time, but says that even "if I'd really been able to crystallize my thinking, I don't know if I'd have had the guts to put that forward anyhow, because it just wasn't the climate."[99]

Nonprofessional chores were less onerous in secondary schools; secondary teachers already had prep time, and hall duty wasn't hard. Still, Beth Blackmon favored freeing teachers from nonteaching duties. She felt management was taking advantage of teachers, asking them to do too many things. But "many people twenty-five years later consider that victory for the teachers a real loss for the schools and for the kids." They say, " 'When teachers gave up hall duties, then the kids were in the halls going crazy.' " Blackmon's own perplexity emerges in her language: "These duties were taken away from the teachers."[100] Teachers did not take them away. The Union took them away from teachers.

Like Blackmon, Marion Bolden taught at Barringer. Bolden opposed the change. Before, "we would always confront a child who was using vulgar language." When teachers stopped patrolling the hall, cursing and running became routine. "How can you teach in a classroom when there are kids running around the hall?" At the time, many teachers privately indicated they agreed with her. In hindsight, Bolden believes that the elimination of nonprofessional chores has been a disaster. "There are a couple of good security people that bond with kids. But it certainly is not the same thing. And you want to know what? I think that when there's another contract, that is the one issue that the strike is going to be about." She adds, musing, "If I were the superintendent, teachers wouldn't get a contract until. . . . I would compromise on other issues, to make that more palatable." In 1999, Marion Bolden became superintendent.[101] This story isn't over.

In May, June, and September of 1970, most teachers ignored their Union and performed the duties, but on October 15, the arbitrator upheld the Union's interpretation of the contract provision. Soon battle lines were drawn. Moving swiftly to enforce the arbitrator's ruling, Carole Graves set a deadline. On Monday, November 2, "all teachers *must cease performing nonprofessional duties.*" On November 4, the Newark PTA adopted a resolution condemning the arbitrator's ruling. Now teachers would have to protect their contract not only against the Board—they had proven they could do that—but against Black parents as well.[102]

An accident triggered the explosion. South Eighth Street, in the West Ward, was the largest elementary school in the state. The students were almost all Black; 77 of the 117 teachers were white. On November 17, after leaving South Eighth Street, an eight-year-old girl was hit by a car. The girl was hospitalized in fair condition. Parents blamed teachers for exposing children to risks by no longer escorting them out of the building. On November 19, the school's PTA began a boycott of the school. Only 134 of the 2,200 children came the next day. Parents said they would continue to boycott until teachers agreed to resume all nonteaching duties. In addition, they demanded the transfer of three white teachers, equalization of the number of Black and white teachers, the power to hire and fire all school personnel and select the books, and the right to participate in future negotiations between the Board and Union.[103]

In fact the South Eighth Street PTA did not formulate its comprehensive program in response to the accident. At the beginning of the school year, militant parents organizing at the school gained control of the PTA. What they hoped to do was smash the contract. Before the accident, they had already made the same demands. But by dramatizing the apparent selfishness of teachers in abandoning nonteaching duties, the accident gave the militants a powerful tool for bringing more moderate parents into the movement.[104]

Dr. E. Wyman Garrett, the leader of Black militants at the school, hated the Union. He saw it as fundamentally white, racist, and focused on power rather than on educating Black children. A member of the Board of Education under Mayor Addonizio, Garrett voted against the contract in February; he had physically threatened Carole Graves during negotiations. In March, he twice visited the South Eighth Street School and "proceeded to threaten, intimidate, harass and insult several members of the faculty," according to Graves. In April, Garrett promised that every time Graves spoke at Board meetings he would bring up a NTU contract proposal to show how selfish teachers were.[105]

When Gibson refused to reappoint Garrett to the Board in July, Garrett blamed the Union. In fact, Graves had urged Gibson to eliminate from the Board any member who had "engaged in maudlin or malevolent histrionics that inflamed the public and encouraged unnecessary confrontations." She meant Garrett. Garrett also blamed Baraka for using his influence with Gibson to settle old scores with Garrett. Nobody's follower, an "independent" and "articulate" advocate of Black Power (as Saunders later described him), Garrett made the South Eighth Street PTA his new power base.[106]

After the accident, Garrett led more than one hundred PTA members to Board headquarters, where they demanded the transfer of the three teachers who were "insensitive to the community." One was rumored to have referred to Black children as monkeys. Another was Pete Petino, who, as building rep, defended the teacher. There were no formal charges against the three, no way they could defend themselves. When the contract was adopted, Jesse Jacob had warned that parents would boycott schools to get rid of teachers they didn't want. Jacob believed the contract, by acknowledging the needs of "the community," gave the Board leeway to transfer teachers whom parents condemned. The Board agreed to transfer all three teachers.[107]

The PTA members wanted more: they wanted teachers to resume nonteaching duties. Board members explained that the contract tied their hands. "We're not interested in contracts," Garrett replied. "We're interested in our kids." He denounced binding arbitration for taking control of the schools out of the hands of the community. Jacob agreed, promising Garrett and the parents that in the upcoming negotiations, "We are going to fight the Newark Teachers' Union with everything we have."[108]

Jacob and Saunders used the parents' energy to build a citywide movement against the Union. Saunders held the first of his public meetings three days after the boycott began. Elayne Brodie, Rose Spencer (head of the Newark PTA), and a South Eighth Street PTA representative criticized the arbitrator's ruling, citing the harm to children. After meeting privately with Saunders to shape a common strategy, Spencer raised the specter of a citywide boycott of the schools if Newark teachers did not resume their duties. Saunders spoke at South Eighth Street: "It is a question of whether a union contract can stand up in the face of community concern for the welfare of the children."[109]

The contract and Union had been denounced before. When teachers were given makeup days for pay lost during the 1970 strike, some Black leaders correctly criticized the idea as educationally worthless, and African American Board members voted against it. But there was no Black majority on the Board and no grass-roots movement, and the teachers got their makeup days.[110] Now conditions were different. Saunders seized on the parent movement at South Eighth Street, shaping it into a weapon. For the first time, the Union was on the defensive. Some teachers called for an immediate strike as the only way to block the involuntary transfer of the three teachers. But Graves said no. She did not want to be perceived as striking against the community, like Shanker's union in Ocean Hill–Brownsville.[111]

The PTA ended the boycott and turned to stronger tactics. It told teachers to come to school willing to do cafeteria and playground duty or not to come at all. One teacher said, "I'm going to go to school tomorrow, but if there is any violence, I'm leaving and never coming back. They just don't want us." On December 9, teachers tried to meet with parents. The meeting was mediated by Saunders, Jacob, and Superintendent Titus, and went nowhere. That day, only 50 of the 117 teachers reported to school. The others went to the Board with demands of their own: confirm our right not to perform nonprofessional chores, hire aides to carry out these duties, suspend the principal, protect us from harassment and intimidation.[112]

When the teachers who went to the Board returned to school the next day, they were blocked by parents, who asked if they were willing to resume their former duties. Eight said yes, and were allowed in the building. After consulting Jacob, parents denied entrance to forty-eight other teachers. The following day, Jacob and the parents allowed them back. But the precedent of barring large numbers of teachers from South Eighth Street would be used again, after the 1971 strike.[113]

Jacob and Saunders made the school the first battleground of the coming war. Believing he had no money to offer, Saunders successfully played the race card. He encouraged the struggle at South Eighth Street, using it as an excuse not to negotiate. After wasting November, he cited the events at the school as the reason for not beginning negotiations in December. Unrest in the community over the current contract was not conducive to negotiating, he stated.[114] Saunders's community strategy made it impossible for teachers to negotiate, and dangerous for them to strike.

Taking his cue from Saunders and Jacob, Garrett shifted his focus from challenging the current contract to going to war over the next one. "Let's face it, we have nothing to lose," he told the Board in the simplifying language of 1970 activism. "The children aren't being educated now so if the teachers want to strike . . . then let them go, close down the schools, and give them a fight." Jacob was pleased. "You may not be accountable to the board," he told teachers, "but you are to the community."[115]

When Vic Cascella insisted on taking nonprofessional chores to arbitration, NTU leaders feared "damage in the community." Graves tried to contain the damage in a memo to Newark parent and community organizations. Citing reports of growing unemployment in the nation, she pointed out that many Newarkers would be employed doing nonprofessional chores as aides, clerks, and security guards. "Apply now."[116] In the long run, Newark parents took the jobs and joined NTU. But in the short run, race trumped class. In the winter of 1970–71, led by the South Eighth Street PTA, many Black parents were angry enough to join Jacob's and Saunders's crusade against the Newark Teachers Union.

As the end of the contract drew closer, NTU leaders saw, unhappily, that their only choices were to tell teachers to work without a contract (which was, for a union, no choice at all) or tell them to strike. They were being pushed into a war against Newark's first nonwhite Board majority and first Black mayor, with few allies of their own. Aside from the leaders of other unions, they enjoyed little support within the city. Their own national union doubted they should strike again. Their chance of victory was slim. Graves complained that the Board was forcing the NTU to strike in order to "break the union."[117]

Then Saunders made a mistake. On January 11, arguing in a bargaining session for making Martin Luther King's birthday a Newark holiday, he became carried away with his own rhetoric. The new contract would serve Black children. It would "be responsive not only to their needs but to their parents as well. It will be a contract of Black orientation." It was a crucial mistake, he later admitted. The Union immediately publicized Saunders's statement in the Italian community. Soon Louis Turco, the city council's new president, called on Saunders, pressing him to yield on binding arbitration and nonprofessional chores. Countering, Saunders pressed Turco to approve Gibson's tax proposals. The two men had "a massive confrontation."[118] Turco versus Saunders, council versus Board: split along ethnic/racial lines, the city was ready for the 1971 strike.

In 1970, teachers chose to strike. In 1971, facing what Graves described as an unfavorable climate resulting from the election of Gibson, they were forced to strike.[119] The 1970 strike, despite a tendency toward racial polarization, was a class conflict, pitting a grass-roots workers' movement against a powerful employer. The 1971 strike would be a race war, pitting two grass-roots movements against each other.

Chapter 5

The 1971 Strike

In form, the 1971 strike was similar to the 1970 strike: picketing, morning meeting, Sunday rally, occasional downtown demonstration. The feeling was different, however, frequently summed up in one word. "The second strike was vicious," says Phyllis Salowe. "That was vicious," says Martha Nolley. "The feeling that I got between the first strike and the second strike was totally different," says Beth Blackmon. "I mean this became vicious, incredibly vicious."[1]

Either/Or

There were not just two sides in 1971; there were also two ways of seeing. Striking teachers saw their struggle as one of working people against management. Their opponents saw Black parents and citizens against white teachers. There was tremendous pressure to choose between these competing views, rather than to seek what was true in each. Few people were able to look at the strike from both perspectives. Either the strike was seen through the lens of class, or it was seen through the lens of race.

E. Wyman Garrett looked through the lens of race. To Garrett, there was prehistory, when whites ruled Newark. And then there was Gibson's election and Jacob's appointment and his own push at South Eighth Street, when Blacks began to shape their own history, and teachers went on strike to reverse the progress of Blacks. In his view, the Board's power was never challenged, "but all of a sudden when it is controlled by black members, there is talk of taking that power away."[2] What Garrett didn't see was the 1970 strike. In 1970 the

140

teachers fought for a share of power against a white-controlled Board. He was on that Board; he was there. But through the lens of race, the 1970 strike became invisible.

And Carole Graves became a race traitor. In 1970, many Blacks saw her ascendancy as a sign of progress. Not in 1971. In reality she was more of a leader in 1971. But now she was seen as creating a major problem for the city's first Black mayor. Kenneth Travitt, the new head of ONE, denounced Graves and Clara Dasher as "colored lackeys." Travitt correctly interpreted some support for the strike as opposition to Mayor Gibson. He did not stop there; he believed the purpose of the strike itself was to hurt Gibson. "All of this rabble rousing is to discredit the Gibson administration."[3]

Either/or: workers against management, or whites against Blacks? Graves argued, defensively, "We are not a part of the establishment. We are workers." Seen through the lens of class, striking teachers were working people, underdogs against the establishment. "WHO ARE WE?" asked NTU, in a leaflet aimed at Newark citizens. "THE STRIKING TEACHERS ARE BLACK & WHITE *WORKERS*."[4]

Given the racial climate, NTU leaders worried that teachers would not want to strike. The Board of Education wouldn't negotiate a new contract, and the old one expired January 31, 1971. If teachers didn't strike, they would lose the gains they had won in 1970. If they did strike, they would strike against a non-white Board of Education, a Black mayor, and Black parent groups. "Gibson was the mayor," Jim Lerman recalls. "Baraka had been doing all this stuff about striking this time is a strike against the community. And the Black teachers for sure didn't want to go on strike. And the white teachers were afraid to go on strike."[5]

The decisive moment, Lerman says, occurred at a mass meeting at the end of January.

> Carole Graves walked into that hall and gave the performance of her life. She got pissed at everybody—the mayor, the commissioner of education, the superintendent of schools—and she was naming names, just like chapter and verse, and she was spitting mad. And for all these white people in that audience, to hear someone who was Black tell them that they had better go on strike, made that strike.[6]

Naming white as well as Black enemies of the teachers, the superintendent and commissioner as well as the mayor, Graves was saying that the dividing line between those who supported the teachers and those who opposed them was not the color line. The dividing line was the line between labor and management.

Before the strike, when a teacher had asked what would happen if they didn't strike, Graves had answered that going to work without a contract would subject teachers to the Board's power. To Graves, unions were in the forefront of the battle against bondage; the real Black freedom movement flowed with— not against—the movement of working people to organize. During the strike, she identified the "two great struggles in the history of the American people, the struggle of *my people* against slavery, culminating in the Thirteenth Amendment, which prohibited involuntary servitude, and the struggle of the labor movement for the right to create unions to obtain freedom *from the arbitrary power* of employers."[7]

Jim Brown, who began teaching in January, embraced the Union position. "We won, or else we went back to the master—or to the boss/employee type of thing, where the boss would tell you everything." He recalls an elegant formulation of the meaning of the strike. "I remember Bayard Rustin and to this day his saying: 'A boss is a boss is a boss.'" Brown remembers "everybody cheering, applauding."[8] Teachers were cheering because Rustin, as a Black, was saying that their strike was about class, not race.

NTU leaders always presented the struggle as labor versus management. When they distributed the Board's list of forty-eight demands to teachers, they put a star next to its rejection of binding arbitration. They did not star its rejection of the whole concept of nonprofessional chores; nonprofessional chores, as an issue, was already racialized. But they starred "There will be no time limit on any faculty meeting" and "Newark Board of Education will install in each school a time clock wherein all personnel are required to punch in and out, and pay will be based on the time clock."[9] In short, a boss is a boss is a boss.

The Board was boss. But was it the same boss, the same Board? Black activists like Garrett argued that Gibson's appointments made the Board new. They stressed the discontinuity in Board membership. Striking teachers stressed the continuity in Board function; they argued that despite appearances, the Board had not changed. "I've seen a lot of people come and go on the Board of Ed," says Beth Blackmon. "Somehow my perception of the Board of Ed remains constant through time," as if the Board has "a life of its own."[10]

Looking through the lens of class, Union leaders saw the conflict as union busters against Black and white workers. Young Black men attacked striking teachers on February 2, the second day of the 1971 strike, and sent several to the hospital. Graves insisted that the attack was not a racial incident but "strictly an anti-union incident."[11] The attackers did not discriminate. "What was heard was not 'Let's get the white b——' or 'Let's get the Black b——' but 'Let's get the union b——.'"[12]

NTU leaders believed that Gibson and Jacob wanted to bust their Union. They told other unions that "the City Administration and this Board of Education have set out to break any effective public employee union and trade union in the city and to turn back the clock for union members to pre-1930 days." This view of the strike was effective in reaching out to labor. "Help Stop Union Busting," urged a flyer signed by the local Teamsters, United Automobile Workers (UAW), and Building and Construction Trades, as well as by the New Jersey AFL-CIO and New Jersey Industrial Union Council.[13]

Local union leaders recognized that the Union was in danger and gave it crucial support. The UAW sent pickets. The Teamsters refused to cross the picket line to deliver food and heating oil. The New Jersey AFL-CIO, headed by Charles Marciante, lobbied local and state government, and gave between three hundred and six hundred dollars a day to support the strike, according to Ron Polonsky. "We couldn't do a thing without Marciante." Felix Martino adds: "The trade unions supported us to the extent that they could. They supplied speakers, they supplied moral support, they even supplied money and placards. Sometimes they even came on the picket line."[14]

There were limits to labor support, however. These limits derived from the limits of the trade union movement itself. Most trade unions, especially the old craft unions, were primarily white. Most were organized and controlled from the top down. And most had not been militant for years.

Local union leaders threatened to be militant in 1971. They called a one-day general strike in Newark to support the teachers. Newark business and political leaders pressed them to call it off. Two days before the general strike, claiming there had been progress in negotiations, Marciante cancelled it. Some teachers were bitter, saying labor leaders shouldn't threaten to strike if they didn't mean it.[15]

The Organization of Negro Educators (ONE) focused on another limit of labor support when it charged that the unions backing the teachers strike were "predominantly lily-white." By the rules governing the discourse on race in 1971, only a Black could respond. Mae Massie, a civil rights director of the International Union of Electrical, Radio and Machine Workers, defended labor's effort to integrate Blacks, accused ONE of adding racial overtones to the strike, and asserted that the strike involved "pure and simple labor-management issues."[16]

The most serious limitation of the support provided by local trade unions was that it came from the top. Connie Woodruff, community affairs director of the International Ladies Garment Workers Union (ILGWU), helped striking teachers present their side to the Black community, spoke at their rallies, raised money for them, lent them the ILGWU office for their strike headquarters, and let them use the phones and auditorium for free. But she couldn't get her own members in Newark to support the strike, or even keep their own children home. Woodruff concluded, unhappily, that only union leaders backed the teachers; the Black community in Newark, including union members, did not support the teachers.[17]

Desperately seeking community support, striking teachers took it where they could get it, from the Italian communities of the North, East, and West Wards. And from Tony Imperiale, as Carole Graves acknowledged. "As far as welcoming support, I think when someone is drowning and going down for the third time, you don't look at where that hand is coming from, or what color it is."[18] In fact, the 1971 strike was never simply labor versus management. It was also Italian versus Black.

Imperiale had made his name in 1967 as the leader of Italian vigilantes, dedicated to saving Newark from the Black menace. His great strength as a leader, besides his readiness to use violence, was that he could not be shamed. After the 1970 mayoral election, he announced he was forming a conservative organization to fight Gibson and seeking help from supporters of George Wallace, the former Alabama governor and leading segregationist. Charges of racism bounced off Imperiale. "If racism means to be against communists, to be against those who are for insurrection, to be against those who advocate anarchy, then I'm proud to say I'm the head of a racist organization."[19]

Striking teachers accepted an alliance with Imperiale rather than let Jacob and Saunders strip away the gains made with such sacrifice in 1970, but because of his racism most accepted his help reluctantly. Carol Karman was troubled by the alliance with Imperiale; Graves clung to the pretense that his help was unsolicited. Polonsky took Imperiale's support but wouldn't let him speak at daily strike meetings.[20]

Tom Lawton was grateful to Imperiale for helping him when he was accused of attacking a Black strikebreaker, but Lawton's gratitude never translated into support for Imperiale. Growing up in Newark, Lawton made friends with the little girl next door. "I didn't know I wasn't supposed to like her, until my father told me I wasn't. And when I asked why, he says: 'She's Black.' . . . At that time, in the fifties, they didn't say Black. She was 'a nigger.' " Tom's father feared for his son's safety in the Black family's house. "His concept of a Black family was distorted." Lawton recognized that in many ways the 1971 strike "was becoming a Black and white situation," but he kept his distance from Imperiale, because he could not subscribe to Imperiale's distorted concepts about Blacks.[21]

Pete Petino embraced Imperiale. "Tony was a tremendous help," Petino says.

> I did like him. I have a lot of respect for him. In fact if it wasn't for Tony
> Imperiale and his men, when we demonstrated with Bayard Rustin at South

Eighth, if it wasn't for Tony, I think we would have been in deep shit, quite frankly. Tony was there. He wasn't out on the line. He was there with his men, in cars and in trucks, making sure when the groups that came and converged on us that day—that even though the police were there, it didn't get out of hand. And we had known Tony was going to be there. In case.

Petino, Dominick Bizzarro, and Joe Del Grosso were the Italian connection, quietly assigned by NTU to coordinate activities with Imperiale. "We kind of were a liaison with him. We reached out," says Petino. The alliance with Imperiale heightened the danger of large-scale racial violence. It could not be publicized. "I think the correct term for that is 'covert.'"[22]

Italian Americans gave the strike the mass base in the community that it otherwise lacked. First Avenue School in the North Ward embodied Italian power, as South Eighth Street embodied Black power. Two women crossing the First Avenue picket line were hurt as they entered school, and hospitalized; the next day, Imperiale and a group of parents turned everyone away from the school, including the principal. One Black teacher still tried to go to work. Police escorted her through the line, using force to hold parents back, but she left after seeing no one else was in school. The Board assigned her and three other nonstriking Black teachers to another school. Imperiale, parents, and teachers kept First Avenue closed tight.[23]

Closing First Avenue was a communal effort. Almost everyone from the school was on the picket line, including the secretary, who lived in the neighborhood. Merchants opened their shops to pickets on cold mornings and gave free coffee. Parents brought doughnuts and coffee for pickets and sent their children to the alternative schools set up in basements and staffed by striking teachers. Closing the school helped the strike, because the Board only received state aid for schools that were open. A co-chair of the newly formed North Ward Community for Unity extended the logic of First Avenue to other schools. She said, "We should force the closing of the schools by any means—I mean any means."[24]

In Newark, Italian Americans appropriated the rhetorical style of Black Power. Across America, the heightened consciousness of white ethnics grew out of their encounter with Black pride and assertiveness; they reacted against, and borrowed from, Black nationalism. Deliberately quoting parents at South Eighth Street, First Avenue parents accused the Black teacher who went into school of "insensitivity to the community." Petino observed that when Blacks spoke at Board meetings and bargaining sessions, they claimed to speak "for the community," but only spoke for Blacks. Calling on North Ward residents to assert their power, he made the point that the idea of community was at least as meaningful to Italians as Blacks. "You're the community," thundered Petino.[25]

Italian Americans in Newark rose as a community in support of the strike. Their rallying cry was that they must stop Blacks in general, and Baraka in particular. Some already resented the preponderance of Jewish principals, especially in high schools. Were Blacks now going to take over the school system? During the strike, a group from the East Ward asked North Ward residents to join in defending the educational rights of "the white citizens of Newark."[26]

The strike was strong in the North Ward, where Imperiale was based, and even stronger in the East Ward, in the Ironbound district. The Ironbound was an industrial area with a strong blue-collar tradition and an Italian American core. A number of teachers crossed picket lines in the North Ward during the 1971 strike, but very few crossed in the Ironbound. Parents and teachers at Ann Street School were particularly aggressive, preventing anyone—teachers, aides, substitutes—from crossing the line. When nearly four hundred Ironbound residents met at Our Lady of Fatima Church to declare support for the strike, Louis Turco, the East Ward councilman and city council president, urged them to march on City Hall. Turco said, "Other people get together and make a lot of noise and they get the goodies."[27]

Turco had opposed the 1970 strike; a victory by teachers would cost the city too much money, he said. After Gibson's election, Turco became a leader of the opposition, and after Saunders framed the Board's stance as Black, he became a supporter of the teachers. He received a standing ovation when he unexpectedly showed up at a strike meeting in February. During the strike, he defended binding arbitration against "the radicals in Newark like Jesse Jacob, E. Wyman Garrett and LeRoi Jones."[28]

Imperiale, Turco, and John Cervase gave leadership to the Italian community's support of the 1971 strike. Imperiale, with his paramilitary organization, led Italians in the street. Turco, as the most politically powerful Italian in Newark, led the council against the Board. Cervase became the voice of the Italian community on the Board.

Cervase was a wealthy lawyer, with a beautiful home in the Forest Hills section of the North Ward and a traditional management perspective, reinforced by social conservatism. Appointed to the Board of Education by Addonizio, he became the first president of the Independent Board Members Association of New Jersey, founded in 1968 to combat subversive activity in the schools and prevent racial integration. Cervase condemned student demonstrations, sex education, forced busing, and the ban on school prayer; he blamed liberal teachers for fostering drug addiction and disrespect for lawful authority. He strongly opposed the 1970 strike, accusing the Union of wanting to share power with the Board. After the settlement, he helped block an effort to gain leniency for arrested teachers and shaped Board resistance to the new grievance procedure.[29]

But after Gibson's victory and Jacob's appointment, Cervase reversed his stand toward the teachers, their Union, and their contract. He saw the conflict in 1971 from the perspective of race, not class. Abandoning his management perspective, he now feared Black power more than teacher power. Above all, he was afraid of Baraka. Baraka wanted to teach Newark children to be African, not American; he "writes the word 'American' with a small letter, but uses a capital letter for the word 'Black.' "[30] Cervase embraced the Union in 1971 as a bastion of American civilization against Baraka and the militant hordes.

Cervase became the lone Board member to break publicly with Jacob, denouncing him as the captive of Baraka, Garrett, and Elayne Brodie. Jacob, who took direction from no one, called Cervase a liar. But Cervase lumped all angry Blacks together. Although he carefully made distinctions between Italians— criticizing Imperiale as too extreme, and dismissing a colleague on the Board as too working-class—he reduced all Blacks to followers or opponents of Baraka. The real battle in the strike, he said, was not between the Union and the Board but between the Union and Black militants.[31]

In 1971 the tendency to simplify was very powerful on both sides. People looked through the lens of class and saw conspiracy: Gibson wanted to break the Union and deprive teachers of their rights. Or they looked through the lens of race, and saw conspiracy: striking teachers were trying to undermine Gibson and prevent Blacks from coming into their own.

There was no middle ground. Early in the strike, Larry Hamm and the leaders of the Newark Student Federation claimed not to be on either side and to speak for white students as well as Black, but they too were affected by the spirit of 1971. Hamm, who was independent in 1970, identified with Baraka in 1971. He led the Student Federation to embrace a nationalist program of Black power in school curriculum and staffing. In April, the Federation urged the Board to reject a settlement with the teachers, even though not settling meant the strike would continue.[32]

Teachers, seen exclusively through the lens of race, were not working people, subject to the arbitrary decisions of bosses, but privileged persons. They were possessors of wealth and power greater than most Blacks, and they were the enemy. David Barrett, director of Newark's antipoverty program and an ally of Baraka, defended the violence against teachers on February 2 as "the desperate actions of an abused, offended and aroused community." Barrett rejected the idea that teachers were working-class. "If they are members of the working class, then what class do the 25 percent unemployed, and the rest of us who are underemployed, then what class do they—do we—belong to?"[33]

The unemployed, the powerless, and those who spoke for them were good. The teachers were bad. An activist denounced the "so-called professional teachers" and their "so-called union." Elayne Brodie labeled NTU "a sick, barbaric teachers' union." The new Central Ward councilman, Dennis Westbrook, said teachers were "foreigners," meaning they didn't belong in the community. New Ark Community Coalition distributed a drawing of four white teachers. One wore a mini skirt; one had long sideburns. The four were holding hands and clutching money. The flyer proclaimed: "RUNT (Racist Union of Non Teachers) wants our community dollars for suburbs."[34]

The word "community" became reified, as if it was a thing, rather than a web of relationships. One activist said, "Too often the community is left out, and it is the community's children who are affected by the contract." The community's children: the community was not children. Nor was it parents. Most parents were not involved in the issues and did not attend PTA meetings, Don Saunders said; if he randomly stopped Blacks in Newark and asked them what they thought of nonprofessional chores, they probably wouldn't know what he was talking about. Saunders nevertheless claimed that the community wanted power over the schools. "The community didn't want to participate, they wanted control. . . . They wanted to control the school system."[35]

The idea of community was, finally, not about people. Community was the nationalist ideal: militant, Black, powerful. It was a weapon to use against teachers, the insensitive foreigners. The idea of community articulated by Garrett, Baraka, and Saunders tended to smother differences within the actual Black community. It pushed members of that community to simplify, or at least keep quiet.

Graves and Polonsky simplified too. They attacked the integrity of Black activists and blamed all racial conflict on them. "The issues have been intentionally muddled by unethical, irresponsible, and self-serving politicians and 'poverty pimps,'" asserted Graves. An NTU leaflet identified Baraka, Jacob, Saunders, Brodie, and others as "poverty pimps" and detailed the money they received from federal programs and city agencies. They were in a conspiracy with the powers-that-be. Polonsky asked whether "Dr. Garrett and LeRoi Jones might not be Agnew-type frontmen, saying the things ex officio that those in office would want to say." Graves told the teachers, "Once again it has become convenient to inject racism into a struggle which unites the working men and women of this country. The government and the courts, assisted by reactionary nationalists, have formed an amalgamation to destroy your dignity."[36]

There was a tendency to demonize opponents of the strike, especially

Baraka. Many striking teachers regarded him as an evil genius and, without evidence, blamed him for the violent attack on February 2. In court, arguing against an injunction against the strike, the Union's lawyer asserted that the strike was necessary to block Baraka's attempt "to take over the schools and the board of education." Angela Paone, speaking at Fairleigh Dickinson University, was asked why Mayor Gibson wasn't doing more to settle the strike. She responded that the mayor was under Baraka's influence. A reporter telephoned Dasher, who verified that Paone was articulating the Union position.[37]

Just as opponents of the strike saw Graves and Dasher as puppets of whites, Union activists saw Jacob and Gibson as puppets of Baraka. They ridiculed Gibson, calling him "Mayor Jones." This view of Gibson cemented the Union's alliance with Italian Americans in the North and East Wards. "The union's charge that Jones is attempting to take over the school system and its references to 'Mayor Jones' have reinforced the belief of some persons that Gibson is in fact being directed by militant blacks," observed the *Newark News*. "In the North and East Wards . . . , those who had warned during the campaign that Gibson was the puppet of Jones and other black militants, are quick to say, 'I told you so.' "[38]

Each side in the 1971 strike attacked the motives and decency of the other. Neither saw the other merely as partisan, or even as wrong, but also as lacking integrity. Graves and Dasher were colored lackeys, Baraka and Brodie were poverty pimps. Those who insisted that class was central to the conflict were derided as "so-called professional teachers." Those who insisted that race was central were derided as "so-called leaders." It was hard for participants on either side to regard people on the other side as fully human. And the fact that, week after week, your side denied the humanity of my side was taken as proof that your side was humanly deficient.

Some participants managed to keep their balance. They knew the struggle was about both race and class. They took sides, but tried not to demonize their opponents. One NTU leaflet took a historical approach: many Black activists rejected unions because the labor movement had failed to integrate construction unions, to organize in the South, and to fight for jobs and housing for Blacks. These Black activists allied themselves with the establishment instead of allying with teachers and other working people. Written by someone who knew labor history and Black history, the leaflet granted Baraka's sincerity. "It would be wrong to dismiss Leroi Jones as an unrepresentative figure in Black America, or, as has been suggested, as an 'agent' of the city power structure."[39]

Not all Black groups joined in the condemnation of the strike. The Black Panthers picketed West Side High in support of the teachers and read a statement at a morning strike meeting. "We see the Board of Education as being one of the many oppressors located in our community," they said. "We view the present struggle of the Newark Teachers Union as one for progressive change for black and all oppressed people." The Nation of Islam also supported the strike. The Panthers, who always emphasized class as well as race, were a tiny group in Newark; the Nation of Islam, which was nationalistic, was larger. But what the two groups had in common was that their opposition to Baraka led to their support for the teachers. According to *Muhammad Speaks*, newspaper of the Nation of Islam, Baraka "tended to pit parents and students against teachers and place the Black community on the same side as the racist Board of Education."[40]

The teacher power movement and the Black Power movement both emerged during the 1960s. Each achieved its first major success in Newark in 1970: the teachers strike and the election of Gibson. In 1971, both movements were trying to protect what they had won. Neither felt secure or established. So they tore at each other. Hoping to gain legitimacy, each dismissed the other as illegitimate. In April, each side characterized the other as fascist.[41]

Either/or. The 1971 strike put terrible pressure on people to choose, not only between two sides, but also between two ways of viewing the struggle: Either solidarity with union brothers and sisters, or solidarity with Black brothers and sisters. Either Baraka was being used by the corporations, or Graves was being used by the white establishment. Either Gibson was trying to crush the Union, or the Union was trying to destroy Gibson.

Even before 1971, as Clara Dasher recognized, some Blacks tended to regard NTU as "a white racist union."[42] During the 1970 strike, teachers challenged this tendency, limiting its growth. But in 1971, they seemed to be striking against Black Power. As the strike continued, week after week, many intelligent and idealistic teachers felt increasing pressure to simplify. The chorus of Black voices portraying them as selfish, as striking in order to benefit their own kind at the expense of others less fortunate, challenged their understanding of themselves.

In 1971, Bob Lowenstein wrote to the *Newark News*, questioning the way that Black parents and community activists portrayed teachers. Lowenstein, who always advocated a teacher unionism that benefited students and the larger community, asked adults who had attended Newark schools whether their competent and devoted teachers "can have, almost overnight, become incompetent, negligent, and indifferent to the needs of their charges." His point was that teachers were not to blame for the failures of the school system. And then he too fell into blaming. Citing student absence, lateness, and lack of study, Lowenstein blamed the home and community.[43]

In 1970, Phyllis Salowe struck to help students. She didn't care about binding arbitration; she wanted more supplies. But 1971 was different. "There was more of a white/Black division in the second strike. And the parent groups, the community was making it that way." The hostility from parents bothered her. "The worst thing was being attacked as not caring about the children and only caring about ourselves. I guess that was the part that was most difficult for me to bear." Salowe's sense of innocence was shaken. "I couldn't understand why these people didn't think I was their ally. It was distressing, obviously. Distressing's the wrong word. I couldn't understand."[44]

For Salowe, 1971 had a terrible, clarifying effect. Feeling "torn," she observed, in herself and other young teachers, the narrowed choices, and the process of choosing. "There were a lot of people who were striking for very idealistic reasons the first time who didn't go out the second time. Or there were people who went out in the beginning and came back, because of . . . the effect that they thought it was going to have on the kids." But there was another group of young people who stayed out, who became less idealistic and "much more . . . militant, as a result." She was one of them. "The second strike was much more a strike of workers for better working conditions, and it was much clearer to me. . . . By the second strike, I wasn't striking for more pencils or different books."[45]

Dave Lieberfarb felt in 1970 that he was bringing "power to the people." By "people," he meant the teachers and parents. But in 1971, activist parents were saying that his struggle was opposed to their struggle, that he was the enemy. "We found much to our chagrin, especially in the second strike, that most local groups were against us." Lieberfarb stayed out again but was "probably a little less sure of myself that God was on our side." His uncertainty was heightened by the alliance with Imperiale. "Knowing that people like that were on our side was very disillusioning at times. [If you] judge people by who their friends are and who their enemies are, you have to wonder about your position sometimes, if you have more respect for some of your enemies than for some of your friends."[46]

Carol Karman had faith in the Union as one of the few places in the society where Blacks and whites could come together, and together struggle toward a better world. During the 1971 strike, she clung to that faith. Unlike Salowe or Lieberfarb, Karman was not shaken by charges that the strike was hurting the Black community. "I never felt guilty for one minute. I didn't buy that bullshit. I knew LeRoi Jones was being paid by Prudential Life Insurance, and that Gibson was out to break my Union, and was just using the race question to try to beat the Union. I was very convinced. I didn't waver at all."[47]

Most teachers who stayed out in 1971 or who crossed the picket line were hurt by the experience. The pressure was greatest on Black teachers. Torn between the conflicting solidarities of race and class, Black teachers faced painful decisions over and over again.

Phyllis Cuyler stayed out for a while. Afraid of violence, she didn't picket much. She was single, living alone, worried about her bills, paying off a loan from the 1970 strike, and confused because "there was so many viewpoints." Then she went back. She was pelted with eggs as she crossed the picket line. "I didn't feel good about it either way, because I didn't think I should be going in, but I didn't feel that anybody should throw eggs at me."[48] Cuyler's previous analysis, in which racial and class struggle converged, gave her little comfort in 1971. She was caught in the middle, between two solidarities.

Marion Bolden had stayed home in 1970. "I kind of followed the crowd, just being new." She didn't call in sick and didn't bond with other strikers; she supported the Union, but not in a passionate, transforming way. As the 1971 strike drew near, "I agonized more." She feared it would drag on and become "unfair to the kids." She decided to keep working. Inside Barringer, with a dozen Black teachers, Bolden experienced a camaraderie she had not felt in 1970. They took turns bringing food for lunch and became "a support group." She who had been shy found her voice in the group; it was the beginning of becoming a leader. But the decision to work did not end her choices. A striking Black teacher called her at home and asked her to stay out for just one day. She talked to others in the group, and they agreed: "Let's give our colleagues one day."[49]

To Avant Lowther, 1971 was "Black *versus* white." He decided to cross the picket line. "Here I am, a new young Black teacher. . . . And here you have this Union with a Black president that's a figurehead, and you have Petino and all of these others, the Italian white males who were behind her." But inside West Kinney, the question of Black identity reemerged. Baraka was there, coaching volunteers. "It was always a constant conflict, because he was trying to push Black Black Black Black Black at the expense of everything else." Lowther's father didn't want Baraka and his volunteers in the school, because they taught Swahili, instead of skills the students needed to survive in America. Once Baraka "threatened my father, and one of the kids ran upstairs and got me." Lowther was so angry at Baraka that he could have killed him.[50]

Zenobia Capel was a veteran teacher. She told the Union rep at Peshine Avenue School that she would not strike. Although she thought the Union did more than the Association for teachers, she was not a joiner. And she had a baby, and bills to pay. Capel went to work during the 1971 strike, as she had in 1970. But she resisted the racial arguments used against the 1971 strikers. "When Jesse [Jacob] says that they're doing it to our kids, . . . I know that I don't sound really Black when I say it, but you can use that too often. After a while it doesn't mean anything. If everything is done to you because you're Black, then it gets to be a crutch for you, and also, no one pays attention to it."[51]

Janice Adams held on to her belief in the Union as a force for social progress. She knew many people saw the 1971 strike as " 'those horrible teachers against the Black kids,' but that's not the way I felt about it. I felt that by forcing the issue, that an awful lot of substantive changes would take place"—such as new reading programs and counseling services, smaller classes, a better physical plant. She refused to believe there was no money for the schools. She told *Muhammad Speaks*: "Mayor Gibson is being manipulated by the corporate power structure. . . . He doesn't want big business to move out of Newark and so the corporations have had their property value reassessed downward. And then the cry is made that there is no money in the city." As a Black and a worker, Adams was a strike activist in 1971. "Nationalism was very strong, and I was a part of that also. I didn't see what I was doing as a contradiction."[52]

Harold Moore was active in the strike, picketing most days. One day he went to Seton Hall University to speak to a Black Studies class. "There were a lot of young militant Blacks in that program who had some opinions about the strike. . . . A lot of them felt that the fact that I was supporting the strike made me less Black." The charge annoyed him but didn't really get to him. "I never let anyone else define Blackness for me." Moore told the students how he felt about the strike. "I don't think I changed everybody's mind, but I think they saw that it wasn't just a black and white issue. I mean that in more ways than one. When young people become militant, it becomes very difficult for them to see any way but their way."[53]

Blessed with an inner calm and robust spirituality, Moore charted his own course through the ups and downs of the struggle. He was emotionally sustained by the camaraderie of strikers: "We were so close." Financially, he scraped by; Pat Piegari found him work on the docks. But the strike eventually hurt Moore. His wife, Alison, was worried about the violence. "We were getting warnings from people all over," she says. "I don't want anything bad to happen to him, because he's too good." Then came threats of suspensions and firings. Though Alison put no pressure on him, Moore felt "what the strike was doing to her." He went to Piegari and Paone and, in tears, told them he was going back. The principal waited until school was over the next day before telling Moore he was suspended. Moore was furious at him for hiding the suspension all day. But he was also joyful. "He was so happy that he was suspended," Paone remembers. "He was thrilled because now the decision had been made, and that's it."[54]

The 1971 strike was brutal for everyone, especially for those who experienced conflicting claims of race and class. The longer it lasted, the more brutal it became; it seemed it would never end. Yet finally, in April, people torn by the conflicting claims would help end the strike.

Violence

The 1971 strike began on Monday, February 1. Half of the teachers—including most Black teachers—crossed the picket line on the first day of the 1971 strike.[55]

Few strikers picketed on Monday, February 1. They were afraid to picket because of the mood in the city, the free-floating anger. At most elementary schools, strikers were outnumbered by teachers who went to work, and they did not want to confront angry parents by themselves. Also, teachers arrested in 1970 had been warned by the Union's lawyer that their bail would be revoked if they were arrested again; they could go to jail for a long time. NTU leaders decided not to try to put pickets at every school, but rather to concentrate them at selected schools. Teachers willing to picket reported to the Union office on Clinton Avenue to get their picket assignment.[56]

It was still early on Tuesday, February 2, when fifteen teachers left the office with their assignments. Cars pulled up, surrounding them. "It was daylight," says Jim Brown. "So it was maybe seven-thirty or something, and we came walking out, with a lot of bravado, you know, high spirits. And that's when the incident happened." Young Black men, twenty or more of them, jumped out of the cars; the men were wearing fatigues and black army boots, running at the teachers, attacking males first. Stunned and terrified, teachers reacted individually. Brown, who had grown up in Newark, fought off one attacker. Then he ran.[57]

Brown had chosen to teach in Newark because he was from the city and knew he would be comfortable there. He was the son of a Newark fireman who had previously worked in a factory and always belonged to a union. Jim, the oldest of twelve children, grew up with the belief that "you wouldn't cross somebody's picket line." In college, he saw himself, with pride, as Nicky Newarker. He learned at a Union meeting in January that the Board refused to negotiate with the teachers. Like other young members of West Side High's math department, he knew what that meant. "We considered ourselves working-class teachers, rather than this high title of a professional. So there was no doubt in our mind that we were going to walk."[58]

In high school he had been on the track team. Now he ran. He ran to the corner of Clinton Avenue and turned left. Two men were after him, one carrying a broom handle, one a milk crate, but they could not keep up with him, "so I feel pretty safe." As he ran, a car pulled up. He imagined the police were on the way, and the car was there to help the two men escape. Instead, more men jumped out of the car, boxing him in. He yelled for someone to call the police. An older Black man came out of his door, and said, "I called the police." One young man threw the milk crate but missed. Brown looked for guns or knives and didn't see any. "I figured this is going to be a street fight." He blocked some punches and threw some but didn't connect. Blows from the broom knocked him to the ground. The men jumped in the car and left.[59]

He got up and walked the two blocks back to the Union office. After the attack, the office was locked tight. "I didn't realize how actually scared I really was until I walked back." He banged on the door, and someone let him in. "Carole Graves was there at the time, and Clara [Dasher] was there, and they look and they see that I'm all cut up, so they start washing my arms. Next thing you know I had to excuse myself, and I went in the bathroom and I threw up."[60]

Six teachers were taken to Beth Israel Hospital; two were kept overnight. Helen Cornish, who suffered a fractured skull, was released the next day. Terry Elman, who had fought back against the attackers, was kept longer. "I myself was hit in the back of the head with a whiffle bat that had nails coming out of it, causing 126 stitches," he explained. "I was hit in the face with a pipe that broke my nose, broke my elbow, knocked me to the ground." One of the young men straddled him when he was on the ground and was going to hit him with a fire extinguisher. A striking teacher, a Black woman, ran over and pushed the attacker aside.[61]

Tuesday night, at a mass meeting, Brown told his story. One or two other victims also spoke. Television cameras were present. (Only when he was watching the TV news did Brown notice a teacher in the front row weeping as she listened to him.) To further publicize the incident, the Union distributed a leaflet with a photo of a battered Terry Elman entering the hospital, and the words: "WE CARE! DO YOU?"[62]

Teachers cared. The attack shocked and angered them. Many were indignant that there were no arrests. On Wednesday, 227 more teachers stayed out to protest the violence; 20 more were out at Weequahic, 15 more at West Side. Nonstriking teachers at Sussex Avenue School decided to show sympathy with striking colleagues because of the assault; the Sussex Avenue PTA agreed to a one-day boycott, and on Thursday the school was closed. Pete Petino thinks the attack "gained us a lot of support, because those people that weren't out then decided to go out, because they were outraged that that would happen."[63]

But the increase in the percentage of striking teachers was only temporary. By the middle of the second week, the percentage was again hovering around 50, where it remained for a long time, before slipping even lower. The attack on February 2 scared some teachers away from picketing and hardened others. "That [assault] pretty much set the tone, that it was going to be a very hardball strike," says Jim Lowenstein. The violence against the teachers on the second day "cemented the strike" and "actually made the strike," according to Graves. Only 50 percent or fewer of the teachers were out, but after the attack, "they vowed to stay out forever."[64]

Petino says February 2 "triggered" a lot of violence. Tom Lawton says "everyone was fearing for their lives" after hearing what happened to Terry Elman. "We figured there would be roving bands of parents out there, beating teachers up. So everyone had something to protect themselves." Pickets began to carry screwdrivers, ice picks, knives. Carloads of strike opponents cruised around Newark in the mornings, intimidating pickets. "Teachers started retaliating," said Graves. "The picket lines were vicious scenes."[65]

Violence became characteristic of the 1971 strike. Cars were the preferred target for both sides. Someone poured soap powder down the carburetor of Carole Graves's 1970 Plymouth, then stuffed newspaper in the interior and set it on fire. The 1961 Cadillac of Elayne Brodie—a leading opponent of the Union, who helped Saunders with his community strategy—was burned at night. Someone broke the windows of Jesse Jacob's car, which made him even angrier at the Union.[66]

Attacks on the cars of strikebreakers became commonplace as the weeks went on, and striking teachers became more desperate. At East Side High, on the first day of the strike, teachers who crossed the picket line found the tires of their cars punctured by an ice pick. After the assault on the Union teachers, there were reports from around the city of tires punctured, windows smashed, convertible tops slit, bodies scratched with keys or spray-painted. Violence against the cars of teachers who refused to strike was both an outlet for the anger of striking teachers and a picket line strategy. In 1970 there were enough pickets to intimidate teachers who wanted to work, but wanted even more to avoid trouble. In 1971 violence made up for the lack of numbers.[67]

"Oh yeah, cars were expendable," says Petino, laughing. "Windows. Tires. You name it." Petino was one of a number of young activists who kept up their spirits by punishing teachers who crossed the picket line. Other strikers vicariously enjoyed the tales of revenge. The destruction was so widely accepted in the subculture of striking teachers that people who were not ordinarily violent became drawn into it. Elena Scambio called in sick in 1970, when she was not yet certified. In 1971, to retaliate against "people who were breaking the picket line," she gave flat tires. "I was a young teacher caught up in the activity of the moment. Because members of my family had always been strong union members, I wouldn't think of not participating."[68]

Tom Lawton, who drove a Rheingold beer truck during the strike to support himself, would stop in front of Garfield School to snarl traffic. To slow down teachers trying to get into school before the line formed, the band of young activists at Garfield would loop a chain (without a lock) around the gate and put bubble gum in the lock of the school door. They put objects in the tailpipes of cars belonging to teachers who were inside. "Not enough to ruin it, but just enough to foul them up for a while." The point was "to harass" strikebreakers without getting caught. "Little devious activities. We weren't really pugilists that would get out there and fight with people."[69]

Joe Del Grosso began teaching at Garfield late in 1970 and quickly became active in the Union. He used a BB gun. "When we could find teachers' cars that were scabbing, we would ventilate their windows." He shot out the windows of one car seven times, because the owner was a leader of those going in. "Finally after the seventh time, the teacher knew I did it, came to me, and said, 'That's it. I'm not going in any more. I surrender.' "[70]

Scambio, Lawton, and Del Grosso are unusual only in talking openly about what they did, when they were very young. Most activists felt the same way about people who were crossing the line. The feeling was: if we all stayed out, we would win quickly, and we could all go back. By going in, you prolong the strike. You collect a paycheck, while we go without. Yet you want it both ways. When we win, you'll benefit from the new contract as much as we will. If there's a raise, you'll take that too. But we are going to make you pay.[71]

Much of the violence was low-level vandalism. But it was intended to hurt. Pat Piegari and Angela Paone had a baby to feed, and they were not getting paid. "As the 1971 strike went on, I became more pissed and more militant," Piegari says. He threw pennies on the ground in front of teachers who were going in. "People hated that." He spray-painted the cars of teachers who were working and abused husbands who dropped off wives. Once he picked up a wooden police barricade and hurled it at the car of a teacher driving through a picket line.[72]

Many Americans treat cars almost as sacred objects: if you hurt my car, you hurt me. Charles Malone never supported the NTU or its strikes, going to work in 1965, in 1970, and in 1971. "But in the last one, I went in, and somebody banged my car. I'll never forget that." He was driving through the picket line at West Side High School when a picket struck the side of his car. Malone tried to shrug it off. Then the picket did it again. Malone got out of the car. "I'll tell you what," said Malone, who was a Tuskegee airman during World War II. "You touch the car again and your ass is mine." Although he protected his car, he still felt aggrieved. To him, the picket had gone too far. "We disagree, you call me scab. But don't touch my car."[73]

Ellen Cunniff was always critical of the Union and loyal to the Association. She and her mother drove to work at Abington Avenue during the strike. At night, she parked in her driveway in Belleville, just north of Newark. One night, someone took the trouble to find her house and puncture all four of her tires. She thought she knew who did it, a striker she knew and liked. As she saw it, it wasn't personal. It was because she and her mother were going to work.[74]

Unlike Cunniff and Malone, Phil Basile was a Union teacher. Basile struck in 1970 and was arrested. In 1971, he and his wife were trying to adopt a child; any further trouble with the law could ruin their chances. "I really felt bad. I certainly didn't want to cross—to this day, I won't cross a picket line." Painfully, he explained to friends at Barringer, and they said they understood. But that was before the strike began. After a few weeks, a friend took the distributor wire out of Basile's car. Basile confronted him. The friend was not apologetic. "'What are you going to do about it?'" asked the friend. "I didn't do anything," says Basile.[75]

Anyone on the "scab list" was fair game. At most schools, the building rep sent a list of strikebreakers to the Union office, where home addresses and telephone numbers were added. At night, strikers found and spray-painted the cars of some of the fifty-seven teachers and teacher aides on the Barringer list. During the day, Carmine Cicurillo, one of the oldest teachers, drove into the parking lot at Barringer. Pickets surrounded his car and wouldn't let him out. They rocked the car, terrifying him. Nick Cammesa had his tires shot out, apparently with an air pistol.[76]

Throughout the city, where activists gathered, conversation turned to violence. Violence didn't seem wrong to teachers who had grown up within the labor movement and knew that people who crossed picket lines were likely to suffer bodily harm. "A lot of us felt: uh-uh—we were just like the Teamsters—don't cross my picket line," says Jim Brown. "You cross my picket line, you're gonna get hurt." Others believed the situation required extraordinary measures. "It is very clearly a question of survival of the union—and when your survival is at stake, you don't play nice," said a striker from South Eighth Street.[77]

The violence of the 1971 strike developed during violent times in America. One nonviolent Newark teacher, arrested for striking in 1970, observed that people were setting off bombs nationally because they were frustrated by the seemingly endless Vietnam War and the plight of Blacks, particularly in central cities.[78] More bombs went off after the Cambodia bombing and the killing of students at Kent State and Jackson State in the spring of 1970. On the left, many young Americans romanticized violence. Violence against things, rather than against people, was particularly celebrated.

In practice, the line between violence against things and violence against people is hard to maintain. One woman, who asked me not to use her name, is still shocked that two male strikers conceived an idea involving explosives, directed against an older colleague who was crossing the line. "It was a terrible plan, really to immobilize this man's car." She emphasizes that they did not carry out the plan. Another discussion took place between NTU activists in a teacher's apartment. One said, "Something's got to blow." Asked to explain, he did: blow up a school building. Carol Karman loudly protested. Karman objected to violence on that scale, Carole Graves recalls, "because people who weren't a part of this were going to get hurt."[79]

Graves adds, "I don't think that the people who were fanning these flames understood the potential for real disaster that was in the making." She lived in the city, in the midst of the conflict, and so perhaps had a more realistic view of the danger. She feared an escalation of violence on both sides. "The rhetoric was heating, the physical attacks were heating up, our people were being roughed up by certain community people," threats were being made against families. "It had gone out of control very quickly." She tried to limit Union violence. But she was jailed for half the strike, which restricted her influence. And Graves too was affected by the overall atmosphere of the times, and the place. "Everybody suddenly seemed to be in a movie, playing some role in a movie, maybe myself included."[80]

The most violent thing done to cars in Newark was loosening the lugs on tires. A few male teachers who were crossing the line told Phyllis Cuyler that it had been done to them. According to Ellen Cunniff, the same thing was done to three nonstriking teachers at Garfield. One was Vicky Middleton. On the handwritten "scab list" from Garfield, Middleton was the one name underlined, because she was taking an active role against the strike. According to Cunniff, one of Middleton's tires came off on Route 22 as she drove home to Plainfield; she plunged into traffic, was so badly injured that she never returned to work, and later died as a result of her injuries.[81] Cunniff was ready to believe anything bad about the Union. But if she is right, and one teacher died as a result of violence in the strike, it would not be surprising. What would be surprising is that only one teacher died.

"It was an armed camp in Newark," said Graves. "Nobody talked about it. No one knows how close someone on either side came to being killed." She herself was a target. Her niece, the niece's husband, and their baby were visiting her on a Saturday evening in November, during the struggle at South Eighth Street. Someone shot out the windows at the back of the house, and the baby was cut on the foot by glass. Later, after the assault outside the NTU office and numerous bomb threats, its windows were sandbagged, and it became "a fortress." Newark assigned plainclothes detectives to Graves as her bodyguards. When a friend, a teacher activist, was attacked, two detectives guarding Graves broke it up.[82]

Newark was indeed an armed camp. Don Saunders had his own bodyguard. "I'm walking alone with a bodyguard who, when the pressure got so great, pulled a weapon on me. That's how jumpy people were." An anonymous caller to the house of Board member Tom Malanga complained that Malanga had once been "a good union man." Then a shot was fired through Malanga's living room window. A teacher's father was angry about how she had been treated; he was arrested with a gun before he hurt anyone. Another man was arrested with a gun at Franklin Street School, where he was interfering with pickets. Harold Moore knew several striking teachers who carried guns. He himself was not violent and carried no weapon. "But there was so much passion and so much anger, you could understand somebody being fearful enough to carry a gun."[83]

Bob Hirschfeld wanted a gun. He was an activist, arrested in 1970, a member of the Union's new executive board. He received anonymous phone calls threatening his family and asked the Livingston police to watch his children as they walked to school. But he still didn't feel they were safe. He himself just missed being in the group of teachers who were attacked on February 2; he arrived at the Union office late because he was arguing with his wife, who feared what would happen if he were arrested again. Now she put her foot down, saying he was not going to bring a gun into the house. As a compromise, he borrowed a dog, a German shepherd. "I kept the dog here for the next two weeks. . . . That was sort of my answer, or my wife's answer, to buying a gun."[84]

One reason the violence in 1971 wasn't worse is that guns were not as common then as they have become. Men and women carried less decisive weapons, and sometimes used them. For example, Cynthia O'Neal was picketing at South Tenth Street, and Hattie Black wanted to go through. Black stabbed O'Neal in the arm with a small, sharp instrument. Janice Adams was there. "We were all shocked that an educator would do that."[85]

People on the picket line, and people crossing it, felt less vulnerable if they were armed with a weapon of some kind—a sharp or blunt instrument in their pocket, purse, or car. "Whether it was a pocket knife, or a set of brass knuckles, or a baseball bat, a lot of people were arming themselves for their protection," says Lawton.[86] In this way, violence created fear, and fear created the potential for more violence.

Jim Lowenstein picketed at South Eighth Street. "Talk about face-to-face confrontations with violence." About seventy teachers, and Bayard Rustin, faced community members. Jesse Jacob was personally serving injunctions. He served one on Rustin, who was hit with all kinds of insults—including signs saying "Fag go home"—but he maintained his dignity and composure. Garrett was threatening pickets: "Just stop one teacher or child, and even the police won't be able to help you." Lowenstein recognized some of the men on the other side. "They were the enforcers, the thugs," the Black equivalent of Imperiale's men, he says. No one was hurt. "But you could see—it could have been triggered off—someone could have thrown a punch."[87]

Lowenstein was afraid during the confrontation. After that day, he carried a weapon. "On a daily basis, it was either a screwdriver, [or] some kind of tool or implement with me, just in case. Nothing lethal, but something to give me a little more leverage, a little more of an edge. A screwdriver, possibly a little wrench, or something—just if I needed to buy a step or two between me and somebody else."[88]

Dave Lieberfarb hadn't been violent since the eighth grade, when he punched his friend Lowenstein, who was too shocked to hit back. But you didn't have to be particularly violent to pick up a weapon during the 1971 teachers strike. Lieberfarb was passing out leaflets at Weequahic, publicizing alternative schools run by strikers for students who weren't going to school. A man snatched away the leaflets; Lieberfarb went to get more from the other side of the building. "And I picked up an empty soda bottle . . . and stuck it in my pocket. And he came back—he came back at me again, and I pulled the empty soda bottle out, and he thought better of it, and he left."[89]

Zenobia Capel carried shears to protect herself. (To protect her car, she parked two blocks from school, in the alley of a friend of her mother's. "The car was never touched, because they didn't know where it was.") Once a woman picket angrily denounced Capel for being selfish. "But she never got too close," because the shears were sticking up out of Capel's bag. Capel, who taught physical education, thinks she would not have used the shears on a woman. "I'm too big, and I'm too strong." However, "I would have, on a man."[90]

It was hard for Avant Lowther to cross the line. "A lot of mornings I was actually physically sick for coming in." But he thought strikers would respect his decision. Instead, he and his wife received calls at home. "They were harassing my wife and it was making me angry." He was also angry because he heard rumors of pickets beating female teachers at other schools. He arrived at work one morning, already angry, and ran into a picket line. A white teacher from another school, a big man, blocked his way. He said to the teacher, "If you're not going to pay my bills, you're going to have to get out of my way." The teacher called him a scab and other names. Lowther told him to get out of the way, or he would go through him, and the teacher pulled a knife. In the ensuing scuffle, before others separated them, the teacher was wounded in the neck. "I cut him with his own knife, but he didn't die."[91]

A white teacher assaulted a young Black teacher trying to enter Ann Street School. A security guard was injured in a melee at Robert Treat School. Four striking teachers were attacked in their homes. Two reporters for the Liberation News Service were roughed up by teachers at a mass strike meeting. Pat Piegari confronted a Black substitute who was crossing the line. "We're trying to make things better for young Black kids," he said. "And you're in there for money, and I'm losing money." The substitute surprised him by punching him in the face, and a brawl began between the two men. Ellen Cunniff and her mother, driving to Abington, were blocked by pickets. Acting on impulse, her mother got out of the car, squared her shoulders, and advanced toward the line, where she was met by a young teacher. "All of sudden, my mother and this young girl are on the ground."[92]

Violence tended to drive away people, on either side, who were not prepared to get rough. Mary Abend, born in Spain, was in her first year of teaching in Newark, at Arts High, which was small and friendly. She was striking because she had grown up pro-union in Gary; her father, a steelworker, was in several strikes. NTU called for pickets at Arts High, and Abend went. A chair or table was hurled out of a third-floor school window, landing near the pickets. "I never in my wildest dreams expected that there would be danger." No one was hurt. But she never picketed again.[93]

Teachers felt safer when they were surrounded by people who seemed tough. Carol Karman, who picketed every day, picketed her own school once or twice. Clinton Avenue was a new elementary school in a Black neighborhood and no one else was striking. Parents harassed Karman when she picketed, but she wasn't afraid. Her closest girlfriends from other schools came to her picket line. Her brother, a per-diem sub in Newark, also picketed with her and yelled right back at the parents. "He was very tough and loud, so that made me feel good, having him there."[94]

Anna and Marty Blume crossed the picket line during the 1971 strike. They identified more with Black students and parents than with teachers; in a larger sense, they were more committed to the Black struggle than to the labor movement. They could park in the playground. But they first had to get their car through the line. "We had a lot of people in our face," says Anna. High school teachers and dockworkers pressed against the car. "They weren't messing around. You could get hurt over there, serious hurt. I'm not just talking about cars." But the Blumes were not alone. Most Bergen Street teachers were crossing the line. "We also had a lot of community people who were looking out for us," adds Marty. "We almost felt some kind of protection from them."[95]

Sometimes the protection was professional. When a young picket was assaulted, her brother, a powerful man in the labor movement in New Jersey, summoned Felix Martino. "This was the type of guy who when he said come now, you came." The man gave instructions. His sister would picket at Barringer, where Martino could look out for her. Just to be safe, the man would bring his own people, construction workers. " 'And if they show up,' " said the man, referring to strike opponents, " 'we're going to break heads.' "[96]

The strike went on and on, past the three and a half weeks of the 1970 strike, stretching into a second month, then into a third. The Board continued to take a hard line, insisting on gutting the contract. Striking teachers grew desperate. Their numbers were dwindling. The more fortunate found work at local breweries. Most ran out of money. Some used food stamps; some collected welfare; some cashed in life insurance. Jesse Jacob cancelled all the benefits of striking teachers, including health benefits: "I had stopped paying them and I had taken away their insurance. I was prepared to do what was necessary. If it meant that they had to stay out there in them streets until the next September, it had been all right with me."[97]

"First of all, we all went broke. I had five kids and I went broke," says Gene Liss. "Every single penny that I had in savings, which wasn't much, probably two thousand dollars, was gone. I borrowed money from my father." In the ninth week, he received a letter, suspending him. "We thought we were gonna lose our jobs." Jacob and the Board suspended 347 striking teachers and asked the New Jersey Commissioner of Education to determine whether they should be fired. Still Liss stayed out. After all, his father was a member of the Teamsters Union. But he worried: who would hire a teacher who was fired?[98]

The concern was real. During the summer of 1970, Superintendent Titus noted, without irony, "We haven't had any trouble recruiting teachers since we agreed on our new teacher salary guide." Nationally, there was a surplus of qualified teachers. Jacob told community groups that given the job market, it would be easy to replace striking teachers. Mayor Gibson, at the time of the suspensions, said it was "inevitable" the Board would fire strikers. "If the teachers who are supposed to do it won't, then we will get teachers who will."[99]

"Seventy-one was such a long strike," Angela Paone remembers, "and there were people who were breaking ranks at the end, and that was very painful. . . . People started folding very much at the end. We didn't know it was going to be the end, but we were folding toward the end." Ron Polonsky, the strike organizer, never gave the true figures of how many were still striking. Publicly, he continued to be optimistic. Costumed at the morning meeting in black leather jacket, sunglasses, and long hair, he would raise both arms, make a V with the fingers of each hand, and chant: "The strike is strong! The strike is strong!" His energy, enthusiasm, and humor helped some strikers keep going. But after so many weeks, Polonsky himself wondered when it would end, and how. Privately, he confessed to a national AFT organizer that he didn't know how much longer the strikers could go on; even the most dedicated were beginning to get demoralized.[100]

One day after the Board suspended teachers, the superior court of Essex County issued arrest orders for pickets. Sheriff's men invaded the morning meeting on April 1 to arrest two pickets, and Polonsky lost control. "The next time they'd better come with guns," he said in front of a TV camera. "No more teachers are going to be locked up. No more sacrificial lambs. If they want to come back, bring the National Guard."[101]

Under threat—financial, legal, physical—more and more teachers returned to work. The Board knew that its pressure was working. "I felt our position was good, because more teachers were going back," said Don Saunders. "Until we got to the hard core in the Union."[102]

Pete Petino observed the same shrinking numbers, and the same core.

> As the weeks went on, more and more people went back. People started to go back. It got tougher and tougher economically for people. That's why I always used the figure—I don't know if it's right—when it came down to the settlement on April 19, we were like five hundred out there. We were just five hundred hard-core people in the whole district that no matter what happened that five hundred would never go back.[103]

Under pressure, the hard core became harder, angrier, more violent. "The first few weeks of the strike, for me, I was very calm, and not overly aggressive on the picket line," says Joe Del Grosso, who began teaching during the fall of 1970. "I was single, I was living home with my mother, I could survive. But I discussed with my colleagues who were trying to feed a family, who had to go drive a beer truck at night or take a second job to try and support the family." As time went by, "I have to say I succumbed, and became part of the violence myself."[104]

Del Grosso's initiation into violence began when he was a child in the North Ward. "I had to fight a lot of street battles myself, and if you ran home to Mommy you would have to fight a lot more battles, because then you would be a Mama's boy." On the first morning of the strike, he was driven to Garfield by Dominick Bizzarro, his building rep and mentor in unionism. "We got out of the automobile, and there is someone trying to get into the school. I saw Dominick tackle the person. . . . Then it really dawned on me that it was not a game." Once, leaving the Union office, Del Grosso and a few colleagues were threatened by young Black men. "We drove away, and they actually chased after us. And they caught me and they sideswiped my car, and . . . forced me into another car, and my car was pretty much banged up. It was an awakening.

We learned that we had to be very, very careful, and not go anywhere alone, and be in groups, because it was getting very dangerous."[105]

At first, Del Grosso felt bad about what was happening to teachers. A Black teacher approached the picket line at Garfield, intending to cross, early in the strike. Imperiale had men at Garfield, "to make sure that we were protected." One of Imperiale's men began to shout at the teacher, which led to pushing and shoving, and eventually punching. "The police ironically arrested the teacher who was crossing the picket line, for assault, and they took him away. Because Mr. Imperiale's men were very close to the police." Del Grosso liked the teacher; before the strike they sometimes went to lunch together. As the teacher waited in the police car, Del Grosso went over to the window. "I just said to him, 'I'm sorry,' because he was still a teacher, and it was still tragic in the circumstances."[106]

Del Grosso's sense of tragedy diminished as the struggle went on. He knew he was headed for jail, because he was very militant and was photographed many times by the authorities. Giving himself to the battle of the picket line, he made it into a kind of game. "We had to become inventive. And we invented what we called the wild bus ride. The wild bus ride was where we rented a bus, and we got fifty of the craziest pickets we could find." A bus or a big truck would descend on a school. At Ridge Street School on March 24, for instance, pickets arrived suddenly in a bus and pelted the school with eggs. No one knew where the bus might show up, or what the teachers riding it might do.[107]

Del Grosso's inventiveness went further. He proposed a wild bus ride to his own school, to trap strikebreakers inside. Teachers parked in the Garfield playground during the strike. So when the wild bus, with fifty or sixty of the most militant teachers inside, swooped down and pulled into the parking lot, the cars were there. "I could see the teachers in the building, watching their cars being trampled." When the pickets finished with the cars—"like shooting fish in a barrel"—they formed a circle around the building. Several had attack dogs with them. Teachers could not leave the building. Some police arrived, but not enough; teachers were still afraid to come out. Husbands came to try to get their wives out, and pickets fought them. Teachers were captive in the building until four-thirty or five o'clock.[108]

As a guerrilla tactic, the bus ride worked. Only a handful of people returned to work at Garfield the next day. Tom Lawton agrees that guerrilla tactics at Garfield were successful in keeping many teachers home. "A lot of them were afraid that we were crazy and would cause them bodily harm, so they stayed out." The fear lasted. Two years after the strike, Ellen Cunniff was assigned to Garfield by the Board. She had heard how the wild bus riders came to Garfield "and sealed in the school" and had heard about other violent activities there. "They had so many bad things happen that when I was assigned there, I asked if there were any other openings. I was afraid to go there."[109]

Many parents kept their children home because of the violence. Though teacher attendance rose over time, pupil attendance remained low. "We wore 'em out," says Pete Petino.

> We disrupted the system. Even though we were small, we got into the trucks—you must have heard the stories about the trucks, the buses. And each day that passed, schools didn't know when they'd be hit. Either going in, in the morning, or in the afternoon. And it was a constant disruption. And then at the time, kids weren't going to school either, because there was a fear of violence.[110]

Petino coordinated the violence. Asked which side was more violent, he doesn't hesitate. "I think we were more violent." Hurting or harassing teachers as they went into school was difficult. "Of course there was a lot of that going on, but we had such heavy police presence, it became very difficult. So we did other things as it wore on, and that's where the nighttime rides and the nighttime visits and all that came in."[111]

Teachers were vulnerable at home. They received letters sarcastically urging them "to be in school on Monday to operate in my self-interest and not in the interest of my colleagues, the students, and the educational system." Then the anonymous calls began. Finally, for some teachers, there were nighttime visits, not only for their cars but for themselves. "Visits to their homes also," says Petino, laughing. "You paid people visits. It depends on how many people you had . . . who could make visits, who were into that."[112]

The nighttime visits were both secret and legendary—more legendary for being secret. Jerry Yablonsky heard stories about Union teachers shooting at houses at night. "I didn't know the details . . . and then didn't want to, once I found out what was going on." But Yablonsky felt sympathetic to the violence. His uncle led the Painters Union, and he grew up knowing that unions punish people who cross their picket line.[113]

Carol Karman liked the stories about the night visits.

> There were these brigades of guys who would go around at night and do mean things to scabs. Then we'd hear about them. It was almost mythological. There was no evidence and no proof, and no one knew exactly who they were talking about. . . . You'd hear about so-and-so got a punch in the nose, and so-and-so decked somebody else, and then they went to somebody's house, and they put his door on fire, and they put sugar in that guy's gas tank.[114]

Many of the myths of the strike are about violence. "You must have heard the stories," Petino said to me, referring to the wild bus rides. "To this day . . . , people will have anecdotes about do you remember the '71 strike, when we did this, and we did that," says Jim Brown. "Talking about when we were all young, and maybe a little bit more brave." At the time, Graves disclaimed knowledge of violence toward cars or people; it was not NTU policy, she said. But it was policy. Three decades later, she acknowledges that teachers were armed; there were guns. "It was only a 50 percent strike, barely 50 percent," she explains. "Those that didn't get scared in just hunkered down, and said we're in this to the death."[115]

The 1971 Newark teachers strike was not incidentally but essentially violent. Both sides were violent, but the strikers used more violence. The Board had allies in the Black community who used violence, but the Board didn't need to rely on that kind of violence. It took away health insurance from all strikers, suspended most, and threatened to fire them. Everyone arrested in 1970 was threatened with a long sentence if arrested again; Graves and two NTU vice presidents were locked in jail during much of the strike. The Board had not only law but also time on its side. Unlike a private employer hit by a strike, it lost no money; only the striking teachers lost money—about three thousand dollars each, or 30 percent of a yearly salary. Jacob and the Board were in no hurry to settle. They could afford to turn up the pressure on teachers, one twist at a time. Their violence was institutionalized.

Teachers had no legal remedy. The 1968 law that created the Public Employment Relations Commission (PERC) gave it no power to force good-faith negotiations or determine unfair labor practices.[116] The violence by striking teachers effectively discouraged teachers from going to work and parents from sending children to school. Union leaders quietly embraced violence, even organized it, because the Board would not negotiate. They hoped the violence and disorder of 1971 would lead Mayor Gibson to intervene. Getting him to intervene, as Mayor Addonizio had intervened in 1970, was their last hope.

The Peace Movement

Mayor Gibson tried to make peace three times. He failed the first time, and Carole Graves was jailed. He failed the second time, and 347 teachers were suspended. But the third time, with the help of Clarence Coggins, he created a popular movement for peace. This time Graves was released from jail, the suspensions were rescinded, and the contract was signed.

Like Kafka's K, who tried to ascend to the Castle in his first day in the village, Gibson naively set out to make peace on the evening of the last day of the contract. On January 31, he summoned Graves, the NTU lawyer, and the

AFT representative to a secret meeting. He did not invite Jesse Jacob. He held the meeting not at the Downtowner Motor Inn, where three weeks of useless negotiation had taken place, but at the Ballantine House, which was connected to the Newark Museum. The press did not learn for weeks that the NTU and Gibson agreed that night to avoid a strike.[117]

Earlier in January, NTU leaders let Gibson know that they understood the city's financial plight and were willing to sacrifice most of their demands. Meanwhile, he had met his payroll obligation, and hoped to raise additional money through his tax package. Gibson called the meeting because the city could afford a modest raise and the Union would settle for it. The agreement reached on January 31 gave teachers no raise in the first year and a moderate raise in the second. The discussions, which lasted all night, focused on issues other than money. Graves and Vinnie Russell, the AFT negotiator, insisted that the teachers could not give back what they had won in 1970. The mayor conceded binding arbitration and suggested a ten-day extension of the existing contract to work out remaining differences. Graves reluctantly agreed to the extension.[118]

By seven in the morning, Gibson believed he had averted a strike. He asked his chauffeur to take the three Union representatives to the Union mass meeting, and he himself went to a diner to explain the terms of the agreement to Jacob. Jacob raised no objections, and left. Now it was his turn to exclude the mayor. Calling an executive session of the Board, he denounced Gibson's agreement as capitulation to the Union and instructed the Board to vote against it. Somehow the mayor heard that the Board meeting was not going well. He rushed over and was made to wait. When he was finally allowed to speak, Jacob responded defiantly. Only Cervase supported the agreement. The agreement was dead, and the strike began.[119]

The breach between Gibson and Jacob never closed. Within days, the press reported that the mayor was willing to grant binding arbitration but the Board was not. Don Saunders commented, brutally and publicly, that "the mayor doesn't know much about education." Within weeks, the mayor sent Pete Curtin, his staff coordinator, to tell Saunders to settle the strike. Saunders threw Curtin out, saying he took instructions only from Jacob. Gibson descended on Saunders's hotel room with his bodyguards, insisting that he was in charge. Saunders, knowing Jacob was behind him, was not intimidated and told Gibson that he wouldn't want to be mayor, because he, Saunders, made more money.[120]

Gibson did not make another attempt to end the strike for six weeks. Nor did he pressure Board members. Respecting the Board's autonomy, he let the strike run its ugly course. Then, on March 16, he met alone with the Board. On March 19, at his direction, everyone moved into the Downtowner Motor

Inn: Board team, Union team, himself, and a state-appointed mediator. The teams lived there, meeting in separate rooms; representatives of the press and community were excluded. Gibson thought that with the Board insulated from community groups he could push through a settlement.[121]

The mediator, Jonas Silver, recommended slightly modified versions of binding arbitration and nonprofessional chores. Money was still not the issue, although the teachers, who had lost so much by striking, were offered a bit more than on January 31. The Board and the Union both read Silver's recommendations as favoring the Union. Jacob's reaction was characteristic: "I'm sorry but I'm just not giving them [the teachers] my school system." The intensive negotiations ended March 25. Defying Gibson again, the Board rejected Silver's recommendations. Gibson's new attempt failed, like a slow-motion replay of January 31, because nothing essential had changed. Jacob still controlled the Board, and diehard opponents of the Union still spoke for the Black community.[122]

From the point of view of peace, there was nothing wrong with the content of Silver's recommendations; indeed, they would become the basis for the eventual settlement. What was wrong was Silver's process. He did nothing to alter the dynamic on the Board or in the community. Experienced in labor mediation, he did not take the Board's position seriously. The Board demands, he said, went beyond normal management concerns: "All the contract terms in their position are related to the attempt of nationalist and certain community elements to gain control." To Silver, the Union's demands seemed traditional and legitimate, the Board's demands nontraditional and illegitimate. It was not that he was on labor's side as opposed to management's. It was that he assumed community concerns were an abnormal intrusion into labor/management negotiation.[123]

Silver did not establish a personal connection with Jacob or other Board members. He believed that Jacob was not really shaping Board policy. Like the Union, he saw Baraka and Gibson behind Jacob; behind Gibson, he saw Baraka again.[124] Lumping Blacks together, Silver failed to give either Jacob or Gibson credit for being his own man. Only someone who took Jacob's independence seriously could help Gibson undermine Jacob's hold on the Board. Only someone who did not imagine Baraka to be all-powerful could help Gibson build a counterforce to Baraka in the Black community. Only someone who recognized Gibson's autonomy and goodwill could help him end the strike.

That someone was Clarence Coggins. In the summer of 1970, Gibson hired Coggins as his director of community organization. Coggins was a trade unionist who was also a Black community activist. Involved in grass-roots labor struggles since the thirties, he became active in the Black movement in the fifties and sixties, in Newark and Jersey City. He remained attuned, throughout his long and often brilliant career as a community organizer, to the possibility of alliances across race of working and poor people. Agitator, organizer, outsider, former Communist, Coggins was now, for the first time, on the inside. His job, federally funded, was to organize the residents of Newark to take advantage of the services provided by federal, state, and local agencies. He was charged with preventing racial explosions by bringing people together on a grass-roots level. From his perspective, the conflict in the city over the strike was in danger of producing an explosion worse than 1967.[125]

In the fall, Gibson assigned Coggins to the Board's negotiating team, representing the community. Coggins thought Jacob and Saunders were out of control. "They were drunk with power." In the street, which was Coggins's territory, Black militants were applying the struggle in Ocean Hill–Brownsville to Newark. Militants denounced NTU "as a white racist union. However, the one thing that stuck in their craw—and they had to turn flips to deal with— was [that] the leadership of the Newark Teachers Union was a Black woman." On the Board and in the street, Jacob and Saunders, Baraka and Garrett seemed caught up in the new nationalistic way of thinking. "It was a kill-the-teachers atmosphere."[126]

From the beginning, Coggins was afraid of violence. Graves regarded him as the only member of the Board negotiating team who really wanted to settle the strike in January, because he knew the havoc it could unleash. Once the strike began, he recognized there was little he could do. "There are times to fish and times to cut bait." He bided his time, watching the brutality grow, waiting for others to see the danger. He talked to Silver, and found Silver was a professional. "That was his problem." In a "racially tainted confrontation," you couldn't just make recommendations. You had to change the situation. You had to isolate "the nut element on each side" and create forces for peace. You had to reach into the Black community, said Coggins, and tell them "Garrett's crazy." And reach into the Union, and say "Carole's all right, but calm her down."[127]

Jacob later said of Coggins: "I needed him like Custer needed more Indians." Having repulsed Gibson's second intervention, Jacob and the Board removed Coggins and Curtin (Gibson's aides) from the negotiating team. Now Coggins was free to throw himself into the struggle for peace. He thought that both the Union and Board were "set for a death stand." Neither would listen to reason. Jacob was prepared to go it alone, to become a martyr; he perceived the mayor's desire to settle the strike as a conspiracy to give the Union a victory it could not win in the street. On the other hand, Graves and Dasher perceived the mayor's failure to settle the strike as proof that he wanted to break the Union. With the emergence of the forces mobilized by Imperiale and Turco,

Newark was at the brink. "The only reason available was the mass of the people."[128]

Coggins and Gibson worked with a new mediator, who was sophisticated in his approach to race. Ron Haughton entered the strike negotiations at Gibson's invitation immediately after Silver failed. Haughton, who was white, added Dee Watson and Warren Taylor, who were Black, to his team, in order to gain the Board's trust. He was certain he could win the NTU's trust. "With my having extremely good relationships with the AFT, you know, I was completely confident of my credibility [with NTU]. But Jacob didn't know this. So Jacob confidentially told me that our panel was dead because it was too Black. [Laughs.]"[129]

Haughton, Watson, and Taylor consciously developed personal ties to individuals. Watson cultivated Jacob and other Board team members; even though she never won Jacob to the cause of peace, she probably helped prepare him for his eventual defeat. Taylor reached out to the other Board members, who were not on the negotiating team but would vote on any settlement. Haughton built relationships with people on the Union negotiating team. Clara Dasher noticed the difference. "Jonas Silver was a little more impersonal, let me put it that way. Much more impersonal than Ron Haughton was."[130]

Negotiations broke down at one point. In the crisis, Haughton fell back on his strength, which was personal relationships. George Brickhouse, who was Black, was the new AFT negotiator. Haughton, drawing on their common roots, quickly became close to Brickhouse. "He was fantastic. And he came from Detroit. And he came out of an auto plant. So we could relate." Haughton arranged a meeting between Brickhouse and Gibson in a hotel room in Jersey City. "There's only one thing to do when things fall apart, and that's for the mediator . . . to suggest that the top two people get together."[131] The top people were the AFT negotiator and the mayor—not Graves, and definitely not Jacob. Because what Haughton wanted, and got, was the mayor's commitment to pressure Jacob and the Board to settle.

The top people, however, could not end the strike. One problem was that Graves did not trust Brickhouse. She had instructed Vic Cascella to make sure AFT did not sell out NTU while she was in jail. The coming of Brickhouse, in place of Russell, only made her more suspicious. "She figured Brickhouse would make a deal with the mayor; that's why he was here, to get a Black man to get along with the mayor," explains Cascella. The Jersey City meeting was a meeting of two men Graves did not trust, one of whom claimed to represent her. She felt better when the judge released her from jail to allow her to participate in negotiations. She was fearful of traps, however; at the end, Dee Watson had to soothe her.[132]

The bigger problem was with the other side. Saunders was forced out, under pressure from the mayor, as Fox had been in 1970.[133] But the Black community activists Saunders had encouraged could not be turned off. They vehemently resisted the settlement.

The new terms of settlement were similar to what Silver had proposed, and only marginally less offensive to strike opponents. Instead of a single arbitrator, there would be a tripartite panel of arbitrators; instead of teachers being relieved from all nonteaching duties, they would be required to perform a few minor ones. Haughton's aim was to end the strike, not to increase racial understanding. "This was part racial, part community, and part labor dispute. And I made a conscious move to pour it right into a labor-dispute mold, simply because it became easier to handle it, or if you want to be cynical about it, to maneuver it."[134]

Gibson pushed the settlement and put together a majority of Board members for peace. The solid majority that had supported Jacob turned out not so solid after all. To Jacob, beating the Union was a holy cause, worth any sacrifice. To most Board members, the issues were pragmatic. They shared Jacob's concerns about binding arbitration. The Union had usurped management prerogatives in 1970; they wanted to right the balance in 1971. "We wanted to be able to run the system, not allow the teachers to run it," said Fernando Zambrana, the lone Puerto Rican on the Board. But they didn't want to break the Union, they didn't want a war of attrition, they didn't want to be martyrs. And some wanted to be reappointed, which only Gibson, not Jacob, could do.[135]

Jacob began to lose control of the Board at the end of March, when the Board suspended the 347 teachers. Gibson did not oppose the move, but three Board members—Cervase, Dr. Michael Petti, and Charles Bell—voted no. Cervase always voted against Jacob. Petti was a political ally of Turco, who pressured him to vote no. Bell's vote was the big surprise. He was African American. For the first time, a member of the nonwhite majority of the Board stood up to Jacob, casting a vote against escalation.[136]

On April 1, believing he had the votes to end the strike, Gibson summoned the Board to his office. Tom Malanga and Alan Krim, after pressure from the mayor, were ready to support the settlement; their terms were ending and they wanted to stay on the Board. With Bell, Petti, and Cervase, the mayor now had five votes lined up for peace. And when the Board voted in the mayor's office, that's the way it went: five supporting the settlement, four opposed. The efforts of Haughton, Watson, and Taylor seemed to be paying off. All that remained was a public Board meeting to ratify the agreement.[137]

Jacob delayed calling the meeting for five days. Community activists used the time to put pressure on Bell to change his vote. The two other Black Board members and Zambrana remained loyal to Jacob. If Bell opposed the proposed settlement, the vote would be along racial lines, and the mayor would lose. Nine weeks of struggle between the proponents of race and the proponents of class now came down to an internal struggle within Bell.[138]

Gibson had appointed Bell to the Board as a Black activist and as a representative of labor. As a North Carolina high school student, Bell had been a leader of civil rights protests; as a Newark parent, he was a PTA leader in Miller Street School. During the 1970 strike, he escorted teachers who wanted to work into the school. For that reason, Clara Dasher considered him an enemy of the Union. But as a wage earner, Bell was an official with District 37 of the State, County, Municipal Employees Union in New York. He believed in unions, took labor relations courses, and was looking forward to a career in the trade union movement.[139]

Bell didn't want to choose. He felt connected to activists in the Black community and shared their belief that Blacks should control the institutions in their community. At the same time, he saw the labor movement as a way of empowering Black workers. He felt strongly that teachers should resume their nonteaching duties. And he felt strongly that it was wrong to try to break the Union. As a Board member, he complained about the polarization in the city. "We've already had letters from the North Ward parents giving lists of teachers not striking whom they want replaced, and letters from South Ward parents giving lists of striking teachers whom they also want replaced."[140]

Bell was caught, like Black teachers, in the cross fire of 1971. Before the vote in Gibson's office, NTU contacted leaders of District 37 in New York, and asked them to pressure Bell to honor union solidarity by supporting the settlement. Before the public Board meeting five days later, Black community activists pressured Bell to honor racial solidarity by opposing the settlement. A leaflet asked "HOW LONG ARE WE GOING TO BE ENSLAVED? Mr. Bell has the answer. His vote can unlock the chains of bondage!!" The leaflet urged Bell to "RISE UP AND VOTE *NO* ON RATIFICATION."[141]

Almost one thousand people crowded into city council chambers on the evening of April 6, with many left outside. They were chanting "Cervase must go," or "Jacob must go." Signs pleaded "Bell don't sell us out." One hundred eighty-four people signed up to speak, and Jacob allotted ten minutes to each. "Come on niggers," said Garrett, who took forty minutes, "get off your knees and stand up." He addressed whites in the audience: "You Honkeys run your schools the way you want to on your side of town and we'll run our schools on our side of town." Garrett and other speakers were interrupted by shouting, as whites and Blacks insulted each other. The few people who tried to speak in favor of ratification were shouted down. A white woman spoke directly to the Board, "asking if they knew what it was all about here tonight, BLACK AGAINST WHITE, WHITE AGAINST BLACK." She too was shouted down.[142]

Around eleven o'clock, a white teacher ran toward the podium, screaming, "Jesse, here I am, come and get me." A fight broke out. Some people were knocked to the floor, others pushed against the walls. Male teachers told female teachers to leave; one gave his gun to a woman who was leaving, in case he was arrested. Only fifteen people had spoken, and the Board had not voted. But the meeting—the most tumultuous public hearing in Newark's history, according to one observer—was over. The violence was not over, however. Garrett ordered a white *New York Times* reporter to turn over his notebook, and when the reporter refused, Garrett instructed three Black men to assault him. They punched him in the stomach, taking his notebook and his wallet.[143]

The violence also wasn't over for Joe Del Grosso and a few other teachers sitting upstairs. "As we came downstairs there was a group waiting for us at the bottom of the stairway, and you could tell that they weren't going to be hospitable toward us. And as we came down the stairwell, there was a shoving match, a pushing match that went on." Del Grosso and his friends moved quickly outside. "All of a sudden we heard what sounded like fireworks. But then we saw the glass of the car shattered, that we were running past to get to our car."[144]

Harold Moore was at the meeting. Throughout the strike, he was never scared, except at Board meetings. "The Board meetings were so very hostile"—especially on April 6.

> Very frightening. I don't like crowds anyway, and unruly crowds really upset me. It's funny, there just didn't seem to be any reason in those days. I mean it was them and us. We were all right and they were all wrong. And that's scary. It was scary then, but not nearly as scary as it is now, as I think back to it. How we were really out of control, both sides. . . . It just seemed like the strike had a life of its own, and we were being carried along by it.[145]

The depth of violence during the strike was hard to comprehend, said Clarence Coggins; he was able to understand it only because he spanned the decades. It reminded him of the thirties, "when we used to strike, where the man intended to kill you." If there were no deaths in 1971, it was because "the man lacked the ability or the circumstances to kill. Not the will." From the beginning, Coggins had warned Gibson the strike "could precipitate a bloodbath which would drown Newark forever." Now, in April, his warnings seemed to be coming true.[146]

What Coggins saw, what most journalists and historians have been reluctant to see, is that the potential for violence was greater in 1971 than in 1967.

"'Sixty-seven was the outbreak of people whose aspirations had been stifled." In 1971, "you're talking of the active, virulent intervention . . . from both sides of the fence." Two angry, frustrated, and organized peoples—Italian and Black—faced each other. Or as Bob Curvin put it, the danger in 1971 was of "communal violence."[147]

Violence between Italians and Blacks could "mushroom not only into a riot but into a race war," Dasher said at the time. "I think a real bloodbath would have resulted, had the strike gone on," she explained later. "Imperiale was ranting and raving, and he was getting his troops together; they were going to go on the warpath." It wasn't just Imperiale's paramilitaries. The Italian community as a whole was mobilizing. "We had the East Ward and we had North Ward parents who had now really come out in support of the teachers. . . . They were discussing all kinds of activities so far as going into Board meetings and direct confrontation with some of the community leaders. It was really getting out of hand. I think that played a major part in having the strike end."[148]

As Moore says, both sides were out of control. The Board planned to resume the meeting on April 7 at Symphony Hall, to hear from more citizens and take a vote. Both sides were planning to show up in force. Then Gibson interceded. His police chief arrested Garrett. Gibson spent April 7 on the phone, "reaching out for those people who may have influence in order to lower the heat level." Some Black activists resisted his appeal. A hastily written leaflet urged "all Blackmen" to get to the meeting early. "We *must not* allow striking Suburban Beast unnion [sic] 'Teachers' to *beat our* women and children *again*."[149]

Gibson had more success with the teachers. He called George Brickhouse and made an offer: if the teachers prevented violence by staying away from the Symphony Hall meeting, he would find a way to work out a settlement on binding arbitration and nonprofessional chores. Brickhouse talked to Vic Cascella, who had already issued a directive for teachers to go to the meeting en masse. "I made Brickhouse swear that he would cut his throat if the mayor backed down on him," says Cascella. "And he assured me, and Ron Haughton assured me, that the mayor was sincere." The teachers did not go to Symphony Hall, and for one last time Jesse Jacob had things his way.[150]

The crowd was Black. The first speaker told Board members, "You're looking at an angry group of people out here tonight. We ain't playing and we ain't shucking. I'm telling you if you're asking for trouble, goddamn it, we're here to give it to you." She was cheered. The second speaker was more direct: "Brother Bell, if I can call you brother. . . . They're using you, brother, they're using you, they're using you." Thirteen different speakers implored or warned Bell.[151]

The Board voted in alphabetical order. Bell was first. He insisted on the complexity of the conflict: the Union was not all wrong and the Board was not all right. Still, it was necessary to choose. "There comes a time in life when one must not do what is best but what is necessary." Some people who had not yet caught his drift made a small disturbance. Looking grim, Bell continued. "Mr. President, my vote tonight is for the survival of a city. Therefore Mr. President, I vote no." The audience broke into joyful applause. Bell didn't smile. Jacob cast the tie-breaking vote, then embraced Bell and wept. The settlement was defeated, five to four. The next day, at NTU's request, Bell's union fired him.[152]

Bell's vote was the high point of drama in the strike. His agony was public. He was caught in the either/or between racial solidarity and class solidarity. There was no third way. In voting no, he said he was doing not what was best in an ideal sense, but what was necessary for the survival of Newark. He gave Black rage a victory, almost a catharsis. In that sense, his vote was the climax of the campaign by the opponents of the strike. But in a deeper sense, it was anticlimactic, because they had already lost.

Cascella knew Jacob was celebrating. "But at that point I knew that we had won." Bell's vote, said Ron Haughton, was "interpreted as a vote against the Union. I'm saying 'interpreted,' because Charlie Bell had an agenda . . . which was very constructive." Bell's agenda was to avoid violence and make peace. After voting no on April 7, he joined Haughton and Coggins on Gibson's unofficial peace team.[153]

Each played a key role. Haughton and his two associates were the bridge between the Board and Union teams, which still did not like each other and never met together. Haughton worked closely with Graves, Dasher, Cascella, and Brickhouse, and with Bell, because "it was important to get behind Jesse Jacob." Bell was the Board member who worked hardest on contract language, although he was never officially on the negotiating team. Coggins urged the mayor to take the case for peace directly to the people. He knew most Black people had not yet been brought into the debate, contrary to the claims of Baraka and Garrett. Together, Coggins and Gibson reached into the Black community and altered the dynamic.[154]

Gibson went on television on April 12. Following Coggins's advice, he spoke as a Black against the activists who loudly maintained that continuing the struggle was good for Black children and parents. "Those being quoted" did not speak for the majority in Newark. There was "a certain amount of racism" in the schools, but the current "emotionalism" was not making anything better for anybody. Most Newark parents wanted their children back in school. They wanted "something better for their children than they have for themselves."[155]

Four days later, Gibson published "A Call to Reason," which began, "Newark is in a crisis." After eleven weeks of strike, and fourteen weeks of negotiation, "we are again at an impasse." Gibson insisted: "Only the moral pressure and action of the people can create an atmosphere which will lead both sides to a fair and just settlement." A fair settlement would keep binding arbitration, adding one arbitrator chosen by each side to the neutral arbitrator, for a total of three. It would remove the term "nonprofessional chores" from the contract, requiring elementary teachers to lead students from the building entrance to class, and secondary teachers to stand outside the door of their rooms when students were changing classes. It would lift the suspensions of the teachers.[156]

The Call to Reason—which Coggins, Haughton, and Pete Curtin had created at an all-night brainstorming session—became the charter of the peace movement. Coggins took the statement and orchestrated a campaign aimed at creating popular support. His community organization set up phone banks, sent out sound trucks, and distributed thousands of copies door to door, "just like we were running an election campaign." For Coggins, the purpose was simple: "to end this thing before there is a catastrophe."[157]

In the second and third weeks of April, Haughton reached behind Jacob to Bell, Gibson publicly called for a settlement, and Coggins organized people around the mayor's call. The three-pronged attack was overwhelming. Resistance to a settlement collapsed. Community leaders who had spoken so passionately on April 6 and 7 saw the tide turning against them, and began to urge Jacob to settle.[158]

Elayne Brodie thought the conflict had gone too far. She told Carole Graves that they were both Black women with power, and " 'we don't need this.' " Baraka too pulled back from the brink. "We shouldn't even be fighting with the Italians," he said on April 9. "We're as stupid as they are. The business community takes out $3 billion a year from Newark, and we're fighting over crumbs." He contacted Dasher and helped get Graves out of jail. Dasher thought Baraka was motivated by a desire to avoid civil war, "for his own safety and the safety of his people."[159]

But Imperiale was angry that the strike was going to end. At First Avenue School, he criticized Graves and Dasher publicly for the first time, accusing them of "selling yourselves out to a bum," meaning Baraka. Imperiale objected to compromise, preferring all-out war. "It is time to declare war against Mayor Gibson." At a large and emotional meeting at East Side High, he called Gibson an "idiot"; if the mayor wouldn't act, people should take over his office. Cervase, however, urged the crowd to support the mayor.[160] Imperiale contributed to peace by scaring people into their senses. He was left out of the peace process and at the end appeared to feel his own irrelevance.

Jacob also felt isolated. "I got no backing from anybody in this raggedy city of mine." Before the Board voted on April 18, Jacob signed off on the contract language. He had lost, because the popular movement for peace had transformed the climate in which he was operating. Coggins brought people who supported the mayor's position to the April 18 Board meeting. Ladies came from church in their Sunday best and reacted with disdain when anyone shouted; there were no real disturbances. Bell voted yes, as did Zambrana. By six to three, the Board ended the strike. In a remarkable admission, Jacob later acknowledged that popular pressure was decisive on April 18. "The community came down full force"; the majority on the Board "couldn't stand the pressure."[161]

Gibson, Coggins, and Bell defeated Jacob by refuting his claim to speak for the Black community. Haughton, the white mediator, was able to draw on the wisdom of Coggins and Bell, who felt the conflicting pulls of race and class. But Haughton simplified the strike, in order to end it. He fooled Jacob into thinking he was sympathetic. Haughton's previous ties were with labor. To the extent that he shifted the focus away from race, pouring the complex conflict "into a labor-dispute mold," he favored NTU. Haughton kept people from meeting face to face and fostered no dialogue on race. When the strike was over, they understood each other as little as when it began.

There was peace in the city, but no peace in the schools. As the end drew near, Garrett and fifty other PTA leaders warned teachers they would be allowed back only "after intensive screening and interviewing by the black community." Jacob said at the April 18 Board meeting: "I speak to you this afternoon not as a man who has lost a war but as a man who has suffered a temporary setback."[162] Unable to stop the peace movement, Jacob and Garrett kept fighting, school by school.

"It was the most bitter and savage teacher strike ever seen in the history of this country," said a subdued victory statement of the Newark Teachers Union. The Union won the war but was unable to protect its returning veterans. Jacob turned away thirty teachers at South Eighth Street, including Clara Dasher; a group of parents watched approvingly. The few teachers who had been on strike at Bergen Street and Robert Treat were not allowed back by parents. At Maple Avenue School, thirty returning teachers had to take refuge in a classroom. The president of the Maple Avenue PTA explained, "We don't want criminals teaching our children." At South Tenth Street, parents waited for teachers with baseball bats. Jacob joined them as they turned away four or five white teachers. A young Black teacher at South Tenth who had worked during the strike defended the right of colleagues to return. She argued with parents. "I was appalled. I thought the strike was over, but they said I was taking sides." The parents ordered her out, too.[163]

Bob Hirschfeld was turned away from Quitman Street School by a Black community group and transferred to a school where there was not enough for him to do. After ten years in teaching, he began to think that "perhaps my future was marked in Newark. I was taking graduate courses at the time, working on a master's, and I just wondered where I was going to go in Newark, if this was going to hold me back, just the fact that I had been an activist in the Union." At the end of the school year he left Newark, and left teaching. He has never taught again.[164]

Carol Karman was the only one on strike at Clinton Avenue. When she came back after the strike, she says, "I don't remember how much Valium I took, to just get my nerve to walk up there. And this lady came up to me, with her fingernail this long, and pointed it this close to my eye, and said get out of here." Karman was "evicted" from her building and eventually transferred to Wilson Avenue in the East Ward. She is still teaching in Newark.[165]

White parents turned away teachers too. At First Avenue and at Alexander Street in the Vailsburg section of the West Ward, parents prevented teachers who had worked during the strike from entering. A Black teacher, reassigned during the strike, attempted to return to First Avenue, saw angry white mothers outside, and thought better of it. True to its principles, the Union defended the right of every teacher—from South Eighth Street or First Avenue, "who was on strike or who was not on strike"—to return to her or his school.[166]

The Board reassigned teachers who were turned away from predominantly Black schools. Ninety former strikers from seven schools refused to accept reassignment. They protested outside Jacob's office. "If it comes to transferring the teachers," he said, "they will have to remember that we still have management prerogatives, such as determining where our employees should work." The Union, which read the contract differently, urged them not to accept transfer. But it could not force the issue, because it could not strike again. More than half of the ninety were involuntarily transferred by the Board in May.[167]

The wounds inflicted by teachers on other teachers went deeper and lasted longer than the wounds inflicted by parents. Some nonstriking teachers were able to return to First Avenue, says Elena Scambio, but "there was tremendous hostility" toward them from other teachers. "There was real tension, and a split staff. And the principal was not respected, and did nothing, and could not do anything, to pull the staff together." At some schools, the split between faculty members lasted ten or fifteen years. It manifested itself in things like being unable to get people to come to someone's retirement lunch. And it manifested itself in the silences between people.[168]

The strikers were angry when they came back to Barringer, says Beth

Blackmon. "They felt as if they made tremendous sacrifices in eleven and a half weeks; they never recouped what they lost." One teacher would say to another, " 'You never supported it to begin with.' Or 'You chickened out.' And it's horrible, horrible. People didn't talk for years. For years they never spoke." The rift between strikers and nonstrikers did not heal. "In fact, sometimes the rancor will surface even now." Because most Black teachers crossed the picket line in 1971, this terrible silence between teachers has sometimes been a silence between races. "Even today, in the third-floor teachers room at Barringer High School, very few Black teachers go in there; most of them go to other teacher rooms."[169]

Striking teachers were angry at teachers who crossed the picket line at West Kinney Junior High. "This was the first really big split between a lot of Blacks and a lot of whites," says Avant Lowther. "The aftermath of that strike is what really began to tear this school apart." There too the rancor lasted for years. It took Lowther himself at least five years to regain his standing in the Union. "I was on the outs because I had come in." As part of making amends he went through a sort of reeducation about unionism. Then the Union sent him and other Black teachers—"I don't know if you would call us emissaries"—into the Black community to speak at churches and other gathering places. "I went back to my church and I explained to them what the Union was about. . . . So that was part of the healing process."[170]

Sometimes friends created their own healing process. At Peshine Avenue, Zenobia Capel and Ronald Denner were friends. But he went on strike, and she didn't. When he brought his class down for physical education after the strike, he didn't speak to her. He just turned around and walked away. She called him back.

"Mr. Denner, may I speak to you a minute please?" And he came back, and I sent the class inside, and I said to him that this was the United States, and that each person was supposed to be able to make a decision for themselves, and he made his decision, and I made my decision. That he had over the weekend to get himself together. This was Thursday, and the children had gym every other day. So when he brought his class back on Monday, either he was going to say good morning to me, or he would never speak to me again. . . . When he brought his kids down on Monday, he was his old jolly self again, and he said "Good morning Mrs. Capel," and I said "Good morning Mr. Denner," and we remained friends until I left, and even after.[171]

Union leaders carried a grudge. At the end of 1971, NTU gave only $5 as its annual contribution to the national NAACP. "Our contribution is limited for two reasons," wrote Cascella. "First, the courts of the State of New Jersey have fined us $270,000 and brought us to a near bankrupt condition. Second, the officers and members of the Newark Teachers Union object to the actions and statements of the N.A.A.C.P. Education Chairman of your Newark branch, one Elaine Brody." Elayne Brodie, like Baraka and Garrett, had spoken against the strikers. Cascella, as acting president of the Union with Graves back in jail, spoke for the strikers against the Black activists. We are still hurting, he seemed to be saying, still angry.[172]

As he wrote, 178 rank-and-file teachers were preparing to join Graves and her fellow officers in jail.

Chapter 6

Teachers in Jail

Teachers postponed jail, hoping to avoid it. By the time they went to jail, the original meaning of the 1970 strike and the teachers' arrests had begun to fade. For many men, prison became an individual challenge, an experience to survive. But many women became close in prison; drawing on each other's strength, they re-created in jail the meaning of their strike.

To Go or Not to Go

Should the teachers appeal the sentences, or just go to jail? Arguments about appealing exacerbated the split in NTU and heightened the tension between NTU and national AFT.

The Essex County Sheriff's Department arrested 188 Newark teachers during the 1970 strike and charged them with contempt of court for violating the injunction against striking. That many teachers had never before been jailed in the United States. The arrested teachers imagined their sentences would be suspended after the strike, as sentences were suspended after the NTU strike of 1965 and the Association strike of 1966. But Judge Nelson Mintz, who helped on the 1965 and 1966 cases, argued that the 1970 strike proved that previous restraint had been ineffective. This time there would be no leniency.[1]

Mintz and two colleagues tried teachers in batches during March 1970. They convicted 185 of the 188 teachers, and two nonteachers. Teachers made statements at the sentencing about the wrongs of the school system and the right of public employees to strike, but Mintz was not impressed. He said there was no excuse for teachers to strike, regardless of their grievances. They had known about the injunction and willfully violated it. Most rank-and-file teachers received ten-day sentences. Most NTU officers received either thirty days or three months.[2]

Dave Selden, the AFT president, was one of the two nonteachers sentenced. Arrested in February 1970, he chose to go directly to jail, posting bail only when the strike was settled. Sentenced to sixty days in March, he didn't appeal, returning to jail to finish his time. Selden wanted to make a point: "The United States is the only democratic country which prohibits strikes by public employees." Going to jail was his way to demonstrate the unfairness of the law. He hoped the NTU officers would follow him to jail rather than appeal. A failed appeal could solidify the prohibition against strikes. New Jersey law neither expressly prohibited nor permitted strikes by public employees, leaving it to the courts. Better to keep a certain ambiguity in the law and to make political capital out of teachers in jail. Selden predicted the officers of NTU would soon join him in jail.[3]

NTU officers were advised by their lawyers not to appeal. National AFT warned them that it would not pay for an appeal to the Supreme Court, which would cost one hundred thousand dollars. "Go to jail now," AFT urged them, according to Andy Thorburn. "You're probably going to go anyway, so why waste one hundred thousand dollars? But if you do go two years later, it ain't going to do crap for anybody." Given the legal advice, Selden's example, and AFT's warning, NTU officers began to pick a date and make arrangements with their families.[4]

Then, during the last week in March, Graves changed her mind. She didn't want to go to jail and knew many teachers didn't want to go. She hoped an appeal to the Supreme Court would help establish the rights of teachers everywhere. She knew she was going against the strategy of AFT, but counted on its financial support. "That's the beginning of the break with AFT," says Thorburn.[5]

NTU needed support because its members' dues were all going to pay its enormous fines from the 1971 strike. AFT gave NTU fifty thousand dollars for the appeal. In April 1971, the Appellate Division of the Superior Court of New Jersey rejected the appeal. NTU appealed to the state supreme court, which refused to hear the case, and, separately, to the United States Supreme Court. On October 15, 1971, Graves and several others went to Washington to ask Selden and AFT Secretary-Treasurer Bob Porter for more money. Selden and Porter said no. The relationship between NTU and AFT turned ugly, in a public way.[6]

Selden and Porter came to Newark and told the convicted teachers why they did not want to back the appeal to the United States Supreme Court. Teachers felt betrayed. One protested, "[T]he AFT leadership is out of touch with the rank and file of the Newark Teachers Union." Back in Washington, Selden wrote to NTU members, describing the attitude of Graves and others who came to Washington as "uncooperative, even truculent." He listed the aid provided by the national to the local: $88,000 for legal expenses, $65,000 to replace the dues that the court impounded after both strikes, other grants and loans. "Our assistance has rarely been acknowledged. Instead, we have been constantly subjected to criticism and abuse for not doing more."[7]

Graves was outraged that Selden wrote directly to NTU members. The real issue, she shot back, was whether the AFT was going to keep its promises. "The AFT had promised us during both strikes to back us 'all the way'—and 'all the way,' to the NTU teachers means their day in Court, up to and including the highest court in the land." She went further, accusing Selden of plotting to overthrow her. "You have never recognized me as the effective head of the N.T.U. . . . You have treated the NTU like a 'banana republic.' You have honeycombed it with your agents coordinated by John Schmid. . . . I submit to you, Mr. President, that the root cause of the acrimony lies in the fact that I refused to assume the role of a figure-head president."[8]

Graves's relationship with the AFT leadership had never been easy. From the beginning of her presidency, she backed the Black Caucus in AFT against Selden and Shanker. At the 1970 AFT convention, she joined an unsuccessful effort to overthrow Selden. National AFT leaders initially opposed a strike in Newark in 1971 because they feared more fines and jailings; when the strike went on and on, Graves worried that they would settle it over her head. On the eve of Selden's visit to Newark in October, she wrote an AFT vice president in Denver about her "increasing difficulties with A.F.T.," which was using its control of money "to make the N.T.U. 'fall in line.' " She asked to "meet as soon as possible in order to make preliminary plans for the convention." She was plotting to overthrow Selden.[9]

In her mind, her enemies within NTU and her enemies in AFT were linked in a single conspiracy. She knew that members of the defeated NTU faction enjoyed better relations with AFT staff than she did, and she sensed, correctly, that some AFT staff did not respect her abilities. John Schmid, a former NTU leader and current AFT representative, was the link between her enemies. She believed that both sets of enemies had wanted her to be a figurehead, and that once she took effective control of the local in 1970, they began working together to topple her. Her belief in a continuing conspiracy of internal and external enemies did not bode well for democracy in the Union, because she tended to see anyone who disagreed with her as an agent of the AFT. Her rift with national AFT, intensified by the conflict over the appeals, would last for many years.[10]

In the fall, the United States Supreme Court refused to hear the appeal. Now there was nothing to do but make arrangements for jail. But Graves would not give up. Desperately, she wrote to Charles Marciante, "[T]he only recourse at this point would be through political channels." Not even the political clout of organized labor could save the teachers from jail. At the end of November 1971, the officers began to serve their long sentences. In the second half of December, the rank and file joined them in jail.[11]

The appeals proved costly in three ways. They wasted a lot of money. The conflict over the money, in turn, hurt the relationship between the local and the national. And the length of the appeal process deprived the strategy of getting arrested of much of its original point.

Teachers went to jail twenty-two months after their "crime" was committed. When six teachers—including Andy Thorburn, Esther Tumin, and Bob Hirschfeld—went to jail, they were no longer teaching in Newark. Some teachers crossed the picket line in 1971 before going to jail for picketing in 1970. Phyllis Salowe, Dave Lieberfarb, and other idealistic young teachers went to jail not on the emotional high of 1970, when they knew right was on their side, but after the unsettling experience of 1971, when parents of the students they wanted to help were on the other side. The long delay robbed jail of much of the political or personal meaning it might once have had.[12]

For Thorburn, going to jail was a strange experience, because he was no longer a teacher. But even for those still teaching in Newark, it was disorienting. Teachers were "crestfallen and pretty much astonished," says Jim Lowenstein. "The idea of going to jail was still pretty shocking." Jim Lerman, an NTU officer with a three-month sentence, "never thought we were going to go to jail." His father, a prominent doctor, worried that money spent on Jim's Ivy League education would be wasted, because now he would have a criminal record. Earlier, when Lerman faced jail for refusing to fight in Vietnam, his father hired a lawyer who won him conscientious objector status. But his father could not help him now.[13]

Betty Rufalo had already served her sentence. In late March 1970, when other officers changed their minds about jail, Rufalo went ahead. "I thought that if I went, it would help dramatize our cause." Also, she'd already talked to her children about being gone for three months and didn't want to do it again. Thorburn argued for publicizing Rufalo's time in jail: attractive mother of three goes to jail, due to the archaic law that punishes teachers for striking. But Graves thought that Rufalo, a leading member of the group controlling the Union's executive board—was grandstanding, by going to jail after Graves decided not to. In an early test of Graves's power, during the weeks in which the 1970 coup was being prepared, most convicted teachers supported Graves.[14]

Rufalo went to jail alone. The Essex County penitentiary in North Caldwell was ten miles from Newark. Outside, it seemed old and depressing. Inside, Rufalo was told to strip and given a worn striped shift. Then she was taken into the heart of the jail. "We go through one door and it's locked behind us. Through another door . . . locked. Then I see a row of cells. Iron bars." She felt how alone she was. "It's an eight-by-four cell. . . . No light except from the cellblock tier. It's horrible. I sit down on the cot and think: This is it; here I am. I'm already sorry."[15]

Rufalo went on strike with other teachers, was arrested and convicted with others, but went to prison by herself. "I didn't think I'd be going alone." For days, she was in shock. She didn't eat. She had expected to write letters and read, but couldn't concentrate. In her cell, she cried and told herself, "I'm not going to make it; I'm just not going to make it." She developed diarrhea and became depressed. At the end of a week, her husband visited and was pained to see how pale and forlorn she looked, with sunken eyes. After two weeks, unable to remember why getting arrested once made sense to her, she wrote in her journal, "I've made up my mind. I'm quitting all causes." After three weeks: "I am slowly fading away physically and mentally."[16]

Rufalo was thirty-seven. She had grown up in Newark and had been teaching there since she was twenty-one. When she was a new teacher, the student body at her elementary school was changing from white to Black. Children were behind grade level in reading, if they could read at all. There were no books or supplies. She had forty-two children in one class. "Discipline problems were fantastic and there was nowhere to turn for help." She turned to the Union, joining in 1956 and becoming a leader in the campaign for collective bargaining. When the Union beat the Association in the election, "We had power!" But in jail she was powerless. She was taking orders from people who called her by her first name, whom she respectfully called Mrs. "I became a little sheep, a mouse. . . . Jail is designed to humiliate you, strip you of dignity, and it works."[17]

The other inmates were Black. Most were young women from Newark, school dropouts, arrested for drugs or prostitution. "I was scared of them at first." At recreation time, they played rock-and-roll records and danced with each other. She watched. Gradually she came to appreciate how "everybody shared." One woman got money from her man and bought cigarettes, candy, and ice cream from the prison store for the others. "I began to understand about homosexuality in prison. It's just two girls taking care of each other. . . . Once I sat down on a bench and a girl's leg touched mine. And you know what?

I liked it. A human body touching me, warm and nice. If I'd been outside, I'd have moved away. But in there, I needed that contact."[18]

Life outside was far away. If a prisoner got a letter saying her child was in the hospital, she wouldn't cry. Rufalo explained that "in order to survive you've got to find a life and friends within the framework of jail." Rufalo herself cried when she got letters and felt awful when her husband left after a visit. She did not complete the transition to prison life. Her lawyer, citing her deteriorating health and the illness of two of her children, gained her release after thirty-two days. "If I were going to be in jail for any length of time, I would do what most of the other girls did—divorce myself from life outside."[19]

Rufalo was the first woman teacher in the nation to go to jail for striking.[20] Her experience was horrible, because she went alone, without the support that would later sustain women who went to Caldwell together. But Rufalo's jail experience anticipated that of many teachers. They too were surprised how hard it was to be locked up. They could not eat the food. They suffered from the same learned helplessness. They were unprepared for a world of hierarchy, where they were at the bottom, accorded no dignity. And they were afraid of, and drawn to, the other inmates, the Black students from Newark who hadn't graduated and had no future.

Carole Graves also went to jail alone. During the 1971 strike, when she was charged with defying the injunction, again she announced she would not go quietly. On Thursday, February 4, 1971, the sheriff went to arrest Graves and two NTU vice presidents at the motel where negotiations took place. They were gone. They had fled Newark, and New Jersey. The Union and the sheriff searched for Graves. There were reports on Friday that the sheriff was going to put out a thirteen-state alarm.[21]

"I ran away with her," says Carol Karman. "The whole thing was nuts. We went to Manhattan, and we went to a hotel. Like Angela Davis. It's ridiculous. You're going to hide out, so you go to a hotel in midtown?" Graves felt like a political fugitive in a movie. "That was just a crazy time," she says, "the ride through the tunnel, and Carol Karman and . . . the getaway car. It was like a movie." In New York, she turned to Al Shanker. "He was Big Al, he was the leader." Graves and Karman, with the two vice presidents, went to Shanker's office on Friday. Shanker didn't want them there—"because we were like fugitives"—and convinced them to turn themselves in. They surrendered to the sheriff in Newark, shortly after midnight. Exhausted, Graves told a reporter: "I felt like many of the country's political fugitives, except I am a school-teacher."[22]

She spent a total of forty-one days in the jail in Caldwell during the 1971 strike. In the tradition of political prisoners, she staged a hunger strike, taking only liquids and vitamin pills for at least a week. A judge released her several times, hoping she could call off the strike; when it continued, he ordered her back. Like Rufalo, Graves drew some comfort from other inmates. "Not one inmate believes that teachers should be imprisoned for striking," she wrote from jail. Freed when the peace process gained momentum, she was stoical about her experience. "It's jail. . . . It's not the Hilton."[23]

She returned to jail six months later, after the appeals of the 1970 convictions failed. At the end of November, she entered the courthouse dressed in black, was given flowers by a supporter, and began to cry quietly. Six other officers and one rank-and-file teacher also went to Caldwell that day. But all were men. Like Rufalo, who had gone to jail twenty months earlier, Graves began her three months in the women's wing alone. "I had wished that at least one other woman would have been with us," she wrote in her prison diary.[24]

"Really *hate* to go back to that place," she noted. "I got that sinking feeling just looking at the grim buildings." Her two striped seersucker dresses were "just like I remember—early refugee." During her previous stay, there had been the constant possibility she would be released. This was going to be different. "I can see that my time is going to be 'hard' this time around."[25]

Her response to jail was more political this time. She had visited Angela Davis in jail in California over the summer. Before going to Caldwell, she had written to Essex County Freeholder Wynona Lipman and Warden John Rush, asking to discuss prison reform. Now Rush and Lipman came by and said she could teach. Graves planned to teach prisoners about their rights. "I saw another mission coming. That helped me a lot to endure." At prayer meeting, most inmates would sob convulsively, from shame. Graves was dry-eyed. "I could not get emotional because I know what put me in prison. . . . When I begin teaching I shall start with the nature of the prison system in this country."[26]

Her first day of teaching "went beautifully." She read from Bayard Rustin's selected writings, and the women responded. But from the beginning, her aims and the warden's were in conflict. "I do not think that I will be allowed academic freedom because when I mentioned teaching Civics & the rights of individuals inside & outside prison the warden was visibly disturbed." He wanted her to help prisoners get their high school equivalency degrees. That was fine with Graves. But she also wanted inmates to get a sense of their rights and of the forces that put them in prison. She wanted them to reclaim their self-respect, stop cursing all the time, and organize. This proved too ambitious. Five weeks after she began teaching, Graves gave up. "I've decided that I will not attempt to teach formal classes any longer because of the tension and the obvious attempts to thwart the entire program."[27]

She gave up organizing too, concluding bitterly, "There is no such thing as solidarity here." There was a fight between an inmate who supported her efforts at prison reform and one who opposed her. Most inmates turned against her. "You can't liberate a people who are not ready to be liberated. . . . Although they have the intelligence, they lack values, commitment & determination— they are sheep." The prison authorities successfully isolated her, locking her in her cell and threatening her with loss of time off for good behavior. "I was so frustrated & disgusted that I didn't know what to do. I even tried to cry but I couldn't." She would have felt rage, if she had allowed herself to feel. "I just went into that mode of detaching myself." Graves rolled herself into a fist, beating on the prison before it beat her down. She tried to be a leader inside as she was outside; she fought for self-respect and dignity, "exactly the same battle that I had fought against the Newark Board of Education." By February, she was defeated and depressed.[28]

She was infuriated that inmates to whom she'd become close were beaten down or bribed, that she herself was isolated and threatened. "I have become so cynical and even hardened & bitter by this whole experience." Prison, she concluded, did not rehabilitate. Rather, it was an integral part of the crime system. "Girls get high from pills. I have played numbers. The officers themselves bring in lottery tickets & sell them and they also play numbers given them by the lottery inmates. Arrangements are made before certain inmates leave here to sell stolen goods to certain officers."[29]

Rank-and-file teachers joined Graves in jail in the last two weeks of December. She had become used to acting alone. She called a hunger strike, without consulting other teachers. "I was furious," says Carol Karman. "I said, 'Carole, this is ridiculous. If you're going to have a hunger strike, at least tell people like one meal in advance, so they can stock up on bread.' " Karman thought Graves was changing, developing an inflated view of her role.[30]

Graves had mixed feelings about the presence of the teachers. Afraid of losing detachment, she fought against the temptation of taking pleasure in their company. "It's awful to say this, but I really wish that the other teachers didn't have to do the 8 days, because it was not until their arrival, that my mind concentrated so much on time counted by days. I had got into the habit of looking back on weeks." She began to feel again. "When I saw the others I almost felt 'Happy to be here.' I really had to snap back and think of the purpose of jail & that is to break the individuals spirit thru brainwashing." She became angry at the teachers right before they left. "Well thank god this is the last day for all of them." Yet the next morning, when they left, "I tried not to show any emotion but what the hell, I'm no machine & it's just unnatural to continuously keep a stiff upper lip."[31]

With the teachers, Graves asserted leadership yet kept somewhat aloof. "She wasn't afraid while we were there," says Esther Tumin, "but when she was there alone she was very afraid, because she didn't know what they might plant on her or what they might accuse her of." Refusing to give in to helplessness and fear, Graves became tougher in prison, more self-reliant and mistrustful. She learned (in Rufalo's phrase) "to find a life and friends within the framework of jail." According to Phyllis Salowe, "She had become almost like a regular prisoner person. She was friendly with the prison population." She was there before the teachers and would be there when they left. "And had a strange attitude toward us. Like ' . . . you're only here for two weeks; you come and go.' "[32]

Graves was primarily responsible for the decision to appeal the 1970 convictions all the way. As a result of that decision, Rufalo went to jail alone, and so did she. There is no way to know who lost more. Rufalo couldn't eat the food; Graves wouldn't eat, as a matter of principle. Rufalo was overwhelmed by the experience. "Jail is designed to . . . strip you of dignity, and it works." Graves fought for dignity and self-respect. She regarded Rufalo's story—in *Redbook*, before Graves went to jail—as "whimpering," which "trivialized" the teachers' struggle and "made it soapish."[33] Seen as a troublemaker, she ended her time alone, locked in her cell.

Graves attacked the prison system in the same way she attacked the Board of Education. But she didn't defeat the Board alone, and she couldn't make a dent in the prison. There was no prison rebellion, except when other teachers were there, to fight alongside her.

The Women in Jail

The Essex County Corrections Center at Caldwell housed men and women guilty of misdemeanors. Many returned over and over. Most sentences were not for days, like the teachers' sentences, but for months. Normally there were 450 to 700 men prisoners and 30 women. The women's wing was too small to accommodate the women teachers, so the teachers—men as well as women—were divided into two shifts. The first shift of 29 women teachers arrived on December 15.[34]

Phyllis Salowe's grandfather drove her to the courthouse in Newark, where teachers would be taken as a group to Caldwell. "That was a big deal for him, to drive his granddaughter to jail." No longer opposed to her activism, Salowe's parents were proud of what she had done, "but they were absolutely appalled that I was going to jail." Salowe herself was not worried. "I thought it was going to be like a hotel," not a Hilton, "but I figured I would be in a Day's Inn for a while."[35] Her parents, in their hysteria, were more in touch with reality.

The Union told teachers what to bring. Salowe followed instructions about what to bring to jail, as she followed instructions about what to bring to the picket line in 1970. When she entered the prison, guards went through her stuff. She was surprised on the picket line when the policeman yanked her earring through her skin; she was surprised in jail when the matron termed her hairbrush "contraband" and took it from her. "I couldn't get anybody to tell me why it was contraband. I started to object about it. And whatever happened around my objection, I remember a sense of: these are not people you argue with. This is not having a fight with your principal, or your father or your mother. These guys had guns. This was not going to be a joke."[36]

Salowe planned to read a lot, but it was too noisy; the radio and phonograph blared, not soul or Motown, "just loud brassy music." She planned to lose weight, but the food was too starchy. All the drinks were too sweet, including something that seemed like iced tea. In the big room where teachers and other inmates went when released from their individual cells, the television was always on. "There was nothing to do." Salowe, who never played cards, learned to play. She spent most of her time with teachers, but sometimes talked with other inmates. They were in prison for drugs, prostitution, running numbers, robbery. In addition to the shock of the noise, and of the loss of the freedom to argue, she experienced culture shock. "I remember talking to a person who was telling me how she used to shoplift steaks down her pants in the supermarket on Bergen Street, near where I lived. She was giving me helpful hints."[37]

Salowe's system went into shock. "I couldn't go to the bathroom, I couldn't urinate. . . . I didn't urinate six days or something, out of being there, which was out of panic. It shut down." She developed a major urinary tract infection and had to be hospitalized for almost two weeks after she left jail. Newark teachers remember what was important to them about jail. Only when I asked about the protests in jail did Salowe remember; then she recalled teacher actions in some detail. But when asked initially about jail, she answered, very quietly, "It was awful." What she remembers, without prompting, are the shocks to her system that caused it to shut down.[38]

Carol Karman remembers the noise and the heat. "They kept the heat at about 90 degrees. And we were on the second tier, and heat rises, so it was really hot up there. And also they kept the rock and roll blaring, from 7 AM until lights out. Those were the two things. What was striking about it was you couldn't think." Another teacher decided that the excessive heat, day and night, was "deliberate, in order to put us into a kind of stupor, out of which we will not make much of a noise." Karman made less noise in prison than she did outside. Remembering how Malcolm X and others read a lot in jail, she brought books with her, but it was too hot and noisy. "I can't imagine how anyone could read in Caldwell. It wasn't made for reading." She was not afraid anyone was going to beat her up. But the environment was brutal in another sense. "It almost felt like physical punishment."[39]

Like Salowe and Karman, Alice Saltman was in the group of teachers who went to jail on December 15. But her experience was different. Somehow she found the space to observe, to think, to keep her balance. She was an artist. With time on her hands, she embroidered a pillow with "Essex County Penitentiary" and the date. It was the only time in her life she embroidered, except for the time she spent waiting at her gynecologist's office. She also made a beautiful and stark sketch of her cell, showing the toilet (there was no privacy) and the little cot. She never regretted jail. "It was a very interesting experience."[40]

Saltman observed the effect of the prison routine. By rule, prisoners were supposed to wait when going from one room to another; even if the door was not locked, someone had to open it for them. After a few days, teachers "stopped automatically when they came to a door." This was one of the "astounding things" she learned in jail about people—"how fast you can make them conform." Saltman never conformed, never allowed others to shape the meaning of her experience. At her sentencing, the judge "gave a little lecture on morality. You could throw up. I wrote him a letter [laughs] and I told him everything I thought." In prison, she joined the fight to improve conditions. "We got a lot of things changed in there." On the last day, she was still judging the judges, still questioning authority. "We were given a tin cup when we came in. . . . When we left, they searched our bodies. I said, What did they think we were going to take, that fucking tin cup?"[41]

Physically, Saltman had a harder time in prison than Rufalo, Salowe, or Karman, because she was much older. The heat and noise hurt her, as they hurt everyone. The presweetened drinks—cocoa and coffee, as well as tea—hurt her more, because she was hypoglycemic. What hurt her most was that the authorities deprived her of medication. She had recently undergone major stomach surgery for an ulcer. Her medication was not a matter of life or death, "[b]ut still, not to let medication through, I thought that was pretty ridiculous." Even where her health was at stake, Saltman kept her sense of the absurdity of injustice. She drew strength from her history of activism, stretching back to her mother, who had also gone to jail, and forward to her children. After her husband visited, he wrote, "I know now you were concealing your feeling sick, your stomach or hypoglycemic attack. Brave girl!" She knew her children were proud of her too. "My kids thought I was terrific. . . . They've all enjoyed the stories."[42]

Saltman was arrested with her best friend, Hannah Litzky, and they went to jail together. Like Saltman, Litzky had a personal history of teacher activism reaching back to the 1930s, and a family history of political egalitarianism reaching back to the early years of the twentieth century. Like Saltman, Litzky observed the prison environment, as a way of keeping balance. Saltman, the art teacher, sketched her cell; Litzky, the English teacher, wrote in a diary. "Prison *very hot*," she wrote on the first day. At supper, she saw Carole Graves. Back in her cell, she tried to read. "Blasting music makes reading impossible." Refusing to give up, she put her finger in her ear and read until lights went out.[43]

Her cot was narrow and hard. The heat was intense, lights from the corridor shone in, and she could hear other women snoring. "A miserable night!" In the morning, she found that her medication was not there. The head matron, "Miss Ott.—superb charac.—perfectly cast," promised the medication would be brought by evening. Lunch was "abundant slop." For exercise, she did yoga. Although the weather was warm for December, the prisoners were not allowed out. "Beautiful day—but no one ever goes out!"[44] Litzky did not realize it, but even as she was recording the lack of medication and of outdoor exercise, she was preparing her response.

When Saltman, Litzky, and a teacher with diabetes arrived in prison, they were told that the medication they had mailed in advance was in the pharmacy on the men's side (there was no pharmacy on the woman's side) and that the pharmacy was closed. On the second day, they became impatient. "All day clamored for medication," noted Litzky. Saltman, her best friend, was feeling bad, and she was angry on her own behalf too. "Had a tantrum after supper & threatened not to return to my cell unless med. was given." Other teachers began to mutter. Then Carole Graves stepped forward, and turned Litzky's individual threat into a collective action. "Carole Graves told matron *all* of us would stay out unless med. delivered to Alice, ill after supper." Litzky and Graves led the first collective revolt together, and won the first victory. "Med. delivered by special messenger about 8 pm."[45]

Looking back at what she did, Litzky could not explain it. "I don't know where I had the guts to do that. I have the feeling that I'd been reading about some—maybe the Attica prison riot. Or maybe some defiance in some jail. I don't know where my defiance came from." The Attica uprising, which was brutally suppressed, took place about three months before the teachers went to jail. But the rebellion in the women's wing in Caldwell, although inspired by prison rebellions, grew directly out of the dynamics of teacher activism. Litzky's defiance came from decades of struggle in Newark. "Like many schools, this place, with its antiquated building, is trapped in a rigid, out-dated routine," she wrote from jail.[46] Graves's language—"all of us would stay out"— evoked a teacher strike more than a prison rebellion. The focus on personal connection and on helping each other ("unless med. delivered to Alice") was especially characteristic of the activist style of women teachers.

In jail for striking in 1970, after the vicious 1971 strike, women teachers re-created the original meaning of their Union activity. In 1970, most striking teachers wanted to help their students as well as themselves. In jail, they tried to help the other prisoners. The rebellion that Litzky sparked on the second day was about medication, an issue that affected teachers more than other inmates, who were mostly very young. But successes, even little successes, encourage people to hope and organize. As they gained confidence, the teachers reached out and connected with other inmates, who were there when they arrived and would be there when they left. On the third day, during a recreational hour in the big room, teachers met with other prisoners and together drew up a list of demands. Then Jeanette Lappé told the matron that they wanted to see the warden.[47]

Lappé, like Litzky and Saltman, was a regular in the old third-floor teachers room at Weequahic, where women wove their personal, professional, and political lives together. It was she who had flunked Seymour Spiegel for not doing the work, then overrode his despair and made him go to college. Lappé died in 1986, but shortly after leaving jail, she recorded her memories in response to questions submitted by a niece for a school project. Like Saltman's drawing and Litzky's and Graves's diaries, Lappé's tape is important evidence of the way some women brought the same talent, principles, and passion to jail that they brought to teaching and striking.

When Lappé requested a meeting with the warden, the matron didn't know what to do. "She was startled and said, 'He's busy.' We said, 'We will wait here until he comes.'" It was one thing to handle a single defiant inmate like Graves; it was another thing to face a group. "Again, when she said that he couldn't come, we said, 'We will not leave the recreation floor until he does come.' We were in effect staging a sit-in." Put in a new situation, the matron contacted Warden Rush, who came to the women's wing with his bodyguard. "He said 'All right, let's sit down and talk.' We said, 'How can we sit down, there are no chairs for us to sit on . . . ?' He ordered the guard to bring us chairs. This was the first time that everybody had a chair on which to sit."[48]

In classic organizing style, the teachers asked a leader among the other prisoners to read the demands. As she read, the warden agreed to better medical attention, writing materials and a program of arts and crafts, privacy when undressing at admittance, better visiting arrangements. "To each [demand] he made some response of a positive sort, because he saw that we were well organized and well unified."[49] Possibly he too had been reading about prison rebellions.

After the demands, Lappé, in her polite way—she seems always to have been civil—continued the offensive. "I raised my hand and said, 'Why can't we go outside?' He looked startled." Warden Rush evidently thought he'd been conciliatory enough. To end the discussion, he stated that women prisoners did not go outside. "I said, 'Why not?' " The discussion became an argument, with the warden getting the worst of it. Like most long-standing policies in the women's wing of the prison, the policy of not going outside in winter could not be rationally defended. It depended on women just going along. But the prison authorities hadn't reckoned on the teachers. "Finally he said, 'You can go out.' This was a remarkable victory. For the next three days, all of us went out, every afternoon. We played volleyball, or we sat around, or we talked. The guards were furious with us, because we were giving them extra work to do, but we had a marvelous time."[50]

Just as they reached out across the color line to parents in 1970, so mostly white teachers reached out to prisoners who were almost all Black. These personal contacts made the coordinated actions possible. On the second evening, Litzky heard a "long exchange of jokes, in a competition between teachers and kids. Hilarious!" On the third day: "Indiv. persons emerging." She mentioned Marie, middle-aged, "who invited me to eat w/her first night"; Mary, serving ten months for running numbers, whose mother worked at Beth Israel Hospital; and Ruth, white and alcoholic, whose husband was also in jail. A new relationship was developing, in which teachers and other inmates learned from one another. Teachers went to listen to four young inmates on a panel about drug addiction. Some prisoners began to crochet, and teachers "pounced on this as an opportunity to help them learn." Meals gave teachers some of their best opportunities, according to Lappé. "At dinner time, breakfast time, lunch time, we always made it our business to sit with some of the regular inmates, and we learned a great deal from them."[51]

On the fifth day, the women came together to put on a talent show. It was Lappé's idea. To find those who had talent, "We canvassed all the inmates, both the old and the new ones." The old and the new: a new way of talking about the inmates and the teachers, reflecting a new experience. Just before the evening began, the authorities raised objections, but "after some fussing and some veiled kind of threats of a sit-in or a sit-down, we finally had our talent show." Lappé's language—sit-in or sit-down—linked the civil rights struggles of the sixties to the labor struggles of the thirties. Drawing on their history of activism, the teachers won the right to have the show. The room was decorated with bits of paper found in corners of the jail. A pregnant prisoner presided. The old inmates sang songs, the new inmates put on skits, and everyone sang Christmas carols.[52]

The relationship between old and new inmates was never easy. Some prisoners resented the teachers. "Evidently the inmates had been required to do weeks of cleaning and spiffing up, in preparation for us coming," explains Salowe. "There was a food change when we came. People—inmates—told us that the food was actually better when we were there." Teachers were given special treatment. Litzky described it as a "Policy of divide & conquer." Teachers were given real towels, whereas other inmates had dishtowels; their striped shifts were not old or torn. "*New* towels and *new* nightgowns," noted Graves. "Divisive? yes, but it's not going to work." The professional status of teachers could have resulted in class privileges for them and class resentment against them. "The authorities may have wanted to treat us differently," said Lappé. "We refused to be treated differently." Teachers demanded, and won, real towels and new uniforms for the other inmates. "We were very conscious of the fact that we did not want to appear like a group apart from them."[53]

Two things were happening simultaneously: the teachers were becoming a group themselves, and as a group, they were reaching out to other inmates. Litzky wrote to her husband and daughter that jail was "an invaluable experience." On the one hand, "we've come to know one another—teachers whom we knew only by sight or not at all—very well; we've developed an esprit de corps & a loyalty, a mutual support & concern." On the other hand, "we've seen at close hand 'the other America,' poor & victimized, submissive & inarticulate. Many, even the youngest—late teens, early 20's—are recidivists for whom prison is a way of life; almost all—this bothers me *so* much!—have rotting teeth &/or big gaps in their mouths." Bad teeth were an indicator of class, a visible sign of a lack of money and education. So were submissiveness and recidivism. The point, however, was not just to observe inequalities but to change them. "We try to mingle with them, talk to them, encourage them."[54]

One issue did divide teachers from other inmates. Litzky noted: "Other inmates told that teachers had complained about their washing of dishes." Everyone ate directly off metal trays. Inmates washed the trays by hand in a tub with lukewarm water, rinsing them in another tub; the water quickly became dirty. By the sixth day, many teachers were ill with sore throats, headaches, dysentery. They called a strategy meeting. "C[arole Graves] reported conversation w/ Miss Ott. who said she's been requesting a dishwasher for years to no avail." They reached consensus. "We all agreed to eat only liquids & bread to protest unsanitary conditions." For the rest of their stay, teachers did not use trays, eating only what they could put on pieces of bread.[55]

Complaints about the washing of dishes could separate teachers from other inmates. But there was another aspect of the issue, one that involved the old union principle of no pay, no work. When a teacher was assigned to wash trays, Lappé recalled, "We said, 'fine, how much will you pay her for this work?' The guard said, 'What do you mean pay? We don't pay for this kind of work.' " Here was a working-class issue, one that could unite the prisoners. At the meeting, teachers agreed to wash only if paid. Litzky recorded what happened next. "At supper call, specific cell occupants named to do dishes, including 7 teachers. They refused unless promised payment. Other inmates shocked but applauded. Much confusion, screaming, uncertainty. Threats of being locked in. All agreed to stay in but then others would have to serve us in cells. Better to carry out the original plan & eat only bread & liquid. This we did." At supper, a guard announced washers would be paid. That evening, "Some of the girls on tier A sang carols to us."[56]

"But then others would have to serve us": teachers like Litzky, Lappé, and Graves recognized the danger of class privilege, and consciously strove to find, or create, common ground. They saw themselves as organizers. "Until we came, the existing inmates had no idea of how to organize themselves or how to develop any kind of power that would make them effective in getting some changes to be brought about," said Lappé. She hoped that having "seen how it was done," the prisoners would organize themselves after the teachers were gone. After the successful protest against not being paid, Litzky wrote in her diary, "CG. reported that Tiers A & B have learned the lesson of solidarity." Litzky saw the protest as "a fascinating exercise in group dynamics!" The few cents a day did not matter to teachers, who were leaving soon. They were modeling protest for the other prisoners. "All this to educate other inmates to demand their rights."[57]

The key was acting as a group. Otherwise, according to Lappé, jail would break you down. She became convinced that the goal of the prison system—despite the rhetoric of rehabilitation—was to dehumanize and demoralize the prisoner. It was supposed to break you down. That's why the rules were so arbitrary, the heat so high, the medical care so bad. That's why the guards and management treated prisoners with contempt. "You are not treated as a human being, but rather as a thing, to be manipulated, to be pushed around, to be abused." Because women teachers treated each other as human beings, prison was not nearly as damaging to them as it was to Graves or Rufalo, who went alone.[58]

The authorities blamed Graves for the protests. Two young inmates who were close to her joined the fast; others became involved in other ways. "I was given a subtle threat that if I don't stop organizing I could possibly be sent to Clinton or Trenton. Shit! They never learn & I guess neither do I. If I had any sense I would just sit off to myself and let this time pass." But she couldn't let it pass. It was too exciting. "The teachers have had a profound effect on the inmates and administration of this institution. . . . For a while the apathy, so prevalent was shaken." It reminded her of the strikes. "Very tired since the other teachers came. . . . Our days are now filled with the kind of atmosphere that was prevalent during the strikes."[59]

The teachers were released after eight days; like other prisoners, they were given credit for the day they were arrested and a day off for good behavior. Because of their behavior, they were threatened with a ninth day, but the warden wisely let them go. On the teachers' last night, Graves noted, "Tina, Sharon & Betty [inmates] stayed up later than usual, assembling the demands. Bobbi, Lucy and Catherine [teachers] helped with the typing. It was an organized & joint project from beginning to end." Bobbi would carry the demands outside: a dishwasher; recreation; higher pay for cleaning, laundry, and kitchen work; the right to keep personal possessions and to have a grievance committee. The next morning, "Sharon shed tears when the teachers were called from the dining room to prepare to leave."[60]

Lappé was sad too. She worried about the people the teachers were leaving behind. It was horrible to know what the prison system did to them. "We knew that once they would be released from this jail they would go back to the same crimes and the same conditions, under the same circumstances, as when they entered." At the same time, she was greatly relieved to be free. "I can tell you that when I saw my husband and my sons and their wives and my grandson, it was one of the most happy and the most sad days of my life."[61]

That same day, December 23, the second shift of thirty-seven women entered the prison. Dorothy Bergman was in the second group. She thinks the authorities may have been a bit more lenient as a result of the activism of the first group. Everyone, teacher or not, had a new uniform. But nothing fundamental had changed. Prisoners were theoretically allowed outside, but pretexts were found to keep them in. Women in the second group never went out. They spent all day in their individual cells and the big recreation room where the music blared. Bergman saw how huge the speakers were, almost floor to ceiling. When she asked why the music was so loud, a guard told her it kept the minds of the prisoners off their problems; they would not make trouble.[62]

Bergman did not make trouble. As a young teacher at Weequahic in the 1950s, she had still felt like a student. She confronted her principal in the late 1960s and her sister in the 1970 strike. But in jail, she was, again, intimidated. The intimidation began right away. She brought one paperback for each day, but the guards simply took away five. They searched incoming prisoners in a room with a window. "What they did—not to me but to others, because I saw— was they left the shade up, and you stripped, so you're naked against the wall, and they stick their hand in your vagina." She was taken to her cell and became a number. "You feel dehumanized as soon as you get your number, practically."[63]

The second group of women recognized that the tendency of the system was to numb people. The doctor, who came only on Monday, carried no stethoscope and gave no examinations, "but he freely gives out tranquillizers and sleeping pills," observed Helen Klayman. "They like the women to take pills," she concluded, "because it keeps them quiet." Pills and pounding music kept people docile. So did the way they were treated as things. "It's worse than being in a zoo, because even animals aren't treated that badly," said Betty McEachin.[64] The second group of teachers did not fight for their rights. They resisted the dehumanizing tendencies of the system in quieter ways.

Bergman made the best of prison, focusing on the concrete. She disliked most of the food but enjoyed the beets, which were grown on the grounds, and the bread, which was baked by male prisoners. The Union provided a real holiday meal on Christmas, a chicken dinner she ate with a spoon, the only silverware allowed. Warned by the first group, she brought earplugs to counter the music. She was also warned to bring a lot of soap for the shower. Showering twice a day became her way of keeping busy. Like other prisoners in the women's wing, she had nothing to do. "I was very clean that week."[65]

Teachers took care of each other. One came down with the flu. "I don't know how she got through that week," says Bergman. There was no nurse or infirmary on the women's wing. "We took care of her, wiped her brow, dried her clothes." The second group protested only once, on behalf of a diabetic teacher. All drinks were presweetened and there was too much sugar in the food. To get the teacher alternative foods, teachers stood out in the hall and refused to enter the dining room. The diabetic was given—for the eight days—a total of five hard-boiled eggs and two slices of American cheese.[66]

Like the first group, the second group of women became a kind of community. Bergman knitted and played Scrabble with other teachers. "We became very close in jail." For years after, she went to reunions of jailed teachers. At night, after the lights went out, she would reach out to her friend, the colleague from her school who was arrested with her. It was "lovely, . . . because she had the cell next to me, and at night I could just reach out and hold her hand." Bergman also held hands with the teacher on the other side of her. "You couldn't do both sides at once; you had to do one, then go to the other side of the cell."[67]

But there was another kind of touching that she found disturbing. In the recreation room, inmates would dance, rubbing against each other. "It was not nice to watch." Sometimes a prisoner would ask a teacher to dance. "They did it purposely to get us upset." Bergman saw the overtures by other prisoners as a kind of hostility, not as a kind of reaching out.[68]

Carole Graves's perceptions were very different. Before the teachers arrived, Graves noted that there were about five lesbians among the inmates.

"One has taken a fancy to me but it is not difficult for me to handle because I am much older." After the teachers left, she returned to the problem of "how to keep out of the middle of advances made by the gay sect." The inmate closest to her was a young lesbian; what worried Graves was being framed. She feared "attempts to set me up in a homosexual relationship." But while the second group of teachers was there, Graves was pleased by the readiness of a gay teacher to dance with inmates. "My sisters in the Union are sisters here—with all the inmates," she wrote. "During recreation time the[y] mingled with the others—even dancing. One dyke can spot another."[69]

The high point of sisterhood for Graves was the Christmas celebration. Her mother visited that day: "Mama sad-faced the first time in 33 years that I have not been home for Christmas." But Graves was almost happy. "Something good has happened in this awful place." A teacher coordinated the program of Christmas carols, spirituals, and skits. There was "complete silence—This in jail," when she sang "O holy night." The celebration brought teachers together, creating "more solidarity among the NTU women than ever before." And many other inmates "moved up a fraction and reached a higher level of understanding." "People have touch[ed] each other and made impressions. Questions, evaluations, solidarity even. Replacing 'Mother Fucker' 'Suck my Dick.' "[70]

An art teacher in the second group made sketches of prisoners. A striker who was a school nurse gave first aid to an inmate who suffered convulsive seizures. Teachers began a calisthenics group, and some inmates joined. Graves began a program in which teachers tutored other inmates, but the authorities intervened, again accusing her of making trouble. Two teachers organized musical chairs and a chair race, and most inmates joined in the fun and laughter; Graves noted that the matron, who seemed disturbed by the camaraderie, told the other inmates to " 'act like ladies.' " On the last night, the "other inmates and teacher inmates" cried when "the kids sang Auld Lang Syne and the teachers sang back 'For all we know.' "[71]

But teachers in the second group made no systematic effort to organize the other inmates. Why not? Probably the question is wrong. Given how the prison system tended—still tends—to create disorientation and passivity, no one can fault prisoners who count the days and stay sane. The women on the second shift took care of each other and became a group, protecting and strengthening their connection to each other. Some formed connections with particular inmates. If some saw the prisoners as "other," because of their own assumptions about class or race or sexual orientation, and were a little afraid, no one should be surprised. The question is rather why the first group was able to go beyond stereotypes. Why were they able to act consistently as a group, and not only for themselves but for the other prisoners?

Litzky, Saltman, and Lappé had not taught that fall. They were not tired like the second group of teachers, who went to jail during the Christmas break, straight from teaching; nor did they have to worry about their own children, who were grown. They were able to focus their considerable energies on jail, even to look forward to it.[72] They brought to Caldwell the egalitarianism, the questioning of authority, the emphasis on rights and dignity, the culture of resistance that hundreds of teachers developed over decades of struggle in the old Newark Teachers Union. In prison, Lappé and Litzky saw themselves as activists who had a special responsibility. Leaders of the old Union, rooted in Weequahic, joined with Graves, the leader of the new Union. Together, they challenged the system and accomplished more than Graves could accomplish on her own.

Teachers in the second group tried to support each other, but some individuals were left exposed. Because women in the second group were less forceful about articulating a critique of the prison environment and less insistent about claiming their rights, individual teachers became vulnerable to the dehumanizing aspects of the prison system.

For Esther Tumin, the experience was traumatic. Tumin thought of herself as a strong person. Yet in jail, she fell apart. "For me it was horrendous. Others took it much better than I. I was ashamed of myself for caving in." Her strength worked against her, because it was tied to her sense of having control of her life. In jail she had none. On the first day, the authorities withheld medication she needed for a painfully bad back. They confiscated the earplugs she had brought to combat the loud music. "I keep thinking of those earplugs I brought with me, and they took them away. Someone else they left with knitting needles!"[73] It made no sense, and there was nothing she could do about it. From the first day, Tumin experienced helpless, impotent rage.

She tried to make sense of the inconsistencies, the arbitrary rules and even more arbitrary exceptions, and concluded that it was all "purely whimsical" and nothing made sense. "You stood on shifting sands. You never knew the rules, because they would change them whenever they wanted to: the rule about going outside, the rule about mingling in the afternoon, about being released from your cell. And if you questioned it, they just shrugged it off, and nobody paid any attention to you."[74] They shrugged her off because they had all the power and she had none. Tumin, who became a professional to have respect and a striker to regain control of her work, found herself completely under the control of people who didn't respect her.

Her sense of status, of her place in the world, was assaulted. "One of the more humiliating experiences was on Christmas Eve. One of the Black churches came in. And we all stood in line with the other prisoners, mostly all these little Black girls. . . . We passed a table where there was a Black preacher, and he was giving each person a little bag, and in the bag there was an orange, and maybe a bag of mints, and a toothbrush. And we took it and we said thank you." The experience was humiliating because she was put on the level of "little Black girls," a charity case, receiving alms from a Black church. At Weequahic, as teacher and advisor, she tried without great success to help Black girls and boys so they would not end up on the streets, or in jail. Now she was in jail herself, at the bottom of the heap, saying thank you for an orange. And meaning it: "The orange was the one piece of fresh fruit we saw for eight days, so we appreciated it [laughs]."[75]

Tumin was sensitive to the nuances of the prison hierarchy. "The record player was in the charge of some of the more dominant Black girls; prison always has its own hierarchy." The authorities allowed some inmates, but not teachers, to wear jewelry. They also "watched us like hawks. When we had visitors they were on top of us, as if someone was going to slip a hacksaw or drugs in for us, something they didn't do for the other girls." Other inmates were sometimes allowed "in each other's cells; there were some lesbian relationships there. We never were allowed in each other's cells." The matron and guards gave privileges to other inmates to keep them docile. They acted differently with teachers, either "oversympathetic and smiling" or overly harsh and suspicious, because teachers represented a potential challenge. "Most of the girls in jail were young and Black, and they were in jail for drugs and thieving and shoplifting. . . . The women in charge were used to lording it over these kids. They were in control. But when all these women poured in, they didn't know what to do with us."[76]

The authorities did not, in fact, know what to do with the women teachers. The first group, sensing weakness, demanded their rights. (Probably that's why the second group was watched so closely.) Tumin was too appalled to demand anything. In her cell, she felt powerless and exposed. "Anybody—people, wardens, some of them males—came back and forth along the catwalk that was outside our cells, and we might be sitting on the bathroom. There was no curtain, no nothing to protect our privacy." Tumin experienced prison as a topsy-turvy world in which the people with education, the ones who knew how to use power to benefit society, were nakedly exposed to the power of lower-class people. The matron and guards were "uneducated, very lower class, very ignorant people. . . . These are not people who are interested in benefiting society. These are people who take these jobs because the jobs don't demand from them any training or any education, and they don't know what to do with the power that they have. Because they have power. They can keep you locked in your cell for a hundred hours."[77]

She began to break down. She never got the medication her doctor prescribed for her back. She was in the middle of menopause. She missed the earplugs. "The music pounded day and night. I was getting severe headaches." In physical and psychological pain, she medicated herself. "My next door neighbor, who was a colleague of mine from Weequahic High School, ordered cigarettes. I had quit then, but I started again. We went through her cigarettes, she and I; we would pass them around the corner into each other's cells." Relief was temporary. "The music was driving me absolutely mad." The back pain became worse, pushing her toward the edge.[78]

When a lawyer friend visited, Tumin told him that her back was in trauma but the prison would not release her medicine. He told her husband, who contacted her doctor, who phoned the prison. During a meal, Tumin was called to the matron's office. The matron told Tumin she would be allowed to see her own doctor, "which made me very happy, because I needed some kind of relief."[79] Her professional, middle-class network—lawyer friend, doctor—was working at last.

But there were conditions. In the police van, she would have to wear her prison dress and one of the raggedy prison coats. And she had to go in handcuffs.

> At which point I absolutely lost control. I never—my friends heard of it, they couldn't believe it—I never in my life lost control the way I did then. I screamed. I used blasphemies. I used vulgarities. My language was horrendous. I accused her of being trained in Auschwitz. . . . I said in the beginning: could you believe, in thongs and a prison dress and a ratty jacket, that I'm going to run away free in the middle of Maplewood? What's the matter with you? . . . I ended up not going. I screamed myself into hysteria, and they put me back in the cell. Because I just wouldn't go under those conditions. And I paid for it. I was in pain, in very bad pain, for a few days. But it had its funny side. Because everyone said: "You? That language? You?" It was the one outburst of my whole life, and I couldn't help it. I just couldn't help it.[80]

The professional middle-class identity that she had constructed so painstakingly cracked. Deprived of control of her life, she lost control of herself. No other teacher experienced such rage, or ended up feeling so ashamed. But in her honesty, Tumin reveals an aspect of what many teachers experienced. Betty Rufalo and Phyllis Salowe also suffered emotional depression and physical deterioration. Dorothy Bergman came through prison much less scarred than Tumin, but she too felt as if she lost not only her privacy but her identity. "You're nothing," says Bergman. "When people are in prison, or concentration camp, I can see very easily—of course we didn't suffer like they suffered—I can see, you have no name, they had a number on their arm, I had no name. If I had any complaints or any worry or anything I had to ask about, don't ask. You're nobody."[81]

It was no accident that Bergman and Tumin thought of the camps. Other teachers, entering the showers, joked that they wanted to be sure it was water that was going to come out. Teachers experienced prison as a world in which they didn't matter; their identity and status did not count. They were stripped of their rights and treated like nonpersons. Tumin in particular felt bullied and humiliated by people who didn't care about her, or even about their own rules. She thought of the Holocaust for the same reason that Charles Nolley, enduring the arbitrary power of the principal, thought of slavery. Jail tapped into that nightmare place deep inside where Auschwitz still existed. In the last days in prison, after her outburst, Tumin tried to talk herself out of depression. "I think the last few days I was simply badly depressed. I was saying to myself, 'Look, there are people who have gone through concentration camps, Esther, so take it. This is going to be over, etc., etc.' But it left its scars."[82]

She came home on New Year's Eve. There were welcome-home presents from friends: a new azalea bush, and a beautiful picture of birds. "I saw them both and I burst into tears. I cried for three days thereafter. I just couldn't stop it." She returned to work, looking "gaunt and sorrowful and depressed." She would go to the lunchroom, grab something, and bring it back to her desk. She had been teaching in Livingston for a year and a half, having left Newark because of the way it treated teachers. Now she couldn't face her new colleagues. They asked if something was wrong. "I said, 'I just can't eat in public.' The tears kept getting ready to rise the minute I thought about it, much less spoke about it." For years, she was not able to talk about what happened to her, even to her husband. Much later, she began to talk, as a way to relieve the trauma. "I'll never be over it. You saw I got a little teary before."[83]

Tumin blames herself. "Some of the women were much braver than I, especially in the first group." But bravery was not the issue, as she has proven by courageously facing her collapse. The difference between Tumin's experience in jail and the experience of Saltman, Litzky, and Lappé—all four were friends from Weequahic—did not turn on bravery. The difference went back to the 1960s. As Weequahic's student body changed to predominantly Black, the assumptions of Jewish liberals and radicals on the faculty were challenged. Were they indeed fighting for a better world, or were they fighting to keep their place in the existing world? Was their Union advancing the interests of working people everywhere, or was it primarily a way to protect their own status? And when they struck in 1970, were they striking to make the schools better, or to be paid better for a job that was becoming less and less meaningful?

Tumin tended to answer these questions differently than her three friends, who remained radically egalitarian. They responded to prison, and to the other prisoners, as a new opportunity to challenge injustice and hierarchy; she responded to prison as the latest example of a world gone mad.[84]

After they were released from jail, many women teachers campaigned for prison reform. They joined the Fortune Society, which helps people find jobs after coming out of jail; Graves introduced them to it. From prison, Litzky wrote, "The Fortune Society will have many new members as a result of our experiences." (Decades later, Litzky was still a member.) Litzky and Lappé wrote letters to local newspapers about conditions at Caldwell and spoke wherever they could. So did many others, from both groups. Salowe spoke on the radio. Even Tumin spoke twice, at local temples. But her heart was not in it. To her, the teachers' attempts at prison reform were "a lot of noise." Her friends "were gung-ho about prison reform. I just didn't want to care about anything. I wasn't interested in prison reform."[85]

Two years after the teachers left, a reporter visited the women's wing and found conditions virtually unchanged. The only improvement was temporary: Dr. Garrett, a gynecologist, spent four hours a week at the prison doing internal exams, in fulfillment of the terms of his punishment for assaulting the *New York Times* reporter.[86] Women teachers did not succeed in changing the system. What they changed was themselves. In prison, some women continued the process of self-transformation that had begun when they joined the Union and affirmed the spirit that had landed them in prison in the first place.

The Men in Jail

Men teachers had an easier time in prison than women, because their conditions were better. Yet in some ways, they had a rougher time, because they were men.

They were treated less harshly. Their prison clothes were not striped; they wore blue shirts and khaki pants. They went outside for exercise. They saw movies and went to religious services of their choice. They had the dishwasher and pharmacy and doctor's office. Most importantly, they were not in individual cells. They were lodged dormitory-style, about twenty to a cage, in a special wing of the prison. Bob Hirschfeld explains that the cage was "very large," maybe as large as his house. "So at least within your confined area, you had, if not freedom, you had some movement." Pete Petino agrees that the men who went to jail in December had a less difficult time than the women. "We weren't with the general population, except to eat," he says. "We were isolated together, so it wasn't that bad."[87]

What hurt was the loss of freedom. Many men hated being locked up, even if it wasn't in a cell. Steve Shaffer knew that the officers, who had gone to jail alone in November, had a worse time. "But with us, we were all together in a bunk area. I won't say it was easy time, 'cause that would be a very serious mistake, but neither was it extremely hard time. 'Cause we had the camaraderie." It wasn't easy, because they were not free. "I couldn't go to a store. I couldn't go to a movie. If I was to take a shower, it was with everybody. If I was to go to the bathroom, it was with everybody. There was no sense of privacy."[88] Loss of freedom and loss of privacy were manifestations of the loss of control of one's own life.

For Shaffer, who grew up poor, who worked to help his mother and advance himself, the loss of freedom was intolerable. He felt he was losing the self he had become. One prison guard was also a security guard at Shaffer's school. Desperate for a taste of home, Shaffer asked the guard to buy him a corned beef sandwich, forgetting to request no mustard. "I hate mustard. Do you think it made a difference? I ate the sandwich. That's the feeling: something was taken away from me. I still remember it to this day. I will never let anyone take it away from me again."[89] Like all of us, Shaffer had developed values and tastes that defined his identity. In jail, those values and tastes, and that identity, did not count for very much.

The heat and noise were not so bad on the teachers' special wing. But still they couldn't move about as they pleased. They played catch with rolled-up socks. Some jogged in the hall. One broke the lock on the cage. It was a symbolic act, a kind of joke: the gates were locked, and there was nowhere to go. Fred Barbaro, who interviewed teachers after they left jail, observed that they were used to moving freely around the classroom, and to controlling the movement of others; for them, "forced confinement was a terrible experience."[90]

Six male officers of the NTU began serving three-month sentences at the end of November. They had no camaraderie to sustain them. Eddie Tumin, brother-in-law of Esther Tumin, felt isolated. Most men teachers came in contact with other inmates only at meals. Tumin, however, lived with them. One, who was a former student of Tumin's, glared at him every time they met. When Tumin asked why he was angry, he said it was because Tumin had given him detention. Tumin made the connection: there was "a tremendous similarity between jail and school—the inability to resist wrongful authority, the constant threat of punishment, the lack of control over your own actions."[91]

As a leader of NTU during the collective bargaining campaign, Tumin sometimes antagonized teachers with his aggressive style. But in jail with the general population, he was circumspect. On his first day, the inmates demanded music on a radio program; they began to beat on the bars of their cells with their tin cups. "I joined in tentatively, first checking that no guard was in a position to observe me." He joined not because he liked the music ("It drives me to distraction. I find it impossible to think sometimes.") but out of rebelliousness. He joined tentatively, because he was not sure where he stood with the guards, or the inmates.[92]

Battling the heat that first night, suffering disorientation, Tumin made it through. When morning came, he was "inordinately proud in having survived." Alone, like Graves and Rufalo, he looked forward to visiting day. His wife and three young children were coming; the youngest was turning five. "I tried to steel myself for that first visit. But when I saw them, and my little girl said, 'I miss you, Dad, I wish you could come to my birthday party,' well, it touched me and . . . I cried."[93]

The heat and noise of Tumin's wing wore him down. He asked to move to another area of the prison and was sent from warden to captain to doctor to psychologist. Finally, he was moved to the hospital wing, which housed not only ill prisoners but also those who didn't fit in. Conditions were better. Now he began to wonder how most inmates adjusted to the heat and noise. "How? Lower mentality levels? Some connection between the sluggish state of air and sluggish, thuggish mentality?" In contrast to the first group of women, who refused to be treated "like a group apart," Tumin looked down on the other inmates from his privileged position in the hospital wing. Emotionally and intellectually, he kept his distance.[94]

Like the women, men teachers found prison dehumanizing. But they did not fight for their rights or for the rights of other inmates. Instead, many sought privileges. Shaffer asked for a sandwich, Tumin to relocate. Bob Hirschfeld knew the brother of a guard, so the guard looked in on him occasionally and asked how he was doing; even this minimal concern meant something in the depersonalized context of prison. Another jailed teacher was himself a county freeholder-elect. In the county prison, he enjoyed many special privileges and was frequently out of his cage. Sometimes he did favors for other teachers.[95]

Men teachers sought privileges partly because they did not identify with other inmates. Women teachers, especially in the first group, developed relationships with other inmates, learned from them, and cared about them. Most men teachers felt an unbridgeable gulf between "the prison people," as one teacher called them, and themselves. They did not know the other inmates and felt intimidated by them. Phil Basile was part of the large group of sixty-seven men who went to jail on December 23. He was bored hanging around with teachers but did not identify with the other prisoners. "It wasn't like I stole something or murdered somebody or was a criminal." The other prisoners, the real criminals, seemed hostile. "Like all these people were laughing at us.

We'd come down the stairs and they'd be laughing at us. . . . They did intimidate us in a lot of ways."[96]

Pat Piegari suffered the same disorientation as other men. "I was ND31! That was the biggest shock: no one called you by your name. Another thing: you got your clothes and you got a spoon—no knife or fork, because you're in jail. . . . And there were no napkins." But Piegari reacted differently. He made a conscious effort to spend time with other prisoners. They were wary at first. "Some were laughing: 'You'll be out in a few days. We are in for a long time.' " Also, there was a racial difference. "We had to be a little careful. We weren't welcomed. . . . We had to be careful what we said, not to alienate people."[97]

Most men teachers spent their time solely with each other. But Piegari's instinct was to reach beyond the confines of race and class. "Other people in jail didn't do that. But I felt comfortable crossing over." His after-school experience helped. "I could relate, from working on the playground, in rec, at night at Abington. It gave me a kind of savvy." One prisoner was a former student who liked him and "passed the word around that I was OK. I had some credibility. Also I could play ball." Acting on his own, Piegari was not trying to change anything. He just wanted to keep up his own spirits and not become depressed.[98]

Jim Lowenstein was also able to cross over, because he got sick. For the first four days, he was in a large cage with twenty-three other teachers, most of whom he already knew. Then he came down with a stomach ailment, probably as a result of the food, and was moved to a little medical ward. "That was interesting, because this was the first chance I had to meet anyone other than a teacher who was an inmate. So for four days I had some very interesting conversations with some of these guys." One inmate was absorbed in history, and they "talked about history a lot."[99]

Jim Lerman, an officer with a three-month sentence, lived with other inmates. "Several men with whom I have become friendly (and who have been here on the average of five times each) tell me that the best way to jail (Yes, it is a verb) is to 'forget about the outside.' " The problem was that life inside was pretty meaningless. "Each day is the same," he wrote at the end of the first month. "The essential quality that obtains here is boredom." Already he had lost ten pounds. The psychological, or spiritual, dimension of the experience was far worse. "Our lives begin to lose meaning and even to ourselves we begin to become less of a person."[100]

It was hard for men teachers to keep up their spirits in captivity. The routine got them down, the combination of regimentation and boredom. "You're cooped up," says Basile. "Go down to breakfast; it was horrible. Then we'd come back, had to clean our area. Then you'd hang around. Go to lunch. Then you come back, hang around. . . . There was absolutely, positively nothing to do." To break the routine, to have something to do, teachers who rarely or never went to church or temple went to the weekly service in jail. Tumin, who was not religious, met some teachers "at the weekly Thursday night visit of the rabbi who lit Chanukah candles and expounded at some unnecessary length on that story and its meaning. I felt like an old-timer—me and my 19 days in jail—explaining to these, the innocents, how to be prison-wise."[101]

The leaders among the women, like Litzky, Lappé, and Graves, reached out and organized. The leaders among the men were more focused on showing that they weren't intimidated, that they were prison-wise. Don Nicholas, who served three months, claimed that jail was easier for him than picketing. Pete Petino was given special responsibilities for the group of twenty-two men who went to jail on December 15. "The way we organized, it was to have certain people go with groups, to keep their morale up. . . . And I was a staff rep, so I was there to keep everybody boosted."[102]

Petino struggled to keep his own morale up. He thought the warden had told the guards to harass him. "They would push me around a little bit, trying to get me to mouth back or raise my hands—shit like that." One time he forgot the rule against bringing anything out of the dining room. "I was walking out with the tea and one guard smacked it out of my hand and pushed me. Told me to clean it up, and I told him to go fuck himself." But fighting back could lead to more time, so Petino relied on the Union lawyer. "Paul [Giblin] was always in the warden's office to make sure they got off my back." Looking back, Petino plays down his struggle: "It wasn't a bad experience." But at the time, a fellow prisoner heard him, visibly upset, tell a visitor he was having a terrible time.[103]

Petino lost fifteen pounds during his eight days. He didn't eat; he just drank tea. He says he didn't like the food and wanted to lose weight. "That pissed 'em off too." Like many men, he experienced prison as a contest, in which someone won and someone lost. Unlike leaders on the women's side, he did not reach out to other inmates. They became instead part of the environment against which he tested himself. "We played a football game against them and we beat them too, pretty handily, as I remember. We beat them. . . . We kicked some ass that day."[104] Petino's role in the strikes carried over to jail. He had to act like a hard guy, probably to believe it himself.

Jerry Meyer was disappointed in Petino for not calling meetings or offering leadership. Meyer went to jail with the teachers even though he was not one of them. He had joined in the downtown march during his lunch hour, alongside two strikers who were his friends. One was arrested, and Meyer yelled, "Why don't you arrest the Mafia, and leave the teachers alone?" An officer waded into the crowd and arrested him. Unlike the labor leaders arrested at the march, Meyer made no effort to get his case separated from that of the Newark teachers. He believed in what they were doing and hoped his case would help the Union to expose the unfairness of the injunction. He was disappointed there was little effort to use the jailings to organize opposition to the injunction, and no effort at organization in jail. He felt almost as if he had gone to jail for nothing.[105]

Two things disturbed Meyer about most teachers in the first group. Instead of showing solidarity, they ostracized two of their own: a Black teacher who went to work in 1971, and a white teacher who supported Black nationalism. The second disturbing thing was that teachers showed little empathy for the other inmates. Meyer suggested they needed a prisoners union, but teachers reacted negatively. He was sympathetic to the inmates and noticed that some of them showed more organization than the teachers. A group of Black Muslims would turn their trays over whenever pork was served. He found their protest moving.[106]

As an outsider, Meyer saw things about teachers that they couldn't see. At the same time, he lacked an understanding of the context. It was hard for teachers to show solidarity with those who had crossed the picket line in 1971; the polarization would last for years. It was hard, too, for teachers to organize against the injunction, almost two years after their arrests. By then, the expansive spirit of 1970 was fading. Looking out the window one day, on the way to the dining room, Meyer saw women teachers across the way. He yelled, "Carol! Carol!" Carol Karman was one of his closest friends, and a major reason he had joined the downtown march in 1970. She did not hear him. "Get back in line," snapped a guard. "What do you think this is, a college campus?"[107] Meyer would have felt better if he had known that the women were reviving the spirit of 1970, reaching out to other inmates, and organizing resistance.

Men teachers were less oppressed by the prison than were the women, but they oppressed each other more. "I saw deterioration in my colleagues," says Piegari, who was in the large second group. "After three days, they began to look and act like prisoners, . . . arguing with each other and fighting with each other. Picking verbal confrontations. And depression: I saw a lot of depression. People isolating themselves and staying by themselves and becoming depressed."[108] The men did not, as a group, support each other, or connect with other inmates. "Isolated together," in Petino's apt phrase, they felt trapped and frustrated, and took it out on each other.

Jerry Yablonsky kept a prison diary that demonstrates the deterioration of which Piegari speaks. As an organizer, Yablonsky had shown sensitivity to teachers who feared losing professional status by becoming part of the labor movement. In jail, he lost, or hid, that sensitivity. The difference between his diary and Hannah Litzky's diary embodies the difference between how men and women teachers responded to jail.

During their third day in prison, which was Christmas, the men "discussed union matters & possible prison reform—no consensus." That night, Yablonsky was nauseous and had a hard time falling asleep. "The cage next to me kept talking all night." Two colleagues, whom he named, kept talking. "They & others acted like assholes (perhaps they weren't acting)."[109]

On the fifth day, teachers agreed to write a letter detailing their complaints about the prison, but they did not follow through. Still, there was cause for celebration. Prison regulations required all prisoners to be clean-shaven. "Several guys refused to shave their beards. [Their] punishment is no more recreation—which does not exist anyway. Chalk up a victory for our side."[110]

On the sixth day, he observed, "We have all settled down to prison life." He played Twenty Questions "& got the answer in 15 questions." He felt a growing revulsion toward other inmates. "I am becoming fed up with the kind of life the regular inmates lead. They seem to accept being treated like shitheads & many act like zombies. I occasionally see the inmates when I go to meals & their cell-blocks give me a sickening feeling." Perhaps recoiling from the harshness of his judgment, Yablonsky tempered it with understanding. "If you treat men like animals they are likely to respond in kind." That night, after lights out, "we were yelling, talking, laughing as usual, when the Guard came by & told us if we didn't shut up he would report us & have our one day good time taken away & send those who talk to another wing. We shut up."[111]

On the seventh morning, teachers played football and basketball outside. Afterward they were cold but couldn't get back in until a guard opened the door. "I suggested that we nicely ask the guard—"please let us back into jail, mother-fucker." At night, "Some of the men complained about my snoring, but I can't help it, so fuck them." The deterioration in Yablonsky's language accurately reflects his experience. (A reporter who saw Eddie Tumin's diary noted a similar deterioration over time.)[112] Yablonsky was hurt and confused by being locked up like a criminal. But he could not name his feelings and instead reacted in manly fashion, cursing and getting angry.

On the eighth day, WNBC-TV came to the men's wing. The reaction of teachers to this opportunity to publicize their cause shows that the deterioration was indeed general. The warden walked down the hall with the people from NBC. "I shouted 'the food stinks,' and the warden's steps faltered, while the TV men laughed. Once the camera started to work, several of us sang a song asking Cahill to let the teachers go & the others applauded." NBC interviewed one veteran teacher and left. "The teachers then erupted into internecine arguments."

An "idiot" was angry because he feared that the singing might antagonize Governor Cahill, who could still grant clemency to teachers with long sentences. (The "idiot" was serving a twenty-day sentence and facing six months for the 1971 strike.) Others were angry at men in Yablonsky's cage because "we looked too happy and cooperated too willingly." Stung by the criticism, one man screamed, "[T]his is war, you assholes." The teachers became so aggressive toward each other and out of control that the guards locked them in their cages, "to avoid fist fights."[113]

That evening, the teachers were told that NBC would return in the morning with live coverage of their departure. Yablonsky wrote, "I think the prison authorities are afraid of us & what we might say. Despite the whole week, we beat these fucks & they know it. The jailor is afraid of their prisoners! This is not a small victory."[114] Yablonsky was right that the prison authorities were afraid. What is perplexing, however, is what he meant by beating them. By his own testimony, the men teachers were unable to reach consensus on how to respond to prison and did not take advantage of the fear they inspired in the authorities. Instead, they ended up attacking each other. What is clear is that Yablonsky framed the experience of men in jail—playing Twenty Questions, refusing to shave, being televised—in terms of winners and losers.

Most men were burdened by the need to be rough, to be tough, to be competitive. Instead of comforting each other, they tended to take the pain of prison out on each other. In all of Yablonsky's prison diary there is not a kind word about another human being. It was as if, in traditional masculine fashion, he feared he would break down if he were kind or gentle. Released on the ninth morning, he ended his diary with what he'd learned and how he felt: "Fuck New Jersey."[115]

One teacher was unfailingly gentle. Asa Watkins came from a Quaker background. During World War II, as a conscientious objector, he was responsible for one hundred beds on the night shift in a hospital. He took his eight days in jail in stride, hanging out with Jerry Meyer and Bernie Zimmer. They would walk the halls, singing the populist ballad "The House I Live In." Bob Hirschfeld found Watkins "a very gentle guy" and "a very, very interesting guy" who did something constructive every minute. "He sketched, he wrote, he was not bored." He drew Hirschfeld and four other teachers playing cards and gave the picture to Hirschfeld, who still has it. Watkins did not conform to the competitive and tough masculine type. If he had not had a family, Hirschfeld would have thought he was homosexual.[116]

Hirschfeld himself did not act tough or cool. On the first night in jail, he made a key distinction: "We really haven't been treated badly but the system itself is certainly demeaning." Or as he later said, "You weren't a teacher. You were a prisoner." Hirschfeld himself was no longer a teacher even before he went to jail. Refused entrance to his school after the 1971 strike, he was selling educational materials to school systems at the start of the 1971–72 school year. But he was not bitter and still identified with the teachers. "Spirits are high and we've been laughing regularly," he wrote to his wife. "However I think I'd consider Denver if I had 6 mo. to do." One teacher had fled to Denver rather than face a long sentence for the 1971 strike. Hirschfeld was attuned to the laughing, and the pain beneath. "Terry [Elman], [Bernie] Zimmer & Co have been keeping everyone in stitches but Bernie is facing 6 mos. and I suspect he's not laughing on the inside."[117]

The characteristic response of the men was to make jokes. A popular joke was about the food: "[T]hey beet us to death." Jerry Meyer suggested that the lawyer who had argued their cases was "0 for 189." Another joke mocked the rhetoric of strike meetings: "2,800 out today—we're stronger than ever." Hirschfeld, playing with his jail identity, told his wife that "for the next 8 days your name is Mrs. N.D.16 and the kids are little N.D.16s." Many jokes were about Governor Cahill. When the guard's phone rang, teachers would say, "That's Cahill." The joke was on them: after twenty-three months of waiting, appealing, and hoping for pardon, the teachers were in jail.[118] The first group of women teachers traded jokes with the other inmates as part of creating common ties. The prison humor of men teachers was a way for them to express their pain without becoming too vulnerable.

The humor in Hirschfeld's letter was also a way to protect his wife. Like Alice Saltman, he didn't want his spouse to worry too much. He cautioned her that she would find the visiting area "dismal" and reassured her that his living quarters were "considerably more presentable." He warned her that to talk to him, she would have to bend down to a grating below the glass. The visiting areas on both the men's and women's sides were designed so that visitors could not, at the same time, look at prisoners and talk to them. He asked her to come anyway. At the end of his letter, he added a postscript: "Did Cahill call yet?" Later, he was more blunt. "Once you were there it was no joke. It was prison."[119]

Hirschfeld had contact with other prisoners only once, in the touch football game between teachers and inmates. He always loved sports but was never very good, except that morning. "I scored 2 touchdowns, intercepted 3 passes, and the fellows have changed my name from N.D.16 to Crazylegs Hirschfeld," he wrote to his wife. "I was voted the Bnai Brith Most Valuable Inmate Award." He didn't tell her that he was knocked down in the game. Bleeding but happy, he went to the nurse, where he encountered inmates he found scary: "Bruisers." Except for the game, he kept his distance from the inmates.[120]

But he made two interesting observations about them. Male inmates were split into three shifts for meals and given only ten minutes to eat because "there were uprisings going on in prisons." He also observed that inmates had different values from mainstream society. Watching the 1967 remake of *Hotel*, in which Karl Malden played the thief, "the prisoners were all rooting for Karl Malden." Hirschfeld's final action in jail might have won approval from other inmates if they'd known about it. He stole his tin cup. He smuggled it past the authorities and has it still. Perhaps he wanted something to show for his ten years of teaching in Newark.[121]

The heroic period of mass picketing, mass arrests, and mass jailings ended when the second group of men and women left prison on December 31, 1971. Six months later, ten teachers—including Graves, Lerman, Watkins, Zimmer, Nicholas—returned to jail. They had violated the injunction a second time in the 1971 strike; their sentence was three months (reduced from six months, upon appeal.) In addition, four teachers went to jail for the first time. Joe Del Grosso and Dom Bizzarro, who were neither officers of NTU nor repeat offenders, were given one month each. Clara Dasher and another officer were given three-month sentences. Graves was finally no longer alone: Dasher and two other women were with her this time.[122]

These fourteen remembered what the mass of women had demonstrated— that the authorities were afraid of their organizing of other inmates. "We made bold statements in the paper when we knew we were going to jail, saying that we would unionize the place, we'll take all the grievances of the prisoners, etc.," says Del Grosso. Perhaps as a result, they got better treatment. They were allowed out on work release, coming back to Caldwell to sleep at night. The men were placed in the hospital wing rather than with the general population. They were given privileges. One of the guards told Del Grosso his hair was too long and he had to get a haircut. "Then one of the other guards pulled him aside and told him that I was a teacher . . . , and he let me go."[123]

But prison was still prison. What Del Grosso found hardest was what most male teachers found hardest. At the courthouse, before being transported to Caldwell, he was locked in a cell. The loss of freedom was almost physically painful. "When I heard that iron door close, I almost . . . lost my balance. A very strange sense came over me. . . . I've never been a person that could stay still for a long period of time or be confined in that way. Then it really hit me that this was not going to be an easy thing to go through."[124]

The other inmates were shocked when Del Grosso told them why he was in Caldwell. "'Oh, we read about you. You're one of the teachers. All you did was carry a sign. At least I did this.'" In fact, during the 1971 strike, Del Grosso did much more than carry a sign. In jail, his street savvy helped the teachers. Their purchases from the prison store (cigarettes, cake) were stolen when they were out of their cells. "I'll never forget the look on some of the teachers' faces." He advised teachers to let it go. "I knew some of the prisoners that were in jail from the streets, and they had said don't make no big issue of it, because then you'll be a mark and they'll just keep stealing from you." The tendency of men teachers to act tough was not only psychological, he points out. Some men inmates were aggressive and violent. He met men in jail who were there for assault, and one who (in a separate case) had used a gun. "You had to keep up a certain image in jail, because if you were weak they would prey upon you. So we had to do that."[125]

Men teachers in prison could not be vulnerable. Women teachers comforted each other and rallied to those who needed help, acting as a kind of support group and creating a community. Relationships were central to the women, who were sustained by people inside and outside. Touch was vital. Dorothy Bergman held hands with teachers at night. Betty Rufalo felt the warmth of an inmate's leg. Hannah Litzky, in her diary, commented on her second visit with her husband and daughter: "So frustrating not to be able to touch them." By contrast, Dave Lieberfarb welcomed jail as an opportunity to end a relationship. Another man, bitter about going to jail, would not let his wife visit him.[126]

Women teachers in jail were consoled by men but also burdened by them. Even in jail, teachers were still wives, responsible for taking care of their husbands. Catherine Boardman cooked and froze meals for her husband and their two teenagers before she went to jail; when she came out, she was behind on the laundry. Betty Rufalo's husband was angry. "The kids got chicken pox and it was a drag. I had much more responsibility than I normally do, and—I'll be honest—I felt resentful. I resented the law and the judge and I resented my wife." Even men who wanted to help were likely to make it worse by taking the experience of their own helplessness so personally. "I visited my wife on Sunday," said one. "The room was crowded and noisy. We were separated by glass and had some trouble communicating. I left angry and frustrated. Who could I turn to? Who could I call? How could I spare my wife this indignity?"[127]

Activist women teachers in jail, like activist women in other sixties movements, practiced a more personal, more democratic, and more effective style of organizing than men. In the southern civil rights movement, Ella Baker and other Black women avoided the top-down approach of male ministers and succeeded in fostering grass-roots leadership. In the northern urban projects of Students for a Democratic Society, young women organizers were more successful than young men in building sustainable ties with neighborhood people. At decade's end, women made decentralized, personal consciousness-raising groups into the core of their movement for liberation.[128]

During the thirty-five-year-long history of the Union, stretching back to the Christmas Eve when the Union was born, women acted with men, often following their lead. Jail in 1971 gave women a chance to show what they could do on their own. For the first time since the sex-segregated faculty rooms of the forties and fifties, women had a space of their own. Conditions were worse on the women's side, overwhelming some. But on the whole, the women's style of activism worked better in prison than the men's. In the third-floor teachers room at Weequahic, women forged a type of activism that blended the personal and political, the functions of a support group and a union. In jail, some of these same women connected with younger teachers and other inmates and proved it was possible to fight back in prison, even if you were only there for eight days.

Epilogue

Power to the People?

Striking teachers had high hopes. They hoped to limit the power of the Board of Education and create a real process for decision making. Many hoped to make the schools better, for themselves and students. In the decades after the strikes, teachers benefited from better salaries and fringe benefits, and especially from the grievance procedure, which gave them rights for the first time. But many striking teachers were disappointed when the Union stopped fighting for students, and most were disappointed when the Union stopped fighting hard for teachers.

Newark teachers do not agree upon when the decline of their Union began, because they do not share a single concept of what a teacher union should be. Those who believe it should be a democratic forum with a play of ideas and a multiplicity of viewpoints began to be disillusioned as early as 1972. Those who believe it should fight as hard for students as for teachers became disillusioned by the mid-1970s. Those who believe it should vigorously advance the rights of teachers became disillusioned during the 1980s. And many of those who only ask that the Union get them raises and protect their gains became disillusioned by the mid-1990s.

Carol Karman thinks the first step in the decline of the Union was the silencing of dissent. Karman forced herself to attend executive board meetings after the 1971 strike, pressing Janice Adams, Angela Paone, and other activists to go with her. It was a losing struggle. "I was fighting for something very abstract. I think that's why we lost. We were fighting for democracy." Carole Graves was stronger than democracy. "She was the hero," says Karman.

"Nobody wanted to hear one bad word about her. She really could write her own ticket. And who she took along with her was who was in power."[1]

The 1970 coup, in which Karman participated, set a precedent. The power concentrated in Graves could be used against anyone who disagreed with her. Differences could be resolved by purging dissidents. Jim Lerman, who was active in the democratic opposition within the Union, and Graves disagreed at an executive board meeting in February 1972. Graves regarded opposition as conspiracy and treason. In her mind, the dissidents were part of an AFT plot. She wrote to Lerman, denouncing him for spreading dissension, threatening to bring him up on charges, and concluding bitterly: "Congratulations and success in your well earned job with the American Federation of Teachers."[2]

Graves and her supporters won the 1972 elections. The democratic opposition faded and the Union began to ossify. Janice Adams no longer felt welcome. "Ideas which were not in keeping with some of Carole Graves' ideas were not encouraged. I mean there wasn't any real dialogue." Other former strikers also missed the atmosphere of the old Union. "I experienced the Union as becoming less and less democratic," says Marty Blume. "The Union wasn't there anymore," says Dorothy Bergman, "the Union wasn't what I joined, . . . where you reason things out, you give your opinion, they vote on it, they listen to you." Increasingly, people were shouted down, cursed, or felt a heavy hand on their shoulder at meetings. Many stopped attending at this time.[3]

Jim Lowenstein could not walk away. He had grown up in the Union, which had been his extended family. During the 1970s, he pushed the Union to honor its commitment to help students. The New Jersey Supreme Court ruled in 1973 that unequal funding for Black urban and white suburban schools was unconstitutional. How could the Union use the court decision to improve Newark schools? Lowenstein kept raising this question until the leadership appointed him to head a committee. Working hard with other teachers, he wrote a report. And that was the end of it. He thinks the report was never read. He began to doubt that the Union would ever tackle school reform.[4]

At School Within a School, Lowenstein was part of reform. "We made curricular decisions. We met on a daily basis." Teachers were invited to initiate change. "It wasn't simply: 'here's a textbook, go teach the program.'" Students read Euripides in English class while studying the Greeks in history; they read Dickens as they studied the Industrial Revolution. "There was an attempt to integrate the curriculum. With the math people, with the art and music people. It was fabulous. It was so exciting. Not only that, but we were encouraged to develop new courses."[5]

Lowenstein thrived at SWAS. He would argue with Seymour Spiegel, the director, who says Lowenstein helped keep him honest. Lowenstein's arguments were less effective, however, with the Union. "I tried to have the Union subscribe to and advance the position that the entire system should be restructured—at least the high schools—[along the lines] of the School Within a School." Again he experienced the leadership's indifference to school reform. "That went nowhere with the Union. 'Very nice Jim, thank you very much.' "[6]

SWAS was killed by Board hostility and Union indifference. The Board opposed any program that did not fit its hierarchical and bureaucratic structure. Leo Litzky, the supportive principal of the school in which SWAS was housed, was pushed out in 1972; Spiegel was forced out in 1976. "They were replaced by hacks who didn't have the same vision or commitment to the program," Lowenstein observes. SWAS teachers were used to fending off attacks by the Board, but now they had to fight their own administrators as well. Teachers lost their meeting time and the right to choose books. The school lost the right to suspend students. "It was being changed back into a regular high school."[7]

Lowenstein was hurt by the direction of change in both SWAS and the Union. He was losing hope. He joined a dissident group in the Union in 1978 and ran for election, but the group lost in a landslide to Graves. After years of fighting for children and teachers, in the tradition of his father, Jim Lowenstein began to run dry. "I could see incipient burn out hitting me." In 1982, he left SWAS, the Union, and teaching. He became a lawyer.[8]

Teachers who wanted the Union to be a force for improving the schools were defeated during the 1970s and date the decline of the Union from that period. Felix Martino, Tom Lawton, and Jim Brown had a more bread-and-butter view of the Union. As they walked the picket line, they hoped the Union would fight for their rights, advance their interests, and protect their professional dignity. They were happy with the Union in the 1970s.

"That was the golden era of the Union, between say 1974 to about 1980, something like that," says Martino. He cites the generous fringe benefits, the elimination of nonprofessional chores, and the grievance procedure, which became deeply embedded in the contract. Martino never hoped the Union would enable teachers to shape educational policy. His hope was rather that the Union would make up for the decline in the status of teachers and the increased difficulty of teaching by protecting their rights and interests. He liked the way Graves aggressively represented teachers in bargaining with the Board during the 1970s. After 1980, "the Union, I think, got overconfident; it became less concerned with the needs of teachers."[9]

There was a one-week strike in 1976 and a two-day strike in 1980; there were no strikes after that. Union leaders settled into a working relationship with Board members and began to pay less attention to what their own members wanted. The Union was "useful to teachers" until the mid-1980s, says Beth

Blackmon. "Then what happened was that the Union, although the bargaining agent for the teachers, was no longer really the voice of the teachers. So that teachers in my building . . . had nothing to say to the Union rep. The Union rep was—instead of a voice of the teachers in the building, was a voice of the Union."[10]

The transformed role of the building representative epitomized the change in the Union. Reps played a pivotal role from 1962 to 1971, involving teachers in Union activities and forwarding teachers' concerns to the Union office. Through the 1970s, reps kept teachers involved, in case there was a strike. There was little for them to do after 1980. Tom Lawton, who became a rep in 1973, started to feel useless then. "I don't think there was communication down at my level," he says. The two-way relationship between the Union and the members became one way. "I would have Union meetings in the building, pass out information, take back information. And when I would bring information back and ask questions at the next meeting of the NTU, I wasn't getting answers." He began to skip Union meetings, and gradually withdrew.[11]

Jim Brown was a building representative for fifteen years. He remained loyal and grateful to Graves. But like many other strike activists, he felt frustrated. "In the beginning, there was a lot of interaction between the rank and file and the Union leadership. There were frequent meetings; issues got discussed." In the 1980s, "There weren't as many meetings. There was a heavy-handedness in the way the meeting was run. 'That's out of order.' There weren't discussions about what you want to do. Slowly but surely, more and more people got frustrated, because you didn't have any input in the decisions the Union would make."[12]

Brown saw a turning point when the Union went into politics. Election of Board of Education members began in 1983. In place of "us against them, the Union against the Board of Education," the Union was sponsoring candidates for the Board. Most candidates were backed by someone on city council, so "to get involved with the school board elections, you had to be involved with the council people. Interestingly enough, the council people were involved with the county people." The Union became involved in Board politics, Newark politics, Essex County politics. Graves herself ran twice for city council, unsuccessfully, before being elected to county office. "The first time Carole Graves decided to run for office, she sent each building rep in the mail two tickets to her political affair, and the tickets were $150 each. That was the first indication to me that: wait a minute! This lady is not serious about what teachers can afford."[13]

Within the Union, no one challenged Graves. Earlier, there were a succession of dissident groups, including Karman's group in the early seventies and the group containing Lowenstein in the late seventies. Steve Shaffer was involved in a dissident group and so was Bob Clark. A 1975 challenge led by Vic Cascella came closest to unseating her. All these groups opposed Graves for different reasons and did not join together. She was able to consolidate power and prevent further public expression of disagreement. The Union became a top-down organization, and participation declined at all levels.[14]

Most teachers who were involved in the strikes stopped participating during the 1980s; younger teachers never began. NTU stopped holding regular monthly membership meetings and folded the reps meeting into the executive board meeting. Joe Del Grosso was on the executive board. "The whole meeting would take thirty minutes. Everything: 'Yes. Yes.' " The silence disturbed Graves. She said to Karman, " 'You know Carol, people just aren't like they used to be. They're apathetic. They're not interested.' " Karman comments, "She never got the connection between what she did and what happened."[15]

NTU's involvement in Board elections led to an alliance with the Board. The Union "made peace with the Board of Ed at the expense of the teachers," says Blackmon. "And more and more, over the past few years, we began to think of them as one, almost." NTU leaders began to live like Board members. They dined in restaurants on the Union's credit card, took frequent trips, rode in leased cars. "The Board of Education and the Newark Teachers Union were mirror images of each other," says Eugene Liss. "One was using taxpayers' money and the other was using dues-payers' money." To Liss, "It's criminal." But Blackmon is reluctant to judge Graves or her associates. "I don't think they're bad people. I just think that's simply the way business is done."[16]

A strike activist, Liss went on to serve as the Union's lawyer. "By '76, '77, and '78, we were solving the money problems of the Union. And money became more accessible. And the people who were responsible for the money . . . didn't recognize the serious business that's involved when you handle public people's money." The State of New Jersey investigated and found the treasurer was using Union funds for his own profit. Another strike activist was bitter: "Ten or twelve years after all this commitment, the scumbags were lining their pockets!" Rumors of corruption swirled around the Union, which gave no financial statements to members. "No reports to the membership, no questions about finances," says Pete Petino. "No one came forward and questioned anything."[17]

Robert Braun later wrote of Graves: "She wanted to change the city, and those who knew her well a quarter-century ago believed she could. Instead, it changed her." Charles Bell, a key figure in the peace movement in 1971, became Board president in 1985. Once he, like Graves, had hoped to reform the Newark school system. Now Bell and Graves supported and campaigned for each other, protecting the status quo. Teachers connected to a Board or Union leader prospered. Marty Blume was assigned as a guidance counselor to East Side High in 1985. His new colleagues assumed he had a godfather in the Board or Union. They asked whom he knew, whom he paid off; when he said no one, they didn't believe him. "What I found out from Newark," says Blackmon, "is that if you have a godfather you're protected no matter what you do. I mean people do outrageous things. They have sex with students in closets. They do all kinds of incredible things and say all kinds of incredible things to kids. If they're protected."[18]

The Union did not create this systematic corruption; rather, it gradually accommodated to it. But precisely because the Union was different in the beginning, its participation in the system of favors and protection created despair in teachers who once believed in the possibility of change. The resulting cynicism is painful for people who, deep down, still care. The Union deprived teachers of hope. In that sense, the Union hurt them more than the Board, because teachers never believed in the Board.

Race solidified the Union leadership and the Board-Union alliance. In the 1970s, neighborhood people hired as aides to do nonprofessional chores and teachers recruited in the South became Union members. The majority of NTU members were Black. Black solidarity and white fear of being accused of racism discouraged teachers from confronting Union or Board leaders. "Everyone seemed to want to lay off racial issues, because they were explosive or very volatile kinds of things," says Blackmon. "If somebody was doing something wrong and he was of a particular race, well, you didn't say anything."[19]

In the early 1970s, a Black woman raised a critical voice. In a continuation of the tradition of 1971, someone slashed all four of her tires, and she stopped challenging the Union leadership. A Black man planned to run against the leadership, later in the 1970s, but intimidation was again effective. Later, in 1995, Martha Nolley joined an insurgent group led by a white man, and anonymous notes were put in her box, calling her racist; the insurgent group was publicly attacked as racist. The purpose, explains Charles Nolley, was to get Blacks to support Graves. "Because historically, it's always been the white master who put his foot down on Blacks. So here's a white guy running for something against a Black person. So you stick with the Black person. So you want it to be a racist thing."[20] Racial politics enforced the status quo.

Nationally, the labor movement was on the defensive in the 1980s, and the range of issues for collective bargaining became increasingly narrow. In New Jersey, the State Supreme Court ruled in a 1978 Ridgefield Park case that teacher unions could not bargain over involuntary transfer and most other working conditions. The Newark Board of Education invoked the Ridgefield

Park decision in 1980. Later the Board removed from the contract the protection against involuntary transfer, and the Union chose not to fight. Both Janice Adams and Tom Lawton were simply transferred against their wishes, more than twenty years after they thought they had won forever the right to due process.[21]

The decline of the Union paralleled the decline of the industrial unionism of the 1930s and the social movements of the 1960s. Like CIO unions, particularly the United Automobile Workers, NTU lost its rich, democratic culture. UAW members in the 1950s and NTU members in the 1980s ceased playing a significant role in their union, and settled for wage increases and one-person rule. Like movement organizations, particularly SNCC, NTU lost its capacity for bringing forth new leaders, its belief in people, its ability to listen, and its internal sense of community, even as it became more racially homogenous.[22]

The Newark Teachers Union promised in the 1960s to help teachers gain the control over working conditions that professionals traditionally enjoyed. Measured against that promise, the Union failed. It stopped pressing the Board for better working conditions, concentrating on a better working relationship with the Board. Teachers were left to struggle on in their individual classrooms.[23]

Before the Union era, students needed individual attention, but classes were too large; there were serious discipline problems; most teachers were unable to bring students from where they were to where they needed to be. Nothing changed on this level, except everything got worse.

As students became more challenging, Edith Counts believes, teachers became less qualified. The written exam was abolished in 1968. In the 1970s, to replace departing white teachers, the Board recruited heavily from traditionally Black colleges in the South. By the end of the seventies, half the teachers in Newark were not certified. Meanwhile, Counts points out, teachers with experience and training often used their connections to get out of teaching. "That was the biggest thing, to become something else other than a classroom teacher, and many times that was completely political."[24]

Teachers who stayed in the classroom burned out. When Phil Basile was young, he reached out to students, even outside school. "Now I refuse to get that close. I won't allow the kids to get that close to me." Colleagues say Basile is still a better-than-average teacher. But the chaos of students' lives fills him with despair. "I'm not going to take it seriously any more. I just can't. Every time you take something seriously, you work with a kid, work with a kid, you do good, the kid's doing good—she's pregnant. Now where are you going? Or he's in jail. I've had my heart torn out a lot of times. . . . You become hard at heart over the years, because then you don't want to be that close."[25]

It's hard for teachers in Newark to feel successful. Their best students disappear. Or teachers try to impose limits on students who are not serious, who attend occasionally, who are always late and never prepared, only to be undercut by administration. One senior came to Basile's class only twice all spring term. He would see her in the park with boys during school hours. Two days before graduation, the guidance counselor asked him to help her make up the work. Basile refused. The assistant superintendent called, leaning on him. He realized someone was looking out for the girl. Though he failed her, he became more bitter. His feeling was: No one cares, so why should I?[26]

Janice Adams continued to feel successful in the classroom through the 1970s. "I've had some lovely kids, real sweethearts." In the 1980s and 1990s, more and more of her energy went into discipline. Drugs were more prevalent, violence more common. The change was gradual, cumulative, and overwhelming. "Now there's a hardness from some of the kids," she says. "It's like a protection, I think." What would she do if she had the power? "First of all—it sounds terrible—I would remove the disruptive kids." She has not given up or become cynical. She still teaches junior high, still lives in Newark, still enjoys the energy of the city and the energy of the kids. But even Adams is running out of hope.[27]

Most Newark teachers do not feel they are growing. Teachers told a school reformer that faculty development programs have been ineffective because the programs generally ignore the problem of discipline. Parents defend disruptive children; principals back away. "A lot of people are afraid of the kids," says Charles Nolley. "But more of them are afraid of the parents." Martha Nolley and her colleagues moved to restore order at Weequahic in the 1990s. A team of teachers swept the school and pulled students from halls or bathrooms. "We took over the school and showed him [the principal] how to get the kids under control. And he didn't back us. . . . We'd catch the kids and take them to the holding place. He'd send them right back to the class." She adds: "They always destroy whatever works."[28]

What Carol Karman finds exhausting is trying to help students learn while dealing simultaneously with behavior problems. Just two or three out-of-control children can disrupt a class. Karman thinks that students often misbehave because they cannot read. Once, teaching fifth grade, she searched for and found a discarded set of third-grade books. Her students took the book home every night and wrote a summary of a story. The next day, they discussed the story, and she could tell they understood. "I told them what functional illiteracy was, and I told them that they were going to learn to be real literate people." They were ready for a fifth-grade book at the end of a month; at the end of the year, they gave her a plaque. "They learned how to read. Not every single kid, but the overwhelming majority. Some of them went up two grade levels that year. That was about 1974. That's one of my best stories. I don't have that many great stories."[29]

The Board of Education, in the name of raising standards, later barred teachers from using books below grade level. Teachers were bitter. Karman protested to her principal, pointing out that the new policy led both students and teachers to fake it, to pretend students understood what they were reading. How do teachers' ideas reach the people who make policy, she asked? " 'Well,' " said the principal, " 'when I go to the principals' meeting, the principals can bring them up.' " Karman is skeptical. "What if the principals are scared shit of the superintendent? If you saw how the principal runs the [faculty] meeting, you'd see how the superintendent runs the meeting. The faculty meetings are just top-down lectures. Boring, boring lectures."[30]

Ideas for change, rooted in classroom experience, almost never reach the top; after a while, many teachers stop having ideas. In Karman's vision, the undemocratic nature of the system, the demoralization of teachers, and the misbehavior of students are all linked. "I haven't had much experience of principals who wanted feedback. The thing is, what are they going to do with it? They have bosses too. The whole system is set up top down, but nobody has the right to say anything. We all have this big army up there, and the kids are acting crazy. They're the only ones that have the nerve to say no." Blackmon has a similar vision. Board and Union leaders, showing no respect for dialogue, "groomed a generation of kids in the schools now that have no respect for dialogue. Which is one reason that schools in places like Newark are violent and disruptive places."[31]

Desperate for reform, some teachers welcomed the takeover of the Newark school system by the State of New Jersey in 1995. So far, observers describe the changes as primarily cosmetic. The state government, dominated by suburban interests, has not shifted resources toward urban centers. Nor has it questioned its top-down approach to educational reform. Edith Counts, who retired in 1993, predicted a state takeover would have little impact on the schools. "Teachers know now that they can't look forward to next year being any different from the previous year." Elena Scambio, who represented the state in Newark for many years before the takeover as the assistant commissioner of education, thinks many Newark teachers simply have lost hope.[32]

Marty and Anna Blume long ago gave up their belief in the possibility of educational reform in Newark. Still idealistic, Anna left the Newark school system and now teaches elsewhere. Marty studied psychology and became a guidance counselor, learning to count success one student at a time. "We kept on narrowing and narrowing our focus." Once they hoped for more. In 1970, the strike victory, the leadership of Carole Graves, the election of Gibson, the alliance of teachers and parents at Bergen Street—all seemed to the Blumes to be ushering in a new era of interracial cooperation and educational reform.[33]

Walking the picket line in 1970, many teachers hoped to make teaching possible. They knew their Union was itself a democratic institution, within which teachers debated ideas with each other, and they believed it would be a force for democratizing the school system. But the process worked the other way. The Union, instead of changing the top-down system, became an integral part of it.

The Union never stopped helping teachers in some ways, though. Many teachers found Pete Petino especially helpful with grievances. A call to the Union office could end an abuse. The grievance procedure puts "a lot of checks" on people in power, Mary Abend says. "I know from having seen relatives and friends who work where there is no union . . . if you have somebody who doesn't like you as a boss, you have no recourse. It's you and them. And unfortunately there are too many people who abuse power." The Union "still gives us some dignity," said Karman in 1994. "You mention the Union, and they think twice. You mention a grievance, and they might cringe. That gives a teacher a certain amount of self-respect."[34] As if still arguing with Tony Ficcio, sounding eerily like Bob Lowenstein, Karman insists, "That's not just bread and butter, that's not just bread and butter. That's self-respect."[35]

In 1995, teachers fought to reclaim the Union as their own. The cry of racism was no longer effective. Martha Nolley and other teachers stood their ground: "It wasn't about color." A Black NTU leader who called the insurgents racists was confronted by Nolley's Weequahic colleagues. "They're showing this paper to him, shoving it in his face. He's just standing there. These are women now doing this, teachers. They say, 'How dare you put this in the boxes? . . . How dare you send us this garbage in the mail?' And said, 'We know Martha Nolley. . . . ' And then they called him everything, cursed him out something awful."[36] The insurgents proved that the power that teachers won in 1970 was never entirely lost. The story of how they took their power back is the last one in this book.

Like many teachers, Nolley loyally backed Graves for a quarter of a century. But in the summer of 1994, NTU lent the Board of Education $411,000 to fight the impending state takeover. Petino opposed giving teachers' money to management. "When she fired Pete, that was her downfall." In the winter, Graves began receiving a $71,000 salary as county register of deeds and mortgages, in addition to her salary of $96,000 as NTU president. Teachers, working for six months with no contract, asked for a strike vote, but Graves signed a contract with no raise in the first year. Nolley was angry. "I went to a meeting and asked a question, and she told us we were silly." Nolley reluctantly concluded that Graves had become "almost like a dictator."[37]

At the first meeting of the insurgent group in February, Joe Del Grosso raised the fundamental question. "Years ago, the management intimidated us. How can we live with a union that intimidates?" The group, spearheaded by Del Grosso, was Teachers About Change (TAC). Most teachers were afraid to join, afraid of retaliation, of being forced out of their schools. The teachers who were not intimidated were those with roots in the teacher strikes and sixties activism. "The first people that joined the movement were the very people that I was on strike with in the seventies," says Del Grosso. "It was the veteran teachers who came to the vanguard of the movement. The younger teachers were reluctant. They were afraid. And we discussed that. And when we discussed it, we reminisced about our colleges—our college experience. And we came up with that rationale: we came from this era."[38]

Del Grosso's mission was to restore democracy to the Union. He was peculiarly suited to the task because he encompassed most of the different strands in the Union. He was a sixties person who was influenced by oppositional movements in college but was not opposed to the war in Vietnam. He was a Catholic who converted to Judaism while dating a Jewish woman and remained Jewish when they broke up. He was an Italian street fighter who learned how to become a teacher and leader from a Black mentor.[39]

Del Grosso was assigned to teach with a Black man named Frank Hoggard by his principal in 1971. Instead of punishing Del Grosso, as the principal intended, the experience transformed him. "I finally was with someone who was a really professional teacher." He learned by observing Hoggard that showing respect for students worked: "You didn't need to lose your temper to keep discipline." Hoggard put poems on the board for the children to copy and learn to recite, "and I would say they'll never do that, because I didn't understand that you could bring children up to that level, if you, like I said, used dignity."[40]

Hoggard also mentored Del Grosso in his Union career. Away from school, they worked the *New York Times* crossword puzzles together to extend Del Grosso's vocabulary. Del Grosso learned to use correct English when speaking publicly, instead of Newark colloquialisms and street language. Hoggard told him he was intelligent and did a good job as building rep, but "'you can't always be the person's hatchet man, because that's what you'll be labeled.'" He said, "'You have to come to grips with who you can become and what you can become.'" Del Grosso learned that "there were other ways besides always exploding and having a temper."[41]

Del Grosso rose to NTU executive vice president, but Graves abolished the position. Already disenchanted, he was ready when she alienated core supporters in 1994–95. TAC argued that Graves ran a closed union and kept finances secret, that she was too distant from the members and too cozy with the Board. Union leaders fought back. With Union funds, they hired a detective agency to spy on people who went to TAC meetings. They called Del Grosso a bar fighter and a racist. Thinking with his head instead of his fists, Del Grosso ran a campaign rooted in respect for teachers. "I never got angry. I knew that that was a trap, and that Carole was thinking about the old Joey from the old days."[42]

TAC put together a slate of thirty candidates, half of whom were Black or Latino. In the election, in June 1995, all TAC candidates, including Martha Nolley, won easily. Del Grosso defeated Graves for the presidency by 1,809 to 1,015.[43]

Winning was only the first step; the habits of democracy had been lost. Del Grosso appointed teachers to determine his salary. "They came to me and told me they were going to pay me $90,000 a year. I said, 'No. That's not acceptable to me.'" They thought he wanted more. He explained that $90,000 was too much; no teacher made nearly that. They offered him $85,000, then $82,000. They justified $82,000 by pointing to his long hours and short summers. He accepted. Del Grosso put through a resolution at his first executive board meeting that no staff member, including the president, could get a larger percentage raise than teachers.[44]

It was easy for Del Grosso to get resolutions passed at that first meeting. His problem was getting people to disagree. On the first three motions, everyone just said yes. "So I turned off the tape recorder, and I say: ' . . . When a motion is on the floor, just because you think in your mind that I, as president, or Roz [Samuels], as the secretary-treasurer, are in favor of that motion, that doesn't mean that you have to vote for that motion. You could go against it.' And they all just like looked at me." Gradually debate began. On one motion, Del Grosso offered strong arguments. The motion carried, but eleven people voted no. "At the end of the meeting they sat very quiet and they looked at me, and one of the executive board members walked over to me, and said, 'You're mad at us, Joey, right?' 'No. Mad at you? I'm proud of you.' And I walked over to the ones that voted against the motion, and I hugged all of them, and I said, 'You didn't do anything wrong. You disagreed. That's what unions are for.'"[45]

Not all union presidents agreed that disagreements are good for unions. Some criticized Del Grosso for exposing Graves's practices. "They say to me . . . I'm giving unions a bad name. And I take great umbrage to that because I feel *they* gave unionism a bad name, and what I'm trying to do is give unions a good name." One of the presidents who criticized Del Grosso was his national president, Al Shanker. "I think that presidents of unions have their own union," comments Del Grosso. He e-mailed Shanker, criticizing him for backing AFL-CIO head Lane Kirkland to the end. As leader of the reform forces within the Newark Teachers Union in 1995, Del Grosso supported John Sweeny, leader of the reform forces in the AFL-CIO.[46]

How far might reform carry the Newark Teachers Union? In some cities, teacher unions have become forces for school reform, and there has been an increasing convergence of teacher activists working on union reform with teacher activists working on school reform. "The Union should become more involved with the direction of education," says Tom Lawton, who was elected on TAC's slate. Having reformed the Union, teachers can help reform the schools. "We're doing more and more paperwork, but not improving education. The teachers aren't asked what to do. Maybe through the Union, who has more access to the teachers, who will be freer to talk to the Union than the Board, we can generate some ideas."[47]

School reform becomes possible when teachers and parents work together. Initiatives by teachers at School Within a School, Bergen Street, and Barringer only succeeded because of alliances with parents. But teachers did not know how to share their power with parents. Nor did they realize they would lose their power if they entrusted it to others, even to those whom they elected. If Newark teachers become powerful again, will they build alliances with parents? If teachers and parents join together, which issues will they tackle? Discipline, surely. And then?

Real school reform nurtures the hopes of teachers, and draws on their energy and insights. Teachers know a lot about teaching. Most schools isolate them in their classrooms, discourage their initiatives, use up their youthful idealism and turn them into cynics. Much of what claims to be educational reform takes even more initiative away from teachers, forcing them to teach prefabricated curriculums that prepare students for standardized tests. Real school reform enables teachers to talk to each other, learn from each other, and together shape the curriculum and schedule.

Not all Newark teachers, even at the height of their power, wanted their Union to get involved in school reform. There were different, vital, and competing visions of what the Newark Teachers Union should be. There was the bread-and-butter tradition of Tony Ficcio, and the more expansive and socially committed tradition of Bob Lowenstein. Clearly, however, no version of unionism will amount to much without democracy. Without democracy, teachers in the traditions of Lowenstein and Ficcio could not argue with each other, learn from each other, and evolve their own vision. The loss of democracy cut short the learning process of the teachers. Democracy comes first. What happens next is up to the teachers themselves.

Appendix

Teachers in the Book

Mary Abend. Began teaching autumn 1970. From Gary, Indiana. Picketed in 1971 until discouraged by violence against strikers.

Janice Adams. Began in 1964, junior high. Strong NTU striker, 1970 and 1971. For Union democracy, 1971–72. Still teaching in Newark in 2001.

Phil Basile. Barringer teacher. Arrested in 1970, crossed picket line in 1971. Later became discouraged about teaching.

Dorothy Bergman. Began teaching at Weequahic, 1950s. Active in NTU as elementary teacher in 1960s, and went on strike in 1970. Went to jail.

Marty Bierbaum. Taught in Newark during the Vietnam War. Part of "basement experiment" at Bergen Street. Struck in 1970 but not in 1971.

Beth Blackmon. Barringer history teacher. Began teaching in 1969. Active in NTU and strikes. At Barringer until 1994 and still working in Newark.

Anna Blume and Marty Blume. Bergen Street teachers. Experimental as teachers, hopeful about change in Newark. Struck 1970, not 1971.

Marion Bolden. Began at Barringer in 1969. Stayed out during 1970 strike. Went to work during 1971. Differed on "nonprofessional chores." Now superintendent of schools in Newark.

Jim Brown. Called "Nicky Newark" by students in local college. Began teaching 1970–71, beaten up as a striker in 1971. Later taught at SWAS.

Zenobia Capel. Physical education teacher in 1950s, and again from 1960s to 1980s. Not a striker. Protected herself during 1971 strike.

Vic Cascella. Began teaching 1950s. "Young Turk" in NTU in 1960s. Fought for elementary teachers' rights. Acting president of Union during 1971 strike.

Joe Ciccolini Sr. Barringer teacher of business. Union member and striker. From a labor background.

Bob Clark. Funeral director, elementary teacher, striker in 1965 and 1970–71. Part of 1970 coup. Later critical of NTU leadership.

Edith Counts. Elementary teacher. Grew up in Newark. Began teaching there in 1961. Member of Association. Crossed picket line in 1970 and 1971. Retired 1993.

Ellen Cunniff. Elementary speech teacher. Association member. Hoped to go into administration. Crossed the line in 1970 and 1971.

Phyllis Cuyler. Began teaching at Arts High, 1969. Graduate of Howard University. Struck 1970, and briefly in 1971, then went back. Still teaching in Newark.

Clara Dasher. South Eighth Street teacher. Vice president of NTU from 1969 until her death in 1990s. Worked closely with Carole Graves for twenty-five years.

Joe Del Grosso. Began elementary teaching before 1971 strike. A leader of "wild bus rides." Arrested. Became NTU president in 1995.

Ben Epstein. Weequahic teacher and NTU activist in the 1940s and 1950s. Principal, then assistant superintendent during the 1960s. Died 2000.

Ralph Favilla. Navy veteran. Elementary teacher. Began teaching 1958. "Young Turk" in 1960s. Skilled organizer of teachers. Striker 1970 and 1971.

Tony Ficcio. Began teaching in the 1950s. Led bargaining push in 1960s. After 1969, on staff of state teacher federations in New Jersey and New York.

Walter Genuario. Began teaching at West Side High School in 1968. Labor movement background. Striker. Later SWAS teacher. Still in Newark as administrator in 2001.

Carole Graves. Elementary special education teacher. Picketed in 1965. President of NTU, 1968–1995. Jailed for long periods, 1971–72.

Bob Hirschfeld. Elementary teacher, picketed 1965. Arrested 1970. Participated in 1970 coup. Driven out by hostile Newark parents after 1971. Salesman since 1971.

Carol Karman. Elementary teacher. Picketed in 1965, 1970, 1971. Went to jail. Hopeful of change in 1969–71. Active in 1970 coup. Still teaching.

Jeanette Lappé. Began teaching at Weequahic in 1940s. Active in third-floor teachers room. Demanding teacher. Striker. A leader of jail rebellion.

Tom Lawton. Self-described "Nicky Newark." Garfield Elementary teacher. Active in strikes. Elected to executive board of NTU on reform slate in 1995.

Jim Lerman. Brown University graduate, 1968. Began teaching in Newark in

1968. Hoped to change the world of education. Active as striker, NTU newsletter editor. Jailed.

Dave Lieberfarb. A journalist at heart, a teacher during the Vietnam war. Idealistic. "Power to the People." Struck in 1970 and 1971.

Gene Liss. Elementary teacher, active in both 1970 and 1971 strikes. A lawyer for NTU during 1970s, and again since 1995.

Hannah Litzky. Weequahic teacher. Active in third-floor teachers room. NTU activist from 1937. Active in 1970 strike and in jail. Died in 1999.

Bob Lowenstein. Ph.D. in Romance languages. Weequahic teacher and NTU leader from 1930s to 1960s. Outspoken, articulate, principled.

Jim Lowenstein. Bob's son. Taught at Weequahic and SWAS. Picketed in 1970 and 1971. Arrested. Active in school and Union reform in 1970s.

Avant Lowther Jr. Began teaching at West Kinney Junior High, 1968. Son of a Newark teacher. Militant striker 1970. Torn in 1971; went to work.

Charles Malone. Tuskegee Airman. High School teacher. Crossed the picket line in 1965, 1970, 1971.

Felix Martino. Barringer teacher. Son of Newark teacher. In 1970, on strike to get a grievance procedure, and in 1971 to keep it.

Harold Moore. Elementary teacher of the deaf, beginning in the 1950s. Couldn't get supplies, left Association. Active in strikes. Retired 1988.

Don Nicholas. Secondary teacher, began teaching in 1960. Labor background. "Young Turk" in 1960s. Arrested in 1970 and in 1971. Served in NTU until 1995.

Charles Nolley and Martha Nolley. Secondary school teachers, active strikers. Charles began teaching in 1950s, joined NTU in 1960s, as a result of on-the-job experience. Martha elected on NTU reform slate in 1995.

Angela Paone. Began teaching 1964. Attracted to larger issues raised by NTU. Stayed with same students two years. Striker in 1970 and 1971.

Pete Petino. South Eighth Street School. Arrested in 1970 strike. Driven from school, became full-time NTU staff. Still on Union staff.

Pat Piegari. Elementary teacher. Frustrated by lack of supplies. Called for 1970 strike. Active picket, 1970 and 1971. Arrested 1970.

Ron Polonsky. West Kinney Junior High. Recruited for NTU. Worked on 1969 election campaign. First full-time NTU staff member. Strike organizer 1970, 1971. Purged from NTU, 1972.

Phyllis Salowe. Elementary teacher, began 1969. Idealistic striker in 1970. Not-so-idealistic striker in 1971. Arrested 1970. Currently a citizen action leader.

Alice Saltman. Weequahic art teacher since the 1930s. Active in Union. Litzky's best friend, picketed with her in 1970 and went to jail.

Elena Scambio. Began teaching at First Avenue School, 1969. Stayed home during 1970 strike. Active picket, 1971. Later educational leader in Newark and state.

John Schmid. Secondary teacher, NTU leader, in 1960s. On AFT staff during 1970 and 1971 strikes. Graves's enemy, early 1970s. Still a labor organizer.

Steve Shaffer. Secondary teacher, began 1969. Arrested 1970. Strong trade union and Democratic Party commitment. Still teaching in Newark.

Seymour Spiegel. Secondary teacher, began teaching in the 1950s. NTU member. SWAS founder and director, 1969–76. Still an educational reformer.

Andy Thorburn. Led Barringer faculty self-organization, 1968–69. Worked with Polonsky on 1969 NTU campaign. Left NTU and teaching after 1970 coup.

Esther Tumin. Weequahic science teacher, began teaching in 1959, in midlife. Participant in third-floor teachers room. Arrested 1970. Had bad time in jail.

Jerry Yablonsky. Began teaching at East Side High in 1961. Part-time NTU organizer in 1960s. Picket captain in 1970. Arrested. Left Newark teaching, 1989.

Notes

Abbreviations

NN	*Newark Evening News*
NTU files	Newark Teachers Union files
NTU membership book	Newark Teachers Union membership book, Newark Teachers Union files
SL	*Newark Star-Ledger*

Introduction

1. Carol Karman, interview with author, Bloomfield, N.J., March 17, 1994.
2. Erich Auerbach, *Mimesis: The Representation of Reality in Western Literature* (Princeton, N.J.: Princeton University Press, 1953), 547–548.
3. Norman Eiger, "The Newark School Wars: A Socio-Historical Study of the 1970 and 1971 Newark School System Strikes" (Ed.D. diss., Rutgers University, 1976); Robert J. Braun, *Teachers and Power: The Story of the American Federation of Teachers* (New York: Simon and Schuster, 1972).
4. Eiger, "The Newark School Wars"; editorial, "Toward Newark School Peace," *New York Times*, April 3, 1971, 28.
5. Fred Barbaro, "The Newark Teachers' Strike," *The Urban Review* (January 1972): 3–10; Ron Porambo, *No Cause for Indictment: An Autopsy of Newark* (New York: Holt, Rinehart, and Winston, 1971), 370–381; William M. Phillips Jr., *Participation of the Black Community in Selected Aspects of the Educational Institutions of Newark* (New Brunswick, N.J.: Rutgers, the State University, 1973), 191; William M. Phillips Jr., and Joseph M. Conforti, *Social Conflict: Teachers' Strikes in Newark, 1964–1971* (Trenton: New Jersey Department of Education, 1972), 58.
6. Marjorie Murphy, *Blackboard Unions: The AFT and the NEA, 1900–1980* (Ithaca, N.Y.: Cornell University Press, 1990), 198–208; David Selden, *The Teacher Rebellion* (Washington, D.C.: Howard University Press, 1985), 109.

7. Charles M. Payne, *I've Got the Light of Freedom: The Organizing Tradition and the Mississippi Freedom Struggle* (Berkeley: University of California Press, 1995), 68, 100, 101, and 362; Clayborne Carson, *In Struggle: SNCC and the Black Awakening of the 1960s* (Cambridge: Harvard University Press, 1981), 20, 30, and 43.

One   The Teacher Activists

1. The original charter of Local 481 hangs on the wall of the Newark Teachers Union.
2. Marjorie Murphy, *Blackboard Unions: The AFT and the NEA, 1900–1980* (Ithaca, N.Y.: Cornell University Press, 1990), 83–85 and 123; Newark Teachers Union, *Teaching*, n.d., 3.
3. Newark Teachers Union, *50th Anniversary Celebration*, video, November 29, 1986; Ben Epstein, interview with author, Toms River, N.J., August 7, 1995; Bob Lowenstein, interview with author, West Orange, N.J., June 14, 1993; Murphy, *Blackboard Unions*, 87–88; Sidney Rosenfeld, "Memo to Elem. School Teachers," n.d., NTU files; David Selden, *The Teacher Rebellion* (Washington, D.C.: Howard University Press, 1985), 13.
4. Epstein interview with author; Bob Lowenstein interview; Newark Teachers Union video; William B. Helmreich, *The Enduring Community: The Jews of Newark and MetroWest* (New Brunswick, N.J.: Transaction Publishers, 1999), 115.
5. Bob Lowenstein interview. Lowenstein heard this comment at a meeting of Local 481.
6. Allen Ginsberg, "To Aunt Rose," in *Bluestones and Salt Hay: An Anthology of Contemporary New Jersey Poets*, ed. Joel Lewis (New Brunswick, N.J.: Rutgers University Press, 1990), 65; Hannah Litzky, interview with author, West Orange, N.J., August 25, 1993.
7. Litztky interview; Hannah Litzky, telephone conversation with author, November 11, 1995.
8. Litzky interview; Bob Lowenstein interview; NTU membership book.
9. Philip Roth, *I Married a Communist* (New York: Vintage Books, 1999), 5; Litzky interview.
10. Bob Lowenstein interview.
11. Michael Denning, *The Cultural Front: The Laboring of American Culture in the Twentieth Century* (London: Verso, 1996), xvi–xvii and 90; Bob Lowenstein interview.
12. Bob Lowenstein interview.
13. Alice Saltman, interview with author, Livingston, N.J., June 13, 1995; Dorothy Bergman, interview with author, New York City, October 11, 1995; Helmreich, *The Enduring Community*, 110–113. The memory of Weequahic as an almost 100 percent Jewish neighborhood is a simplification of the kind people often make, looking back. Robert W. Snyder, "The Neighborhood Changed: The Irish of Washington Heights and Inwood since the 1940s" (paper presented at Oral History Association conference, 1996).
14. Saltman interview.
15. Andy Thorburn, interview with author, Somerset, N.J., July 14, 1992; Litzky interview. Kathleen Casey interviewed women who taught in inner cities, saw themselves as skilled workers, drew on the Old and New Lefts, and focused on social

change. But unlike Weequahic women, they were not strong unionists, because they saw their unions as not dealing with teaching/learning issues. Kathleen Casey, *I Answer with My Life: Life Histories of Women Teachers Working for Social Change* (New York: Routledge, 1993), 4, 90, and 100.

16. Esther Tumin, interview with author, Livingston, N.J, December 4, 1992; NTU membership book.

17. Tumin, interview with author, Livingston, N.J., December 14, 1992.

18. Seymour Spiegel, interview with author, Watchung, N.J., September 21, 1995; Jeanette Lappé, letter to the editor, *NN,* May 22, 1970, 24.

19. Spiegel interviews, September 21, 1995, and September 22, 1995; NTU membership book.

20. Spiegel interview, September 21, 1995; Vic Cascella, Ralph Favilla, and Don Nicholas, interview with author, Newark, December 1, 1995; John Schmid, interview with author, Bloomfield, N.J., February 28, 1997.

21. Bob Lowenstein interview; Tony Ficcio, interview with author, New York City, November 29, 1995; Murphy, *Blackboard Unions*, 151–152.

22. Epstein interview; NTU membership book; Murphy, *Blackboard Unions*, 87–88; Steve Shaffer, interview with author, Fair Lawn, N.J., November 19, 1994; Bergman, interview with author.

23. Schmid interview; Ellen Cunniff, interview with author, Bloomfield, N.J., August 14, 1995.

24. Spiegel interview, September 22, 1995; Murphy, *Blackboard Unions*, 167–171; Denning, *The Cultural Front*, 89–90. The Teachers Union of New York was a local union similar in many ways to the early Newark Teachers Union. This was the union to which my mother belonged, but it was expelled from the AFL in 1941 and went out of existence in 1964. Paul Buhle, "Albert Shanker: No Flowers," *New Politics* (Summer 1997): 51–52.

25. Lowenstein, quoted in Donald A. Gsell, "Teacher Unionism in New Jersey: A History and Current Analysis" (Ed.D. diss., Rutgers University, 1967), 101–102.

26. Bob Lowenstein interview; Litzky interview; Cascella, Favilla, and Nicholas interview; Gsell, "Teacher Unionism in New Jersey," 102–103; Murphy, *Blackboard Unions*, 194.

27. Angela Paone, interview with author, Roseland, N.J., August 8, 1995; Epstein interview; Robert Braun, *Teachers and Power: The Story of the American Federation of Teachers* (New York: Simon and Schuster, 1972), 184; Cascella, Favilla, and Nicholas interview; Schmid interview.

28. Marc Gaswirth, William M. Weinberg, and Barbara E. Kemmerer, *Teachers' Strikes in New Jersey: Studies in Industrial Relations and Human Resources, No.1.* (Metuchen, N.J.: Scarecrow Press, 1982), 6; Marc Gaswirth, "Teacher Militancy in New Jersey: An Analysis of Organizational Change, Public Policy Development, and School Board–Teacher Relationships through January, 1975" (Ed.D.diss., Rutgers University, 1977), 25 and 58–59. The New Jersey Education Association did make important gains, including tenure laws, by lobbying the state legislature.

29. Murphy, *Blackboard Unions*, 217–218; Epstein interview; Norman Eiger, "The Newark School Wars: A Socio-Historical Study of the 1970 and 1971 Newark School System Strikes" (Ed.D. diss., Rutgers University, 1976), 29.

30. Joseph F. Cascella, "Speech to the Board of Education," Newark, August 27, 1963, NTU files, 7–8; "Report on Newark Teachers Union NTU-IUD Program," n.d., NTU files, 1; Ficcio interview.

31. Ficcio interview; Paone interview; Schmid interview.

32. Ficcio interview.

33. Cascella, Favilla, and Nicholas interview; Vic Cascella, telephone conversation, July 11, 2000.

34. Cascella, Favilla, and Nicholas interview.

35. Cascella, Favilla, and Nicholas interview; NTU membership book. The membership book shows Favilla winning a recruiting competition.

36. Vic Cascella, interview with author, Newark, August 6, 1996.

37. Cascella, Favilla, and Nicholas interview.

38. Cascella interview; Cascella, Favilla, and Nicholas interview; Eiger, "The Newark School Wars," 64.

39. Don Nicholas, interview with author, Newark, September 1, 1992, and Newark, December 1, 1995; Cascella, Favilla, and Nicholas interview.

40. Ficcio interview; Cascella, Favilla, and Nicholas interview; Gaswirth, "Teacher Militancy," 92; Selden, *The Teacher Rebellion*, 85 and 88; Alan Rosenthal, *Pedagogues and Power: Teacher Groups in School Politics* (Syracuse, N.Y.: Syracuse University Press, 1968), 14; Kim Moody, *An Injury to All: The Decline of American Unionism* (London: Verso, 1988), 210.

41. "Report on Newark Teachers Union NTU-IUD Program," 1–4 and 6. The Board of Education unofficially reserved membership slots for a Jewish representative, a Black representative, and other specific ethnic groups. Jacob Fox, interview with Norman Eiger, Montclair, N.J., December 24, 1974.

42. *NTU Bulletin* (October 1962), 3; Cascella, Favilla, and Nicholas interview.

43. Cascella, Favilla, and Nicholas interview; "Report on Newark Teachers Union NTU-IUD Program," 7.

44. "Where We Are," n.d., NTU files, 3; Ficcio interview; Cascella, Favilla, and Nicholas interviews; Andy Thorburn, interview with author, Somerset, N.J., July 28, 1992.

45. "Where We Are," 3.

46. Litzky, telephone conversation with author; Jim Lerman, interview with author, Hoboken, N.J., September 22, 1993; Cascella, Favilla, and Nicholas interview,.

47. Sidney Rosenfeld, "Memo to Elem. School Teachers"; *NTU Bulletin* (October, 1962), 2; Rosenthal, *Pedagogues and Power*, 33–35.

48. Jerry Yablonsky, interview with author, Springfield, N.J., November 7, 1995.

49. Yablonsky interview; Thorburn interview, July 28, 1992; Cascella, Favilla, and Nicholas interview, 1995.

50. Yablonsky interview; Cascella, Favilla, and Nicholas interview; Schmid interview.

51. Ficcio interview.

52. Ficcio interview; Yablonsky interview.

53. Cascella, Favilla, and Nicholas interview; Murphy, *Blackboard Unions*, 23 and 34.

54. Daniel J. Walkowitz, *Working with Class: Social Workers and the Politics of Middle Class Identity* (Chapel Hill: University of North Carolina Press, 1999), 119–126; Stanley Aronowitz, "White Shirt, Blue Collar," *The Nation* (June 14, 1999): 57–58. The thoughts at the end of the paragraph come from my reading of Jacques

Rancière, *The Nights of Labor: The Workers' Dream in Nineteeth-Century France* (Philadelphia: Temple University Press, 1989), 3–23.

55. Ficcio interview; "Where We Are," 1.

56. Schmid interview; Yablonsky interview; Ficcio interview. Ficcio, Sidney Rosenfeld, and Don Nicholas also helped.

57. NTU membership book.

58. "Where We Are," 3; "Why Teachers Must Strike Now," n.d. [1964], Exhibit Q, Board of Education of Newark *vs.* Newark Teachers Union [et al.], n.d. [1965], in NTU files.

59. Cascella, Favilla, and Nicholas interview; Ficcio interview; Schmid interview; William M. Phillips Jr. and Jospeph M. Conforti, *Social Conflict: Teachers' Strikes in Newark, 1964–1971* (Trenton: New Jersey Department of Education, 1972), 4.

60. Edith Counts, interview with author, East Orange, N.J., August 9, 1993; Clara Dasher, interview with Norman Eiger, New Brunswick, N.J., June 21, 1974.

61. Counts interview.

62. Dasher interview; NTU membership book; "Vote the Presidential Slate," pamphlet, n.d. [1970]. Bob Hirschfeld gave me a copy of the pamphlet.

63. Ellen Cunniff, interview with author, Bloomfield, N.J., August 14, 1995.

64. Cunniff interview.

65. Cunniff interview. On why women often preferred the National Education Association, see Richard A. Quantz, "The Complex Visions of Female Teachers and the Failure of Unionization in the 1930s: An Oral History," in *The Teacher's Voice: A Social History of Teaching in Twentieth-Century America*, ed. Richard J. Altenbaugh (London: Falmer Press, 1992), 140–148.

66. Pat Piegari, interview with author, Caldwell, N.J., 1995; NTU membership book. On teachers using their own money to pay for supplies, see *SL*, February 22, 1970, sec. 1, 1+; *American Teacher/Special Issue* (February 16, 1970): 3.

67. Piegari interview.

68. Joe Ciccolini Sr., interview with author, Nutley, N.J., September 27, 1995.

69. Felix Martino, interview with author, Roseland, N.J., August 4, 1995; NTU membership book.

70. Martino interview.

71. Pete Petino, interview with author, Newark, November 5, 1995.

72. Martino interview.

73. Ficcio interview.

74. Bob Lowenstein interview.

75. Thorburn interview, July 28, 1992; Schmid interview; Selden, *Teacher Rebellion*, 5 and 248; Robert Lowe and Howard Fuller, "The New Unionism and the Very Old: What History Can Tell Bob Chase and His Critics," *Education Week* (April 1, 1998): 46 and 50.

76. Carol Karman, conversation with author, New York City, May 8, 1996; Jim Lowenstein, letter to author, February 21, 1996, 2; Peter D. Dickson, "The Sources of Italian Politics: The North Ward of Newark, New Jersey" (senior thesis, Princeton University, 1973), 79.

77. Paone interview; NTU membership book.

78. Janice Adams, interview with author, Newark, September 7, 1995; Paone interview.

79. Kenneth T. and Barbara B. Jackson, "The Black Experience in Newark: The Growth of the Ghetto, 1870–1970," in *New Jersey since 1860: New Findings and Interpretations*, ed. William C. Wright (Trenton: New Jersey Historical Commission, 1972), 45 and 49; Clement A. Price, "The Beleaguered City as Promised Land: Blacks in Newark, 1917–1947," in *A New Jersey Anthology*, ed. Maxine N. Lurie (Newark: New Jersey Historical Society, 1994), 440–441 and 449; Jean Anyon, *Ghetto Schooling: A Political Economy of Urban Educational Reform* (New York: Teachers College Press, 1997), 61 and 103; *NN*, May 6, 1970, 14, and September 27, 1970, sec. 1, 12; Nicholas interview.

80. Charles Nolley and Martha Nolley, interview with author, Montclair, N.J., September 14, 1995.

81. Nolley and Nolley interview; NTU membership book.

82. Harold Moore, interview with author, Montclair, N.J., August 21, 1995.

83. Moore interview; NTU membership book.

84. *NTU Bulletin* (June 1965): 2; Cascella, Favilla, and Nicholas interview, 1995.

85. Cascella, Favilla, and Nicholas interview; *NTU Bulletin* (June 1965): 2.

86. *NTU Bulletin* (June 1965): 1; Gaswirth, "Teacher Militancy," 73–74, 242–244, and 334; Selden, *The Teacher Rebellion*, 96 and 99.

87. Sidney Rosenfeld, letter to Newark teachers, November 5, 1965, exhibit N in "Board of Education of Newark *vs.* Newark Teachers Union [et al.]," n.d. [1965], in NTU files; Eiger, "The Newark School Wars," 40–41.

88. Schmid interview; "Complaint by Board of Education against Newark Teacher Union et al," n.d. [December 3, 1965], NTU files; Phillips and Conforti, *Social Conflict*, 7–8; Marshall O. Donley, Jr., *Power to the Teacher: How America's Educators Became Militant* (Bloomington: Indiana University Press, 1976), 102.

89. "Complaint by Board of Education against Newark Teacher Union et al.," n.d. [December 3, 1965], NTU files.

90. *The New Jersey Teacher* (November–December 1965): 1; *NN*, December 6, 1965, 1.

91. *Directions for Picket Captains*, leaflet, NTU files; "School Representatives Confidential Report on Strike Preparation," n.d. [1965], NTU files.

92. *NN*, December 6, 1965, 1; Phillips and Conforti, *Social Conflict*, 9; Eiger, "The Newark School Wars," 45 and 48; Fox interview with Eiger.

93. Bob Clark, interview with author, Glen Ridge, N.J., October 17, 1995; NTU membership book.

94. Carol Karman, interviews with author, Bloomfield, N.J., March 17, 1994, and June 2, 1994. Her name in 1965 was Najarian.

95. Karman interview, June 2, 1994; NTU membership book.

96. Carole Graves, interview with author, Newark, May 24, 2000.

97. Untitled strike pledge list, Dayton Street School, in NTU file "Dollars for Dignity"; NTU membership book; Karman interview, June 2, 1994; Carole Graves, "Biographical Sketch," September 21, 1970, in NTU files.

98. *NTU Bulletin* (June 1965): 1; Eiger, "The Newark School Wars," 51; Phillips and Conforti, *Social Conflict*, 7–9.

99. Gaswirth, "Teacher Militancy," 187 and 189–190; Eiger, "The Newark School Wars," 51–53; Phillips and Conforti, *Social Conflict*, 8–9; Schmid interview.

100. Phillips and Conforti, *Social Conflict*, 8–10; Gaswirth, "Teacher Militancy," 87–89;

T. M. Stinnett, *Turmoil in Teaching: A History of the Organizational Struggle for America's Teachers* (New York: Macmillan, 1968), 298; *NN*, February 23, 1966, 1.

101. Edith Jaffe, "Address to Board of Education," January 24, 1967, 1–2 and 5, NTU files; Eiger, "The Newark School Wars," 55–56; Phillips and Conforti, *Social Conflict*, 11.

102. Donald A. Gsell, "Teacher Unionism in New Jersey," cited by Eiger, "The Newark School Wars," 57; NTU membership book.

103. "Big Deal on Green Street," leaflet, in NTU files (emphasis added by the Union); Newark Board of Education and Newark Teachers Association, "Agreement," July 28, 1965, to July 27, 1966, 11; Ficcio interview; Phillips and Conforti, *Social Conflict*, 5 and 7.

104. Jaffe, "Address to Board," 3; Phillips and Conforti, *Social Conflict*, 12.

105. Selden, *The Teacher Rebellion*, 85.

Two   After the Riot / Rebellion

1. Kenneth T. and Barbara B. Jackson, "The Black Experience in Newark: The Growth of the Ghetto, 1870–1970," in *New Jersey since 1860: New Findings and Interpretations*, ed. William C. Wright (Trenton: New Jersey Historical Commission, 1972), 41; Robert Curvin, "The Persistent Minority: The Black Political Experience in Newark" (Ph.D. diss., Princeton University, 1975), 13 and 21; Jean Anyon, *Ghetto Schooling: A Political Economy of Urban Educational Reform* (New York: Teachers College Press, 1997), 99.

2. Curvin, "The Persistent Minority," 13–14 and 21.

3. Anyon, *Ghetto Schooling*, 62–64, 74, 79, and 127; Clement A. Price, "The Beleagured City as Promised Land: Blacks in Newark, 1917–1947," in *A New Jersey Anthology*, ed. Maxine N. Lurie (Newark: New Jersey Historical Society, 1994), 452–453; Jackson, "The Black Experience," 58 n. 39; Curvin, "The Persistent Minority," 148–151; K. Komozi Woodard, "The Making of the New Ark: Imamu Amiri Baraka (LeRoi Jones), the Congress of African People, and the Modern Black Convention Movement; A History of the Black Revolt and the New Nationalism, 1966–1976" (Ph.D. diss., University of Pennsylvania, 1991), 84; George Lipsitz, *Rainbow at Midnight: Labor and Culture in the 1940s* (Urbana: University of Illinois Press, 1994), 258.

4. Norman Eiger, "The Newark School Wars: A Socio-Historical Study of the 1970 and 1971 Newark School System Strikes" (Ed.D. diss., Rutgers University, 1976), 10 and 504; Anyon, *Ghetto Schooling*, 59–60, 78, and 104; *Where Is the Money? Financing Quality Education in Newark (or New Jersey)*, n.d. [1971], 1, NTU files; *NN*, June 7, 1970, 7+.

5. Newark Teachers Union, *Teaching: A Vanishing Profession* (Newark: Newark Teachers Union, n.d. [1954?]), 14 and 15.

6. For a clear summary of the process of urban decline in northern cities, see Thomas J. Sugrue, *The Origins of the Urban Crisis: Race and Inequality in Postwar Detroit* (Princeton, N.J.: Princeton University Press, 1996), 7–9.

7. Affidavit of Franklyn Titus, November 30, 1965, in "Board of Education of Newark *vs.* Newark Teachers Union [et al.]," n.d. [1965], NTU files.

8. Affidavit of Franklyn Titus, November 30, 1965.

9. Price, "The Beleagured City," 439–440 and 454; Edith Counts, interview with author, East Orange, N.J., August 9, 1993.

10. Anyon, *Ghetto Schooling*, 93; Curvin, "The Persistent Minority," 25–26 and 82–83; William M. Phillips Jr., *Participation of the Black Community in Selected Aspects of the Educational Institutions of Newark* (New Brunswick, N.J.: Rutgers, the State University, 1973), 180–184; Charles Malone, interview with author, Orange, N.J., June 12, 1995; Frank Green, interview with author, Montclair, N.J., August 29, 1995; Eiger, "The Newark School Wars," 82–83.

11. William M. Phillips Jr. and Joseph M. Conforti, *Social Conflict: Teachers' Strikes in Newark, 1964–1971* (Trenton: New Jersey Department of Education, 1972), 2; Anyon, *Ghetto Schooling*, 94.

12. Phillips and Conforti, *Social Conflict*, 10, 13, and 20; Eiger, "The Newark School Wars," 81; Anyon, *Ghetto Schooling*, 124.

13. Phillips, *Participation of the Black Community*, 153; Fred Means, interview with Norman Eiger, New Brunswick, N.J., December 3, 1974; Avant Lowther Jr., interview with author, Newark, June 14, 1995; Anyon, *Ghetto Schooling*, 94–95 and 121–122; Andy Thorburn, interview with author, Somerset, N.J., July 28, 1992; John Schmid, interview with author, Bloomfield, N.J., February 28, 1997.

14. Robert J. Braun, *Teachers and Power: The Story of the American Federation of Teachers* (New York: Simon and Schuster, 1972), 182–183; Phillips and Conforti, *Social Conflict*, 20–23; Eiger, "The Newark School Wars," 60 and 115; Anyon, *Ghetto Schooling*, 125–126. Ten white teachers appealed to the New Jersey Supreme Court, which upheld the Board. *NN,* September 24, 1970, 1, and October 27, 1970, 27.

15. Joseph Cascella, speech to the Board of Education, August 27, 1963, 8, NTU files; minutes of NTU Executive Board meeting, May 2, 1968, 2, NTU files; Eiger, "The Newark School Wars," 50. Nationally, AFT supported the civil rights movement more than did NEA. Marjorie Murphy, *Blackboard Unions: The AFT and the NEA, 1900–1980* (Ithaca, N.Y.: Cornell University Press, 1990), 201–206.

16. Bruder and Graves, quoted in *NTU Bulletin* (November 1967): 1; Eiger, "The Newark School Wars," 59.

17. Carole Graves, interview with author, Newark, May 24, 2000; Schmid interview; Victor Cascella, Ralph Favilla, and Don Nicholas, interview with author, Newark, December 1, 1995; Andy Thorburn, interview with author, Somerset, N.J., July 14, 1992; Means interview with Eiger; "Dollars for Dignity," pledge forms, n.d., NTU files.

18. Carole Graves, letter to Harold Ashby, July 16, 1968, NTU files.

19. Phillips and Conforti, *Social Conflict*, 17.

20. Curvin, "The Persistent Minority," 50; Phillips and Conforti, *Social Conflict*, 14–15; Anyon, *Ghetto Schooling*, 110; *NN,* October 11, 1967, 1; *SL*, November 18, 1967, 1.

21. Imamu Amiri Baraka, "Newark—Before Black Men Conquered," in *Raise Race Rays Raze: Essays since 1965* (New York: Random House 1971), 63; William B. Helmreich, *The Jews of Newark and MetroWest: The Enduring Community* (New Brunswick, N.J.: Transaction Publishers, 1999), 112; David Shipler, "The White Niggers of Newark," *Harper's* (August 1972): 82; Peter D. Dickson, "The Sources of Italian Politics: The North Ward of Newark, New Jersey" (senior thesis,

Princeton University, 1973), 42; Gwendolyn Mikell, "Class and Ethnic Political Relations in Newark, N.J.: Blacks and Italians," in *Cities of the United States: Studies in Urban Anthropology*, ed. Leith Mullings (New York: Columbia University Press, 1987), 88 and 91; Ron Porambo, *No Cause for Indictment: An Autopsy of Newark* (New York: Holt, Rinehart, and Winston, 1971), 34–36 and 202; Sandra Garrett Shannon, "Baraka, Black Ethos, and the Black Arts Movement: A Study of Amiri Baraka's Drama during the Black Arts Movement from 1964 to 1969" (Ph.D. diss., University of Maryland, 1986), 152; Eiger, "The Newark School Wars," 15 and 508; Curvin, "The Persistent Minority," 63–65; Phillips and Conforti, *Social Conflict*, 58.

22. Thorburn interview, July 14, 1992; Felix Martino, interview with author, Roseland, N.J., August 4, 1995; *SL*, February 22, 1970, sec. 1, 1+; Angela Paone, interview with author, Roseland, N.J., August 8, 1995; Woodard, "The Making of the New Ark," 425.

23. Thorburn interview, July 14, 1992.

24. Thorburn interview, July 14, 1992; *SL*, November 18, 1967: 1; *Newark Teachers Union Bulletin* (November 1967), 4; Curvin, "The Persistent Minority," 63.

25. Thorburn interview, July 14, 1992.

26. Thorburn interview, July 14, 1992.

27. Thorburn interview, July 14, 1992.

28. Thorburn interview, July 14, 1992.

29. Phillips and Conforti, *Social Conflict*, 14; Thorburn interview, July 14, 1992; *Newark Teachers Union Bulletin* (November 1967), 4.

30. *Newark Teachers Union Bulletin* (November 1967), 2; Thorburn interview, July 28, 1992. On discipline as a key union issue in urban districts, see Susan Martin, "The Impact of a Local Teachers' Union on Educational Policy and Practice: A Case Study of the Cincinnati Federation of Teachers" (Ed.D. diss., University of Cincinnati, 1992), 294–295.

31. *Newark Teachers Union Bulletin* (November 1967), 4.

32. Thorburn interview, July 14, 1992; Malone interview; Anyon, *Ghetto Schooling*, 111–112.

33. Anonymous male teacher, quoted in *SL*, February 22, 1970, sec. 1, 1+; Mary E. Bredemeier, *Urban Classroom Portraits: Teachers Who Make a Difference* (New York: P. Lang, 1988), 47.

34. Esther Tumin, interview with author, Livingston, N.J., December 14, 1992.

35. Tumin interview, December 14, 1992.

36. Anonymous teacher quoted in *SL*, February 22, 1970; Phillips and Conforti, *Social Conflict*, 14; Esther Tumin, interviews with author, Livingston, N.J., December 4, 1992, and December 14, 1992.

37. Tumin interview, December 14, 1992.

38. Tumin interview, December 14, 1992.

39. Tumin interview, December 14, 1992.

40. Tumin interview, December 14, 1992; Alice Saltman, interview with author, Livingston, N.J., June 13, 1995; Phil Basile, interview with author, Verona, N.J., August 15, 1995; Anyon, *Ghetto Schooling*, 112.

41. Anyon, *Ghetto Schooling*, 91; Marty Bierbaum, interview with author, Berkeley Heights, N.J., September 16, 1995.

42. Counts interview.
43. Counts interview.
44. Baraka, "Newark—Before Black Men Conquered," 60; Hannah Litzky, interview with author, West Orange, N.J., August 25, 1993. Weequahic was 19 percent Black in 1961, 70 percent in 1966, and 82 percent in 1968. Anyon, *Ghetto Schooling*, 110.
45. Litzky interview.
46. Litzky interview. In 1995, Litzky was honored as an outstanding educator by the Jewish Historical Society of MetroWest.
47. Paul Lappé, telephone conversation with author, August 6, 1993.
48. "Fact Sheet—School Within a School," n.d. [1971], 1, NTU files; Seymour Spiegel, interview with author, Watchung, N.J., September 21, 1995.
49. Phillips and Conforti, *Social Conflict*, 23; Spiegel interviews with author, Watchung N.J., September 21, 1995, and September 22, 1995; "School Within a School," booklet, NTU files.
50. Spiegel interview, September 22, 1995.
51. Spiegel interviews, September 21, 1995 and September 22, 1995.
52. Spiegel interviews, September 21, 1995, and September 22, 1995; "Fact Sheet—School Within a School," 1; Jim Brown, interview with author, Belleville, N.J., August 17, 1995.
53. Spiegel interview, September 21, 1995.
54. Anna Eng, *Longitudinal Study of University High School Graduates (School Within a School), Newark, New Jersey, 1973–1978* (Newark: Prudential Insurance Company, 1978), 6; Spiegel interview, September 22, 1995; "Fact Sheet—School Within a School," 2; Letter from Carole A. Graves, President, NTU, to Helen Fullilove, September 22, 1971, NTU files; Mayor's Education Task Force, *Report to the Public: Toward a Thorough and Efficient Educational System* (Newark: Mayor's Educational Task Force, 1974), 68.
55. Newark Teachers Union, *Handbook for New Teachers*, 1964, 1, 2, and 8, NTU files.
56. Thorburn interview, July 28, 1992; "Initial Application: Newark More Effective School Program," n.d., NTU files; Eiger, "The Newark School Wars," 184. MES was not really Shanker's program. It was developed by an AFT committee in 1964. Shanker embraced MES as a tactic, hoping to mollify teachers who were former communists. Marjorie Murphy, comment at Organization of American Historians session, Chicago, March 29, 1996.
57. *NTU Bulletin* (November 1967), 2.
58. Ken Waters, quoted in Bredemeier, *Urban Classroom Portraits*, 99. Waters would not give up, and in the early 1970s played a key role in an extraordinary takeover of the administration of West Side prompted by continued violence and drug use, an experiment that did succeed, until the Board killed it. Ibid., 101–106; *SL*, June 25, 1975, 6, and August 27, 1975, 28.
59. Paone interview; *NN*, n.d., clipping in NTU files.
60. Paone interview.
61. Paone interview.
62. NTU membership book.
63. Tumin interview, December 14, 1992.
64. Tumin interview, December 14, 1992.
65. Harold Moore, interview with author, Montclair, N.J., August 21, 1995.

66. *NN*, June 4, 1970, 1+.
67. Phillips and Conforti, *Social Conflict*, 16 and 18–19.
68. Phyllis Salowe, interview with author, West Orange, N.J., August 10, 1995.
69. Beth Blackmon, interview with author, South Orange, N.J., June 26, 1995.
70. Phyllis Cuyler, interview with author, Woodbridge, N.J., July 21, 1994.
71. Cuyler interview.
72. Cuyler interview.
73. Cuyler interview; Salowe interview.
74. Jim Lerman, interviews with author, Hoboken, N.J., September 22, 1993, and October 29, 1993; Jim Lerman, quoted in Bredemeier, *Urban Classsroom Portraits*, 71.
75. Thorburn interview, July 14, 1992; Carole Graves, quoted in *New Jersey Afro-American*, February 6, 1971, Teacher Recruitment sec., 15.
76. Tom Lawton, interview with author, Bloomfield, N.J., June 23, 1995.
77. Brown interview; Marion Bolden, interview with author, Newark, October 2, 1995. Elena Scambio, who commuted to Seton Hall, says the 1960s passed her by. Elena Scambio, interviews with author, Bloomfield, N.J., May 30, 1997, and August 26, 1997.
78. Walter Genuario, interview with author, Glen Ridge, N.J., August 16, 1995.
79. Genuario interview; *NN*, September 27, 1970, sec. 1, 12.
80. Genuario interview.
81. Jim Lowenstein and Steve Shaffer, interview with author, Fair Lawn, N.J., July 26, 1994.
82. Lowenstein and Shaffer interview, July 26, 1994. Shaffer graduated from Rutgers in 1967.
83. Lowenstein and Shaffer interview, July 26, 1994.
84. Anyon, *Ghetto Schooling*, 122–123; Phillips and Conforti, *Social Conflict*, 16; Eiger, "Newark School Wars," 84.
85. Charles Nolley and Martha Nolley, interview with author, Montclair, N.J., September 14, 1995; NTU membership book.
86. Avant Lowther, Jr., interview with author, Newark, June 14, 1995.
87. Lowther interview; Green, interview with author.
88. Lowther interview; NTU membership book.
89. Lowther interview.
90. Jim Lerman, interview with author, Hoboken, N.J., December 10, 1993; Lowenstein and Shaffer interview.
91. Dave Lieberfarb, Jim Lowenstein, and Steve Shaffer, interview with author, Fair Lawn, N.J., November 19, 1994.
92. Bierbaum interview; NTU membership book.
93. Lowenstein and Shaffer interview.
94. Lowenstein and Shaffer interview; NTU membership book.
95. Lowenstein and Shaffer interview; Lieberfarb, Lowenstein, and Shaffer interview.
96. Francis V. Volpe Jr., letter to Hilly Wisot, September 22, 1969, NTU files; Tony Ficcio, interview with author, New York City, November 29, 1995; Aaron Polonsky and Francis Volpe, letter [to building reps], March 20, 1969, NTU files. Volpe was the NTU treasurer.
97. Petitions of Education Employees for an election, NTU files; Ficcio interview; Marc

Gaswirth, "Teacher Militancy in New Jersey: An Analysis of Organizational Change, Public Policy Development, and School Board–Teacher Relationships through January, 1975" (Ed.D.diss., Rutgers University, 1977), 334.

98. Braun, *Teachers and Power*, 183; Eiger, "The Newark School Wars," 56, 60–61, and 502; Anyon, *Ghetto Schooling*, 26; *NN*, October 23, 1969, 1; Phillips and Conforti, *Social Conflict*, 12. The mayor cast the deciding vote on the board of estimate.

99. Limongello, quoted in *SL*, September 19, 1969, NTU leaflet, NTU files; *NN*, September 19, 1969, NTU leaflet, NTU files; *NN*, October 23, 1969; Braun, *Teachers and Power*, 184; Phillips and Conforti, *Social Conflict*, 24; Eiger, "The Newark School Wars," 61. Long after the Association lost power, the courts restored the raise. *NN*, March 28, 1971, sec.1, 8.

100. Nolley and Nolley interview; *SL*, November 11, 1969, 1+; *NN*, September 19, 1969; NTU leaflet, NTU files.

101. Francis V. Volpe Jr., letter to Robert Porter, September 22, 1969, NTU files; Thorburn interview, July 28, 1992; *NN*, November 2, 1969, NTU files; Carole A. Graves, letter to David Selden, December 8, 1969, NTU files; *American Teacher* (December 1969), 5.

102. Lowther interview; Lerman interview, September 22, 1993; NTU membership book; *SL,* November 19, 1969, 1+.

103. Thorburn interview, July 28, 1992.

104. Newark Teachers Union, flyer, NTU files.

105. Edward H. Tumin, letter to Robert Porter, January 26, 1970; NTU membership book. Tumin was an NTU vice president.

106. Lerman interview, October 29, 1993; Thorburn interview, July 28, 1992.

107. *NN*, November 19, 1969, 1+, and September 12, 1969, 12.

108. Newark Teachers Union, leaflet, NTU files.

109. *NN*, September 26, 1969, 12.

110. *NN*, September 26, 1969; Carole A. Graves, letter to building representatives, November 19, 1969, NTU files; letter from New Jersey Public Employment Relations Commission, to Newark Teachers Union, January 6, 1970, NTU files. When they went to vote the second time, aides and subtitutes knew that NTU would represent teachers.

111. *NN*, November 19, 1969; *SL*, November 19, 1969. ONE's combined total in the two November 18 elections exactly equaled the Association's total.

112. Carole A. Graves, letter to David Selden, December 8, 1969, NTU files; Thorburn interview, July 28, 1992; Braun, *Teachers and Power*, 185.

Three   The 1970 Strike

1. Carole Graves, interview with Norman Eiger, Newark, May 21, 1974; Norman Eiger, "The Newark School Wars: A Socio-Historical Study of the 1970 and 1971 Newark School System Strikes" (Ed.D. diss., Rutgers University, 1976), 94; Andy Thorburn, interview with author, Somerset, N.J., July 28, 1992.

2. Bates, quoted in Eiger, "Newark School Wars," 100; Ben Epstein, interview with Norman Eiger, Newark, November 7, 1974.

3. Jacob Fox, interview with Norman Eiger, Montclair, N.J., December 24, 1974.

4. Fox quoted in *American Teacher/Special Issue* (February 16, 1970): 2; Fox interview with Eiger.

5. Bates quoted in Eiger, "The Newark School Wars," 101; Graves quoted in *SL*, February 3, 1970, 7; Eiger, "Newark School Wars," 116 and 172; *SL*, February 13, 1970, 11.

6. Eiger, "Newark School Wars," 105.

7. Epstein, interview with Eiger; Malanga quoted in *NN*, February 4, 1970, 1+; Eiger, "Newark School Wars," 107 and 119.

8. Fox quoted in Eiger, "Newark School Wars," 108; *SL*, February 1, 1970, sec. 1, 28, and February 22, 1970, sec. 1, 1+; Eiger, "Newark School Wars," 106 and 119.

9. Hannah Litzky, "Teachers in Jail," typescript of speech delivered at Northfield, N.J., YM/YWHA, January 14, 1972 (original in Litzky's possession); Dr. Wyman Garrett, quoted in Eiger, "Newark School Wars," 109; *SL*, February 4, 1970, sec. 1, 1+.

10. Fox quoted in *American Teacher/Special Issue* (February 16, 1970): 4; *NN*, February 1, 1970, sec.1, 1.

11. Thorburn interview, July 28, 1992.

12. Thorburn interview, July 28, 1992; Phyllis Salowe, interview with author, West Orange, N.J., August 10, 1995.

13. "Strike Information," leaflet, exhibit E in "Board of Education *vs.* Newark Teachers Union et al., January 31, 1970; Eiger, "Newark School Wars," 107.

14. Thorburn interview, July 28, 1992; *SL*, February 2, 1970, 1.

15. Thorburn interview, July 28, 1992; Vic Cascella, interview with author, Newark, August 6, 1996.

16. Thorburn interview, July 28, 1992.

17. Bates quoted in *SL*, February 2, 1970, 1+; Bates quoted in Eiger, "Newark School Wars," 113; Thorburn interview, July 28, 1992.

18. Piegari's statement, quoted in Newark Teachers Union, *Anatomy of a Strike: February 1, 1970, to February 25, 1970* (Newark: Newark Teachers Union [1970]), 97; Pat Piegari, interview with author, Caldwell, N.J., September 22, 1995; *SL*, February 2, 1970, 1+.

19. Harold Moore, interview with author, Montclair, N.J., August 21, 1995.

20. Moore interview.

21. *SL*, February 3, 1970, 1; *NN*, February 4, 1970, 1; February 5, 1970, 1; February 8, 1970, sec. 1, 18; and February 12, 1970, 1.

22. *SL*, February 3, 1970, 1, and February 4, 1970, 1; *NN*, February 2, 1970, 1; Bob Clark, interview with author, Glen Ridge, N.J., October 17, 1995.

23. *NN*, February 3, 1970, 6; Carole Graves, interview with author, Newark, May 24, 2000.

24. Moore interview; Angela Paone, interview with author, Roseland, N.J., August 8, 1995.

25. Dave Lieberfarb, Jim Lowenstein, and Steve Shaffer, interview with author, Fair Lawn, November 19, 1994.

26. Salowe interview.

27. Joe Ciccolini, Sr., interview with author, Nutley, N.J., September 27, 1995.

28. Avant Lowther, Jr., interview with author, Newark, June 14, 1995.

29. Beth Blackmon, interview with author, South Orange, N.J., June 26, 1995; Alan Rosenthal, *Pedagogues and Power: Teacher Groups in School Politics* (Syracuse, N.Y.: Syracuse University Press, 1969), 37–39.

30. *NN*, February 8, 1970, sec.1, 8. The reporter was William Doolittle.
31. D. Charleton, letter to the editor, *NN*, February 13, 1970, 20.
32. D. Charleton, letter to editor.
33. Clark interview; *SL*, February 4, 1970, 1+.
34. *SL*, February 22, 1970, sec. 1, 1+. The reporter was Robert Braun.
35. Anna Blume and Marty Blume, interview with author, Berkeley Heights, N.J., October 1, 1995.
36. Walter Genuario, interview with author, Glen Ridge, N.J., August 16, 1995; Blume and Blume interview.
37. Felix Martino, interview with author, Roseland, N.J., August 4, 1995.
38. Janice Adams, interview with author, Newark, September 7, 1995.
39. Charles Nolley and Martha Nolley, interview with author, Montclair, N.J., September 14, 1995.
40. Jerry Yablonsky, interview with author, Springfield, N.J., November 7, 1995.
41. Blume and Blume interview.
42. Blume and Blume interview.
43. Blume and Blume interview.
44. Blume and Blume interview.
45. Carol Karman, interview with author, Bloomfield, N.J., March 17, 1994.
46. Karman interview, March 17, 1994.
47. Karman interview, March 17, 1994.
48. *NN*, March 17, 1970, 27, and March 18, 1970, 21; Vic Cascella, Ralph Favilla, and Don Nicholas interview with author, Newark, December 1, 1995; Salowe interview; Frank Green, interview with author, Montclair, N.J., August 29, 1995.
49. Elena Scambio, interview with author, Bloomfield, N.J., May 30, 1997; *SL*, February 11, 1970, 1.
50. Gene Liss, interview with author, August 29, 1995; Cascella, Favilla, and Nicholas interview; Clark interview.
51. Newark Teachers Union, *Anatomy of a Strike*, 28; Thorburn interview, July 28, 1992; Carol Karman, interview with author, Bloomfield, N.J., June 2, 1994; Yablonsky interview; Jim Lowenstein and Steve Shaffer, interview with author, Fair Lawn, N.J., July 26, 1994.
52. Pete Petino, interview with author, Newark, November 5, 1995; Cascella, Favilla, and Nicholas interview.
53. Clark interview.
54. Salowe interview.
55. Adams interview.
56. *NN*, February 3, 1970, 6, and February 7, 1970, 1; *New Jersey Afro-American*, February 7, 1970, 1+; Genuario interview.
57. Piegari interview.
58. Tom Lawton, interview with author, Bloomfield, N.J., June 23, 1995.
59. Lawton interview.
60. Lawton interview.
61. Lawton interview; Lowther interview.
62. Martino interview.
63. *NN*, February 3, 1970, 1; Blume and Blume interview.

64. Salowe interview.
65. Salowe interview.
66. Nolley and Nolley interview; *NN*, October 11, 1970, sec.1, 14; Mary E. Bredemeier, *Urban Classroom Portraits: Teachers Who Make a Difference* (New York: P. Lang, 1988), 102 and 107.
67. Dorothy Bergman, interview with author, New York City, October 11, 1995.
68. Bergman interview; NTU membership book.
69. Bergman interview.
70. Bob Lowenstein, interview with author, West Orange, N.J., June 14, 1993.
71. Lowenstein and Shaffer interview, July 26, 1994.
72. Lowenstein and Shaffer interview, July 26, 1994; Jim Lerman, interview with author, Hoboken N.J., October 29, 1993; Karman interview, March 17, 1994; Blume and Blume interview; Thorburn interview, July 28, 1992.
73. Blackmon interview; Ciccolini interview.
74. *SL*, February 27, 1970, 1+; Martino interview.
75. Marc Gaswirth, "Teacher Militancy in New Jersey: An Analysis of Organizational Change, Public Policy Development, and School Board-Teacher Relationships Through January, 1975" (Ed.D. diss., Rutgers University, 1977), 168–170, 200–201.
76. *SL*, February 4, 1970, 1; February 5, 1970, 1; February 6, 1970, 1; February 7, 1970, 1+; Robert J. Braun, *Teachers and Power: The Story of the American Federation of Teachers* (New York: Simon and Schuster, 1972), 188–189. Nationally, school boards sought injunctions in the 1970s in about 40 percent of teacher strikes. David L. Colton and Edith E. Graber, *Teacher Strikes and the Courts* (Lexington, Mass.: Lexington Books, 1982), 5.
77. "The Board of Education of Newark *vs.* Newark Teachers Union, Local 481," Superior Court of New Jersey, Appellate Division, April 5, 1971, 1–4; *NN*, February 4, 1970, 1, and February 7, 1970, 3; *SL*, February 7, 1970, 1; Eiger, "The Newark School Wars," 135–137.
78. *SL*, February 11, 1970, 1; February 12, 1970, 1+; and February 18, 1970,1+; *NN*, February 1, 1970, 1, and February 11, 1970, 1; Phil Basile, interview with author, Verona, N.J., August 15, 1995; Esther Tumin, interview with author, Livingston, N.J., December 14, 1992; *American Teacher/Special Issue* (February 16, 1970): 2.
79. Yablonsky interview; *NN*, March 12, 1970, 31.
80. Bob Hirschfeld, interview with author, Livingston, N.J., September 28, 1995; *NN*, March 12, 1970, 31; NTU membership book; *Vote the Presidential Slate*, 1970 NTU election pamphlet (original in Bob Hirschfeld's possession).
81. Lowenstein and Shaffer interview; Edith Counts, interview with author, East Orange, N.J., August 9, 1993; Tony Ficcio, interview with author, New York City, November 29, 1995; Yablonsky interview; Thorburn interview, July 28, 1992; *NN*, February 18, 1970, 1+; February 19, 1970, 9; and February 25, 1970, 8; *SL*, February 19, 1970, 8; *The New Jersey Teacher* (November–December 1965): 1 and 11.
82. Moore interview; Blackmon interview; Lawton interview; Ciccolini interview; Thorburn interview, July 28, 1992; *SL*, February 2, 1970, 1.
83. Moore interview; Lowenstein and Shaffer interview; Salowe interview; Cascella, Favilla, and Nicholas interview.
84. Thorburn interview, July 28, 1992; Bergman interview; *SL*, February 17, 1970, 1; *NN*, February 19, 1970, 1+.

85. Coreane Henderson, quoted in *NN*, February 12, 1970, 1; the *News* said 8,000 children—clearly a misprint; Clark interview; Karman interview, March 17, 1994.
86. Lowenstein and Shaffer interview; *SL*, February 13, 1970, 1; *NN*, February 14, 1970, 1; Eiger, "The Newark School Wars," 75 and 154; "Arrests Made by the Sheriff's Department during Newark School Teachers Strike," 2–6, NTU files.
87. *NN*, February 3, 1970, 4; *NN* February 15, 1970, sec. 2, C3, and February 20, 1970, 26.
88. Weintraub quoted in *SL*, March 1, 1970, 1+; Mintz, quoted in *NN*, February 20, 1970, 12; Braun, *Teachers and Power*, 196.
89. Cahill quoted in *SL*, February 17, 1970, 1; Graves interview, May 24, 2000; *NN*, February 11, 1970, 1; *SL*, March 1, 1970, 1+.
90. Salowe interview; Petino interview.
91. Petino interview; "Arrests Made by the Sheriff's Department," 5. All dates of arrest, unless otherwise noted, come from this source.
92. Salowe interview; *NN*, February 17, 1970, 1; *SL*, February 18, 1970, 1+, and February 17, 1970, 1+.
93. Salowe interview.
94. Lawton interview; Seymour Spiegel, interview with author, Watchung, N.J., September 21, 1995; Clark interview.
95. Lowther interview; Nolley and Nolley interview.
96. Blackmon interview; Martino interview; Ciccolini interview.
97. "The Board of Education of Newark *vs.* Newark Teachers Union, Local 481," Superior Court of New Jersey, Appellate Division, April 5, 1971, 5.
98. Basile interview; Lieberfarb, Lowenstein, and Shaffer interview.
99. Bergman interview; "The Board of Education of Newark *vs.* Newark Teachers Union, Local 481," 5. Still in her car, Bergman's friend attempted to escape but was overtaken in a car chase.
100. Karman interview, March 17, 1994; *SL*, February 20, 1970, 1; *NN*, March 18, 1970, 21.
101. Lowenstein and Shaffer, interview; Goeringer quoted in *NN*, February 12, 1970, 4; *NN*, February 20, 1970, 12.
102. Tumin interview, December 14, 1992; and Esther Tumin, interview with author, December 4, 1992.
103. Piegari interview; Paone interview; Bergman interview.
104. Hannah Litzky, interview with author, West Orange, N.J., August 25, 1993; Alice Saltman, interview with author, Livingston, N.J., June 13, 1995.
105. *SL*, February 21, 1970, 1; "Arrests Made by the Sheriff's Department," 1–7. The total of 188 teachers includes NTU officers.
106. [Unknown author], letter to Edward Chervin, March 10, 1971, 2, NTU files; Eiger, "Newark School Wars," 137; *NN*, February 17, 1970, 1+, and February 18, 1970, 1+; *SL*, February, 21, 1970, 1+; Thorburn interview, July 28, 1992.
107. Benjamin Epstein, interview with Norman Eiger, Newark, November 7, 1974; Carole Graves, interview with Norman Eiger, Newark, May 21, 1974; Eiger, "Newark School Wars," 206.
108. Eiger, "Newark School Wars," 189 and 451; Peter D. Dickson, "The Sources of Italian Politics: The North Ward of Newark, New Jersey" (senior thesis, Princeton

University, 1973), 85; Jean Anyon, *Ghetto Schooling: A Political Economy of Urban Educational Reform* (New York: Teachers College Press, 1997), 108–109.

109. Epstein interview with Eiger; Malanga interview with Eiger; Cervase interview with Eiger; *SL*, February 17, 1970, 1; February 19, 1970, 1; February 23, 1970, 1+; March 1, 1970, 1+; Graves interview with author.

110. Marciante quoted in *NN*, February 11, 1970, 1+; Fox quoted in *SL*, March 1, 1970, 1+; Fox interview with Eiger; Eiger, "Newark School Wars," 187–188; *NN*, February 20, 1970, 1.

111. *NN*, February 25, 1970, 8; February 26, 1970, 1 and 9; February 27, 1970, 1+; *SL*, February 18, 1970, 1+; Thorburn interview, July 28, 1992; Eiger, "Newark School Wars," 195 and 198.

112. Fox and Epstein quoted in Eiger, "Newark School Wars," 167–168; *SL*, February 6, 1970, 1; February 11, 1970, 1; February 13, 1970, 11; February 20, 1970, 1; *NN*, February 5, 1970, 1, and February 21, 1970, 1; Eiger, "Newark School Wars," 161–162, 166, and 174–175.

113. Newark Teachers Union, *Anatomy of a Strike*, 102; *NN*, February 26, 1970, 1+ and 7; *SL*, February 26, 1970, 13; Eiger, "Newark School Wars," 116 and 200.

114. Cascella, Favilla, and Nicholas interview; *SL*, February 8, sec. 1, 1; Eiger, "Newark School Wars," 181 and 202.

115. Bates quoted in *NN*, February 26, 1970, 1, and February 26, 1970, 1+ and 7; *SL*, March 1, 1970, 1+.

116. *SL*, March 1, 1970, 1+ (on Petti); *NN*, February 25, 1970, 1, and February 26, 1970, 1; Eiger, "Newark School Wars," 183. The new minimum salary was tied for best in Essex County; the maximum remained the lowest in Essex County. *NN*, March 1, 1970, sec. 1, 1.

117. *SL*, March 1, 1970, 1+; Eiger, "Newark School Wars," 198.

Four   Black Power Between the Strikes

1. *NN*, February 2, 1970, 1+; February 6, 1970, 1+; February 11, 1970, 1+; *New Jersey Afro-American*, February 7, 1970, 1+, and February 14, 1970, 1; *SL*, February 5, 1970, 1+, and February 7, 1970, 1+. McKinley was 60 percent Puerto Rican and 35 percent Black but was just inside the North Ward.

2. Jim Lerman, interview with author, Hoboken, N.J., October 29, 1993.

3. Rustin quoted in *NN*, February 9, 1970, 1+; Andy Thorburn, interview with author, Somerset, N.J., July 28, 1992; Jim Lowenstein and Steve Shaffer, interview with author, Fair Lawn, N.J., July 26, 1994; Lerman interview, October 29, 1993; Bob Hirschfeld, interview with author, Livingston, N.J., September 28, 1995; Gene Liss, interview with author, Newark, August 29, 1995; Seymour Spiegel, interview with author, Watchung, N.J., September 21, 1995; Esther Tumin, interview with author, Livingston, N.J., December 14, 1992; *SL*, February 9, 1970, 1, and February 16, 1970, 1+.

4. Thorburn interview, July 28, 1992, 23; Jervis Anderson, *Bayard Rustin: Troubles I've Seen: A Biography* (New York: HarperCollins, 1997), 314–319 and 323; Stephen Steinberg, "Bayard Rustin and the Black Protest Movement," *New Politics* (Summer 1997), 49–50.

5. Carole Graves, interview with author, Newark, May 24, 2000; Thorburn interview, July 28, 1992; *SL*, February 16, 1970, 1; Robert J. Braun, *Teachers and Power: The Story of the American Federation of Teachers* (New York: Simon and Schuster, 1972), 273.

6. Thorburn interview, July 14, 1992; Graves interview with author; *SL*, April 12, 1971, sec. 1, 12.

7. Carole Graves, letter to Elaine [sic] Brody, January 17, 1970, NTU files; Thorburn interview, July 28, 1992. Graves sent a version of the letter to many heads of organizations.

8. Anonymous Union source quoted in *SL*, February 6, 1970, 9; Baraka quoted in *SL*, February 8, 1970, sec. 1, 1+, and February 19, 1970, 8; Lerman interview, October 29, 1993; Jim Lerman, editorial, *NTU Bulletin*, reprinted in Newark Teachers Union, *Anatomy of a Strike*, Newark, n.d. [1970], 82; *New Jersey Afro-American*, February 14, 1970, 1+.

9. *SL*, February 8, 1970, sec. 1, 1+.

10. *SL*, February 6, 1970, 9; Harold Moore, interview with author, Montclair, N.J., August 21, 1995; Janice Adams, interview with author, Newark, September 7, 1995; Charles Nolley and Martha Nolley, interview with author, Montclair, N.J., September 14, 1995; Phyllis Cuyler, interview with author, Woodbridge, N.J., July 21, 1994; Avant Lowther, Jr., interview with author, Newark, June 14, 1995; Marion Bolden, interview with author, Newark, October 2, 1995; Frank Green, interview with author, Montclair, N.J., August 29, 1995; Charles Malone, interview with author, Orange, N.J., June 12, 1995. See also *NN*, February 19, 1970, 8: South Ward Councilman Horace Sharper, who was Black, "said that some persons felt that the strike had 'anti-black' sentiments but noted that there were blacks on both sides of the situation."

11. Carole Graves, letter to Fred Means, January 26, 1970, NTU files.

12. Means, quoted in *SL*, February 2, 1970, 1+; Campbell, quoted in *New Jersey Afro-American*, February 14, 1970,1+.

13. Fred Means, interview with Norman Eiger, New Brunswick, N.J., December 3, 1994; *NN*, February 3, 1970, 6; *New Jersey Afro-American*, February 7, 1970, 1+; *SL*, February 9, 1970, 1+; Gordon S. Mayes, letter to the editor, *NN*, February 25, 1970, 28.

14. Means, interview with Eiger.

15. M. J. Porter, letter to teachers, n.d., NTU files.

16. Johnson and Lerman quoted in *NN*, February 19, 1970, 1; Lerman interview, October 29, 1993.

17. Johnson quoted in *NN*, February 19, 1970, 1+.

18. *NN*, February 3, 1970, 5.

19. Lerman interview, October 29, 1993; *SL*, February 19, 1970, 8; Newark Teachers Union, *Anatomy of a Strike*, 49, photograph; *NN*, February 20, 1970, 13.

20. Anonymous student quoted in *NN*, February 18, 1970, 22; anonymous student quoted in *SL*, February 19, 1970, 8; *NN*, February 18, 1970, 1; *SL*, February 19, 1970, 1; February 21, 1970, 1+; February 23, 1970, 1+; *NN*, February 19, 1970, 1, and February 20, 1970, 1. Puerto Ricans, with the exception of the Young Lords at McKinley, did not organize separately in relation to the strike. But Aspira, Inc.,

of New Jersey blamed the Board and the teachers for the racism and failures of the schools. *NN*, February 20, 1970, 13.

21. *SL*, February 24, 1970, 1+; *NN*, February 22, 1970, sec. 1, 1+. CFUN was small, energetic, and dedicated, built around Baraka and devoted to him.

22. *NN*, February 19, 1970, 10; *SL*, February 20, 1970, 1+, and February 22, 1970, sec. 1, 1+; Norman Eiger, "The Newark School Wars: A Socio-Historical Study of the 1970 and 1971 Newark School System Strikes" (Ed.D. diss., Rutgers University, 1976), 451.

23. Contract quoted in Eiger, "Newark School Wars," 201; *SL*, February 13, 1970, 11; Eiger, "Newark School Wars," 176–178, 200–201.

24. Titus quoted in *SL*, February 15, 1970, sec. 1, 1+; Thorburn interview, July 28, 1992; *SL*, March 1, 1970, 1+.

25. Eiger, "Newark School Wars," 201–202; *SL*, February 4, 1970, 1+.

26. Jacob quoted in *SL*, February 19, 1970, 1; *SL*, March 1, 1970, 1+, and February 26, 1970, 13; *New Jersey Afro-American*, February 28, 1970, 1+; *NN*, February 26, 1970, 7; Eiger, "Newark School Wars," 193–194.

27. Joseph F. Cascella, "Speech to the Board of Education," Newark, August 27, 1963, 3, NTU files; Eiger, "Newark School Wars," 488.

28. Means, interview with Eiger; David Barrett, speech at Special Board Meeting, April 7, 1971, recorded by Norman Eiger.

29. Ralph Stephens quoted in *SL*, February 26, 1970, 1+; Graves quoted in *NN*, February 27, 1970, 1+.

30. Audience member quoted in *SL*, February 27, 1970, 1+.

31. Thorburn interview, July 28, 1992.

32. Thorburn interviews, July 14, 1992, and July 28, 1992; Vic Cascella, Ralph Favilla, and Don Nicholas, interview with author, Newark, December 1, 1995; Vic Cascella, interview with author, Newark, August 6, 1996; Tony Ficcio, interview with author, New York City, November 29, 1995. Under Graves, NTU did take a stand against the Vietnam war. *SL*, September 22, 1971, 34; and Karman, interview with author, Bloomfield, N.J., March 17, 1994.

33. Thorburn interview, July 28, 1992.

34. Thorburn interview, July 28, 1992; Cascella, Favilla, and Nicholas interview.

35. Cascella, Favilla, and Nicholas interview; Graves interview with author; Hirschfeld interview; Bob Clark, interview with author, Glen Ridge, N.J., October 17, 1995; Pete Petino, interview with author, Newark, November 5, 1995.

36. "Vote the Presidential Slate," leaflet in possession of Bob Hirschfeld, copy in author's possession; Graves interview with author.

37. Nolley and Nolley interview; Thorburn interview, July 28, 1992; Hirscheld interview; Liss interview.

38. Cascella, Favilla, and Nicholas interview; Thorburn interview, July 28, 1992.

39. Graves interview with author; Graves, conversation with author, Newark, June 4, 2000.

40. Cascella, Favilla, and Nicholas interview. Later, Cascella got to know and like Polonsky.

41. Angela Paone, interview with author, Roseland, N.J., August 8, 1995.

42. Karman interview, March 17, 1994.

43. Thorburn interview, July 28, 1992; Means interview with Eiger; Elena Scambio, interview with author, Bloomfield, N.J., August 26, 1997; Braun, *Teachers and Power,* 185; *SL,* June 25, 1995, sec.1, 47; Cascella, Favilla, and Nicholas interview; Petino interview; Carole A. Graves letter to Gladys B. Francis, April 15, 1970; and Carole A. Graves letter to Betty Rufalo, June 29, 1970, NTU files. Former NTU president Sid Rosenfeld soon fell out of favor with Graves. See Carole Graves, letter to Sidney Rosenfeld, November 2, 1970, NTU files.
44. Paone interview; Hirschfeld interview.
45. Cuyler interview; Paone interview; Elena Scambio, interview with author, Bloomfield, N.J., May 30, 1997; and Scambio interview, August 26, 1997; *NN,* February 15, 1971, 1.
46. *NN,* May 10, 1970, sec. 1, 31; Robert Curvin, "The Persistent Minority: The Black Political Experience in Newark" (Ph.D.diss., Princeton University, 1975), 71, 90, and 198; Wilbur C. Rich, *Black Mayors and School Politics: The Failure of Reform in Detroit, Gary, and Newark* (New York: Garland, 1996), 99.
47. Curvin, "The Persistent Minority," 202 and 213; *NN,* June 17, 1970, 1+; K. Komozi Woodard, "The Making of the New Ark: Imamu Amiri Baraka (LeRoi Jones), the Congress of African People, and the Modern Black Convention Movement; A History of the Black Revolt and the New Nationalism, 1966–1976" (Ph.D. diss., University of Pennsylvania, 1991), 212–216.
48. Imamu Amiri Baraka, "Newark—Before Black Men Conquered," in *Raise Race Rays Raze, Essays since 1965* (New York: Random House, 1971), 71; Lloyd W. Brown, *Amiri Baraka* (Boston: Twayne, 1980), 13–14; Woodard, "Making of the New Ark," 186–187.
49. *NN,* June 5, 1970, 15, and June 17, 1970, 1+; Curvin, "The Persistent Minority," 77–78 and 85; Marge McMullen, "The Newark Resident's Budget Crunch: The Tighter It Gets, the Tighter It Gets," *Newark!* (November-December, 1970): 39.
50. Baraka, "The Practice of the New Nationalism," in *Raise Race Rays Raze,* 160, 163, and 164; Woodard, "The Making of the New Ark," 208; Means interview with Eiger; Curvin, "The Persistent Minority," 202. (Baraka's essay was written in January 1970.) Addonizio was convicted in July on 64 charges of extortion and conspiracy. *NN,* July 23, 1970, 1.
51. Gibson quoted in *NN,* October 3, 1970, 1+; Curvin, "The Persistent Minority," 195 and 214; Amiri Baraka, "Ten Years After: Newark/Detroit," in *Daggers and Javelins: Essays, 1974–1979* (New York: William Morrow, 1984), 121.
52. Baraka, "Newark—Before Black Men Conquered," 66–67; Baraka, "Hypocrites," quoted in Henry C. Lacey, *To Raise, Destroy, and Create: The Poetry, Drama, and Fiction of Imamu Amiri Baraka (Le Roi Jones)* (Troy, N.Y.: Whitson Publishing, 1981), 167; Baraka, "The Practice of the New Nationalism," 163; Woodard, "Making of the New Ark," 149, 194, and 383; Ron Porambo, *No Cause for Indictment: An Autopsy of Newark* (New York: Holt, Rinehart, and Winston, 1971), 352.
53. See Baraka, "Hymn to Lanie Poo," in *The LeRoi Jones/Amiri Baraka Reader,* ed. William J. Harris (New York: Thunder's Mouth Press, 1991), 9–10; Lacey, *To Raise, Destroy, and Create,* 25.
54. Baraka, *The System of Dante's Hell,* quoted in Lacey, *To Raise, Destroy, and Create,* 167; Baraka quoted in *NN,* May 16, 1970, 5; Eiger, "Newark School Wars," 239–240.

55. Gibson quoted in *SL*, February 17, 1970, 1+; Gibson quoted in *NN*, July 2, 1970, 11; Gibson quoted in *NN*, October 22, 1970, 15; Jonas Silver, interview with Norman Eiger, New Brunswick, N.J., January 14, 1975.

56. Gibson quoted in *NN*, December 15, 1970, 1; Gibson quoted in Marge McCullen, "Newark's Kenneth A. Gibson: The Man and the Mayor," *Newark!* (September–October 1970), 31; *NN*, January 22, 1971, 1+; Porambo, *No Cause*, 354–355; Eiger, "Newark School Wars," 454.

57. Robert Curvin, "Black Power in City Hall," *Society* (September/October 1972): 56–57; Robert Curvin, "The Persistent Minority," 102 and 126–130; *NN*, July, 21, 1970, 1; November 13, 1970, 1+; November 23, 1970, 22; and December 18, 1970, 1.

58. Curvin, "The Persistent Minority, 100, 104–105, and 131; Curvin, "Black Power," 56–57; *NN*, June 17, 1970, 1; July 2, 1970, 2; and January 27, 1971, 4; Jean Anyon, *Ghetto Schooling: A Political Economy of Urban Educational Reform* (New York: Teachers College Press, 1997), 81 and 100; Woodard, "Making of the New Ark," 117–121; Porambo, *No Cause*, 342; Peter D. Dickson, "The Sources of Italian Politics: The North Ward of Newark, New Jersey" (senior thesis, Princeton University, 1973), 93; Fred Barbaro, "Newark: Political Brokers," *Society* (September–October 1972): 51–52. The three Blacks on the new city council wanted to help Gibson but were outvoted. Puerto Ricans, Newark's third largest ethnic group in 1971, were not yet politically powerful; the Portuguese were fourth in size, ahead of the Jews and Irish.

59. *NN*, March 28, 1971, sec. 1, 8; Eiger, "Newark School Wars," 247. There were political reasons for appointing Jacob as well: he had worked in the 1970 mayoral campaign for a white candidate—John Caulfield—who threw his support to Gibson in the runoff. Porambo, *No Cause*, 370.

60. Jesse Jacob, interview with Norman Eiger, Newark, December 4, 1974; *SL*, February 10, 1971, 22.

61. Jacob interview with Eiger; *New Jersey Afro-American*, February 14, 1970, 1+, and February 21, 1970, 1+; *Sunday SL*, February 15, sec. 1, 6, and February 6, 1970, 1+; William M. Phillips Jr. and Joseph M. Conforti, *Social Conflict: Teachers' Strikes in Newark, 1964–1971* (Trenton: New Jersey Department of Education, 1972), 58.

62. Clarence Coggins, interview with Norman Eiger, Newark, November 7, 1974; Means interview with Eiger; Fred Means, "The Newark Teachers Union *vs.* the Newark Community," May 1970, draft in Mayor Gibson's files, read on tape by Norm Eiger; Eiger, "Newark School Wars," 499.

63. Clara Dasher, interview with Norman Eiger, New Brunswick, N.J., June 21, 1974; Graves quoted in *Muhammad Speaks*, February 26, 1971, sec. 1, 1; William M. Phillips, Jr., *Participation of the Black Community in Selected Aspects of the Educational Institutions of Newark* (New Brunswick, N.J.: Rutgers, the State University, 1973), 33; Jerald E. Podair, " 'White' Values, 'Black' Values: The Ocean–Hill Brownsville Controversy and New York City Culture, 1965–1975," *Radical History Review* 59 (1994): 38; Marjorie Murphy, *Blackboard Unions: The AFT and the NEA, 1900–1980* (Ithaca, N.Y.: Cornell University Press, 1990), 238; Eiger, "Newark School Wars," 498–500.

64. Jerald E. Podair, " 'White' Values, 'Black' Values," 45–46.

65. Graves quoted in *NN*, July 24, 1970, 7; Jacob quoted in *NN*, July 24, 1970, 7 (city/county edition only); Dasher interview with Eiger; Coggins interview with Eiger;

Eiger, "Newark School Wars," 241–243. Personally, Gibson objected to the elimination of nonprofessional chores but not to binding arbitration. Rich, *Black Mayors*, 121.

66. *NN*, September 4, 1970, 1, and October 28, 1970, 1; Jacob interview with Eiger; Coggins interview with Eiger; *NTU Bulletin* (January 4, 1971): 1; "3,000 members, 700 grievances," memo, NTU files; Eiger, "Newark School Wars," 243; Don Saunders, interview with Norman Eiger, East Orange, N.J., July 31, 1975. Harold Ashby, the Board president, resigned to take a paying job as business manager of the Board.

67. Saunders interview with Eiger; Eiger, "Newark School Wars," 245; Jacob interview with Eiger; Fernando Zambrano, interview with Norman Eiger, New Brunswick, N.J., November 18, 1974; Gus Henningberg, interview with Norman Eiger, Newark, November 26, 1974.

68. Saunders quoted in Eiger, "Newark School Wars," 249; Graves interview with Eiger; Saunders interview with Eiger.

69. Saunders interview with Eiger; Peter Curtin, interviewed by Eiger, Trenton, N.J., April 28, 1975; Eiger, "Newark School Wars," 265. At a session later in January, Saunders invited Baraka into the negotiating room. Union leaders were upset by Baraka's apparent influence on negotiations. Graves interview with Eiger; Dasher interview with Eiger; Coggins interview with Eiger.

70. Saunders quoted in Eiger, "Newark School Wars," 464; Saunders interview with Eiger; Curtin interview with Eiger; Coggins interview with Eiger; Ben Epstein, interview with author, Tom's River, N.J., August 7, 1995; Tom Malanga, interview with Norman Eiger, Newark, December 10, 1974.

71. Graves interview with Eiger; Graves interview with author; Dasher interview with Eiger. Graves called the January negotiations "one big filibuster." *SL*, February 1, 1971, 1.

72. Carole Graves, letter to Archer Cole, November 10, 1970, NTU files.

73. Jacob interview with Eiger; Connie Woodruff interview with Eiger, Newark, May 21, 1974; Saunders interview with Eiger; Henningberg interview with Eiger; *NN*, December 20, 1970, sec. 2, 13; Eiger, "Newark School Wars," 262.

74. Marilyn Askin, letter to the editor, *NN*, May 26, 1970, 24; "All about Essex," *NN*, January 2, 1971, 4 (the column was unsigned). The times *were* changing: in the office of an assistant corporation counsel for the city, a women's liberation poster appeared. *NN*, December 12, 1970, 5.

75. *Black Newark*, November 1972, 3; Baraka, *Kawaida Studies*, quoted in Brown, *Amiri Baraka*, 158; Baraka quoted in Sandra Garrett Shannon, "Baraka, Black Ethos, and the Black Arts Movement: A Study of Amiri Baraka's Drama during the Black Arts Movement from 1964 to 1969" (Ph.D. diss., University of Maryland, 1986), 309; Belinda Robnett, *How Long, How Long: African-American Women in the Struggle for Civil Rights* (New York: Oxford University Press, 1997), 180–184. Baraka became a Marxist in 1974 and dropped the prophetic title Imamu from his name. On his relationship with his first wife, see her memoir, Hettie Jones, *How I Became Hettie Jones* (New York: Dutton, 1990).

76. Cuyler interview.

77. Carole Graves, letter to Kenneth A. Gibson, June 24, 1970, 1–2, NTU files; *New*

Jersey Afro-American, August 8, 1970, 6; *NN*, July 24, 1970, 7 (city/county edition only). Gibson originally appointed a Puerto Rican woman, who turned out to be ineligible, so he appointed a Puerto Rican man instead. Later, when Ashby resigned, Gibson replaced him with a Black woman. Like the Addonizio Board, the resulting Board had two women members. *NN*, July 21, 1970, 9, and September 1, 1970, 11; Eiger, "Newark School Wars," 240–242.

78. Fox quoted in Braun, *Teachers and Power*, 176; Marjorie Murphy, Blackboard Unions 1990, 256, 256 n. 11, and 259–260; *New Jersey Afro-American*, February 28, 1970, 1+; Braun, *Teachers and Power*, 267; *SL*, March 28, 1971, sec.1, 1+; Eiger, "Newark School Wars," 500.

79. Jacob quoted in Phillips and Conforti, *Social Conflict*, 38; Jacob interview with Eiger; *SL*, February 7, 1971, sec.1, 1+, and March 28, 1971, sec.1, 12; Braun, *Teachers and Power*, 185, 193, and 267; Jonah Silver, interview with Norman Eiger, New Brunswick, N.J., January 14, 1975. Graves thinks Jacob and Garrett hated her *because* she was a strong woman. Not Gibson: his conflict with her was not personal. Graves interview with author.

80. Joanne Grant, *Ella Baker: Freedom Bound* (New York: John Wiley, 1998), 109 and 122–123; Charles M. Payne, *I've Got the Light of Freedom: The Organizing Tradition and the Mississippi Freedom Struggle* (Berkeley: University of California Press, 1995), 92–94.

81. Anna Blume and Marty Blume, interview with author, Berkeley Heights, N.J., October 1, 1995.

82. Blume and Blume, interview; Marty Bierbaum, interview with author, Berkeley Heights, N.J., September 16, 1995; Phyllis Salowe, interview with author, West Orange, N.J., August 10, 1995. The principal was Herb Lichtman.

83. Blume and Blume interview. Marty was reading many of the new works on educational reform, including Sylvia Ashton Warner's *Teacher* (1962), and he used her term, "organic reading," for the process of teaching reading with students' own words and stories.

84. Blume and Blume interview.

85. Blume and Blume interview; Bierbaum interview; Phyllis Salowe interview. One reason for School Within a School's success was that Seymour Spiegel not only turned power over to teachers but also actively involved parents, who fought for the school at the Board level and protected it. Seymour Spiegel, interview with author, Watchung, N.J., September 22, 1995.

86. *NN*, April 21, 1970, 24; April 22, 1970, 22; April 24, 1970, 56; April 25, 1970, 5; May 27, 1970, 19; June 5, 1970, 29; July 29, 1970, 15; October 16, 1970, 22; October 26, 1970, 8; October 28, 1970, 20.

87. *NN*, May 16, 1970, 5. The superior court ordered the Union's $40,000 fine to be taken from teachers' paychecks, going directly to the court, instead of to the Union as dues.

88. *NTU Bulletin* (January 1971): 7; Newark Teachers Union, "Building Rep. Bulletin," December 3, 1970, NTU files; Eiger, "Newark School Wars," 229.

89. Jim Lerman, interview with author, Hoboken, N.J., September 22, 1993; Cascella interview.

90. Bob Lowry and Sandy Lowry, letter to Ron [Polonsky], November 12, 1970, NTU files.

91. Epstein, quoted in Eiger, "Newark School Wars," 229; Cervase quoted in *NN*, October 28, 1970, 1.
92. *SL*, March 2, 1971, 10; Eiger, "Newark School Wars," 231. When Don Saunders was hired by the Board, he inherited approximately four hundred grievances. Given the contract language, he estimated he could win five. Saunders interview with Eiger.
93. Graves quoted in Eiger, "Newark School Wars," 229. Cascella, Favilla, and Nicholas interview; Dasher interview with Eiger; "These People Went to Jail for You!" leaflet, NTU files. Five hundred grievances reached the Board level, besides the hundreds settled at a lower level. *NTU Bulletin* (January 4, 1971): 3 and 6.
94. Carole A. Graves, letter to Albert Shanker, July 2, 1970, NTU files.
95. Clark interview.
96. Cascella, Favilla, and Nicholas interview. For a similar argument about sacrificing community respect where bread-and-butter issues are concerned, see Philip L. Kerwin, letter to the editor, *NN*, March 9, 1970, 8.
97. *NN*, April 11, 1970, 1; Paul J. Giblin, letter to Harold Ashby, May 14, 1970, NTU files; Paul J. Giblin, letter to Michael A. Petti, June 3, 1970, NTU files.
98. Minutes, Newark Teachers Union executive board meeting, May 21, 1970, 3, NTU files; *NN*, May 12, 1970, 20, and May 15, 1970, 30; Eiger, "Newark School Wars," 224.
99. Moore interview; Carol Karman, telephone conversations with author, November 14, 1998, and April 20, 2000; Clark interview. An elementary teacher had to do half an hour of cafeteria or playground duty twice a month.
100. Beth Blackmon, interview with author, South Orange, N.J., June 26, 1995.
101. Marion Bolden, interview with author, Newark, October 2, 1995.
102. Carole Graves, letter to rep(s), October 29, 1970, NTU files (her emphasis); *NN*, October 28, 1999, 20, and November 6, 1970, 2; *SL*, March 28, 1971, sec.1, 1+; *NN*, October 25, 1970, sec.1, 33.
103. *NN*, November 19, 1970, 36; November 20, 1970, 22; November 22, 1970, sec. 1, 1+; and November 24, 1970, 6.
104. Eiger, "Newark School Wars," 225–227 and 251–252.
105. Dasher interview with Eiger; Carole Graves, letter to Harold Ashby, March 9, 1970, NTU files; *NN*, April 29, 1970, 42; Thorburn interview, July 28, 1992.
106. Carole Graves, letter to Kenneth A. Gibson, June 24, 1970, 1, NTU files; Saunders interview with Eiger; *NN*, July 26, 1970, sec. 1, 25. For a good study of how a group of parents claiming to speak for the whole community seized control of another Newark school, see Carole Sue Layne Willis, "The Educational Aspirations of Parents Who Send Their Children to a Community School: A Case Study of Newark's Springfield Avenue Community School" (Ph.D. diss., University of Wisconsin–Madison, 1976).
107. *NN*, November 24, 1970, 6, and November 30, 1970, 10; Ellen Cunniff, interview with author, Bloomfield, N.J., August 14, 1995. Petino did not report to his new school. Instead he went to Union headquarters, where he was put on staff. The NTU grievance resulted, much later, in overturning the transfer of the three teachers. Meanwhile the Board went after Dasher, who also taught at South Eighth Street. *NN*, November 25, 1970, 21; December 2, 1970, 55; January 23, 1970, 5;

January 24, 1971, sec.1, 4; *SL*, December 2, 1970, 31; Paul J. Giblin, letter to Donald Saunders, January 19, 1971, 2; Cascella, Favilla, and Nicholas interview; Cascella interview.

108. *NN*, November 24, 1970, 6.
109. Saunders quoted in *NN*, December 8, 1970, 24; *NN*, November 22, 1970, sec.1, 1; Phillips and Conforti, *Social Conflict*, 37.
110. *NN*, March 13, 1970, 27; March 26, 1970, 30; June 9, 1970, 20; June 26, 1970, 11; and September 18, 1970, 19; November 1, 1970, sec. 2, C6; Eiger, "Newark School Wars," 218–222. The idea was educationally worthless because attendance was optional for students.
111. Braun, *Teachers and Power*, 270; *NN*, November 25, 1970, 12 and 21; *SL*, March 28, 1971, sec.1, 1+.
112. Anonymous teacher quoted in *NN*, December 8, 1970, 24; *NN*, December 9, 1970, 50. Another Board member, Charles Bell, was also at the December 9 meeting.
113. *NN*, December 10, 1970, 32; Phillips and Conforti, *Social Conflict*, 39.
114. *NN*, December 17, 1970, 36, and January 5, 1970, 1; Eiger, "Newark School Wars," 255.
115. Garrett quoted in *NN*, December 2, 1970, 55; Jacob quoted in *SL*, December 2, 1970, 31.
116. Carole Graves, undated memo, recorded in full by Norm Eiger on tape, "From the File of the Newark Task Force Aftermath of the Strike"; *NN*, November 1, 1970, sec. 2, C6.
117. Graves, quoted in *NN*, December 2, 1970, 55; *NN*, February 18, 1971, 1+; Eiger, "Newark School Wars," 306.
118. Saunders interview with Eiger.
119. Graves interview with Eiger.

Five   The 1971 Strike

1. Phyllis Salowe, interview with author, West Orange, N.J., August 10, 1995; Charles Nolley and Martha Nolley, interview with author, Montclair, N.J., September 14, 1995; Beth Blackmon, interview with author, South Orange, N.J., 1995.
2. Garrett quoted in *NN*, February 23, 1971, 5; *NN*, April 15, 1971, 9.
3. Travitt quoted in *NN*, February 16, 1971, 8; Richard Wesley, interview with author, Montclair, N.J, July 21, 1993; *NN*, March 2, 1971, 6. See also Elayne Brodie, quoted in *SL*, February 26, 1971, 13.
4. Carole Graves, quoted in *Muhammad Speaks*, February 19, 1971, NTU files; Newark Teachers Union, "WHO ARE WE?" leaflet, NTU files (emphasis in the original).
5. Jim Lerman, interview with author, Hoboken, N.J., October 29, 1993.
6. Lerman interview, October 29, 1993. As in 1970, a Black teacher was chosen to make the motion for the 1971 strike. *NN*, February 1, 1971, 1+.
7. "Statement by Carole Graves," press release, n.d., 2, in the possession of Carole Graves (emphasis in the original); *NN*, January 22, 1971, 5.
8. Jim Brown, interview with author, Belleville N.J., August 17, 1995.
9. "Complete Text of Board Demands," *NTU Bulletin* (January 1971), 5.

10. Blackmon interview. A recent study agrees. In Newark, "There was no marked difference between the responses [to the pressure for school reform] of black- and white-dominated Boards of Education." Wilbur C. Rich, *Black Mayors and School Politics: The Failure of Reform in Detroit, Gary, and Newark* (New York: Garland, 1996), 97.
11. Graves, quoted in *SL*, February 3, 1971, 1+.
12. Carole Graves, quoted in *Muhammad Speaks*, February 19, 1971, NTU files.
13. Newark Teachers Union, "Report to Local Labor and Community Groups," n.d., 2, NTU files; "Rally," leaflet, NTU files; "What Does Union-Busting Mean To You?" leaflet, NTU files.
14. Polonsky quoted in *NN*, March 29, 1971, 21; Felix Martino, interview with author, Roseland, N.J., August 4, 1995; *NN*, February 3, 1971, 1+, and March 11, 1971, 23; *SL*, February 4, 1971, 1+, and February 7, 1971, 1+; Pete Petino, interview with author, Newark, November 5, 1995; Brown interview; Norman Eiger, "The Newark School Wars: A Socio-Historical Study of the 1970 and 1971 Newark School System Strikes" (Ed.D. diss., Rutgers University, 1976), 311; Frank Brown, letter to Ron Polonsky, March 11, 1971, NTU files.
15. Eiger, "Newark School Wars," 311–312; *NN*, March 17, 1971, 1; William M. Phillips, Jr. and Joseph M. Conforti, *Social Conflict: Teachers' Strikes in Newark, 1964–1971* (Trenton: New Jersey Department of Education, 1972), 49; Martino interview; *SL*, March 14, 1971, sec. 1, 1; "WORK STOPPAGE RALLY," leaflet, NTU files.
16. Kenneth Travitt, quoted in *NN*, February 19, 1971, 8. Travitt replaced Fred Means as president of ONE.
17. Connie Woodruff, interview with Norman Eiger, Newark, May 21, 1974; Connie Woodruff, "LIKE IT IS," leaflet, NTU files; *NN*, February 25, 1971, 1+.
18. Carole Graves, interview with Norman Eiger, Newark, May 21, 1974.
19. Imperiale quoted in *NN*, July 23, 1970, 8; Anthony Imperiale, letter to the editor, *SL*, February 6, 1971, 20; Peter D. Dickson, "The Sources of Italian Politics: The North Ward of Newark, New Jersey" (senior thesis, Princeton University, 1973), 102–103 and 106–107; Ron Porambo, *No Cause for Indictment: An Autopsy of Newark* (New York: Holt, Rinehart, and Winston, 1971), 339; Robert Curvin, "The Persistent Minority: The Black Political Experience in Newark" (Ph.D. diss., Princeton University, 1975), 102.
20. Carol Karman, interview with author, Bloomfield, N.J., March 17, 1994; Graves interview with Eiger; Robert J. Braun, *Teachers and Power: The Story of the American Federation of Teachers* (New York: Simon and Schuster, 1972), 272 and 273.
21. Tom Lawton, interview with author, Bloomfield, N.J., June 23, 1995.
22. Petino interview.
23. *NN*, February 8, 1971, 12; February 11, 1971, 1; February 16, 1971, 8; March 28, 1971, 1+; and April 21, 1971, 8; *SL*, February 9, 1971, 1, and February 18, 1971, 1+; *New York Times*, April 8, 1971, 50; "Scabs," list, NTU files.
24. Hilda Johnson, quoted in *NN*, March 29, 1971, 21; Elena Scambio, interview with author, Bloomfield, N.J., May 30, 1997. Scambio picketed First Avenue and taught in the basement schools.
25. Parents quoted in *NN*, February 25, 1971, 1+; Petino quoted in *NN*, March 2, 1971, 6; David Shipler, "The White Niggers of Newark," *Harper's Magazine* (August 1972), 77–83.

26. East Ward residents quoted in *NN*, April 6, 1971, 23; Tom Malanga, interview with Norman Eiger, Newark, December 10, 1974; Martino interview; Andy Thorburn, interview with author, Somerset, N.J., July 28, 1992; *NN*, April 1, 1971, 19.
27. Turco quoted in *NN*, February 11, 1971, 26; *New Jersey Afro-American*, March 13, 1971, 1; *NN*, February 4, 1971, 1+; February 24, 1971, 10; February 25, 1971, 1; and March 28, 1971, 1+; Karman interview, June 2, 1994. Italians also organized in support of the strike in the Vailsburg section of the West Ward. *NN*, March 19, 1971, 19.
28. Turco quoted in *NN*, April 6, 1971, 23; *SL*, February 2, 1970, 1+; Don Saunders, interview with Norman Eiger, East Orange, N.J., July 31, 1975; *NN*, March 1, 1971, 1; March 2, 1971, 6; April 1, 1971, 19; and April 8, 1971, 11; *SL*, March 1, 1971, 1+, and March 2, 1971.
29. *NN*, November 29, 1970, sec. 2, C8; Cervase interview with Eiger, Newark, December 24, 1979; *NN*, March 4, 1970, 4; September 11, 1970, 24; and October 28, 1970, 1+; Rich, *Black Mayors*, 95–96; Porambo, *No Cause*, 375.
30. John Cervase, letter to the editor, *NN*, March 3, 1971, 26; Cervase interview with Eiger; *SL*, June 20, 1971, sec. 1, 33. For a good analysis of why Cervase and Turco sacrificed labor-management issues in 1971 and backed the strikers, see Eiger, "Newark School Wars," 509.
31. Cervase interview with Eiger; *SL*, February 3, 1971, 21; *NN*, March 10, 1971, 8; *NN*, February 22, 1971, 5; February 26, 1971, 6; March 10, 1971, 1; and April 6, 1971, 23. Cervase offered to testify that Jacob forced the Union to violate the injunction. *NN*, September 4, 1970, 1; *SL*, February 25, 1971, 1+. Note that Jacob did not support the Black and Puerto Rican Convention candidate in the 1970 mayoral campaign; he supported John Caulfield. Porambo, *No Cause*, 370.
32. Eiger, "Newark School Wars," 314–318; Gus Henningberg, interview with Norman Eiger, Newark, November 26, 1974; Clara Dasher, interview with Norman Eiger, New Brunswick, N.J., June 21, 1974; *NN*, January 24, 1971, sec. 1, 4; January 29, 1971, 1+; February 8, 1971, 8; February 10, 1971, 42; and March 26, 1971, 28; *New Jersey Afro-American*, March 6, 1971, 1+; "Special Board Meeting," anonymous minutes, April 6, 1971, NTU files; K. Komozi Woodard, "The Making of the New Ark: Imamu Amiri Baraka (LeRoi Jones), the Congress of African People, and the Modern Black Convention Movement; A History of the Black Revolt and the New Nationalism, 1966–1976" (Ph.D. diss., University of Pennsylvania, 1991), 141–142. In June 1971, Mayor Gibson appointed Hamm, who had just graduated, to the Board of Education.
33. David H. Barrett, letter to the editor, *NN*, February 5, 1971, 26; Barrett, speaking at the Special Board Meeting, April 7, 1971, audio tape in possession of Norm Eiger.
34. Brodie quoted in Phillips and Conforti, *Social Conflict*, 38; Westbrook, quoted in *NN*, March 2, 1971, 6; Derek T. Winans, letter to the editor, *NN*, March 25, 1971, 26; New Ark Community Coalition, "RUNT," leaflet, NTU files; Eiger, "Newark School Wars," 489. Trying to refute the charge that teachers were suburbanites, NTU claimed that 40% lived in Newark. *New York Times*, April 8, 1971, 50; *American Teacher* (March 1971), 4; "Teachers residing in Newark," list, NTU files. Of the 187 teachers arrested in 1970, one third (63) lived in Newark. "Arrests Made by the Sheriff's Department during Newark School Teachers Strike," annotated list, NTU files.

35. Thomas Carmichael quoted in *NN*, March 17, 1971, 1+; Saunders interview; Robert J. Braun, *Teachers and Power*, 272.

36. Carole A. Graves, letter to Brothers and Sisters, March 14, 1971, 2, NTU files; "The Community's Choice? or Poverty's Pimps?" leaflet, NTU files"; Ron Polonsky, letter to Edward Chervin, March 10, 1971, 5, NTU files; *NN*, March 28, 1971, sec.1, 8, and April 11, 1971, 8; Graves interview with Eiger. Vice President Spiro Agnew was thought to say publicly the outrageous things President Nixon wanted to say but couldn't.

37. Seymour Cohen, quoted in *SL*, February 25, 1971, 1+; *New York Sunday News*, March 28, 1971, J12; Angela Paone, interview with author, Roseland, N.J., August 8, 1995; *NN*, April 20, 1971, 1; Marc Gaswirth, William M. Weinberg, and Barbara E. Kemmerer, *Teachers' Strikes in New Jersey: Studies in Industrial Relations and Human Resources, No. 1* (Metuchen, N.J.: Scarecrow Press, 1982), 79. Many teachers told me Baraka was behind the February 2 attack, but they could offer no evidence.

38. Union activists quoted in *NN*, March 28, 1971, 8; *NN*, February 25, 1971, 1+; Graves interview with Eiger.

39. Newark Teachers Union, "Our Strike and the Two Sides of Black Nationalism," leaflet, NTU files.

40. "Black Panther Party," press release, February 21, 1971, NTU files; *Muhammad Speaks*, February 19, 1971, NTU files; Carol Karman, interview with author, Bloomfield, N.J., June 2, 1994; Petino interview; *SL*, February 23, 1971, 1+; Newark Teachers Union, "Our Strike and the Two Sides of Black Nationalism," leaflet, NTU files; Braun, *Teachers and Power*, 272; Eiger, "Newark School Wars," 510. The Black Panthers had backed the 1970 strike as well. *American Teacher/Special Issue* (February 16, 1970): 2.

41. *NN*, April 9, 1971, 1, and April 11, 1971, 1+; Eiger, "Newark School Wars," 380–381.

42. Dasher interview with Eiger.

43. Robert Lowenstein, letter to the editor, *NN*, February 9, 1971, 16.

44. Salowe interview.

45. Salowe interview.

46. Dave Lieberfarb, Jim Lowenstein, and Steve Shaffer, interview with author, Fair Lawn, N.J., November 19, 1995. Imperiale's support for the strike was one reason Marty Bierbaum decided to cross the picket line. Marty Bierbaum, interview with author, Berkeley Heights, N.J., September 16, 1995.

47. Karman interview, June 2, 1994; Carol Karman, phone conversation with author, May 29, 2000. Prudential contributed funds to the New Ark Coalition.

48. Phyllis Cuyler, interview with author, Woodbridge, N.J., July 21, 1994.

49. Marion Bolden, interview with author, Newark, October 2, 1995.

50. Avant Lowther, Jr., interview with author, Newark, June 14, 1995.

51. Zenobia Capel, interview with author, East Orange, August 12, 1992. Jacob's posture of being the only one who cared about Black children alienated many people. Saunders interview with Eiger; Malanga interview with Eiger; Ron Haughton, interview with Norman Eiger, Princeton, N.J., November 19, 1974.

52. Janice Adams, interview with author, Newark, September 7, 1995; Adams quoted in *Muhammad Speaks*, April 1971, NTU files.

53. Harold Moore, interview with author, Montclair, N.J., August 21, 1995.
54. Harold and Alison Moore interview (Alison participated in parts of the interview); Paone interview.
55. Eiger, "Newark School Wars," 308; Dasher interview with Eiger; Lawton interview.
56. *SL*, February 2, 1971, 1+; *NN*, January 27, 1971, 19; Bob Clark, interview with author, Glen Ridge, N.J., October 17, 1995; Gene Liss, interview with author, Newark, August 29, 1995; Jim Lowenstein and Steve Shaffer, interview with author, Fair Lawn, N.J., July 26, 1994; Lieberfarb, Lowenstein, and Shaffer interview; Jerry Yablonsky, interview with author, Springfield, N.J., November 7, 1995; Dorothy Bergman, interview with author, New York City, October 11, 1995; Karman interview, March 17, 1994; Dasher interview with Eiger; Bob Hirschfeld, interview with author, Livingston, September 28, 1995; Salowe interview; Cuyler interview; Petino interview.
57. Brown interview; *NN*, February 2, 1971, 1.
58. Brown interview.
59. Brown interview.
60. Brown interview.
61. Elman quoted in Newark Teachers Union, videotape, "Newark Teachers Union 50th Anniversary Celebration"; *NN*, February 2, 1971, 1+, and February 3, 1971, 1+; *SL*, February 3, 1971, 1, and February 4, 1971, 1+; Hirschfeld interview; Carole Graves, discussion with author, Newark, June 14, 2000; *American Teacher* (March 1971), 4.
62. Newark Teachers Union, leaflet, NTU files; Brown interview.
63. Petino interview; *NN*, February 3, 1971, 1+, and February 4, 1971, 1+; Superior Court of New Jersey, Chancery Division—Essex County, "In the Matter of Newark Teachers Union Local 481, American Federation of Teachers, AFL-CIO, and unincorporated association, Defendant Charged with Contempt of Court," NTU files. Two months later, one man was indicted for beating Elman. *SL*, April 3, 1971, 4.
64. Lieberfarb, Lowenstein, and Shaffer interview; Graves interview with Eiger; Carole Graves, interview with author, Newark, May 24, 2000; Eiger, "Newark School Wars," 310; Fred Barbaro, "Mass Jailing of Teachers," *The Clearing House* (September 1973), 17; Nolley and Nolley interview.
65. Petino interview; Lawton interview; Graves interview with Eiger; Jim Lerman, "A Question of Survival," *American Teacher* (March 1971), 3.
66. *NN*, February 1, 1971, 1+, and February 12, 1971, 18; *New Jersey Afro-American*, February 20, 1971, 1, and March 13, 1971, 1+; Graves interview with Eiger; *SL*, March 3, 1971, 1+; Ben Epstein, interview with Norman Eiger, Newark, November 7, 1974.
67. *NN*, February 2, 1971, 1; February 4, 1971, 1+; February 16, 1971, 8; February 17, 1971, 1+; and March 13, 1971, 1+; *SL*, February 9, 1971, 1+; Phil Basile, interview with author, Verona, N.J., August 15, 1995; Bolden interview; Bierbaum interview; Capel interview; Hirschfeld interview.
68. Petino interview; Scambio interview, May 30, 1997.
69. Lawton interview. A teacher at another school, who does not want to be identified, put liquid lead on locks, to prevent teachers from going in before pickets got there.
70. Joe Del Grosso, interview with author, Newark, August 24, 1995.
71. Pat Piegari, interview with author, Caldwell, N.J., September 22, 1995; Blackmon interview; Lawton interview; Salowe interiew; Hirschfeld interview.

72. Piegari interview; Blackmon interview.

73. Charles Malone, interview with author, Orange, N.J., June 12, 1995.

74. Ellen Cunniff, interview with author, Bloomfield, N.J., August 14, 1995.

75. Basile interview.

76. Newark Teachers Union, "Scabs" list, NTU files; Basile interview; Blackmon interview.

77. Brown interview; South Eighth Street teacher, quoted in Lerman, "A Question of Survival," 3.

78. Asa Watkins, letter to the editor, *NN*, March 24, 1970, 16.

79. Graves interview with author. A school was firebombed in a New Orleans teachers strike in 1969. Braun, *Teachers and Power*, 15.

80. Graves interview with author.

81. Cuyler interview; Cunniff interview; "Scabs" list, NTU files. Tom Lawton confirms that Middleton died as a result of a crash and that some strike opponents suspected foul play. Lawton interview.

82. Graves interview with Eiger; Graves interview with author; *SL*, December 2, 1970, 31; Ron Polonsky, letter to Edward Chernin, March 10, 1971, NTU files; *NN*, January 25, 1971, 8, and February 8, 1971, 1+; Petino interview.

83. Saunders interview with Eiger; Malanga quoted in *NN*, March 2, 1971, 6; Moore interview; *SL*, March 3, 1971, 1+, and March 7, sec. 1, 16; Malanga interview with Eiger; Andy Thorburn, interview with author, Somerset, N.J., July 14, 1992.

84. Hirschfeld interview.

85. Adams interview; Janice Adams, telephone conversation with author, January 15, 2000; *NN*, March 19, 1971, 1+; *SL*, March 19, 1971, 1.

86. Lawton interview.

87. Lowenstein and Shaffer interview; Garrett quoted in *NN*, February 9, 1971, 1; Lerman interview, October 29, 1993; Phillips and Conforti, *Social Conflict*, 43; *SL*, February 10, 1971, 1+, and February 11, 1971, 1+; *NN*, February 25, 1971, 1+, and February 23, 1971, 5.

88. Lowenstein and Shaffer interview.

89. Lieberfarb, Lowenstein, and Shaffer interview.

90. Capel interview.

91. Lowther interview.

92. Piegari interview; Cunniff interview; *NN*, February 16, 1971, 8, and February 24, 1971, 10; *SL*, March 1, 1971, 1+, and March 26, 1971, 10; Lerman, "A Question of Survival," 3.

93. Mary Abend, interview with author, Newark, June 14, 1995.

94. Carol Karman, interview with author, Bloomfield, N.J., March 17, 1994.

95. Anna Blume and Marty Blume, Berkeley Heights, N.J., October 1, 1995; Bierbaum interview.

96. Martino interview. Graves interview with author: "Some of the biggest names in labor racketeering . . . [were] on our side."

97. Jesse Jacob, interview with Norman Eiger, Newark, December 4, 1974; Arnold Hess, letter to instructional personnel, February 22, 1971, NTU files; *NN*, February 24, 1971, 10, and February 25, 1971, 1; *SL*, February 24, 1971, 7; March 29, 1971, 1+; and April 1, 1971, 1+; Paone interview; Shaffer interview, November 19,

1994; Lawton interview; Scambio interview, May 30, 1997; Hirschfeld interview; Blackmon interview; Dasher interview with Eiger. NTU made interest-free loans available.

98. Liss interview; *NN*, March 31, 1971, 1; *SL*, February 14, 1971, sec. 1, 4.

99. Gibson quoted in *NN*, April 1, 1971, 19; Titus, quoted in *NN*, August 9, 1970, sec. 1, 23; Dasher interview with Eiger. The school board in Minot, North Dakota responded to a 1969 strike by firing all the striking teachers. *SL*, February 7, 1971, sec. 1, 36; Braun, *Teachers and Power*, 121–122.

100. Paone interview; Polonsky quoted in Jim Lerman, interview with author, Hoboken, N.J., December 10, 1993, and in Lowenstein and Shaffer interview; Clark interview; Karman interview, June 2, 1994; Eiger, "Newark School Wars," 349. Polonsky confided in Vinnie Russell, whom Eiger interviewed.

101. Polonsky, quoted in *SL*, April 2, 1971, 1+; *SL*, April 1, 1971, 1.

102. Saunders interview with Eiger.

103. Petino interview; Vic Cascella, Ralph Favilla, and Don Nicholas interview with author, Newark, December 1, 1995.

104. Del Grosso interview.

105. Del Grosso interview.

106. Del Grosso interview.

107. Del Grosso interview; *NN*, March 25, 1971, 1+, and March 27, 1971, 1+. At Broadway Elementary School, "roving busloads of teacher pickets show up two or three times a week." *NN*, March 28, 1971, 1+.

108. Del Grosso interview.

109. Lawton interview; Del Grosso interview; Cunniff interview.

110. Petino interview.

111. Petino interview. Carole Graves agrees that the strikers were more violent. Graves interview with author. Early on, there were only two policemen at most schools. As the mood became angrier, 15 or more police were assigned to schools where violence was anticipated. *NN*, February 24, 1971, 10, and February 25, 1971, 1.

112. Newark Teachers Union, letter to strikebreakers, NTU files; Petino interview; *SL*, February 7, 1971, sec. 1, 36; Cuyler interview.

113. Yablonsky interview. Gerald Meyer heard stories about the house visits from teachers in jail. Gerald Meyer, phone interview with author, February 5, 2000.

114. Karman interview, June 2, 1994.

115. Brown interview; Graves interview with author; *SL*, February 9, 1971, 1+.

116. Eiger, "Newark School Wars," 465–467. The law was changed in 1974 to give PERC more power.

117. Pete Curtin, interview with Eiger, Trenton, N.J., August 28, 1975; *NN*, February 1, 1971, 1; *SL*, February 7, 1971, sec. 1, 1+; Eiger, "Newark School Wars," 293–294; Phillips and Conforti, *Social Conflict*, 40. Curtin was present at the meeting.

118. Curtin interview with Eiger; *SL*, February 7, 1971, sec. 1, 1+; *NN*, March 8, 1971, 1+; Eiger, "Newark School Wars," 291, 295–297, and 303; Gaswirth, Weinberg, and Kemmerer, *Teachers' Strikes*, 79.

119. Curtin interview with Eiger; Cervase interview with Eiger; Dasher interview with Eiger; Malanga interview with Eiger; Saunders interview with Eiger; *SL*, March 8, 1971, 1; *NN*, April 18, 1971, 5; Eiger, "Newark School Wars," 297–299.

120. Saunders quoted in *SL*, February 5, 1971, 1+; Saunders interview with Eiger; Curtin interview with Eiger.
121. Dasher interview with Eiger; *NN*, March 17, 1971, 1+, and April 18, 1971, 5.
122. Jacob quoted in Eiger, "Newark School Wars," 347; *NN*, March 7, 1971, 4, and March 28, 1971, 8; *SL*, March 13, 1971, 2; Eiger, "Newark School Wars," 342–343. Silver was appointed mediator on February 23.
123. Silver quoted in Eiger, "Newark School Wars," 344; Jonas Silver, interview with Norman Eiger, New Brunswick, N.J., January 14, 1975; *NN*, March 5, 1971, 1+.
124. Silver interview with Eiger; Curtin interview with Eiger; Eiger, "Newark School Wars," 346.
125. Clarence Coggins, interview with Norman Eiger, Newark, November 7, 1974; Robert Curvin, telephone conversation with author, June 3, 2001; *NN*, July 30, 1970, 1+, and August 2, 1970, sec. 1, 17; Woodard, "Making of the New Ark," 389. Coggins played a key role in Gibson's election campaign. Curvin, "The Persistent Minority," 203.
126. Coggins interview with Eiger.
127. Coggins interview with Eiger; Graves interview with Eiger.
128. Jacob interview with Eiger; Coggins interview with Eiger; Curtin interview with Eiger.
129. Haughton interview with Eiger, November 19, 1974; Jacob interview with Eiger; *SL*, March 20, 1971, 1, and March 26, 1971, 10; Eiger, "Newark School Wars," 352–353. Haughton knew Dave Selden of AFT.
130. Dasher interview with Eiger; Ron Haughton, interview with Norman Eiger, Princeton, N.J., November 20, 1974; Eiger, "Newark School Wars," 355; Curtin interview with Eiger.
131. Haughton interviews with Eiger, November 19, 1974 and November 20, 1974; Eiger, "Newark School Wars," 358–359. Haughton came from Detroit too.
132. Vic Cascella, interview with author, Newark, August 6, 1996; Eiger, "Newark School Wars," 406–407.
133. Saunders interview with Eiger; Malanga interview with Eiger; Coggins interview with Eiger; Eiger, "Newark School Wars," 399.
134. Haughton interview with Eiger, November 20, 1974; Silver interview with Eiger.
135. Fernando Zambrana, interview with Norman Eiger, New Brunswick, N.J, November 18, 1974; *NN*, February 7, 1971, sec. 1, 1+; Coggins interview with Eiger. Zambrana's ties were to business leaders, and he wanted to put teachers back in their place. But he wasn't out to break the Union.
136. *NN*, March 31, 1971, 1+; Curtin, interview with Eiger; *NN*, April 4, 1971, sec. 1, 8.
137. *NN*, April 4, 1971, sec. 1, 8; Malanga interview with Eiger; Haughton interview with Eiger, November 20, 1974.
138. Eiger, "Newark School Wars," 364–365.
139. Dasher interview with Eiger; *New Jersey Afro-American*, April 29, 1970, 1; *SL*, July 9, 1972, sec. 1, 30; *NN*, April 21, 1970, 24, and July 19, 1970, sec. 1, 1. In 1972, Gibson reappointed Bell but not Jacob; Bell became Board president.
140. Bell quoted in *NN*, March 7, 1971, sec. 1, 1+; Eiger, "Newark School Wars," 376–377.
141. "REVOLUTION 1971!!" leaflet, NTU files; *NN*, April 4, 1971, sec. 1, 8; Eiger, "Newark School Wars," 376.

142. Garrett and others quoted in *NN*, April 7, 1971, 1+; *NN*, April 8, 1971, 1+; *SL*, April 7, 1971, 7; Porambo, *No Cause*, 377; "Special Board Meeting," anonymous minutes, April 6, 1971, NTU files.

143. Paone interview; *NN*, April 7, 1971, 1, and April 8, 1971, 1+; *SL*, April 7, 1971, 1+; *New York Times*, April 8, 1971, 50; Porambo, *No Cause*, 377. The *Times* reporter was Fox Butterfield.

144. Del Grosso interview.

145. Moore interview.

146. Coggins interview with Eiger.

147. Coggins interview with Eiger; Curvin, "The Persistent Minority," 132.

148. Dasher quoted in *SL*, April 10, 1971, 1; Dasher interview with Eiger; Graves interview with Eiger; *NN*, April 1, 1971, 19; April 2, 1971, 5; April 4, 1971, sec. 1, 8; April 7, 1971, 4; April 10, 1971, 1; April 11, 1971, sec. 1, 8; April 12, 1971, 1+; and April 14, 1971, 1.

149. Gibson quoted in *NN*, April 7, 1971, 4; "Calling all Blackmen," leaflet, NTU files.

150. Cascella interview; *SL*, April 8, 1971, 1+.

151. Virginia Scott and David Barrett, speaking at the Special Board Meeting, April 7, 1971, tape in possession of Norman Eiger; *NN*, April 8, 1971, 1, and April 8, 1971, 10; *SL*, April 8, 1971, 1+.

152. Charles Bell, speaking at the Special Board Meeting, April 7, 1971, tape in possession of Norman Eiger; *NN*, April 8, 1971, 1+, and April 13, 1971, 10; Dasher interview with Eiger.

153. Cascella interview, December 1, 1995; Haughton interview with Eiger, November 20, 1974.

154. Haughton interviews with Eiger, November 19, 1974 and November 20, 1974; Graves interview with Eiger; Coggins interview with Eiger; Eiger, "Newark School Wars," 387 and 405.

155. Gibson quoted in *NN*, April 12, 1971, 7.

156. Mayor Gibson, "A Call to Reason," April 16, 1971, reprinted in *NN*, April 17, 1971, 1, and April 18, 1971, 6.

157. Coggins interview with Eiger; *NN*, April 18, 1971, sec. 1, 1; Eiger, "Newark School Wars," 400; Haughton interview with Eiger, November 19, 1974.

158. Jacob interview with Eiger. Jacob gives the example of Virginia Scott, who was the first speaker on April 7, but who now told him that he must go along with the Mayor.

159. Graves interview with author; Baraka quoted in *NN*, April 9, 1971, 1+; Dasher interview with Eiger; Eiger, "Newark School Wars," 394–397.

160. Imperiale quoted in *NN*, April 13, 1971, 10, and in *NN*, April 14, 1971, 1+.

161. Jacob interview with Eiger; Haughton interview with Eiger, November 19, 1974; Epstein interview with Eiger; Graves interview with author; Vic Cascella, phone conversation with author, July 11, 2000; *SL*, April 19, 1971, 1+; Eiger, "Newark School Wars," 407; Porambo, *No Cause*, 379; Board of Education Meeting, April 18, 1971, tape in Norman Eiger's possession; *NN*, April 19, 1971, 1+.

162. PTA leaders quoted in *NN*, April 15, 1971, 9; Jacob quoted in *NN*, April 19, 1971, 1+; Eiger, "Newark School Wars," 408.

163. NTU statement quoted in *American Teacher* (May 1971): 8; Hope Jackson, quoted in *NN*, April 21, 1971, 1+ [Maple Avenue]; Marion Bell, quoted in *NN*, April 19,

1971, 1 [South Tenth]; *NN*, April 19, 1971, 1+, and April 20, 1971; *SL*, May 14, 1971, 19; Fred J. Cook, "Wherever the Central Cities Are Going, Newark Is Going to Get There First," *New York Times* magazine, July 25, 1971, 36; telephone call to author, January 12, 1996. The caller, who taught at South Tenth Street and was transferred after the strike, did not want her name used.

164. Hirschfeld interview.
165. Karman interviews, June 2, 1994, and March 17, 1994.
166. "Newark Teachers Union Newsletter," leaflet, April 23, 1971, NTU file; *NN*, April 19, 1971, 1, and April 21, 1971, 8.
167. Jacob, quoted in *NN*, April 21, 1971, 1+; *NN*, April 20, 1971, 1; May 12, 1971, 44; and May 13, 1971, 1; Newark Teachers Union, "THE POST-STRIKE SITUATION," statement to all labor organizations in the state, NTU files; Clark interview.
168. Scambio interview, May 30, 1997; Clark interview; Cunniff interview; Salowe interview.
169. Blackmon interview. The rift was perhaps less damaging when both striker and nonstriker were white. It took a year or two, but Phil Basile slowly got back to normal relationships with his close friends at Barringer—even the man who removed the distributor wire. Basile interview.
170. Lowther interview. It also took Phyllis Cuyler time to regain her position in the Union. Cuyler interview.
171. Capel interview.
172. Victor Cascella, letter to Roy Wilkins, December 10, 1971, NTU files.

Six   Teachers in Jail

1. *NN*, March 1, 1970, sec. 1, 15, and March 20, 1970, 30; Fred Barbaro, "Mass Jailing of Teachers," *The Clearing House* (September 1973): 13; *American Teacher* (December 1971): 6; Andy Thorburn, interview with author, Somerset, N.J., July 28, 1992.
2. "Arrests Made by the Sheriff's Department during Newark School Teachers Strike," annotated list, NTU; Newark Teachers Union, *The Anatomy of a Strike* (Newark: Newark Teachers Union, n.d. [1970]), 19 and 102–103; *NN*, February 26, 1970, 25; March 17, 1970, 17; and May 19, 1970, 24. The cases against three teachers were dismissed; seven labor officials arrested on the downtown march were acquitted.
3. Selden quoted in *NN*, March 13, 1970, 1; *NN*, March 19, 1970, 56; Jim Lerman, interview with author, Hoboken, N.J., October 29, 1993; Carole Graves, letter to David Selden, November 5, 1971, 2, NTU files; Robert J. Braun, *Teachers and Power: The Story of the American Federation of Teachers* (New York: Simon and Schuster, 1972), 274.
4. Thorburn interview, July 28, 1992; Dorothy Gallagher, "The Teacher Who Chose to Go to Jail," *Redbook* (January 1971), 161.
5. Thorburn interview, July 28, 1992; Braun, *Teachers and Power*, 274.
6. Carole Graves, letter to Colleagues, June 27, 1971, 2, NTU files; Carole Graves, letter to Arrested Teachers—1970, July 7, 1971, NTU files; Carole Graves, memo to Arrested Teachers—1970 and 1971, n.d., NTU files; Marc Gaswirth, "Teacher

Militancy in New Jersey: An Analysis of Organizational Change, Public Policy Development, and School Board-Teacher Relationships Through January, 1975" (Ed.D. diss., Rutgers University, 1977), 269–270.

7. Anonymous teacher, quoted in Carole Graves, letter to David Selden, November 5, 1971, NTU files; David Selden, letter to Newark Teachers Union Members, October 29, 1971, 1–6.

8. Carole Graves, letter to David Selden, November 5, 1971, 1–2, NTU files. Schmid was one of the losers in the 1970 coup; he and Graves were enemies. John Schmid, interview with author, Bloomfield, N.J., February 28, 1997; Carole Graves, letter to Robert Porter, October 5, 1970, NTU files.

9. Carole Graves, letter to Herrick Roth, October 26, 1971, NTU files; Marjorie Murphy, *Blackboard Unions: The AFT and the NEA, 1900–1980* (Ithaca, N.Y.: Cornell University Press, 1990), 256; Braun, *Teachers and Power*, 267 and 269; *NN*, February 18, 1971, 1+; Norman Eiger, "The Newark School Wars: A Socio-Historical Study of the 1970 and 1971 Newark School System Strikes" (Ed.D. diss., Rutgers University, 1976), 306; Jim Lowenstein and Steve Shaffer, interview with author, Fair Lawn, N.J., July 26, 1994. In her letter to Selden, Graves included a threat: "If an accounting is necessary, it will come at the AFT Convention in August of 1972." Graves, letter to Selden, 2.

10. Vic Cascella, Ralph Favilla, and Don Nicholas, interview with author, Newark, December 1, 1995. Vic Cascella, interview with author, Newark, August 6, 1996; Vic Cascella, phone conversation, July 11, 2000; Thorburn interview, July 28, 1992; *SL*, March 24, 1975, 25; Eiger, "Newark School Wars," 420–421.

11. Carole Graves, letter to Charles Marciante, November 12, 1971, 1, NTU files; Carole Graves, letter to labor and AFT leaders, n.d., NTU files. Marciante and other labor leaders organized a clemency drive, which continued after the officers went to jail. Victor Cascella, letter to Carol Karman, January 14, 1972, NTU files; Bob Arey, letter to Local Presidents, February 7, 1972, NTU files; Hannah Litzky, letter to Joachim Prinz, January 26, 1972, in Litzky's possession.

12. "Arrested Teachers: Preferences for Starting of Jail Sentences," memo, NTU files.

13. Thorburn interview, July 28, 1992; Lowenstein and Shaffer interview; Jim Lerman, interview with author, Hoboken, N.J., December 10, 1993; Barbaro, "Mass Jailing," 14–15.

14. Gallagher, "The Teacher Who Chose to Go," 161; Thorburn interview, July 28, 1992; Bob Hirschfeld, interview with author, Livingston, N.J., September 28, 1995.

15. Gallagher, "The Teacher Who Chose to Go," 58 and 162. The official name was the Essex County Correction Center, but no one called it that.

16. Gallagher, "The Teacher Who Chose to Go," 161, 162, and 164.

17. Gallagher, "The Teacher Who Chose to Go," 160 and 162; Newark Teachers Union membership book, NTU files.

18. Gallagher, "The Teacher Who Chose to Go," 162 and 164.

19. Gallagher, "The Teacher Who Chose to Go," 162; *NN*, May 1, 1970, 5; *American Teacher* (May 1970), 2; Schmid interview.

20. Gallagher, "The Teacher Who Chose to Go," 59.

21. *SL*, February 2, 1971, 1+; February 5, 1971, 1+; February 7, 1971, sec. 1, 1+. The two vice presidents were Don Nicholas and Frank Fiorito.

22. Carol Karman, interview with author, Bloomfield, N.J., March 17, 1994; Graves interview with author; Graves quoted in *SL*, February 6, 1971, 1; Carol Graves, letter to Albert Shanker, February 15, 1971, NTU files.

23. Carole Graves, letter to Brothers and Sisters, March 14, 1971, 1, NTU files; Graves quoted in *NN*, April 15, 1971, 9; *NN*, March 19, 1971, 1+; *American Teacher* (April 1971), 5; *SL*, March 18, 1971, 1; March 19, 1971, 1; March 20, 1971, 1+; March 22, 1971, 5; and April 15, 1971, 1.

24. Carole Graves, prison diary, November 29, 1971, 1 (diary in Graves's possession); *SL*, November 30, 1971, 1+.

25. Graves prison diary, November 29, 1971, 1–4, and November 30, 1971, 7.

26. Graves prison diary, December 1, 1971, 8, and December 3, 1971, 10; Graves interview with author; Carole Graves, conversation with author, Newark, June 14, 2000. Angela Davis, a Black revolutionary, was in jail in San Francisco, accused of aiding the violent escape attempt of a prisoner. The AFT was meeting in San Francisco.

27. Graves prison diary, December 7, 1971, 18; December 16, 1971, 32; December 20, 1971, 37; and January 26, 1972, 74; *SL*, December 31, 1971, 4.

28. Graves prison diary, January 26, 1972, 74; February 4, 1972, 91; and February 9, 1972, 99–100, 102, and 103; Graves interview with author; Carole Graves, "SPECIAL TO THE AMERICAN TEACHER," n.d., 2–3, NTU files.

29. Graves prison diary, January 23, 1972, 70.

30. Karman interview, March 17, 1994; *SL*, June 25, 1995, sec. 1, 47–48; Dorothy Bergman, interview with author, New York City, October 11, 1995.

31. Graves prison diary, December 11, 1971, 28, December 16, 1971, 31 and 33; December 29, 1971, 51; and December 31, 1971, 53.

32. Esther Tumin, interview with author, Livingston, N.J., December 4, 1992; Phyllis Salowe, interview with author, West Orange, N.J., August 10, 1995; Lowenstein and Shaffer interview.

33. Graves, conversation with author.

34. "Newark's Black Youth: Outreach toward Freedom," *Newark!* (March/April 1970), 23; Hannah Litzky, prison diary, December 20 [1971] (copy in author's possession); "Arrests Made by the Sheriff's Department during Newark School Teachers Strike," annotated list, NTU files; *SL*, December 16, 1971, 3. Two women served their sentences in June 1971, two began their sentences on December 10, and one spent her ten days in a mental health clinic.

35. Salowe interview.

36. Salowe interview.

37. Salowe interview.

38. Salowe interview.

39. Karman interview, March 17, 1994; Jeanette Lappé, tape recording, n.d. [1972] (tape in possession of Paul Lappé).

40. Alice Saltman, interview with author, Livingston, N.J., June 13, 1995.

41. Saltman interview.

42. Saltman interview; Eli Saltman, letter to Alice Saltman, December 20 [1971], (copy in author's possession).

43. Litzky prison diary, December 15 [1971].

44. Litzky prison diary, December 16 [1971].
45. Litzky prison diary, December 16 [1971]; Hannah Litzky, interview with author, West Orange, N.J., August 25, 1993.
46. Litzky interview; Hannah Litzky, letter to Leo and Paula, December 19, 1971 (copy in author's possession).
47. Lappé tape.
48. Lappé tape; Litzky prison diary, December 17 [1971].
49. Lappé tape; Graves prison diary, December 18, 1971, 34; Litzky, prison diary, December 17, [1971].
50. Lappé tape; Litzky prison diary, December 17 [1971].
51. Litzky prison diary, December 15 and December 17 [1971]; Lappé tape.
52. Lappé tape; Litzky prison diary, December 20 [1971].
53. Salowe interview; Graves prison diary, December 15, 1971, 31; Litzky prison diary, December 20 [1971]; Lappé tape; *News-Record of Maplewood and South Orange*, December 30, 1971, 1+.
54. Litzky, letter to Leo and Paula, December 19, 1971, 1.
55. Litzky prison diary, December 20 [1971]; Graves prison diary, December 19, 1971, 36–37, and December 20, 1971, 37; *SL*, January 9, 1972, sec. 1, 13.
56. Lappé tape; Litzky prison diary, December 20 [1971]; Litzky interview.
57. Lappé tape; Litzky prison diary, December 20 [1971].
58. Lappé tape; Barbaro, "Mass Jailing of Teachers," 15.
59. Graves prison diary, December 21, 1971, 39 and 41, and December 23, 1971, 41–42. Conditions in the state prisons in Trenton and Clinton were worse than Caldwell.
60. Graves prison diary, December 23, 1971, 42; *American Teacher* (January 1972): 3; *SL*, December 31, 1971, 4.
61. Lappé tape.
62. Bergman interview. Five women and four men who were expected to go to jail in December did not. Two received suspended sentences at the last minute; one went to jail the following summer; six failed to surrender. *SL*, December 30, 1971, 4.
63. Bergman interview.
64. Helen Klayman and Betty McEachin, quoted in *SL*, January 9, 1972, sec. 1, 13+.
65. Bergman interview.
66. Bergman interview; Tumin interview, December 4, 1992; *SL*, January 9, 1972, sec. 1, 13+; Graves prison diary, December 27, 1971, 49.
67. Bergman interview.
68. Bergman interview.
69. Graves prison diary, December 5, 1971, 16; December 23, 1971, 43; December 25, 1971, 47; January 2, 1971, 55; and January 30, 1971, 77.
70. Graves prison diary, December 25, 1971, 45–47.
71. Graves prison diary, December 24, 1971, 44, and December 27, 1971, 48; *SL*, January 9, 1972, sec. 1, 13; Bergman interview; Tumin interview, December 4, 1992.
72. Lappé tape; *SL*, January 9, 1972, sec. 1, 13.
73. Tumin interview, December 4, 1992; Esther Tumin, interview with author, Livingston, N.J., December 14, 1992.
74. Tumin interview, December 4, 1992.

75. Tumin interview, December 4, 1992.
76. Tumin interview, December 4, 1992.
77. Tumin interview, December 4, 1992.
78. Tumin interviews, December 4, 1992 and December 14, 1992.
79. Tumin interview, December 4, 1992.
80. Tumin interview, December 4, 1992.
81. Bergman interview.
82. Tumin interview, December 4, 1992; Bergman interview.
83. Tumin interview, December 4, 1992.
84. Tumin interview, December 4, 1992.
85. Litzky, letter to Leo and Paula, December 19, 1971, 2; Tumin interview, December 4, 1992; Litzky interview; *West Orange Chronicle*, January 6, 1972, 10; Lappé tape; Salowe interview.
86. *SL*, April 8, 1974, O–17.
87. Bob Hirschfeld, interview with author, Livingston, N.J., September 28, 1995; Pete Petino, interview with author, Newark, November 5, 1995; *News-Record of Maplewood and South Orange*, December 30, 1971, 1+; *News-Record of Maplewood and South Orange*: 1+ (clipping given to author by Hannah and Leo Litzky).
88. Lowenstein and Shaffer interview.
89. Lowenstein and Shaffer interview.
90. Barbaro, "Mass Jailing," 15; Jerry Yablonsky, interview with author, Springfield, N.J., November 7, 1995; Dave Lieberfarb, interview with author, Fair Lawn, N.J., November 19, 1994.
91. Tumin quoted in *News-Record of Maplewood and South Orange*: 1+. Lucy Bell, who saw two of her former students in jail, left prison thinking of them and trying to promote prison reform. *SL*, January 9, 1972, sec. 1, 1+ clipping.
92. Tumin quoted in *News-Record of Maplewood and South Orange*, December 30, 1971, 1; Thorburn interview, July 28, 1992; Hannah Litzky and Leo Litzky, interview with author, West Orange, N.J., August 25, 1993.
93. Tumin quoted in *News-Record of Maplewood and South Orange*, December 30, 1971, 1+, and by *News-Record of Maplewood and South Orange*: 1+ (clipping).
94. Tumin quoted in *News-Record of Maplewood and South Orange*: 1+ (clipping); *News-Record of Maplewood and South Orange*, December 30, 1971, 1+; Lowenstein and Shaffer interview; Joe Del Grosso, interview with author, Newark, August 24, 1995.
95. Hirschfeld interview; Yablonsky interview; Phil Basile, interview with author, Verona, N.J., August 15, 1995.
96. Del Grosso interview; Basile interview.
97. Pat Piegari, interview with author, Caldwell, N.J., September 22, 1995.
98. Piegari interview.
99. Lowenstein and Shaffer interview.
100. James Lerman, "Letter to Brothers and Sisters," *American Teacher* (February 1972): 23. Lerman was released early when his father died suddenly in a car accident. Graves prison diary, January 16, 1971, 61 and January 17, 1971, 62.
101. Basile interview; Tumin, quoted in *News-Record of Maplewood and South Orange*: 1+ (clipping); Hirschfeld interview; Graves prison diary, November 30, 1971, 7.
102. Petino interview; Don Nicholas, interview with author, Newark, September 1, 1992.

103. Petino interview. The teacher who overheard Petino asked to not be identified.
104. Petino interview.
105. Jerry Meyer, telephone interview with author, February 5, 2000. When arrested, Meyer was teaching at Newark College of Engineering.
106. Meyer phone interview; Barbaro, "Mass Jailing," 17–18.
107. Meyer phone interview.
108. Piegari interview.
109. Jerry Yablonsky, "Impressions on being imprisoned for nothing, Dec. 23–31, 1971," unpublished diary, December 25 and 26, 1971. Copy in author's possession.
110. Yablonsky prison diary, December 27, 1971; *SL*, December 23, 1971, 1+.
111. Yablonsky prison diary, December 28 and 29, 1971.
112. Yablonsky prison diary, December 29 and 30, 1971; *News-Record of Maplewood and South Orange*, December 30, 1971, 1.
113. Yablonsky prison diary, December 30, 1971.
114. Yablonsky prison diary, December 30, 1971.
115. Yablonsky prison diary, December 31, 1971.
116. Hirschfeld interview; Meyer phone interview.
117. Robert Hirschfeld, letter to Janet Hirschfeld, December 16, 1971, 1; Hirschfeld interview; *NN*, April 1, 1971, 1.
118. *SL*, April 15, 1971, 1+, and December 24, 1971, 1; Hirschfeld letter, 1–2; Hirschfeld interview; Meyer phone interview.
119. Hirschfeld letter, 2 and 4; Hirschfeld interview; Lappé tape; Seymour Spiegel, interview with author, Watchung, N.J., September 21, 1995.
120. Hirschfeld letter, 4; Hirschfeld interview.
121. Hirschfeld interview; Yablonsky prison diary, December 25, 1971.
122. *In re* Newark Teachers Union, Local 481 American Federation of Teachers AFL-CIO, February 8, 1972, 4, Superior Court of New Jersey, Appellate Division; *SL*, July 16, 1972, sec. 1, 14. Frank Fiorito served six months, because he was convicted two separate times for violations of the 1971 injunction.
123. Del Grosso interview.
124. Del Grosso interview.
125. Del Grosso interview.
126. Del Grosso interview; Litzky prison diary, December 19, 1971; Lieberfarb, Lowenstein, and Shaffer interview; Felix Martino, interview with author, Roseland, N.J., August 4, 1995.
127. Boardman, quoted in *News-Record of Maplewood and South Orange*, December 30, 1971, 1; Joe Rufalo, quoted in Gallagher, "The Teacher Who Chose to Go," 162; Barbaro, "Mass Jailing," 16.
128. Belinda Robnett, *How Long, How Long: African-American Women in the Struggle for Civil Rights* (New York: Oxford University Press, 1997), 17–25 and 166; Sara Evans, *Personal Politics: The Roots of Women's Liberation in the Civil Rights Movement and the New Left* (New York: Vintage Books, 1980), 134, 140–152, 214–215; Jane Sherron De Hart, "The New Feminism and the Dynamics of Social Change," *Women's America: Refocusing the Past*, ed. Linda K. Kerber and Jane Sherron De Hart (New York: Oxford University Press, 1995), 550–551; Rachel Blau DuPlessiss and Ann Snitow, ed., *The Feminist Memoir Project: Voices from Women's Liberation* (New York: Three Rivers Press, 1998), 14.

Epilogue   Power to the People?

1. Carol Karman, interview with author, Bloomfield, N.J., March 17, 1994.
2. Carole Graves, letter to James Lerman, March 2, 1972, 2, NTU files; Carol Karman, interview with author, Bloomfield, N.J., June 2, 1994.
3. Janice Adams, interview with author, Newark, September 7, 1995; Dorothy Bergman, interview with author, New York City, October 11, 1995; Anna Blume and Marty Blume, interview with author, Berkeley Heights, N.J., October 1, 1995; Beth Blackmon, interview with author, South Orange, N.J., June 26, 1995; Andy Thorburn, interview with author, Somerset, N.J., July 28, 1992.
4. Jim Lowenstein and Steve Shaffer, interview with author, Fair Lawn, N.J., July 26, 1994; Jean Anyon, *Ghetto Schooling: A Political Economy of Urban Educational Reform* (New York: Teachers College Press, 1997), 134–148.
5. Dave Lieberfarb, Jim Lowenstein, and Steve Shaffer, interview with author, Fair Lawn, N.J., November 19, 1994; Elena Scambio, interview with author, Bloomfield, N.J., August 26, 1997. Lowenstein went from Weequahic to SWAS in 1971.
6. Lieberfarb, Lowenstein, and Shaffer interview; Seymour Spiegel, interviews with author, Watchung, N.J., September 21, 1995, and September 22, 1995; Jim Brown, interview with author, Belleville, N.J., August 17, 1995.
7. Lieberfarb, Lowenstein, and Shaffer interview; Spiegel interviews; Honey Litzky and Leo Litzky, interview with author, West Orange, N.J., August 25, 1993; Bergman interview; Brown interview; Frank Green, interview with author, Montclair, N.J, August 29, 1995. Bergman, Green, Brown, and Shaffer all taught at SWAS. Spiegel never fully got over being forced out; for three years, he couldn't even go back to visit.
8. Lowenstein and Shaffer interview; Lieberfarb, Lowenstein, and Shaffer interview; *New Jersey Afro-American*, October 27, 1979, 1.
9. Felix Martino, interview with author, Roseland, N.J., August 4, 1995; Blackmon interview; Norman Eiger, "The Newark School Wars: A Socio-Historical Study of the 1970 and 1971 Newark School System Strikes" (Ed.D. diss., Rutgers University, 1976), 536.
10. Blackmon interview; *New Jersey Afro-American*, October 27, 1979, 1; Eiger, "Newark School Wars," 538; *SL*, September 5, 1980, 1, and September 6, 1980, 1.
11. Tom Lawton, interview with author, Bloomfield, N.J., June 23, 1995.
12. Brown interview.
13. Brown interview.
14. Vic Cascella, Ralph Favilla, and Don Nicholas, interview with author, Newark, December 1, 1995; *SL*, May 6, 1975, 22; Lowenstein and Shaffer interview, July 26, 1994; Bob Clark, interview with author, Glen Ridge, N.J., October 17, 1995. Cascella and Shaffer were disturbed by Graves's poor relationship to AFT, Clark by her seeming loss of integrity.
15. Joe Del Grosso, interview with author, Newark, August 24, 1995; Karman interview, March 17, 1994.
16. Blackmon interview; Gene Liss, interview with author, Newark, August 29, 1995; Scambio interview, August 26, 1997; Martin Bierbaum, "Letter from Newark: Schools for Scandal," *New Jersey Reporter* (October 1985): 37; *SL*, October 23, 1994, sec. 1, 35.

17. Pete Petino, interview with author, Newark, November 5, 1995; Liss interview. The strike activist asked not to be identified.

18. Robert Braun, "Graves' Loss Matters Little to Newark Pupils," *SL*, June 25, 1995, sec. 1, 48; Blackmon interview; Blume and Blume interview; Anyon, *Ghetto Schooling*, 157; Wilbur C. Rich, *Black Mayors and School Politics: The Failure of Reform in Detroit, Gary, and Newark* (New York: Garland, 1996), 120. Bell was also Board president in the 1970s, when the Union and Board were still at odds.

19. Blackmon interview.

20. Charles Nolley and Martha Nolley, interview with author, Montclair, N.J., September 14, 1995; Carol Karman interviews; Vic Cascella, interview with author, Newark, August 6, 1996.

21. Lawton interview; Carol Karman, telephone conversation with author, January 10, 2000; *SL*, September 15, 1980, sec. N, 1; Scambio interview, August 26, 1997; Angela Paone, Janice Adams, Carole Karman conversation with author, New York City May 8, 1996; *SL*, May 4, 1975, sec. 1, 1+; *Ridgefield Park Educ. Ass'n v. Ridgefield Park Bd. of Educ.*, 78 N.J. 144 (1978); Susan Martin, "The Impact of a Local Teachers' Union on Educational Policy and Practice: A Case Study of the Cincinnati Federation of Teachers" (Ed.D. diss., University of Cincinnati, 1992), 230–231; Kim Moody, *An Injury to All: The Decline of American Unionism* (London: Verso, 1988), 152–187.

22. Moody, *An Injury to All*, 45–69; Charles M. Payne, *I've Got the Light of Freedom: The Organizing Tradition and the Mississippi Freedom Struggle* (Berkeley: University of California Press, 1995), 338–390; Clayborne Carson, *In Struggle: SNCC and the Black Awakening of the 1960s* (Cambridge: Harvard University Press, 1981), 234–237 and 287–288.

23. *SL*, June 25, 1995, sec. 1, 48; Paone, Adams, and Karman, conversation with author, May 8, 1996; Scambio interview, August 26, 1997; *SL*, February 2, 1973, 1; Angelo DeTata, letter to Carole Graves, October 17, 1971, 2, NTU files.

24. Edith Counts, interview with author, East Orange, N.J., August 9, 1993; Anyon, *Ghetto Schooling*, 122 and 126; Clark interview; Blackmon interview.

25. Phil Basile, interview with author, Verona, N.J., August 15, 1995; Joe Ciccolini, Sr., interview with author, Nutley, N.J., September 27, 1995.

26. Basile interview.

27. Adams interview.

28. Nolley and Nolley interview; Anyon, *Ghetto Schooling*, 151; Ciccolini interview; Angela Paone, interview with author, Roseland, N.J., August 8, 1995; *New York Times*, September 25, 1995, B7, and March 8, 1998, NJ1+.

29. Karman interview, June 2, 1994.

30. Karman interview, June 2, 1994; Anyon, *Ghetto Schooling*, 24.

31. Karman interview, June 2, 1994; Blackmon interview.

32. Counts interview; Robert C. Johnston, "N.J. Takeover of Newark Found to Yield Gains, but Lack Clear Goals," *Education Week* (May 31, 2000): 17; Anyon, *Ghetto Schooling*, 127 and 181; *NN*, June 4, 1970, 1; Scambio interview, August 26, 1997. Scambio became vice president of the Newark Board of Education, before working for the state. Somehow, she never lost sight of her original commitment to teachers and students.

33. Blume and Blume interview.
34. Mary Abend, interview with author, Newark, June 14, 1995; Karman interview, March 17, 1994; Marjorie Murphy, *Blackboard Unions: The AFT and the NEA, 1900–1980* (Ithaca, N.Y.: Cornell University Press, 1990), 209; Lawton interview; Adams interview; Vic Cascella, interview with author, Newark, August 6, 1996.
35. Karman interview, March 17, 1994.
36. Nolley and Nolley interview.
37. Nolley and Nolley interview; *SL*, October 16, 1994, sec. 1, 12, and February 6, 1995, sec. N: 1+. Graves believes she was right to make opposition to the state takeover a priority. She acknowledges teachers were disappointed in the salary provisions, but thinks her removal of Petino was pivotal; she says she had to do it, because he was violating the law. Carole Graves, interview with author, Newark, May 24, 2000.
38. Del Grosso quoted in *SL*, February 17, 1995, 33; Del Grosso interview; *SL*, February 6, 1995, sec. N, 1.
39. Del Grosso interview; Del Grosso, conversation with author, October 13, 1995.
40. Del Grosso interview.
41. Del Grosso interview.
42. Del Grosso interview; *SL*, June 21, 1995, 17. In the Union office, I saw the detective agency report.
43. *NTU Bulletin* (September/October 1995), 2; *SL*, June 21, 1995, 7.
44. Del Grosso interview.
45. Del Grosso interview.
46. Del Grosso interview; Paul Buhle, "Albert Shanker: No Flowers," *New Politics* (Summer 1997): 51 and 57.
47. Lawton interview; Anyon, *Ghetto Schooling*, 175–176; Ann Bastian, "Teachers Unions on the Brink," *New Labor Forum* (Fall/Winter 1998): 28; Martin, "The Impact of a Local Teachers' Union," 148–305. For a clear articulation of the ways in which teacher unions might still be transformed, see "Social Justice Unionism: A Working Draft—A Call to Education Unionists," *Rethinking Schools* (Autumn 1994): 12–13.

Index

About the Author

Steve Golin teaches at Bloomfield College in New Jersey, where he a professor of history and the coordinator of the teaching center. He is committed both to teachers and to students. He writes about New Jersey working people and is the author of *The Fragile Bridge: Paterson Silk Strike, 1913*.